Early Praise for *Programming Phoenix LiveView*

Programming Phoenix LiveView is action-packed with information and examples to guide you on your journey into LiveView, Phoenix, and Elixir. The authors expertly thread the needle of deep-diving into concepts like generators, forms, Ecto Changesets, Phoenix PubSub broadcasts, and much, much more without overwhelming the reader or losing momentum. Whether you are just getting started or you are looking to accelerate your journey into Elixir and Phoenix LiveView, this book is a great place to start.

➤ **Michael Crumm**
Phoenix Core Team

I love how the example in this book touches nearly every part of a product, from end users to business desires. Sophie and Bruce illuminate how LiveView utilizes functional programming to build fast, interactive web applications.

➤ **Amos King**
Board Member, Erlang Ecosystem Foundation

This book will give you the knowledge to achieve a desired user experience without compromising on your developer experience. As we move into an age where daily interaction with AI is becoming the norm, we need to deliver user experiences reliably and in real time. LiveView gives you the tools to deliver those experiences, and this book is a must-have in your personal library.

➤ **Sam McDavid**
Principal Software Engineer, Dscout

I was on a team tasked with building a strategic project that would be our very first with Phoenix LiveView. With the help of this book and the excellent qualities of Elixir and Phoenix with LiveView, our project came online under budget for both development and operational cost!

The product owner and the company management are extremely happy with the speed of development, the quality of our code, and the performance of the LiveView front end. Additionally, our product is extremely performant and uses minimal resources.

➤ **Bill Tihen**
Developer, Garaio REM

The thorough guide through Phoenix LiveView. Leaving no stone unturned, Sophie and Bruce take you on a journey that will not only ensure you know LiveView but also teach you Phoenix while you're at it. Finally the book to refer people to.

➤ **Lars Wikman**
Founder, Underjord

Programming Phoenix LiveView

Interactive Elixir Web Programming Without Writing Any JavaScript

Bruce A. Tate
Sophie DeBenedetto

The Pragmatic Bookshelf

Dallas, Texas

See our complete catalog of hands-on, practical,
and Pragmatic content for software developers:
https://pragprog.com

Sales, volume licensing, and support:
support@pragprog.com

Derivative works, AI training and testing,
international translations, and other rights:
rights@pragprog.com

The team that produced this book includes:

Publisher: Dave Thomas
Development Editor: Jackie Carter
Copy Editor: L Sakhi MacMillan

Copyright © 2026 The Pragmatic Programmers, LLC.

All rights reserved. No part of this publication may be reproduced by any means, nor may any derivative works be made from this publication, nor may this content be used to train or test an artificial intelligence system, without the prior consent of the publisher.

When we are aware that a term used in this book is claimed as a trademark, the designation is printed with an initial capital letter or in all capitals.

The Pragmatic Starter Kit, The Pragmatic Programmer, Pragmatic Programming, Pragmatic Bookshelf, PragProg, and the linking *g* device are trademarks of The Pragmatic Programmers, LLC.

Every precaution was taken in the preparation of this book. However, the publisher assumes no responsibility for errors or omissions or for damages that may result from the use of information (including program listings) contained herein.

ISBN-13: 978-1-68050-821-5
Book version: P1.0—March, 2026

Contents

Acknowledgments ix

Introduction xi

1. **Get to Know LiveView** 1
   Single-Page Apps Are Distributed Systems   2
   LiveView Makes SPAs Easy   4
   Program LiveView Like a Professional   8
   Install Elixir, Postgres, Phoenix, and LiveView   9
   Create a Phoenix Project   10
   The LiveView Life Cycle   14
   Build a Simple Live View   15
   LiveView Transfers Data Efficiently   23
   Your Turn   26

Part I — Code Generation

2. **Phoenix and Authentication** 31
   CRC: Constructors, Reducers, and Converters   33
   Phoenix Is One Giant Function   37
   Generate the Authentication Layer   42
   Explore Accounts from IEx   49
   Protect Routes with Plugs   54
   Authenticate the Live View   59
   Access Session Data in the Live View   64
   Your Turn   68

3. **Generators: Contexts and Schemas** **71**
   Get to Know the Phoenix Live Generator   72
   Run the Phoenix Live Generator   73
   Understand the Generated Core   80
   Understand the Generated Boundary   87
   Boundary, Core, or Script?   94
   Your Turn   97

4. **Generators: Live Views and Templates** **99**
   Application Inventory   100
   Mount and Render the Product Index   104
   Use Components to Render HTML   111
   Handle Change for the Product Edit   118
   Manage Data with Streams   123
   Phoenix 1.8's Dedicated Form Live View   127
   Your Turn   132

Part II — LiveView Composition

5. **Forms and Changesets** **137**
   Model Change with Changesets   137
   Model Change with Embedded Schemas   139
   Use Embedded Schemas in LiveView   142
   LiveView Form Bindings   154
   Live Uploads   156
   Your Turn   169

6. **Function Components** **173**
   The Survey   174
   Organize Your Live View with Components   176
   Build the Survey Context   177
   Organize the Application Core and Boundary   184
   Build the Survey Live View   189
   Build a Simple Function Component   196
   Build the Demographic Show Function Component   202
   Your Turn   210

7. Live Components   213
    Build the Live Demographic Form Component   214
    Manage Component State   219
    Build the Ratings Components   224
    List Ratings   226
    Show a Rating   231
    Show the Rating Form   233
    Your Turn   239

Part III — Extend LiveView

8. Build an Interactive Dashboard   245
    The Plan   246
    Define the Admin.DashboardLive Live View   247
    Represent Dashboard Concepts with Components   249
    Fetch Survey Results Data   250
    Initialize the Admin.SurveyResultsLive Component State   253
    Render SVG Charts with Contex   254
    Add Filters to Make Charts Interactive   263
    Refactor Chart Code with Macros   275
    Your Turn   279

9. Build a Distributed Dashboard   281
    LiveView and Phoenix Messaging Tools   281
    Track Real-Time Survey Results with PubSub   283
    Track Real-Time User Activity with Presence   290
    Display User Tracking   296
    Your Turn   302

10. Test Your Live Views   303
    What Makes CRC Code Testable?   304
    Unit Test for Survey Results State   306
    Integration Test LiveView Interactions   316
    Verify Distributed Real-Time Updates   327
    Your Turn   331

Part IV — Graphics and Custom Code Organization

11. Build the Game Core **335**
  The Plan 336
  Represent a Shape with Points 338
  Group Points Together in Shapes 350
  Track and Place a Pentomino 352
  Track a Game in a Board 357
  Your Turn 362

12. Render Graphics with SVG **365**
  Plan the Presentation Layer 365
  Define a Skinny GameLive View 367
  Render Points with SVG 368
  Compose with Components 374
  Put It All Together 383
  Your Turn 388

13. Establish Boundaries and APIs **393**
  It's Alive: Plan User Interactions 393
  Process User Interactions in the Core 395
  Build a Game Boundary Layer 399
  Extend the Game Live View 401
  Add Help with JavaScript 404
  Build a Picker to Control Navigation 407
  Your Turn 412

Bibliography **415**

Acknowledgments

This book has been a long journey, and I couldn't have completed it without the support of many wonderful people.

To my wife, Maggie, and my daughters, Kayla and Julia—thank you for your patience during the many early mornings and late nights spent writing and rewriting as LiveView evolved. Your love and support make everything possible.

To my coauthor, Sophie DeBenedetto—thank you for bringing your expertise, energy, and fresh perspective to this project. Your contributions made this book immeasurably better, and working with you has been a genuine pleasure.

➤ *Bruce Tate*

To my coauthor, Bruce—thank you for the opportunity to work on this project with you. Your mentorship, patience, and deep knowledge of the Elixir ecosystem made this collaboration a true learning experience. I'm grateful for your trust and guidance.

To my family and friends—thank you for your unwavering support and encouragement throughout this long process.

➤ *Sophie DeBenedetto*

From both of us:

Our technical reviewers provided invaluable feedback that shaped this book into its final form. Special thanks to Michael Crumm from the Phoenix Core Team, Amos King from the Erlang Ecosystem Foundation, Sam McDavid, Bill Tihen, Lars Wikman, Steven Nunez, Maxim Veytsman, Ulisses De Almeida, Kim Shrier, Meryl Dakin, Samuel Mullen, and Bryan Green. It's been a six-year project, so we are sure we have missed a few people from this list. Your careful reading, thoughtful suggestions, and honest critiques helped us catch errors and improve explanations throughout. Any remaining mistakes are, of course, our own.

The team at Pragmatic Bookshelf has been wonderful to work with, as always. Thanks to Dave Thomas for building a publishing house that truly understands technical authors and readers in this difficult time. Thanks to our editor, Jackie Carter, for guiding us through countless revisions with patience and insight. And as always, thanks to the work of the publishing and marketing teams that helped to get the betas and products out and who keep them rolling through a grinding process. Publishing is changing forever, and the world would be a darker place without you.

This book would not exist without the brilliant work of José Valim, who created Elixir and continues to lead its development with vision and care. Thanks also to Chris McCord, who created Phoenix and LiveView, fundamentally changing how we build interactive web applications. Chris's work on LiveView represents a genuine leap forward for web development, and we're grateful for his continued innovation and leadership. The entire Elixir and Phoenix core teams deserve recognition for building and maintaining such an extraordinary ecosystem.

Finally, thanks to the Elixir community—a group of developers who consistently demonstrate that technical excellence and genuine kindness can go hand in hand. Your enthusiasm for sharing knowledge and helping newcomers makes this community special.

Bruce and Sophie

Introduction

If you haven't been following closely, it might seem like LiveView arrived suddenly, like a new seedling that breaks through the soil surface overnight. That narrative lacks a few important details, such as all of the slow germination and growth that happens out of sight.

Chris McCord, the creator of Phoenix, worked on Ruby on Rails before coming over to the Elixir community. More and more often, his consultancy was asked to use Ruby on Rails to build dynamic single-page apps (SPAs). He tried to build a server-side framework on top of the Ruby on Rails infrastructure, much like LiveView, that would allow him to meet these demands for interactivity. But Chris recognized that the Ruby infrastructure wasn't robust enough to support his idea. He needed better reliability, higher throughput, and more even performance. He shopped around for a more appropriate language and infrastructure and found Elixir.

When Chris moved from Ruby to Elixir, he first learned the metaprogramming techniques[1] he'd need to implement his vision. Then he began building the Phoenix web development framework to support the infrastructure he'd need to make this vision a reality.

At that time, José Valim began helping Chris write idiomatic Elixir abstractions relying on OTP. OTP libraries have powered many of the world's phone switches, offering stunning uptime statistics and near real-time performance, so it played a critical role in Phoenix. Chris introduced a programming model to Phoenix called *channels*. This service uses HTTP WebSockets[2] and OTP to simplify interactions in Phoenix. As the Phoenix team fleshed out the programming model, they saw stunning performance and reliability numbers. Because of OTP, Phoenix would support *the concurrency, reliability, and performance that interactive applications demand.*

---

1. https://pragprog.com/titles/cmelixir/metaprogramming-elixir/
2. https://developer.mozilla.org/en-US/docs/Web/API/WebSockets_API

In functional programming, Chris found cleaner ways to tie his ideas together than object orientation offered. He learned to compose functions with Elixir pipelines and the plugs. His work with OTP taught him to think in the same composable steps we'll show you as this book unfolds. His work with metaprogramming and macros prepared him to build smooth features beyond what basic Elixir provided. As a result, in Phoenix LiveView, users would find a *pleasant, productive programming experience*.

As the web programming field around him grew, frameworks like React and languages like Elm provided a new way to think about user interface development in event-powered layers. Chris took note. Some frameworks such as Morphdom popped up to allow seamless replacement of page elements in a customizable way. The Phoenix team was able to build JavaScript features into LiveView that automate the process of changing a user interface on a socket connection. In LiveView, programmers would find a *beautiful programming model based on tested concepts*, and one that provided JavaScript infrastructure so *developers didn't need to write their own JavaScript*.

And so, that seed germinated and poked up through the surface. Shortly after the seed became visible, we introduced the first version of this book. Six years and hundreds of features later, LiveView hit version 1.0.

In a nutshell, that's LiveView. We'll have plenty of time to go into more detail, but now, let's talk about you.

Is This Book for You?

This book is for advanced beginners and intermediate programmers who want to build web applications using Phoenix LiveView. In it, you'll learn the basic abstractions that make LiveView work, and you'll explore techniques that help you organize your code into layers that make sense. We'll try not to bore you with a tedious feature-by-feature march. Instead, we'll help you grasp LiveView by building a nontrivial application together.

We think this book is ideal for readers who relate to the following descriptions.

You Want to Build Something with LiveView

In this book, you'll learn the way the experts do. You'll write programs that communicate the most important LiveView concepts. You'll take four passes through the content.

- You'll start with a trivial example.
- Then you'll generate some working code and walk through it step by step with the authors.

- After that, you'll extend those programs while tacking on your own code.
- Finally, you'll code some complex programs from scratch.

When you're done, you'll know the base abstractions of Phoenix LiveView, you'll know how to build on them, and you'll be able to write code from scratch because you'll know what code goes where.

You're Having a Hard Time Getting Started

Phoenix LiveView is a brilliant programming model, but it's not always an easy model to grasp. Sometimes, you need a guide. In this book, we break down the basics in small examples, such as what happens when a typical page loads:

```
mount() |> render()
```

Another example represents a running LiveView:

```
def loop() do
  mount()
  |> handle_event()
  |> render()
  |> loop()
end
```

Of course, LiveView is more complicated. Hundreds of lines of Phoenix framework code sit between each of your application functions, but this short example communicates the overarching organization underneath every single LiveView program. We'll show you how this example makes it easier to understand the LiveView layer, and we'll show you tools you can use to understand where to place the other bits of your program.

When you're done, you'll know how LiveView works. More importantly, you'll know how to *think* about events that flow through a LiveView system and why they happen in the order they do.

You Want to Know Where Your Layers Go

LiveView is just one part of a giant ecosystem. Along the way, you'll encounter concepts such as Ecto, OTP, Phoenix, templates, and components. The hard part about coding LiveView isn't building code that works the first time. It's building a layered system that continues to work year after year.

For code that lasts, do what the experts do and break your software into layers. You'll learn how Phoenix developers organize a core layer for predictable concepts and how to manage uncertainty in a boundary layer. Then you'll explore how to apply some of the same concepts in the user interface. Learn to break off major components and also how to write functions that will be primed for reuse.

If you're seeking organizational guidance, you'll be able to fit the concepts in this book right into your mental bookshelf. You won't just know what to do; you'll know why to do it that way.

You Like to Play

If you want to program just for the joy of it, you'll love LiveView. The programming model keeps your brain firmly on the server and lets you explore one concept at a time. Layering on graphics makes this kind of exploratory programming almost magical. If this paragraph describes you, LiveView will give your mind room to roam and the productivity to let your fingers keep up.

This Book Might Not Be for You

While most LiveView developers will have something to learn from us, two groups might want to consider their purchase carefully. Advanced Elixir developers might find this book too basic, and early-stage beginners might find it too advanced. Let us explain.

If you've never seen Elixir before, you'll probably want to use other resources to learn Elixir and come back later. If you don't yet know Elixir, we'll provide you with a few resources you might try before coming back to this book.

Alternative Resources

If you're new to functional programming and want to learn it with a book, try *Learn Functional Programming with Elixir [Alm18]*. For a book for programmers that ramps up more quickly, try *Programming Elixir [Tho18]*. For a multimedia approach, check out Groxio.[3]

Similarly, this book might move slowly for if you're an advanced programmer, so you have a difficult decision to make since there aren't many LiveView books out yet. We won't be offended if you look elsewhere. If you're building APIs in Phoenix but not single-page apps, this book isn't for you, though you'll probably enjoy what *Programming Phoenix [MTV19]* has to say. If you want an advanced book about organizing Elixir software, check out *Designing Elixir Systems with OTP [IT19]*.

If you're willing to accept a book that's paced a bit slowly for advanced developers, we're confident that you'll find something you can use.

---

3. https://grox.io/language/elixir/course

About This Book

Programmers learn by writing code, and that's exactly how this book will work. We'll work on a project together as if we're a fictional game company. You'll write lots of code, starting with small tweaks of generated code and building up to major enhancements that extract common features with components.

As you build the application, you'll encounter more complexity. A distributed dashboard will show a real-time view of other users and processes. You'll even build a game from scratch because that's the best way to learn how to layer the most sophisticated LiveView applications.

Let's take a more detailed look at the plan.

Part I: Code Generation

We'll use two different code generators to build the foundations of the Pento web app—a product database with an authenticated LiveView admin interface.

We won't treat our generated code as black boxes. Instead, we'll trace through the generated code, taking the opportunity to learn LiveView and Phoenix design and best practices from some of the best Elixir programmers in the business. We'll cover how the individual pieces of generated code fit together and discuss the philosophy of each layer. We'll show you when to reach for generators and what you'll gain from using them.

Chapter 2, Phoenix and Authentication, on page 31
 The phx.gen.auth authentication layer generator is a collaboration between the DashBit company and the Phoenix team. This code doesn't use LiveView, but we'll need this generator to authenticate users for our applications. You'll generate and study this layer to learn how Phoenix requests work. Then you'll use the generated code to authenticate a live view.

Chapter 3, Generators: Contexts and Schemas, on page 71
 The phx.gen.live generator creates live views with all of the code that backs them. We'll use this to generate the product CRUD feature set. As the code created by the phx.gen.live generator contains a complete out-of-the-box set of live views backed by a database, we'll spend two chapters discussing it. This chapter will focus on the two back-end layers—the *core* and the *boundary*. The boundary layer, also referred to as the *context*, represents code that has uncertainty, such as database interfaces that can potentially fail. The context layer will allow our admin users to manage products through an API. The core layer contains code that is certain and behaves predictably—for example, code that maps database records and constructs queries.

Chapter 4, Generators: Live Views and Templates, on page 99
> The phx.gen.live generator also generates a set of web modules, templates, and helpers that use the database-backed core and boundary layers detailed in the previous chapter. This chapter will cover the web side of this generator, including the LiveView, templates, and all of the supporting user interface code. Along the way, we'll take a detailed look at the generated LiveView code and trace how the pieces work together. This walkthrough will give you a firm understanding of LiveView basics.

With the LiveView basics under your belt, you'll know how to generate code to do common tasks and extend your code to work with forms and validations. You'll be ready to build your own custom live views using components.

Part II: LiveView Composition

LiveView lets you compose complex change management behavior with layers. First, we'll look at how LiveView manages change with the help of changesets, and you'll see how you can compose change management code in your live views. Then we'll take a deep dive into LiveView components. Components are a mechanism for compartmentalizing live view behavior and state. A single live view can be comprised of a set of small components, each of which is responsible for managing a specific part of your SPA's state. In this part, you'll use components to build organized live views that handle sophisticated interactive features by breaking them down into smaller pieces. Let's talk about some of those features now.

With our authenticated product management interface up and running, our Pento admins will naturally want to know how those products are performing. So we'll use LiveView, and LiveView components, to do market research.

We'll build a survey feature that collects demographic information and product ratings from our users. We'll use two LiveView component features to do this work.

Chapter 5, Forms and Changesets, on page 137
> After we've generated a basic live view, we'll take a closer look at forms. Ecto, the database layer for Phoenix, provides an API, called changesets, for safely validating data. LiveView relies heavily on them to present forms with validations. In this chapter, we'll take a second pass through basic changesets and form tags for database-backed data. Then we'll work with a couple of corner cases, including changesets without databases and attachment uploads.

Chapter 6, Function Components, on page 173
   We'll use stateless components to start carving up our work into reusable pieces. These components will work like partial views. We'll use them to build the first pieces of a reusable multistage poll for our users. In the first stage, the user will answer some demographic questions. In the next stage, the user will rate several products. Along the way, you'll encounter the techniques that let LiveView present state across multiple stages.

Chapter 7, Live Components, on page 213
   As our components get more sophisticated, we'll need to increase their capability. We'll need them to capture events that change the state of our views. We'll use stateful components to let our users interact with pieces of our survey by tying common state to events.

By this point, you'll know when and how to reach for components to keep your live views manageable and organized.

Part III: Extend LiveView

In the next few chapters, you'll see how you can extend the behavior of your custom live view to support real-time interactions. We'll use communication between a parent live view and child components, and between a live view and other areas of your Phoenix app, to get the behavior we want. You'll learn how to use these communication mechanisms to support distributed SPAs with even more advanced interactivity.

Having built the user surveys, we'll need a place to evaluate their results. We'll build a modular admin dashboard that breaks out survey results by demographic and product rating. Our dashboard will be highly interactive and responsive to both user-triggered events and events that occur elsewhere in our application.

We'll approach this functionality in three chapters.

Chapter 8, Build an Interactive Dashboard, on page 245
   Users will be able to filter results charts by demographic info and rating. We'll leverage the functions and patterns that LiveView provides for the event management life cycle and you'll see how components communicate with the live view to which they belong.

Chapter 9, Build a Distributed Dashboard, on page 281
   Our survey results dashboard won't just update in real time to reflect state changes brought about by user interaction on the page. It will also reflect the state of the entire application by updating in real time to include

any new user survey results as they are submitted by our users. This distributed real-time behavior will be supported by Phoenix PubSub.

Chapter 10, Test Your Live Views, on page 303
Once our dashboard is up and running, we'll take a step back and write some tests for the features we've built. We'll examine the testing tools that LiveView provides, and you'll learn LiveView testing best practices to ensure that your live views are robustly tested as they grow in complexity.

When we're done, you'll understand how to use components to compose even complex single-page behaviors into one elegant and easy-to-maintain live view. You'll also know how to track and display system-wide information in a live view. You'll have everything you need to build and maintain highly interactive, real-time, distributed single-page applications with LiveView.

With all of that under our belts, we'll prototype a game.

Part IV: Graphics and Custom Code Organization

We know games aren't the best use case for LiveView. It's usually better to use a client-side technology to solve a pure client-side problem, but bear with us. We strongly believe that games are great teaching tools for the layering of software. They have well-understood requirements, and they have complex flows that often mirror problems we find in the real world. Building out our game will give you an opportunity to put together everything you've learned, from the basics to the most advanced techniques for building live views.

In this set of chapters, we'll prototype a proof of concept for a game. A quick proof of concept is firmly in LiveView's wheelhouse, and it can save tons of time and effort over writing games in less productive environments.

Our game will consist of simple puzzles of five-unit shapes called pentominoes. The final three chapters contain the concepts we'll focus on. By this point, none of these concepts will be new to you, but putting them into practice here will allow you to master them.

Chapter 11, Build the Game Core, on page 335
We'll build our game in layers, beginning with a layer of functions called the *core*. We'll review the reducer method and drive home why it's the right way to model functional software within functional cores. We'll use this technique to build the basic shapes and functions that will make up our game.

Chapter 12, Render Graphics with SVG, on page 365
> We integrate the details of our game into a basic presentation layer. LiveView is great at working with text, and SVG is a text-based graphics representation. We'll use SVG to represent the game board and each pentomino within that board.

Chapter 13, Establish Boundaries and APIs, on page 393
> As our software grows, we'll need to be able to handle uncertainty. Our code will do so in a *boundary* layer. Our boundary will implement the rules that effectively validate movements, limiting how far the pentominoes can move on the page. We'll also integrate the boundary layer into our live view.

These low-level details will perfectly illustrate how the different parts of Elixir work together in a LiveView application. When you're through with this part, you'll have practiced the techniques you'll need to build and organize your own complex LiveView applications from the ground up.

Online Resources

The apps and examples shown in this book can be found at the Pragmatic Programmers website for this book.[4] You'll also find the errata submission form, where you can report problems with the text or make suggestions for future versions. If you want to explore more from Sophie, you can read more of her fine work at Elixir School.[5] If you want to expand on this content with videos and projects to further your understanding, check out Groxio's LiveView course,[6] with a mixture of free and paid content.

When you're ready, turn the page and we'll get started. Let's build something together!

---

4. http://pragprog.com/titles/liveview/
5. https://elixirschool.com/blog/phoenix-live-view/
6. https://grox.io/language/liveview/course

CHAPTER 1

Get to Know LiveView

The nature of web development is changing. For many years, programmers needed to build web programs as many tiny independent requests with responses. Most teams had some developers dedicated to writing programs to serve requests and a small number of team members dedicated to design. Life was simple. Applications were easy to build, even though the user experience was sadly lacking. Frankly, for most tasks, simple request-response apps were *good enough*.

Time passed until yesterday's *good enough* didn't cut it and users demanded more. To meet these demands, web development slowly evolved into a mix of tools and frameworks split across the client and server. Take any of these examples:

- Instead of loading content page by page, modern Twitter and Facebook feeds load more content as a user scrolls down.

- Rather than having an inbox for an email client with a refresh button, users want a page that adds new emails to their inbox in real time.

- Search boxes autocomplete based on data in the database.

These kinds of web projects are sometimes called *single-page apps* (SPAs), though in truth, these kinds of applications often span multiple pages. Many different technologies have emerged to ease the development of SPAs. JavaScript frameworks like React make it easier to change web pages based on changing data. Web frameworks like Ruby's Action Cable and our own Phoenix Channels allow the web server to keep a running conversation between the client and the server. Despite these improvements, such tools have a problem. They force us into the wrong mindset—they don't allow us to think of SPAs as distributed systems.

Single-Page Apps Are Distributed Systems

In case that jarring, bolded title wasn't enough to grab your attention, let the reality sink in. *A SPA is a distributed system!*

Don't believe us? Consider a typical SPA. This imaginary SPA contains a form with several fields. The first field is a select for choosing a country. Based on that country, we want to update the contents of a second field, a list of states or provinces. Based on the selected state, we update yet another element on the page to display a tax amount.

This simple hypothetical SPA breaks the mold of the traditional web application in which the user sends one request and the server sends one response, representing a static page. The SPA would need JavaScript to detect when the selection in a field has changed, more code to send the data to your server, and still more server-side code to return the right data to the client. While these features aren't tough to build, they *are* tedious and error prone. You have several JavaScript elements with multiple clients on your browser page, and the failure of the JavaScript in any one of them can impact the others.

This SPA, and all SPAs, must coordinate and manage the state of the page across the client and the server. This means that single-page apps are distributed systems.

Distributed Systems Are Complex

Distributed systems are software apps whose separate parts reside on multiple nodes of a network. In a distributed system, those separated parts communicate and orchestrate actions such that a single, coherent system is presented to the end user.

Throughout much of its history, most of what we call web development has dodged the distributed systems label because the web server masked much of the complexity from us by handling all of the network communication in a common infrastructure, as in the figure on the next page.

As you can see in this figure, everything is happening on the server:

- Our server-side system receives a request.
- It then runs a server-side program, often through a layer called a *controller*.
- The controller then possibly accesses a database, often through a layer called a *model*.
- The model builds a response, often through a layer called a *view* with a *template*.
- The model delivers the result back to the web browser.

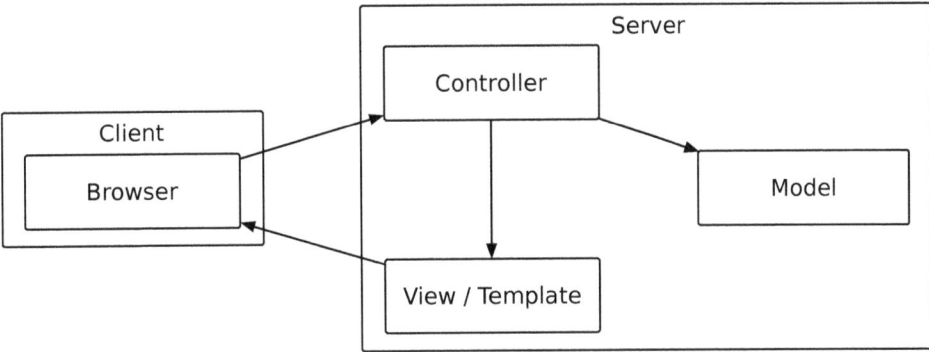

Every bit of that program is contained within a single server and we rarely have to think about code that lives down on the client.

But as we've just discussed, this request-response mindset is no longer sufficient for conceptualizing the complex modern SPA.

If you're building a SPA with custom JavaScript and some server-side layers, you can no longer claim this beautiful, simplified isolation. Web apps are now often multilanguage distributed systems with JavaScript and HTML on the client and some general-purpose application language on the server.

This had made SPA development much more challenging and time-consuming than it needs to be.

SPAs Are Hard

That's another bold, screaming headline, but we're willing to bet it's one that won't get much push back. It's likely that you're living with the consequences of dividing your team or your developer's mind across the client and server. These consequences include slow development cycle times, difficulty observing and remediating bugs, and much more. But it doesn't have to be this way. The typical SPA is complex because of the way we've been thinking about SPA development and the tools we've been using.

In truth, we can't even show a single diagram of a typical SPA because *there are no typical SPAs!* On the client side alone, JavaScript has become frighteningly complex, with many different front-end frameworks applying very different approaches.

Meanwhile, server-side code to deal with requests from client components is still often written with the old, insufficient, request-response mindset. As a result, traditional SPA tooling forces you to think about building each interaction, piece by piece. The mechanisms might vary, but most current approaches to building SPAs force us to think in terms of *interactions*—events that initiate tiny requests and responses that independently change a page in some way. The hardest part of the whole process is splitting our development across the client and server. That split has some very serious consequences.

By splitting our application development across the client and server boundary, we enable a whole class of *potential security breaches*, as a mistake in any single interaction leaves our whole page vulnerable.

By splitting our teams across the client and server, we surrender to a *slower and more complex development cycle*.

By splitting our design across the client and server, we commit to *slower and more complex bug remediation cycles*. By introducing a custom boundary between our browser and server, we dramatically complicate testing.

Want proof? If you've looked for a web development job lately, it's no great wonder that the requirements have grown so quickly. There's a single job—full-stack developer—that addresses this bloat. Developers become the proverbial frogs in their own pot of boiling water, a pot of escalating requirements without relief. Managers have boiling pots of their own—a pot of slowing development times, escalating developer salaries, and increasing requirements.

In this book, we'd like to introduce an idea. SPAs are hard because we've been thinking about them the wrong way. They're hard because we build custom solutions where common infrastructure would better serve. SPAs are hard because we think in terms of *isolated interactions* instead of *shared, evolving state*.

To make this new idea work, we need infrastructure to step into the breach between the client and server. We need tooling that lets us focus strictly on server-side development, and that relies on common infrastructure to keep the client up-to-date.

We need LiveView.

LiveView Makes SPAs Easy

Phoenix LiveView is a framework for building single-page flows on the web. It's an Elixir library that you'll include as a dependency in your Phoenix app, allowing you to build interactive, real-time LiveView flows as part of that Phoenix application. Compared to the traditional SPA, these flows will have some characteristics that seem almost magical to many developers:

- The apps we build will be stunningly interactive.
- The apps we write will be shockingly resistant to failure.
- These interactive apps will use a framework to manage JavaScript for us, so we don't have to write our own client-side code.
- The programming model is simple but at the same time it composes well to handle complexity.
- The programming model keeps our brain in one place, firmly on the server.

All of this means that SPAs built with LiveView will be able to easily meet the interactive demands of their users. Such SPAs will be pleasurable to write and easy to maintain, spurring development teams to new heights of productivity.

This is because LiveView lets programmers make distributed applications by relying on the *infrastructure* in the LiveView library rather than forcing them to write their own custom code between the browser and server. As a result, it's no surprise that LiveView is making tremendous waves throughout the Elixir community and beyond.

LiveView is a compelling programming model for beginners and experts alike, allowing users to think about building applications in a different, more efficient way. As this book unfolds, you'll shift away from viewing the world in terms of many independent request-response interactions. Instead, you'll conceive of a SPA as a holistic state management system.

By providing functions to render state, and events to change state, LiveView gives you the infrastructure you need to build such systems. Over the course of this book, we'll acquaint you with the tools and techniques you'll use within LiveView to render web pages, capture events, and organize your code into templates and components—in other words, everything you'll need to build a distributed state management system, aka a SPA, with LiveView.

Though this is a book about a user-interface technology, we'll spend plenty of time writing pure Elixir with a layered structure that integrates with our views seamlessly.

The LiveView Loop

The LiveView loop, or flow, is the core concept that you need to understand to build applications with LiveView. This flow represents a significant departure from the request-response mindset you might be used to applying to SPAs.

> **LiveView vs. Live Views**
>
> Phoenix LiveView is one of the central actors in this book. It's the library written in the Elixir language that plugs into the Phoenix framework. Live views are another actor. A *live view* is comprised of the routes, modules, and templates, written using the LiveView library, that represent a SPA. In this book, we'll focus more on live views than LiveView. That means we won't try to take you on a feature-by-feature grand tour. Instead, we'll build software that lasts, using practical techniques with the LiveView library.

This shift in mindset is one of the reasons why you'll find building SPAs with LiveView to be a smooth, efficient, and enjoyable process.

Instead of thinking of each interaction on your single-page app as a discrete request with a corresponding response, LiveView manages the state of your page in a long-lived process that loops through a set of steps again and again. Your application receives events, changes the state, and then renders the state, over and over. Don't worry about how your application receives events yet. For now, just focus on this LiveView flow: receive an event, change the state, render the state.

We can break it down into steps:

- LiveView will *receive events*, such as link clicks, key presses, or page submits.
- Based on those events, you'll write functions to *transform your state*.
- After you change your state, LiveView will re-render *only the portions of the page that are affected by the transformed state*.
- After rendering, LiveView again waits for events, and we go back to the top.

That's it. Everything we do for the rest of the book will work in terms of this loop—await events, change state, render the state, repeat.

LiveView makes it easy to manage the state of your SPA throughout this loop by abstracting away the details of client-server communication. Unlike many existing SPA frameworks, LiveView shields you from the details of distributed systems by providing some common infrastructure between the browser and the server. Your code, and your mind, will live in one place, on the server-side, and the infrastructure will manage the details.

If that sounds complicated now, don't worry. It will all come together for you. This book will teach you to think about web development in terms of the LiveView loop: get an event, change the state, render the state. Though the examples we build will be complicated, we'll build them layer by layer so that no single layer will have more complexity than it needs to. And we'll have fun together.

Now you know what LiveView is and how it encourages us to conceive of our SPAs as a LiveView flow rather than as a set of independent requests and responses. With this understanding under your belt, we'll turn our attention to the Elixir and OTP features that make LiveView the perfect fit for building SPAs.

LiveView, Elixir, and OTP

LiveView gives us the infrastructure we need to develop interactive, real-time, distributed web apps quickly and easily. This infrastructure, and the LiveView flow we just outlined, is made possible because of the capabilities of Elixir and OTP. Understanding what Elixir and OTP lend LiveView illustrates why LiveView is perfectly positioned to meet the growing demand for interactivity on the web.

OTP libraries have powered many of the world's phone switches, offering stunning uptime statistics and near real-time performance. OTP plays a critical role in Phoenix, in particular in the design of Phoenix channels. Channels are the programming model in Phoenix created by Chris McCord, the creator of Phoenix. This service uses HTTP WebSockets[1] and OTP to simplify client-server interactions in Phoenix. Phoenix channels led to excellent performance and reliability numbers. Because of OTP, Phoenix, and therefore LiveView, supports *the concurrency, reliability, and performance that interactive applications demand.*

LiveView relies heavily on the use of Phoenix channels—LiveView infrastructure abstracts away the details of channel-based communication between the client and the server. Let's talk about that abstraction and how Elixir made it possible to build it.

Chris's work with OTP taught him to think in terms of the reducer functions we'll show you as this book unfolds. Elixir allowed him to string reducer functions into pipelines, and these pipelines underlie the composable nature of LiveView. At the same time, Elixir's metaprogramming patterns, in particular the use of macros, support a framework made up of clean abstractions. As a result of these Elixir language features, users find a *pleasant, productive programming experience* in Phoenix LiveView.

---

1. https://developer.mozilla.org/en-US/docs/Web/API/WebSockets_API

LiveView doesn't owe all of its elegance and capability to Elixir, however. JavaScript plays a big role in the LiveView infrastructure. As the web programming field grew, frameworks like React and languages like Elm provided a new way to think about user interface development in layers. Meanwhile, frameworks like Morphdom popped up to allow seamless replacement of page elements in a customizable way. Chris took note, and the Phoenix team was able to build JavaScript features into LiveView that automate the process of changing a user interface on a socket connection. As a result, in LiveView programmers find a *beautiful programming model based on tested concepts*, and one that provided JavaScript infrastructure so *developers didn't need to write their own JavaScript.*

By this point, you already know quite a bit about LiveView—what it is, how it manages state at a high level via the LiveView loop, and how its building blocks of Elixir, OTP, and JavaScript make it reliable, scalable, and easy to use. Next up, we'll outline the plan for this book and what you'll build along the way. Then you'll get your hands dirty by building your very first live view.

Program LiveView Like a Professional

LiveView meets all of the interactivity and real-time needs of your average single-page app, while being easy to build and maintain. We firmly believe that the future of Phoenix programming lies with LiveView. So, this book provides you with an on-ramp into not just LiveView but also Phoenix. We'll cover some of the essential pieces of the Phoenix framework that you need to know to understand LiveView and build Phoenix LiveView apps, the right way.

We'll approach this book in the same way you'd approach building a new Phoenix LiveView app from scratch in the wild. This means we'll walk you through the use of generators to build out the foundation of your Phoenix app, including an authentication layer. Having generated a solid base, we'll begin to customize our generated code and build new features on top of it. Finally, we'll build custom LiveView features, from scratch, and illustrate how you can organize complex LiveView applications with composable layers. This generate, customize, build-from-scratch approach is one you'll take again and again when building your own Phoenix LiveView apps in the future.

Along the way, you'll learn to use LiveView to build complex interactive applications that are exceptionally reliable, highly scalable, and strikingly easy to maintain. You'll see how LiveView lets you move fast by offering elegant patterns for code organization, and you'll find that LiveView is the perfect fit for SPA development.

Here's the plan for what we're going to build and how we're going to build it.

We're going to work on a fictional business together, a game company called Pento. Don't worry, we won't spend all of our time, or even most of our time, building games. Most of our work will focus on the back office.

In broad strokes, we'll play the part of a small team in our fictional company that's having trouble making deadlines. We'll use LiveView to attack important isolated projects, such as building a product management system and an admin dashboard, that provide value for our teams. Then we'll wrap up by building one interactive game, Pentominoes.

We'll approach this journey in four parts that mirror how you'll want to approach building your own Phoenix LiveView applications in real life. In the first part, we'll focus on using code generators to build a solid foundation for our Phoenix LiveView app, introducing you to LiveView basics as we go. In the second part, we'll shift gears to building our own custom live views from the ground up, taking you through advanced techniques for composing live views to handle sophisticated interactive flows. In the third part, we'll extend LiveView by using Phoenix's PubSub capabilities to bring real-time interactivity to your custom live views. Then you'll put it all together in the final part to build the Pentominoes game.

Before we can do any of this work, though, we need to install LiveView, and it's past time to build a basic, functioning application. In the next few sections, we'll install the tools we need to build a Phoenix application with LiveView. Then we'll create our baseline Phoenix app with the LiveView dependency. Finally, we'll dive into the LiveView life cycle and build our very first live view.

Enough talking. Let's install.

Install Elixir, Postgres, Phoenix, and LiveView

The first step is to install Phoenix, Erlang, Elixir, Node, and Postgres. Elixir is the language we'll be using, Erlang is the language it's built on, Phoenix is the web framework, Node supports the system JavaScript that LiveView uses, and PostgreSQL is the database our examples will use. If you've already done this, *you can skip this topic.*

Rather than our giving you a stale, error-prone procedure, use the excellent Install Phoenix documentation[2] on the hexdocs page. Make sure you get at least the minimal version of Elixir (>= 1.14 as of this writing), Erlang (>= 25),

---

2. https://hexdocs.pm/phoenix/installation.html

and Phoenix (1.7.18). The correct version of Phoenix is critical. This book will focus on that version, which has Phoenix LiveView 1.0. You'll also pull down PostgreSQL. If you're running Linux or Windows, you'll want inotify-tools for automatic page reloading in development mode.

If you have trouble installing, use this experience as an opportunity to learn about the ecosystem that will support you when things go wrong. Go to the message board support for the framework that's breaking, or ask politely in the Elixir message boards.[3] For more immediate help, you might use Elixir's Slack channels. Get the most recent support options on the Elixir slack community[4] page on Hex. Someone's usually around to offer immediate assistance. When you ask for help, do your homework and honor those who are supporting you.

With the installation done, you're ready to create your project and set up LiveView. We'll use Mix to do so.

Create a Phoenix Project

With all of our dependencies installed, we're ready to start building the Pento app. We'll begin by setting up a new Phoenix project.

Open up an operating system shell and navigate to the parent directory for your project. Then type:

```
[pp_liveview] → % mix phx.new

                              mix phx.new

Creates a new Phoenix project.

...

A project at the given PATH will be created.

...

## Options

...

## Examples

...
```

The documentation embedded within the `mix phx.new` command is excellent. Now you know enough to start. Create a new project, providing a path and taking the defaults for the rest, like this:

---

3. https://elixirforum.com
4. http://elixir-slack.community/

```
[pp_liveview] → mix phx.new pento
* creating pento/lib/pento/application.ex
   . . . more creating messages . . .
Fetch and install dependencies? [Yn] Y
* running mix deps.get
* running mix assets.setup
* running mix deps.compile

   . . . instructions for running app . . .
```

The mix phx.new command runs the Phoenix installer for a standard Phoenix project that includes LiveView. With this, we'll get a brand new Phoenix app that includes all of the library dependencies, configuration, and assets we'll need to build live views.

As we work through this book, we'll point out the dependencies and generated code that generating a new Phoenix LiveView app adds to your project, and we'll examine the directory structure in detail over time. For now, know that back-end code goes in the lib/pento directory, the web-based assets like .css and .js files go in either assets or priv/static, and the web-based code all goes in the lib/pento_web directory.

Create the Database and Run the Server

At the bottom of the installation output, you'll find a few extra instructions that look something like this:

```
We are almost there! The following steps are missing:

    $ cd pento

Then configure your database in config/dev.exs and run:

    $ mix ecto.create

Start your Phoenix app with:

    $ mix phx.server

You can also run your app inside IEx (Interactive Elixir) as:

    $ iex -S mix phx.server
```

(You might see slightly different output depending on your Phoenix version.)

Let's follow those instructions now by performing the following actions. First, make sure you have Postgres installed and running on localhost, accessible with the default username postgres and password postgres. See the PostgreSQL Getting Started[5] guide for help.

---

5. https://www.postgresqltutorial.com/postgresql-getting-started/

Then change to the pento directory and create your database:

```
pp_liveview % cd pento
pp_liveview/pento % mix ecto.create
Compiling 15 files (.ex)
Generated pento app
The database for Pento.Repo has been created
```

Now start the web server:

```
pp_liveview % mix phx.server
[info] Running PentoWeb.Endpoint with Bandit 1.5.2 at 127.0.0.1:4000 (http)
[info] Access PentoWeb.Endpoint at http://localhost:4000
[watch] build finished, watching for changes...
/*! daisyUI 5.0.8 */
≈ tailwindcss v4.0.9

...
```

Notice Phoenix is now using the Tailwind framework, a framework used to program the look and feel of your application. We'll talk more about that later.

For now, point your browser to localhost:4000/, and if you've installed correctly, you'll see the following image.

We're up and running! Let's see what the Phoenix generator did for us.

View Mix Dependencies

You just installed both Elixir and Phoenix and created the application skeleton. Let's take a closer look at the LiveView-specific dependencies that got automatically added to our project now.

Mix installed the libraries LiveView will need as *Mix dependencies*. Every Phoenix application uses the underlying mix tool to fetch and manage dependencies. The mix.exs file contains the instructions for which dependencies to install and how to run them. Crack it open and take a look:

intro/pento/mix.exs
```elixir
defp deps do
  [
    {:phoenix, "~> 1.8.0-rc.0", override: true},
    {:phoenix_ecto, "~> 4.5"},
    {:ecto_sql, "~> 3.10"},
    {:postgrex, ">= 0.0.0"},
    {:phoenix_html, "~> 4.1"},
    {:phoenix_live_reload, "~> 1.2", only: :dev},
    # . . .
    {:telemetry_poller, "~> 1.0"},
    {:gettext, "~> 0.26"},
    {:jason, "~> 1.2"},
    {:dns_cluster, "~> 0.1.1"},
    {:bandit, "~> 1.5"}
  ]
end
```

The mix.exs file ends with .exs, so it's an Elixir script. Think of this script as the configuration details for your app. Each line in the deps list is a dependency for your app. Install these dependencies by running mix deps.get in your terminal. Once installed, these dependencies aren't hidden in some archive. You can see them and look at the code within each one. They're in the deps directory:

```
[pento] → ls deps
bandit              hpax                    phoenix_template
db_connection       jason                   plug
decimal             mime                    plug_crypto
dns_cluster         mint                    postgrex
ecto                nimble_options          req
. . .
finch               phoenix_live_dashboard  telemetry_poller
floki               phoenix_live_reload     thousand_island
gettext             phoenix_live_view       websock
heroicons           phoenix_pubsub          websock_adapter
```

Those are the dependencies we've already installed. You might see a slightly different list based on your version of Phoenix. The LiveView dependencies are phoenix_live_view, phoenix_live_dashboard for system monitoring, and floki for tests. We also have a few dependencies our LiveView dependencies require.

Now that you understand how LiveView integrates into your Phoenix app as a Mix dependency, we're almost ready to write our first LiveView code. First, you need to understand the LiveView life cycle—how it starts up and how it runs to handle user events and manage the state of your single-page app.

The LiveView Life Cycle

As we build our first simple live view, we'll take a deeper dive into the LiveView life cycle we touched upon earlier when we discussed the LiveView loop. We'll walk through how LiveView manages the state of your single-page app in a data structure called a socket and how LiveView starts up, renders the page for the user, and responds to events. Once you understand the LiveView life cycle, you'll be ready to use it to manage the state of more complex live views.

We'll begin by examining how LiveView represents state via Phoenix.LiveView.Socket structs. Understanding how the socket struct is constructed and updated will give you the tools you need to establish and change the state of your live views.

Hold State in LiveView Sockets

Live views are about state, and LiveView manages state in structs called sockets. The module Phoenix.LiveView.Socket creates these structs. Whenever you see one of these socket structs as a variable or an argument within a live view, you should immediately recognize it as the data that constitutes the live view's state.

Let's take a closer look at a socket struct now.

Go to the pento directory and open up an IEx session for your application with iex -S mix. Then request help:

```
iex(1)> h Phoenix.LiveView.Socket

                  Phoenix.LiveView.Socket

The LiveView socket for Phoenix Endpoints.

This is typically mounted directly in your endpoint.

    socket "/live", Phoenix.LiveView.Socket,
      websocket: [connect_info: [session: @session_options]]
```

If you check in lib/pento_web/endpoint.ex, you'll see that, indeed, the socket is mounted there. The socket is more than an endpoint, though. Elixir gives us more tools for understanding code than the h helper. Let's build a new socket:

```
iex(2)> struct(Phoenix.LiveView.Socket)
#Phoenix.LiveView.Socket<
  id: nil,
  endpoint: nil,
  view: nil,
  parent_pid: nil,
  root_pid: nil,
  router: nil,
  ...
>
```

Here, you can see the basic structure of a socket struct and start to get an idea of how socket structs represent live view state. The socket struct has all of the data that Phoenix needs to manage a LiveView connection, and the data contained in this struct is mostly private. The most important key, and the one you'll interact with most frequently in your live views, is assigns: %{}. That's where you'll keep all of a given live view's custom data describing the state of your SPA.

Now you know a bit more about the framework. Every running live view keeps data describing state in a socket. You'll establish and update that state by interacting with the map within the socket's :assigns key.

That's enough talking for now. It's time to put what you've learned into practice and build your very first live view. In doing so, you'll get a first-hand look at the LiveView life cycle.

Build a Simple Live View

The Pento app's first live view will be a simple game called You're Wrong! It's one you can give to your kids to keep them busy for hours. It will ask them to guess a number, and then tell them they're wrong. In this initial pass, we'll define a route, establish our state, and render a page. Then we'll let the user make guesses and tell them they're wrong. Let's get started.

Define the Live View

Most of the time, programmers rely on functions in libraries. We call those functions to build programs. Sometimes we need to provide functions that existing programs must call. This concept is known as *inversion of control*. Elixir provides behaviours, spelled the British way, to describe an inversion-of-control contract between a calling function and receiving function.

LiveView is a *behaviour*, meaning it's a program designed to call into our application's functions to accomplish specific goals. We implement these goals within predetermined functions called *callbacks*. LiveView will call those callbacks when predetermined events happen. For example, LiveView will call our implementation of mount/3 when our process starts, our render/1 function when it's time to render results to send to the user, the handle_event/3 function when someone clicks links, and so on. These callbacks happen in a predetermined order called the *LiveView life cycle*.

To render a live view, we need to understand how the LiveView life cycle starts and when it calls our code. The LiveView life cycle begins in the Phoenix router. That's where you'll define a special type of route called a *live route*. Most Phoenix route definitions use HTTP methods,[6] primarily get and post. The LiveView.live/3 macro maps an incoming HTTP get request to a specified live view. From there, Phoenix starts up a live view process. That process will initialize the live view's state by setting up the socket in a function called mount/3. Then the live view will render that state in some markup for the client. This initial HTTP request and response flows through the live route. After that, a persistent WebSocket connection will handle the LiveView communication.

The following figure tells the story:

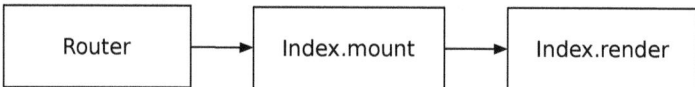

That's simple enough. Each of the arrows represents Phoenix framework code, and we're responsible for writing the boxes with a route and a couple of functions. Let's add our own live/3 route definition first:

```
intro/pento/lib/pento_web/router.ex
scope "/", PentoWeb do
  pipe_through(:browser)

  get "/", PageController, :home
  live "/guess", WrongLive
end
```

The live/3 function allows a final optional argument called a *live action*. Since our app won't need one, skip that concept for now. Our new code means that URLs matching the /guess pattern will invoke the PentoWeb.WrongLive module. Let's create that module now. Open up your editor and create a new WrongLive module and a lib/pento_web/live directory for it to go in, like this:

```
intro/pento/lib/pento_web/live/wrong_live.ex
defmodule PentoWeb.WrongLive do
  use PentoWeb, :live_view
end
```

Notice that our module uses the PentoWeb, :live_view behaviour.

Now, let's look at what happens when the user visits the /guess route.

Mount and Render the Live View

When your Phoenix app receives a request to the /guess route, the WrongLive live view will start up and LiveView will invoke that module's mount/3 function. The mount/3 function is responsible for establishing the initial state for the live view by populating the socket assigns.

---

6. https://developer.mozilla.org/en-US/docs/Web/HTTP/Methods

Let's put two values in our initial socket, a score and a message, like this:

```
intro/pento/lib/pento_web/live/wrong_live.ex
def mount(_params, _session, socket) do
  {:ok, assign(socket, score: 0, message: "Make a guess:")}
end
```

Remember, the socket contains the data representing the state of the live view, and the :assigns key, referred to as the socket assigns, holds custom data. Setting values in maps in Elixir can be tedious, so the LiveView helper function assign/2 simply adds key/value pairs to a given socket assigns, similar to Map.put/2. Our new code sets up our socket assigns with a score of 0 and a message of "Make a guess:".

That means our initial socket looks something like this:

```
%Socket{
  assigns: %{
    score: 0,
    message: "Make a guess:"
  }
}
```

The mount function returns a result tuple. The first element is either :ok or :error, and the second element has the initial contents of the socket.

After the initial mount finishes, LiveView then passes the value of the socket assigns map to the live view's render/1 function. If there's no render/1 function, LiveView looks for a template to render based on the name of the view. Don't worry about these details now. Just know that LiveView calls mount, and then render with those results.

If wrong_live has a render/1 function, LiveView will call it. Add this render/1 function just after mount in wrong_live.ex, like this:

```
intro/pento/lib/pento_web/live/wrong_live.ex
def render(assigns) do
  ~H"""
  <main class="px-4 py-20 sm:px-6 lg:px-8">
  <h1 class="mb-4 text-4xl font-extrabold">Your score: {@score}</h1>
  <h2>
    {@message}
  </h2>
  <br />
  <h2>
    <%= for n <- 1..10 do %>
      <.link
        class="btn btn-secondary"
        phx-click="guess"
```

```
          phx-value-number={n}
        >
          {n}
        </.link>
      <% end %>
    </h2>
  </main>
  """
end
```

This code renders our LiveView. Before we explore it, we should pause to address the interesting ~H""" syntax. The ~H denotes a sigil. In Elixir, sigils are syntactic sugar for a function call to a function named sigil_<sigil_name>/2. The two arguments are the string between the delimiters and the options immediately following the delimiters. In our case, ~H means a function called sigil_H[7] exists. The delimiters are """, a special form of quote wrapping a multiline string. We have no options, so nothing follows the closing """. Note that we don't have to use the """ delimiter. We could choose to use ~H with pipe characters like ~H|Hi, There|, or any other delimiters supported by sigils.[8] You might be asking, What does the ~H sigil do? We'll address that question next.

The Phoenix ~H sigil returns HEEx templates. The HEEx templating engine is an extension of EEx. Just like EEx templates, HEEx will process template replacements within your HTML code. Everything between the <%= and %> expressions is a template replacement and HEEx will evaluate the Elixir code within those tags and replace them with the result. Similarly, everything between {} delimiters is also Elixir. Notice the {@message} expression in our render/1 function. LiveView will populate this code with the value of socket.assigns.message, which we set in mount, and HEEx will evaluate the expression and replace it with the result. It will do the same for the <%= @score %> expression.

HEEx does more than just templating for us though. It also provides compile-time HTML validations, gives us a convenient component rendering syntax (more on that in a later chapter), and optimizes the amount of content sent over the wire, allowing LiveView to render *only those portions of the template that need updating when state changes*. HEEx is the default templating engine for Phoenix and LiveView. Any generated template files in your Phoenix app will be HEEx templates and end in the .html.heex extension. And when using inline render/1 functions in your live views, you'll use the ~H sigil to return HEEx templates. You'll see all of these benefits of HEEx in action throughout the course of this book. For now, let's get back to building our live view.

---

7. https://hexdocs.pm/phoenix_live_view/1.0.0/Phoenix.Component.html#sigil_H/2
8. https://hexdocs.pm/elixir/sigils.html

All right, you've mounted and rendered your first live view. After LiveView finishes calling render/1, it returns the initial web page to the browser. For a traditional web page, the story would end there. In fact, you can see a fully functional old-school web page, as shown in the following image. Make sure to start mix phx.server and then point your browser to localhost:4000/guess.

Your score: 0

Make a guess:

From this page, we can see the mount/3 and render/1 functions work. The mount/3 function sets up the data for the message and score, and then the render/1 function uses the ~H function to present it. After Phoenix renders our web page in the browser, LiveView uses a JavaScript script to establish a persistent WebSocket connection and awaits events over that connection. This page is just the beginning.

LiveView is actively waiting for messages. Our links are already sending messages. To wire them up, all we need to do is tell LiveView what to do, but we're getting ahead of ourselves. Let's look at this next part of the LiveView life cycle now.

> **The Initial Render Respects SEO**
>
> We should take a quick moment to point out a striking benefit of LiveView. The initial render works just like the render for a static page. For the purposes of search engine optimization, your initial page will show Google the same thing it tells your users!

Understand the LiveView Loop

So far, we've seen LiveView receive a request, set up the initial data, and render it. We've not addressed any of the technology that makes a live view interactive. We'll do that now.

When Phoenix processes a LiveView request, two things happen. First, Phoenix processes a plain HTTP request. The router invokes the LiveView module, and that calls the mount/3 function and then render/1. This first pass renders a static, SEO-friendly page that includes some JavaScript. That page then opens a persistent connection between the client and the server using WebSockets.

After Phoenix opens the WebSocket connection, our LiveView program will call mount/3 and render/1 *again*, this time to render the dynamic portions of the page. At this point, the LiveView life cycle starts up the *LiveView loop*. Phoenix LiveView framework code is in control now, calling our application code at strategic times. The live view can now receive events, change the state, and render the page again. This loop repeats whenever live view receives a new event, as this figure shows:

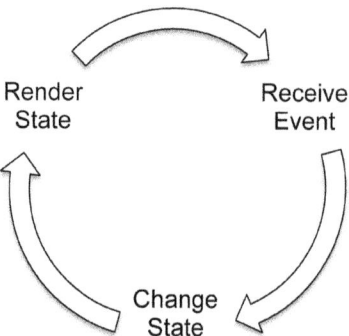

Code structured inline with this flow is simple to understand and easy to build. We don't have to worry about how events get sent to a live view or how markup is re-rendered when state changes. While we do have to implement our own event handler functions and teach them how to change state, LiveView does the hard work of detecting events, such as form submits or clicks on a link, and invokes those handlers for us. Then, once our handlers have changed the state, LiveView triggers a new render based on those changes. Finally, LiveView returns to the top of the loop to process more events.

What you have is a pure, functional render function to deal with the complexities of rendering the user interface and an event loop that receives events that change the state. Most of the hard problems—such as delivering an event from the client to the server, detecting state changes, and re-rendering the page—stay isolated in the infrastructure, where they belong.

Let's use the LiveView loop to add some interactivity to your page. We'll teach the live view to submit an event from the user and respond to that event by updating state and re-rendering the page.

Handle Events

The code in our render function shows a message and then some links. Let's look at one of these links now.

```
<%= for n <- 1..10 do %>
  <.link href="#" class=...
  phx-click="guess" phx-value-number={n} >
    <%= n %>
  </.link>
<% end %>
```

The `for` comprehension will loop over numbers 1 to 10, filling in the value `n` for each of the links. We're left with something like this:

```
<.link href="#" class=... phx-click="guess" phx-value-number="1">1</.link>
```

That's a link that leads to nowhere, but it has two values, a `phx-click` and a `phx-value-number`. We'll use that data when it's time to process events. The page will have similar links for n=2 all the way up through n=10.

Okay, we're ready to run our live view. Make sure you've started your server with `mix phx.server`. Next, point your browser to localhost:4000/guess. You'll see something like the following:

That's the user interface for the game. As expected, we see the message we put into `assigns`, and links for each of the 10 integers. Now click one of the links.

And … it fails. There's good news too, though. The application came back up! That's one of the perks of running on Elixir.

Flip on over to the console and you'll see this message:

```
[error] GenServer #PID<0.649.0> terminating
** (UndefinedFunctionError) function PentoWeb.WrongLive.handle_event/3
 is undefined or private
    (pento 0.1.0) PentoWeb.WrongLive.
    handle_event("guess",%{"number" => "1"}, ...)
...
```

You can see that our program received a message it wasn't ready to handle. When the event came in, LiveView called the function `handle_event("guess"`, some-map-data, our-socket), but no one was home—no such function is implemented by the `WrongLive` module. Let's fix that.

Finishing off our game isn't going to take as much effort as you might expect, because we won't be building routes for our links or building controllers, templates, or models—all of our data will flow over the same socket and be handled by one live view module. We'll simply build a handler for our inbound event.

The tricky part is matching the inbound data. Remember those extra data elements to our <a> links? These will come into play now. Those attributes are called DOM element bindings, or LiveView bindings. By adding the phx-click binding to the link element, LiveView will send a message from the client to the server when the user clicks that element. As you saw, this will trigger the function handle_event/3 with three arguments.

The first is the message name, the one we set in phx-click.

The second is a map with the metadata related to the event.

The last is the state for our live view, the socket.

Let's implement the handle_event/3 function now:

intro/pento/lib/pento_web/live/wrong_live.ex
```elixir
def handle_event("guess", %{"number" => guess}, socket) do
  message = "Your guess: #{guess}. Wrong. Guess again. "
  score = socket.assigns.score - 1

  {
    :noreply,
    assign(
      socket,
      message: message,
      score: score
    )
  }
end
```

Look at the function head first. It uses Elixir's pattern matching to do the heavy lifting. You can see that we match only function calls where the first argument is "guess" and the second is a map with a key of "number". Those are the arguments we set in our phx-click and phx-value link attributes.

The job of this function is to change the live view's state based on the inbound event, so we need to transform the data within socket.assigns. We knock one point off of the score and set a new message. Then we set the new data in the socket.assigns map. Finally, we return a tuple in the shape that LiveView expects—{:noreply, socket}. This update to socket.assigns triggers the live view to re-render by sending some changes down to the client over the persistent WebSocket connection.

Now you can play the game for yourself. If your will isn't strong, be careful. The game is strangely addictive:

If LiveView still seems a little mysterious to you, that's okay. We're ready to fill in a few more details.

LiveView Transfers Data Efficiently

At this point, you know how LiveView operates by handling an initial HTTP request, then opening a WebSocket connection and running an event loop over that connection. Understanding how LiveView transfers data to the client over the WebSocket connection is the final piece of the LiveView puzzle.

You know that LiveView re-renders the page by sending UI changes down to the client in response to state changes. What you might not know, however, is that LiveView sends these changes in a manner that's highly efficient. LiveView applications can therefore be faster and more reliable than similar alternatives composed completely from scratch in lower-level frameworks such as Phoenix or Rails.

We can examine the network traffic in our browser to illustrate exactly how LiveView sends diffs and see how efficient it is for ourselves. In fact, we recommend getting into the habit of inspecting this network traffic when you're developing your live views to ensure that you're not asking LiveView to transfer too much data.

Examine Network Traffic

Open up the developer tools for your browser. We're working with Safari, but other browsers should have similar capabilities. Navigate to the tab showing network traffic. Now, click a number representing one of the links from the game and then click either of the two websocket entries under the open network tab. In one of them, you should see the actual data that's sent up to the browser when the user clicks a number. This data is shown at the top of the next page.

```
[
  "4", "23", "lv:phx-GA8BYcBvYD4PIATD",
  "event",
  {
    "type":"click",
    "event":"guess",
    "value":{"number":"2"}
  }
]         1733606249.970883
```

The data here is formatted with some line breaks, but it's otherwise left intact. Other than a small bit of data in a header and footer, this data is information about the mouse click and the like. We'll get data packets like this only for the links and key presses that we tell LiveView to pay attention to with a DOM element binding.

Next, let's look at the data that goes back down to the client. Clicking the other `websocket` entry should show you something like this:

```
["4","23", "lv:phx-GA8BYcBvYD4PIATD",
  "phx_reply",
  {"status":"ok",
   "response":
     {"diff":
       {"3":
         {"0":"-1","1":"Your guess: 2. Wrong. Guess again. "}
       }
     }
  }
] 1690487105.2571628
```

This is the data that LiveView has sent over the WebSocket connection in response to some state change. This payload only contains a small header and footer along with *changes to the web page*, including the score and message we set in the `handle_event/3` function.

Look at the critical part of the message, the `diff`. It represents the changes in the view *since the last time we rendered!* You can see that LiveView sends the smallest possible payload of diffs to the client—only the information describing what changed in state, and therefore what needs to change on the page, is communicated. Keeping data payloads as small as possible helps ensure LiveView's efficiency.

Now let's see how LiveView detects the changes to send down to the client.

Send Network Diffs

Let's explore how exactly LiveView knows what diffs to send and when. We'll update our view to include a clock.

Update your render function to include the time, like this:

```
<h2>
  <%= @message %>
  It's <%= time() %>
</h2>
```

Add this function right below the render:

```
def time do
   DateTime.utc_now() |> to_string()
end
```

And take a look at your reloaded browser:

```
Your score: 0

Guess a number. It's 2020-01-18 15:53:40.209764Z

1 2 3 4 5 6 7 8 9 10
```

So far so good. You can see the time in the initial page load, 15:53:40.

Now make a guess:

```
Your score: -1

Your guess: 5. Wrong. Guess again. It's 2020-01-18 15:53:40.209764Z

1 2 3 4 5 6 7 8 9 10
```

Even though the page updated, the time is *exactly the same*. The problem is that we didn't give LiveView any way to determine that the value should change and be re-rendered.

When you want to track changes, make sure to use socket assigns values, such as @score, in your templates. LiveView keeps track of the data in socket assigns and any changes to that data instruct LiveView to send a diff down to the client. Diffs describe only what changed in the socket assigns and LiveView re-renders only the portions of the page impacted by those changes.

So although LiveView re-rendered the page when it handled the click event, LiveView did *not* consider the portion of the template that includes the invocation of the time/0 function to have changed. So that portion of the template was not re-rendered, the time/0 was not re-invoked, and the time didn't update on the page.

We can fix this by assigning a time to the socket when we mount, rendering that value in the template, and changing that value when we receive events. Go ahead and make those changes as an exercise.

LiveView's Efficiency Is SEO Friendly

If you refresh the page and then check out your network tab again in your inspector, you'll see that the initial page load *looks like any other page load*. Phoenix sends the main page and the assets as it normally would for any HTTP request/response, as you can see in the following image of the browser's network tab. Pay close attention to the guess request line, which shows that the response is a simple HTML document.

Name	Domain	Type	Initiator	Tran...	Time	50.00ms	100.00ms	150.0ms
guess	localhost	document	—	1.91...	81.8ms			
app.css	localhost	css	guess:8	(me...	2.14ms			
app.js	localhost	js	guess:10	(me...	2.54ms			
data:image/svg+xml,%3C...%3E	—	svg	guess:80	(me...	0ms			
frame	localhost	document	—	13.2...	3.21ms			
frame	localhost	document	—	13.2...	—			
websocket	localhost	socket	—	3.12...	29.3ms			
websocket	localhost	socket	—	431 B	41.9ms			

Many one-page applications render pages that can't be used for SEO (search engine optimization). Because those apps must render the page in parts, Google can't tell what's on the whole page.

Before LiveView, solving this problem was inevitably expensive. With LiveView, the initial page load looks like any other page to a search engine. Only after the initial page load completes does LiveView establish the WebSocket-backed LiveView loop in which your live view listens for events, updates state, and efficiently re-renders *only the portions of the page described in the network diff events*. You get SEO right out of the box, without impacting the efficiency of LiveView.

Now that you understand the basics of LiveView, it's time to put what you know to use.

Your Turn

LiveView is a library for building highly interactive single-page web flows, called live views, without requiring you to write JavaScript. A live view has these characteristics:

- Has internal state.
- Has a render function to render that state.
- Receives events that change state.

- Calls the render function when state changes.
- Only sends changed data to the browser.
- Needs no custom JavaScript.

When we build live views, we focus on managing and rendering our view's state, called a socket. We manage our live view's state by assigning an initial value in the mount/3 function and by updating that value using several handler functions. Those functions can handle input from processes elsewhere in our application as well as manage events triggered by the user on the page, such as mouse clicks or keystroke presses. After a handler function is invoked, LiveView renders the changed state with the render/1 function.

This is the LiveView life cycle in a nutshell. As we build live views that handle increasingly complex interactive features over the course of this book, you'll see how the LiveView framework allows you to be amazingly productive at building single-page apps. By providing an infrastructure that manages client-server communication in a manner that's reliable and scalable, LiveView frees you up to focus on what really matters—shipping features that deliver value to your users.

Give It a Try

Now that you've seen a basic LiveView "game," you can tweak the game so that the user can actually win. You'll need to incorporate the following:

- Assign a random number to the socket when the game is created, one the user will need to guess.

- Check for that number in the handle_event for guess.

- Show a winning message when the user guesses the right number and increment their score in the socket assigns.

- Show a restart message and button when the user wins. Hint: you might want to check out the link/1 function and read this section of the docs on live navigation using the patch approach.[9] You can treat this last challenge as a stretch goal. We'll get into link/1 function in greater detail in upcoming chapters.

---

9. https://hexdocs.pm/phoenix_live_view/live-navigation.html

Next Time

In the next chapter, we're going to start work on the Pento application's infrastructure, beginning with the authentication layer. We'll build out this layer using a code generator. Along the way, we'll take the opportunity to explore how Phoenix requests work, and we'll show you how to use the generated authentication service to authenticate users. Lastly, you'll use the service to authenticate the guessing game live view you just built.

We're just getting started. Let's get to work.

Part I

Code Generation

Both LiveView and the greater Phoenix ecosystem have outstanding support for code generation—you'll use generators often to build a solid foundation for your Phoenix LiveView apps. We'll use a code generator to build a secure and user-friendly authentication scheme that we'll use throughout the rest of the book. Then we'll use a generator to build a LiveView front end for creating and managing a database of products. Along the way, we'll use the generated code to illustrate core code organizational concepts.

CHAPTER 2

Phoenix and Authentication

In this chapter, we're going to use a code generator to build an authentication layer for our Phoenix application. This is an approach that you'll often take when building out a new Phoenix LiveView app. You'll start with a web app essential, authentication, and reach for a tried and tested generator to get up and running quickly.

Let's look a little closer at the role authentication will play in Pento.

While authentication isn't a LiveView concern per se, it will still serve an important purpose for us. On the web, users do things. Authentication services tell us which users are doing which things by tying the id of a user to a session.[1] More specifically, authentication allows us to do the following:

Manage Users
> One important feature of our authentication service is the ability to store users and tokens, look up users by email, and generate secure magic links for passwordless authentication.

Authenticate Requests
> As requests come in, we need a way to check if the user that made the request is logged in or not so our application knows which page to show. A logged-out user might get the sign-in page, a logged-in user might get a game, and so on.

Manage Sessions
> Our application will need to track *session data*, including information about the logged-in user and the expiration of that login, if any. We'll manage this data in cookies, just as web applications built in other frameworks do.

---

1. https://developer.mozilla.org/en-US/docs/Web/HTTP/Session

You don't need to know every detail of how these services work, but you do need to understand in broad strokes what's happening. Because our live views will need to know which user is logged in, we'll rely on these critical responsibilities enacted by the authentication service throughout our LiveView code.

For example, our system will support surveys. We'll use authentication to force users to sign in before taking the survey and to make the signed-in user available to the live view. So we're going to start the work of building our application with authentication—the act of attaching a user's conversation through browser requests to a user in your system.

We're also going to look at how plain old boring Phoenix works with traditional requests and responses. Every live view must start in the browser as a traditional HTTP request. Then the request will flow through many Phoenix services, culminating in the router, where we'll redirect unauthenticated users and attach a user ID to the session before LiveView ever gets involved. That means you need to understand how the Phoenix endpoints and routers work to do even the most basic of tasks.

Before we write any code, let's plan our trip. Let's look at the basic application we've already generated. We'll walk through what happens when a fresh request comes into Phoenix and trace it through the various layers. That journey will take us through an *endpoint* and into the *router* and, finally, into the various modules that make up our custom application.

Then we're going to implement our authentication code. We'll generate the bulk of our code with the phx.gen.auth generator, and then we'll tweak that code to do what we want. This generator is generally the best authentication solution for Phoenix. In Phoenix 1.8, this generator has been enhanced with modern authentication patterns, including magic link authentication by default and a comprehensive user scopes system for secure data access.

After we generate the code, we'll work through the codebase to explore the main authentication service APIs, including the new magic link authentication flow and the innovative scopes system that automatically handles user context throughout your application. We'll demonstrate how the generated code can be used to authenticate a live view with minimal configuration, and we'll take a closer look at LiveView authentication features that allow us to seamlessly authenticate groups of live views using the new scopes pattern.

By the end of this chapter, you'll understand how Phoenix handles web requests, how magic links provide a secure and user-friendly authentication experience, and how the scopes system ensures that user context is automatically and securely threaded through your entire application. You'll experience the recommended way to build and use authentication in your Phoenix app and be able to integrate authentication into your live views using Phoenix 1.8's streamlined approach.

Let's get to work, starting with a common pattern called CRC.

CRC: Constructors, Reducers, and Converters

Pipelines and functional composition play a big role in Elixir. One pattern, called CRC, plays a huge role in many different Elixir modules. Its roots are closely entwined with the common function Enum.reduce/3. Let's take a closer look.

Web frameworks in functional languages all use variations of a common pattern. They use data represented by a common data type and use many tiny, focused functions to change that data, step by step. For example, in the JavaScript world, the state reducer pattern[2] by Kent Dodds uses many of the same strategies. Clojure has a similar framework called Ring.[3]

In Phoenix, the Plug framework follows the same pattern. Let's explore this pattern in more detail.

In Elixir, many modules are associated with a *core type*. The String module deals with strings, Enum deals with enumerables, and so on. As often as possible, experienced Elixir developers strive to make a module's public functions relate to its core type. Constructors create a term of the core type from convenient inputs. Reducers transform a term of the core type to another term of that type. Converters convert the core type to some other type. Taken together, we'll call this pattern CRC, which stands for construct, reduce, convert.

So far, CRC might seem abstract, so let's take a simple tangible example. Let's build a module that has one of each of these functions—a constructor, a reducer, and a converter:

```
iex(1)> defmodule Number do
...(1)>   def new(string), do: Integer.parse(string) |> elem(0)
...(1)>   def add(number, addend), do: number + addend
...(1)>   def to_string(number), do: Integer.to_string(number)
...(1)> end
```

Notice that this tiny module works with *integers* and has three kinds of functions. All of them deal with integers as an input argument, output, or both. The new/1 function is a constructor, and it's used to create a term of the

---

2. https://kentcdodds.com/blog/the-state-reducer-pattern-with-react-hooks
3. https://github.com/ring-clojure/ring

module's type from a String input. The to_string/1 function is a converter that takes an integer input and produces output of some other type, a String in our case. The add/2 reducer takes an integer as both the input and output.

Let's put it to use in two different ways. First, let's use the reduce/3 function with our three functions.

```
iex(2)> list = [1, 2, 3]
[1, 2, 3]
iex(3)> total = Number.new("0")
0
iex(4)> reducer = &Number.add(&2, &1)
#Function<13.126501267/2 in :erl_eval.expr/5>
iex(5)> converter = &Number.to_string/1
&Number.to_string/1
iex(6)> Enum.reduce(list, total, reducer) |> converter.()
"6"
```

We take a list of integers and a string that we feed into our constructor that produces an integer we can use with our reducer. Since Enum.reduce/3 takes the accumulator as the second argument, we build a reducer/2 function using Elixir's capture syntax[4] to flip the order of the arguments in Number.add/2. Then we call Enum.reduce/3 and pipe that result into the converter.

It turns out that the same kinds of functions that work with reducers also work in pipes, like this:

```
iex(7)> [first, second, third] = list
[1, 2, 3]
iex(16)> "0" \
iex(16)> |> Number.new \
...(16)> |> Number.add(first) \
...(16)> |> Number.add(second) \
...(16)> |> Number.add(third) \
...(16)> |> Number.to_string
"6"
```

Perfect! The backslash at the end of each line tells IEx to delay execution because we have more to do. The functions in this Number module show an example of CRC, but it's not the only one. This pattern is great for taking something complicated, like the response to a web request, and breaking it down into many small steps. It also lets us build tiny single-purpose functions that each focus on one thing.

---

4. https://hexdocs.pm/elixir/anonymous-functions.html#the-capture-operator

CRC in Phoenix

Phoenix processes requests with the CRC pattern. The central type of many Phoenix modules is a *connection* struct defined by the Plug.Conn module. The connection represents a web request. We can then break down a response into a bunch of smaller reducers that each process a tiny part of the request, followed by a short converter. Here's what the program looks like at a high level:

```
connection
|> process_part_of_request(...)
|> process_part_of_request(...)
|> render()
```

You can see CRC in play. Phoenix itself serves as the constructor. It builds a common piece of data that has both request data and response information. Initially, Phoenix populates the request data with information about the request, but the response data is empty. Then Phoenix builds a response, piece by piece, with small reducers. Finally, Phoenix converts the connection to a response with the render/1 converter.

Let's make this example a little more concrete. Suppose we want to have our web server build a response to some request, piece by piece. We might have some code that looks like this:

```
iex(4)> connection = %{request_path: "http://mysite.com/"}
%{request_path: "http://mysite.com/"}
iex(5)> reducer = fn acc, key, value -> Map.put(acc, key, value) end
#Function<19.126501267/3 in :erl_eval.expr/5>
iex(6)> connection |> reducer.(:status, 200) |> reducer.(:body, :ok)
%{body: :ok, request_path: "http://mysite.com/", status: 200}
```

Notice the two main concepts at play. First is the common data structure, the connection. The second is a function that takes an argument, called acc for accumulator, that we'll use for our connection and two additional arguments. Our function is called a *reducer* because we can reduce an accumulator and a few arguments into a single accumulator.

Now, with our fictional program, we can string together a narrative that represents a web request. For our request, we take the connection, and then we pass that connection through two reducers to set the status to 200 and the body to :ok. After we've built a map in this way, we can then give it back to our web server by passing it to our render/1 converter to send the correct body with the correct status down to the client.

Now that we have a high-level understanding of how Phoenix strings together a series of functions to respond to a web request, let's look at the specifics. As we go, pay attention to the plugs. Each one is essentially a reducer that accepts a Plug.Conn as an input, does some work, and returns a transformed Plug.Conn.

The Plug.Conn Common Data Structure

Plug is a framework for building web programs, one function at a time. Plugs are either Elixir functions or tiny modules that support a small function named call. Each function makes one little change to a connection—the Plug.Conn data structure. A web server simply lets developers easily string many such plugs together to define the various policies and flows that make up an application. Chris McCord took the Plug toolkit and used it to build Phoenix.

You don't have to guess what's inside. You can see it for yourself. Type iex -S mix to launch interactive Elixir in the context of your Phoenix application. Key in an empty Plug.Conn struct and hit enter. You should see these default values:

```
iex> %Plug.Conn{}
%Plug.Conn{
  ...
  host: "www.example.com",
  method: "GET",
  ...
  resp_body: nil,
  resp_headers: [{"cache-control", "max-age=0, private, must-revalidate"}],
  status: nil
  ...
}
```

We've cut out most of the keys but left a few in place for context. Some are related to the inbound *request*, including the host, the request method,[5] and so on. Some are related to the *response*. For example, the response headers are pieces of data to control caching, specify the response type, and more. The response status is the standardized HTTP status.[6]

So that's the "common data structure" piece of the equation. Next, we'll look at the reducer piece of how Phoenix implements CRC.

---

5. https://developer.mozilla.org/en-US/docs/Web/HTTP/Methods
6. https://www.w3.org/Protocols/rfc2616/rfc2616-sec10.html

Reducers in Plug

Now you've seen Plug.Conn, the data that stitches Phoenix programs together. You don't need to know too much to understand many of the files that make up a Phoenix application beyond three main concepts:

- Plugs are essentially reducer functions.
- They take a Plug.Conn struct as the first argument.
- They return a Plug.Conn struct.
- They can be halted.

The first three concepts allow us to compose a complex concept out of simpler functions. The fourth allows Phoenix to halt a plug. If you're interested, you can read more about how plugs work, including halting.[7]

When you see Phoenix configuration code, it's often full of plugs. When you see lists of plugs, imagine a pipe operator between them. For example, suppose you see something like this:

```
plug Plug.MethodOverride
plug Plug.Head
plug Plug.Session, @session_options
plug PentoWeb.Router
```

You should mentally translate that code to this:

```
connection
|> Plug.MethodOverride.call()
|> Plug.Head.call()
|> Plug.Session.call(@session_options)
|> PentoWeb.Router.call()
```

Said another way, lists of plugs are composed with *pipelines* plus a small amount of boilerplate code to handle failure.

Now, with that background, we're going to look at the heart of your Phoenix infrastructure, and even if you have only a small amount of experience with Phoenix, you'll be able to understand it. Keep in mind that this information will come in handy because it will help you understand exactly what happens when a live view runs.

Phoenix Is One Giant Function

To understand how Phoenix handles web requests, and therefore how LiveView handles web requests, you can think of Phoenix requests as simply one big

---

7. https://hexdocs.pm/phoenix/plug.html

function broken down into smaller plugs. These plugs are stitched together, one after another, as if they were in one big pipeline.

The main sections of the giant Phoenix pipeline are the endpoint, the router, and the application. You can visualize any Phoenix request with this CRC pipeline:

```
connection_from_request
|> endpoint
|> router
|> custom_application
```

Each one of these pieces is made up of tiny functions. The custom_application can be a Phoenix controller, a Phoenix channels application, or a live view. We'll spend most of the book on live views. For now, let's take a few short sections to discuss the first two parts of this pipeline, the endpoint and router.

The Phoenix Endpoint

If Phoenix is a long chain of reducer functions called plugs, the endpoint is the constructor at the very beginning of that chain. The endpoint is a simple Elixir module in a file called endpoint.ex, and it has exactly what you would expect—a pipeline of plugs.

You might not ever change your endpoint.ex file, so we won't read through it in detail. Instead, we'll just scan through it to confirm that every Phoenix request goes through an explicit list of functions called plugs. There's no magic.

Open up endpoint.ex and you'll notice that it has a bit of configuration followed by a bunch of plugs. That configuration defines the *socket* that will handle the communication for all of your live views, but the details aren't important right now.

After those sockets, you see a list of plugs, and every one of them transforms the connection in some small way. Don't get bogged down in the details. Instead, scan down to the bottom. Eventually, requests flow through to the bottom of the pipeline to reach the router:

auth/pento/lib/pento_web/endpoint.ex
```
plug PentoWeb.Router
```

You don't have to know what these plugs do yet. Just know that requests, in the form of Plug.Conn connections, flow through the plugs, making small changes and eventually reaching the Router.

The esteemed router is next.

The Phoenix Router

Think of a router as a switchboard operator. Its job is to route the requests to the bits of code that make up your application. Some of those bits of code are common pieces of *policy*. A policy defines how a given web request should be treated and handled. For example, browser requests may need to deal with cookies, API requests may need to convert to and from JSON, and so on. The router does its job in three parts.

- First, the router specifies chains of common functions to implement policy.
- Next, the router groups together common requests and ties each one to the correct policy.
- Finally, the router maps individual requests onto the modules that do the hard work of building appropriate responses to individual requests.

Said another way, the endpoint *prepares Plug.Conn*. The router *applies collective policies* and then *sends each request to the appropriate custom application module* based on application policy. Then custom *application modules service a request*.

Let's see how that works. Open up lib/pento_web/router.ex. You'll find more plugs and some mappings between specific URLs and the code that implements those pages. Each grouping of plugs provides *policy* for one or more routes. Here's how it works.

Pipelines Are Policies

A *pipeline* is a grouping of plugs that applies a set of transformations to a given connection. The set of transformations applied by a given plug represents a policy. Since you know that every plug takes in a connection and returns a connection, you also know that the first plug in a pipeline takes a connection and the last plug in that pipelines returns a connection. So a plug pipeline works exactly like a single plug! Here's a peek at what the browser pipeline will look like by the time you're done building out the code in this chapter. The pipeline implements the policy your application needs to process a request from a browser:

```
intro/pento/lib/pento_web/router.ex
pipeline :browser do
  plug(:accepts, ["html"])
  plug(:fetch_session)
  plug(:fetch_live_flash)
  plug(:put_root_layout, html: {PentoWeb.Layouts, :root})
  plug(:protect_from_forgery)
  plug(:put_secure_browser_headers)
end
```

The preceding bit of code says we're going to accept only HTML requests, and we'll fetch the session, and so on. The following api pipeline implements the policy for an API:

auth/pento/lib/pento_web/router.ex
```
pipeline :api do
  plug(:accepts, ["json"])
end
```

It has a single plug that means associated routes will accept only JSON[8] requests. Based on business needs, application developers could decide to extend this policy with their own plugs to enforce authentication, preprocess results, and so on.

Now that we know how to build a policy, the last thing we need to do is to tie a particular URL to a policy and then to the code responsible for responding to the request for the particular URL.

Scopes

A scope block groups together common kinds of requests, possibly with a policy. Here's a set of common routes in a scope block.

auth/pento/lib/pento_web/router.ex
```
scope "/", PentoWeb do
  pipe_through(:browser)

  get("/", PageController, :home)
end
```

This tiny block of code does a lot. The scope expression means the provided block of routes between the do and the end applies to *all routes* because all routes begin with /. The pipe_through :browser statement means every matching request in this block will go through all of the plugs in the :browser pipeline. Notice also the PentoWeb argument in the scope directive. The router will prepend this module to every module we specify within the given scope block. Next, we'll move on to the routes within the block.

Routes

The last bit of information is the individual routes. Let's revisit our single custom route for clarity.

auth/pento/lib/pento_web/router.ex
```
live("/guess", WrongLive)
```

---

8. https://www.json.org/json-en.html

Every route starts with a route type, a URL pattern, a module, and options. LiveView routes have the type live.

The URL pattern in a route is a pattern matching statement. The "/" pattern will match the url /, and a pattern of "/bears" will match a URL like /bears, and so on.

The next bit of information is the WrongLive module, which implements the code that responds to the request. The type of route will determine what kind of code does the responding. Since our route is a live route, the WrongLive module should implement a live view. We could have chosen to add an optional live action argument to our route, but we'll wait to do so until the next chapter. For now, let's move on.

Plugs and Authentication

Now we need to think about authentication. Web applications almost always need to know who's logged in. Authentication is the service that answers the question *Who is logging in?* Only the most basic applications can be secure without authentication, and since malicious actors have worked for decades breaking authentication systems, it's best to use a service built by someone who knows what they're doing.

Our authentication service will let in only those who have accounts on our game server. Since we plan to have pages only our registered users should see, we'll need to secure those pages. We must know who's logging in before we can decide whether or not to let them in.

Now, let's put all of that conversation about plugs into action. But first, let's discuss a plan for authentication. We'll build our authentication system in layers, as shown in the figure at the top of the next page.

On the left side is the *infrastructure*. This code will use a variety of services to store long-term user data in the database and short-term session data into cookies, and it will provide user interfaces to manage user interactions.

On the right side, the Phoenix router will send appropriate requests through authentication plugs within the router, and these plugs will control access to custom live views, channels, and controllers.

We'll go into each of these layers in detail throughout the rest of the chapter. Suffice to say we're not going to build this service ourselves. Instead, we'll generate it from an existing dependency. Let's get to work!

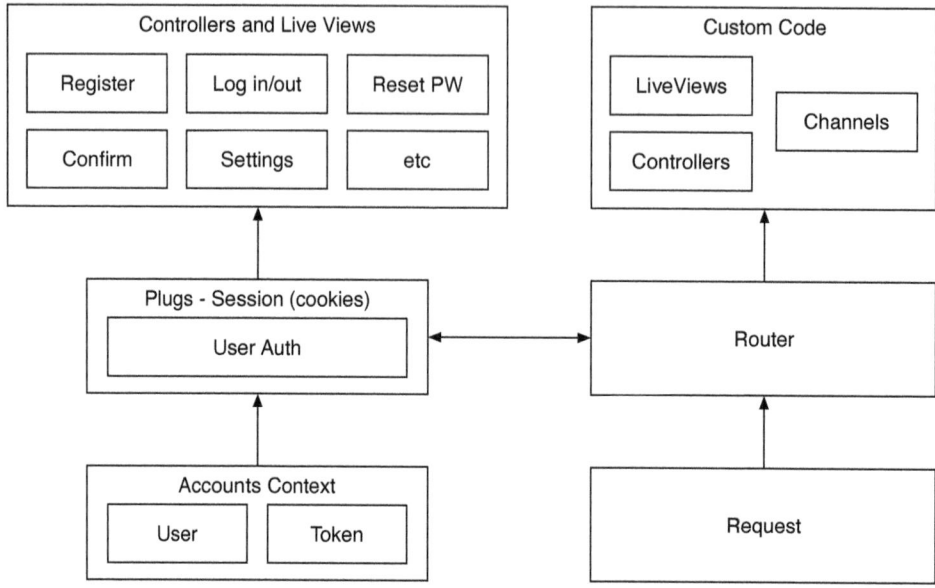

Generate the Authentication Layer

Let's dig down deeper into the phx.gen.auth code generator. Its primary focus is to build a well-layered authentication layer for Phoenix requests. This generator is the authentication standard for all Phoenix applications. We can rely on it to generate, rather than hand-roll, a solution that's mostly complete and adapt it to meet any specialized requirements we might have.

In the following sections, you'll learn how to generate an authentication layer, you'll see how the pieces of generated code fit together to handle the responsibilities of authentication, and you'll even see how LiveView uses the authentication service to identify and operate on the logged-in user.

We'll start by installing and running the generator.

Run the Generator

The version of Phoenix we're using has authentication generation built in. We'll use mix to generate it. Before we generate our code, we'll take advantage of a common pattern for many mix tasks: running them without arguments will give you guidance about any options you'll need. Doing so with mix phx will point you to the phx.gen tasks for generators, and we can apply this technique again to get a list of available generators:

```
[pento] (beta_1_intro *=) → mix phx.gen
mix phx.gen.auth      # Generates authentication logic for a resource
...
mix phx.gen.context   # Generates a context with functions around an Ecto \
  schema
mix phx.gen.embedded  # Generates an embedded Ecto schema
mix phx.gen.html      # Generates context and controller for an HTML resource
mix phx.gen.json      # Generates context and controller for a JSON resource
mix phx.gen.live      # Generates LiveView, templates, and context...
...
mix phx.gen.schema    # Generates an Ecto schema and migration file
```

That's quite a few generators—the first is the one we need.

Run mix phx.gen.auth without any arguments to see what arguments the tool needs, like this:

```
[pento] → mix phx.gen.auth
** (Mix) Invalid arguments

mix phx.gen.auth expects a context module name, followed by
the schema module and its plural name (used as the schema
table name).

For example:

    mix phx.gen.auth Accounts User users

The context serves as the API boundary ...
```

Don't worry about the vocabulary. We'll cover contexts, schemas, and the like in more detail later. For now, know that running this generator creates a module called a *context* and another module called a *schema*. Think of a context as an API for a service, and a schema as a data structure describing a database table. This generator is giving us the command to build an authentication layer. It will generate a context called Accounts and a schema called User with a plural of users. Check out *Designing Elixir Systems with OTP [IT19]* for more detail about building software in layers if you're hungry for more.

The generator's defaults seem reasonable, so let's take that advice. Now we can let it fly.

```
[pento] → mix phx.gen.auth Accounts User users
An authentication system can be created in two different ways:
- Using Phoenix.LiveView (default)
- Using Phoenix.Controller only
Do you want to create a LiveView based authentication system? [Yn] Y
Compiling 16 files (.ex)
Generated pento app
* creating priv/repo/migrations/20250722114420_create_users_auth_tables.exs
```

```
* creating lib/pento/accounts/user_notifier.ex
* creating lib/pento/accounts/user.ex
* creating lib/pento/accounts/user_token.ex
* creating lib/pento_web/user_auth.ex
* creating lib/pento/accounts/scope.ex
* creating lib/pento_web/live/user_live/registration.ex
* creating lib/pento_web/live/user_live/login.ex
* creating lib/pento_web/live/user_live/settings.ex
* creating lib/pento_web/live/user_live/confirmation.ex
* creating lib/pento/accounts.ex
* injecting lib/pento_web/router.ex
* injecting lib/pento_web/router.ex - imports
```

Add the :fetch_current_scope_for_user plug to the :browser pipeline:

```
pipeline :browser do
  ...
  plug :put_secure_browser_headers
  plug :fetch_current_scope_for_user
end
```

```
* injecting lib/pento_web/components/layouts/root.html.heex
```

Make sure to opt in to the LiveView-based authentication. Notice several important new features in Phoenix 1.8's authentication generator:

Magic links by default: Phoenix 1.8 generates magic link authentication as the primary method. Users register with just their email address and receive magic links for login. This eliminates the need for users to remember passwords and provides a more secure authentication flow by default. From a security perspective, magic links offer significant advantages, eliminating common vulnerabilities like password reuse, weak passwords, and credential stuffing attacks, while the time-limited nature of magic links reduces the window of opportunity for potential exploits.

User scopes: The generator creates a new lib/pento/accounts/scope.ex file that implements Phoenix's new scopes pattern. Scopes provide a secure-by-default approach to data access, ensuring that all context functions receive information about the current user and can properly filter data based on ownership.

Scope integration: Notice the instruction to add :fetch_current_scope_for_user to the browser pipeline. This plug ensures that every request has access to the current user's scope, making authorization seamless throughout your application.

Understanding Phoenix 1.8's User Scopes System

Phoenix 1.8 introduces a powerful new pattern called *user scopes* that fundamentally changes how we think about authentication and authorization in

Phoenix applications. Unlike traditional approaches where user context is manually passed around or looked up as needed, the scopes system provides a centralized, secure-by-default way to carry user information throughout your entire application.

What Are User Scopes?

A scope is a data structure that carries information about the current request context, particularly who is making the request and what they're authorized to access. At its core, a scope is simply a struct that wraps user information:

auth/pento/lib/pento/accounts/scope.ex
```
defstruct user: nil
```

This simple structure serves as a secure container for user data that can be threaded through your entire application automatically. The scope is created once per request and then made available everywhere it's needed.

How Scopes Work in the Request Life Cycle

The scopes system integrates seamlessly with Phoenix's request pipeline through a series of plugs and callbacks:

1. *HTTP request level:* The :fetch_current_scope_for_user plug runs early in the browser pipeline, looking up the current user from the session and creating a scope for them.

2. *LiveView level:* When a LiveView mounts, the on_mount callback automatically transfers the scope from the connection to the LiveView socket, making it available throughout the LiveView life cycle.

3. *Context level:* Your business logic functions can accept a scope as their first parameter, ensuring they always have access to the current user's information for authorization decisions.

Here's how the scope gets created and mounted automatically:

auth/pento/lib/pento_web/user_auth.ex
```
defp mount_current_scope(socket, session) do
  Phoenix.Component.assign_new(socket, :current_scope, fn ->
    user =
      if user_token = session["user_token"] do
        Accounts.get_user_by_session_token(user_token)
      end

    Scope.for_user(user)
  end)
end
```

Notice the use of assign_new/3, which ensures the scope is only created once and reused efficiently throughout the request life cycle.

The Security Benefits

The scopes system provides several key security advantages:

Automatic context: Every function that needs user information receives it automatically, eliminating the possibility of authorization bugs where user context is forgotten or incorrectly retrieved.

Centralized logic: All user lookup and scope creation happens in one place, making it easy to audit and secure.

Type safety: By standardizing on the scope struct, you get compile-time guarantees about the shape of your user data.

Prevention of context loss: Because scopes are automatically propagated, you can't accidentally lose track of who the current user is as requests flow through your system.

Scopes in Live Views

In live views, scopes eliminate the need for manual session token handling. Instead of looking up users by tokens in each live view, the scope is automatically available:

```
auth/pento/lib/pento_web/live/wrong_live.ex
def mount(_params, _session, socket) do
  # current_scope is automatically available thanks to on_mount callback
  user = socket.assigns.current_scope.user
  {
    :ok,
    assign(
      socket,
      score: 0,
      message: "Guess a number.",
      current_user: user
    )
  }
end
```

This automatic scope assignment happens through the on_mount callback system, which runs before your live view's own mount function, ensuring the scope is always available when you need it.

Extending Scopes for Authorization

While our current scope only contains user information, scopes can be extended to carry additional authorization data. For example, you might add organization membership, role information, or feature flags:

```
defmodule Pento.Accounts.Scope do
  defstruct user: nil, organization: nil, roles: [], feature_flags: %{}

  def for_user(%User{} = user) do
    %__MODULE__{
      user: user,
      organization: get_user_organization(user),
      roles: get_user_roles(user),
      feature_flags: get_feature_flags(user)
    }
  end
end
```

This pattern ensures that all authorization data is computed once and made available everywhere it's needed rather than being looked up repeatedly throughout a request.

Migration from Traditional Auth Patterns

If you're familiar with previous Phoenix authentication patterns, the scopes system eliminates several common pain points:

- *No more conn.assigns.current_user checks:* The scope is automatically available.

- *No more manual token lookups in live views:* The on_mount callback handles this.

- *No more passing user IDs through function parameters:* The scope carries all needed context.

- *No more authorization logic scattered throughout your codebase:* Everything centralizes around the scope.

The scopes system represents a significant evolution in Phoenix's approach to authentication and authorization, providing a more secure, maintainable, and developer-friendly way to handle user context throughout your application.

Let's continue with setting up our dependencies and database to see this system in action.

The last few instructions tell us to fetch dependencies and run migrations. Our freshly generated code has its own set of requirements, so we'll fetch them now, as shown at the top of the next page.

```
[pento] → mix deps.get
Resolving Hex dependencies...
Resolution completed in 0.125s
New:
  bcrypt_elixir 3.3.2
  comeonin 5.5.1
  elixir_make 0.9.0
Unchanged:
  phoenix 1.8.0-rc.0
  phoenix_live_view 1.0.9
  swoosh 1.18.4
...
```

You'll notice the generator fetched dependencies to encrypt passwords, along with password hashing libraries. Even though Phoenix 1.8 uses magic links by default, it still includes password-hashing capabilities that users can opt into later through their settings page. Also, one of these dependencies requires elixir_make. We don't need to know why.

Run Migrations

Ecto is the database integration layer for Elixir. Ecto separates the concepts of working with database *records* from that of working with database *structure*. Our generator gave us the database structure code in the form of a set of Ecto migrations for creating database tables. Ecto is the framework for dealing with databases within Elixir, and migrations are the part of Ecto that create and modify database entities. Before your application can work with a database table, your migrations will need to be run to ensure that the database table exists, has the right structure for the data you'll put in it, and has the right set of indexes for performance. Check out the excellent advice in *Programming Ecto [WM19]* for more details.

Fortunately, along with the rest of the authentication code, phx.gen.auth built some migrations for us. We need only run them. Head over to your terminal and execute the migrate command shown here:

```
[pento] → mix ecto.migrate
==> pento
Compiling 27 files (.ex)
Generated pento app
07:45:03.302 [info] == Running 20250722114420 \
  Pento.Repo.Migrations.CreateUsersAuthTables.change/0 forward
07:45:03.303 [info] execute "CREATE EXTENSION IF NOT EXISTS citext"
07:45:03.304 [info] create table users
07:45:03.310 [info] create index users_email_index
07:45:03.313 [info] create table users_tokens
07:45:03.317 [info] create index users_tokens_user_id_index
```

```
07:45:03.317 [info] create index users_tokens_context_token_index
07:45:03.319 [info] == Migrated 20250722114420 in 0.0s
```

Perfect. The migration made sure the case insensitive extension exists and then created the tables for users and tokens. Along the way, we created a few indexes for performance as well.

Before we dive in too deeply, let's make sure the overall service is working, end to end. Tests are a great way to do so.

Test the Service

To make sure everything works, run the tests like this:

```
[pento] → mix test
Running ExUnit with seed: 539584, max_cases: 28

.........................................................
..................................................
Finished in 0.4 seconds (0.3s async, 0.06s sync)
106 tests, 0 failures
```

Everything works just fine. We're ready to do some code spelunking!

Explore Accounts from IEx

When you're working with big applications with huge available libraries, it pays to have a few tools in your tool box for exploration. Reading code is one technique you can use, and another is looking at the public functions in IEx. To do so you'll use a function called exports.

Most experienced programmers strive to separate complex code into layers. We'll have plenty of opportunities to explore these layers from the inside in Chapter 3, Generators: Contexts and Schemas, on page 71. In this chapter, rather than focusing on how the code works, we'll look at the various things that it can *do*—starting in this section with the Accounts context. The generated Accounts *context* is the layer that we'll use to create, read, update, and delete users in the database. It provides an API through which all of these database transactions occur.

The Accounts context will handle a few more responsibilities beyond basic CRUD interactions for a user. When a user logs in, we'll need a bit of code that looks up a user. We'll need to store an intermediate representation called a *token* in our database to keep our application secure. We'll also need a way for our user to securely update their email or password. We'll do all of these things in the Accounts context.

View Public Functions

We can get a good idea of what the Accounts context does by looking at its public functions. Luckily, IEx makes this easy. Open up IEx with iex -S mix, alias the context, and get a look at the exports, like this:

```
iex> alias Pento.Accounts
Pento.Accounts
iex> exports Accounts
```

You'll see a ton of functions. We're going to look at them in chunks. The first few functions work with new users. When you expose an application on the web that sends email to users, it's your responsibility to make sure the person on the other end of that email is real and has asked to be included. Confirmation proves a person owns the email address they've used to register:

```
...
confirm_user/1
register_user/1
...
```

The register_user/1 function creates a user, and confirm_user/1 confirms a user.

Let's move on to another responsibility of the code generated by the phx.gen.auth package—managing the user's session. Session management is handled by adding a tiny token to the session stored in a user's cookie when a user signs in and deleting it when they sign out. These generated functions create and delete the session token:

```
...
delete_user_session_token/1
generate_user_session_token/1
...
```

Next up are a few functions that let us look up users in various ways:

```
...
get_user!/1
get_user_by_email/1
get_user_by_email_and_password/2
get_user_by_reset_password_token/1
get_user_by_session_token/1
...
```

The phx.gen.auth library represents authenticated users by adding a token to a session. Using get_user_by_session_token/1, we'll be able to look up a logged-in user using those tokens.

We'll also be able to find our user by email and password when a user logs in, and so on.

In addition, our context provides a few functions for changing users. Here are the most important ones:

```
...
reset_user_password/2
update_user_password/3
update_user_email/2
...
```

We can start the password reset process if a user forgets their password, updates a password, or updates an email.

These functions make up the bulk of the Accounts API. The remaining functions let us validate new and existing users, integrate custom email services, and the like. We have what we need to continue our exploration. Let's put the Accounts API through its paces.

Create a Valid User

Let's see how the email-only registration works under the hood. The register_user/1 function uses a simplified approach that only requires an email:

auth/pento/lib/pento/accounts.ex
```
def register_user(attrs) do
  %User{}
  |> User.email_changeset(attrs)
  |> Repo.insert()
end
```

The following function uses the email_changeset/2, which validates only the email field:

auth/pento/lib/pento/accounts/user.ex
```
def email_changeset(user, attrs, opts \\ []) do
  user
  |> cast(attrs, [:email])
  |> validate_email(opts)
end
```

Notice that no password is required for initial registration—users will receive magic links for authentication instead. The code for this is on the next page.

```
iex> params = %{email: "mercutio@grox.io"}
%{email: "mercutio@grox.io"}
iex> Accounts.register_user(params)
# ...
INSERT INTO "users" ("email","hashed_password","confirmed_at",
                    "inserted_at","updated_at")
  VALUES ($1,$2,$3,$4,$5) RETURNING "id" ["mercutio@grox.io",
  nil, nil, ~N[2025-07-22 11:53:06], ~N[2025-07-22 11:53:06]]
{:ok,
 #Pento.Accounts.User<
    __meta__: #Ecto.Schema.Metadata<:loaded, "users">,
    confirmed_at: nil,
    email: "mercutio@grox.io",
    hashed_password: nil,
    id: 1,
    inserted_at: ~N[2025-07-22 11:53:06],
    updated_at: ~N[2025-07-22 11:53:06],
    ...
 >}
```

Under the hood, the `Accounts` context created a changeset, and seeing valid data, it inserted an account record into the database. Notice the result is an `{:ok, user}` tuple and that `hashed_password` is `nil` since the user hasn't set a password yet—they'll use magic links for authentication! So Mercutio rides!

Try to Create an Invalid User

Now let's try to create an invalid user. If the parameters are invalid, we'll get an error tuple instead:

```
iex> Accounts.register_user(%{})
  {:error,
   #Ecto.Changeset<
     action: :insert,
     changes: %{},
     errors: [
       email: {"can't be blank", [validation: :required]}
     ],
     data: #Pento.Accounts.User<>,
     valid?: false
  >}
```

Since the operation might fail, we return a result tuple. Elixir developers call this data structure a *tagged tuple* because we wrap the result in a tuple and *tag* that result with either an :ok or an :error representing success or failure. We'll get {:ok, user} on success and {:error, changeset} upon error. You'll learn later that a changeset represents change. Invalid changesets say why they are invalid with a list of errors. Don't get bogged down in the details. We'll go more in depth later.

Constraints vs. Changesets

Before we get too much further, we should call out an important distinction in Ecto. One of the most critical responsibilities of any application developer is to make sure data in the databases stays as pure and free of errors as possible. Ecto provides two distinct mechanisms to do so. The first is the *changeset*. We'll provide a more detailed definition later, but for now, think of a changeset as a layer of code that tracks change and enforces valid data at the Elixir level. For example, our first changeset was valid because it provided everything our database schema requires for a valid database row. The second one wasn't valid, because we did *not* provide the required email field. Most of the time, the database doesn't need to be involved at all to determine whether an email is present and whether it's valid.

A *constraint* is a database-level restriction. These restrictions are implemented within the database and exposed in Ecto integrations. For example, Postgres enforces unique constraints with a mechanism called a *unique index*. You can read about them in the Postgres documentation.[9] When we ran mix ecto.gen.migration, the generator created a migration to build our initial database tables. Take a look:

auth/pento/priv/repo/migrations/20250722114420_create_users_auth_tables.exs
```
create unique_index(:users, [:email])
```

Another common use for constraints is to enforce *primary and foreign keys*. Sometimes, relational databases stitch two related rows together by having the same field present in two different tables. A user table might have an id field, a profile table might have a user_id field, and so on. Constraints can not only specify this relationship but also tell our application how to resolve what happens when a user is deleted. A good example of this constraint is in the same migration mentioned previously. In the code we generated, users have user tokens. Here's how they appear in the migration:

auth/pento/priv/repo/migrations/20250722114420_create_users_auth_tables.exs
```
create table(:users_tokens) do
  add :user_id, references(:users, on_delete: :delete_all), null: false
  add :token, :binary, null: false
  add :context, :string, null: false
  add :sent_to, :string

  timestamps(type: :utc_datetime, updated_at: false)
end
```

---

9. https://www.postgresql.org/docs/current/indexes-unique.html

Notice the user_id field of the user_tokens table. The user_id field in each row points to the id in the users table. (By default, Ecto creates id fields on every table.) Our references constraint signifies to Ecto and the database underneath that if any user is deleted, the corresponding tokens should also be deleted.

Most of the time, constraints and changesets each live in their own separate worlds. After the initial migration, constraints are relegated to the database, and changesets need not access the database to work. Sometimes, changesets need to know about constraints to make that information available to the user. For example, Accounts has a changeset that requires emails to be unique. This constraint needs to show up in *both* the changeset and the constraint. The constraint keeps the database data consistent, and the changeset reports any problems to the user. You'll see the full changeset later. For now, here's what the unique constraint looks like in the changeset:

```
changeset
|> unsafe_validate_unique(:email, Pento.Repo)
|> unique_constraint(:email)
```

The unsafe_validate_unique/3 and the unique_constraint/2 functions work together to ensure a unique user. However small, a small chance exists that an email could sneak into the database between the time the unsafe_validate_unique/3 fires and the time the application inserts the changeset into the database. That's the reason for the unsafe prefix. Said another way, don't depend on changeset validations to enforce integrity! Make sure you also add database constraints in your migrations.

Now that you've seen how our new context works, let's move on to the code that will let web requests in to our app or keep them out. That happens in the router.

We'll look at the authentication service and you'll see how it uses plugs that call on Accounts context functions to manage sessions and cookies.

Protect Routes with Plugs

The authentication service we generated integrates with the Phoenix stack to provide infrastructure for session management, including plugs that we can use in the router to control access to our routes.

The authentication service is defined in the file lib/pento_web/user_auth.ex. We could open up the codebase, but instead, let's do a quick review in IEx to see what the public API looks like.

If IEx isn't opened, fire it up with iex -S mix and key this in:

```
iex> exports PentoWeb.UserAuth
__phoenix_verify_routes__/1
fetch_current_scope_for_user/2
log_in_user/2
log_in_user/3
log_out_user/1on_mount/4
redirect_if_user_is_authenticated/2
require_authenticated_user/2
```

All of these functions are plugs. Disregard __phoenix_verify_routes__/1 for now. Functions surrounded by underscores are generally private in nature. The next function fetches an authenticated user and adds it into the connection. The following three functions log users in and out. The last two functions are plugs that direct users between pages based on whether they're logged in or not. Let's first examine fetch_current_scope_for_user/2.

Fetch the Current User

Remember, plugs are reducers that take a Plug.Conn as the first argument and return a transformed Plug.Conn. Most of the plugs we'll use are from the UserAuth module. fetch_current_scope_for_user/2 will add the current user to our Plug.Conn if the user is authenticated. You don't have to take this on faith. Though you might not understand all of the code, you already know enough to get the overall gist of what's happening. Let's take a closer look.

Most of Plug.Conn contains private data we can't change, but application developers have a dedicated place for custom data. Inside Plug.Conn is a key called assigns with a map inside. Just as we did within the LiveView socket, we can use assigns to store custom application data.

The fetch_current_scope_for_user/2 function plug will add a key in assigns called current_user if the user is logged in. You can see that the code generator added this plug to our browser pipeline in the router, here:

auth/pento/lib/pento_web/router.ex
```
pipeline :browser do
  plug(:accepts, ["html"])
  plug(:fetch_session)
  plug(:fetch_live_flash)
  plug(:put_root_layout,
    html: {PentoWeb.Layouts, :root}
  )

  plug(:protect_from_forgery)
  plug(:put_secure_browser_headers)
  plug(:fetch_current_scope_for_user)
end
```

Now whenever a user logs in, any code that handles routes tied to the browser pipeline will have access to the current_user in conn.assigns.current_user.

You may not know it yet, but our pento web app is already taking advantage of this feature in the root layout. LiveView typically specifies the main application layout, called the root layout, in router.ex:

auth/pento/lib/pento_web/router.ex
```
plug(:put_root_layout,
  html: {PentoWeb.Layouts, :root}
)

pipeline :browser do
  ...
  plug :put_root_layout, {PentoWeb.Layouts, :root}
  ...
end
```

Open up the root layout in lib/pento_web/components/layouts/root.html.heex:

```
<ul>
  <%= if @current_user do %>
    <li>
      <%= @current_user.email %>
    </li>
    <li>
      <.link href={~p"/users/settings"}>Settings</.link>
    </li>
    <li>
      <.link href={~p"/users/log_out"} method="delete">Log out</.link>
    </li>
  <% else %>
    <li>
      <.link href={~p"/users/register"}>Register</.link>
    </li>
    <li>
      <.link href={~p"/users/log_in"}>Log in</.link>
    </li>
  <% end %>
</ul>
```

For brevity, we've trimmed the file of some of the CSS formatting, but it's otherwise intact. This file contains nothing special. *Layouts* are simply templates that focus on common elements across all pages. This layout has code to present a basic menu. The snippet uses the current_user, stored in the connection's assigns and accessed in the template via @current_user, to print the email for the logged-in user if one exists. We know the current_user will be present if they're logged in.

Authenticate a User

Remember, Phoenix works by chaining together plugs that manipulate a session. The log_in_user/3 function is no exception. Let's check out the details for logging in a user, like this:

```
iex> h PentoWeb.UserAuth.log_in_user

Logs the user in.

It renews the session ID and clears the whole session to avoid fixation
attacks. See the renew_session function to customize this behavior.

It also sets a :live_socket_id key in the session, so LiveView sessions are
identified and automatically disconnected on log out. The line can be safely
removed if you're not using LiveView.
```

Notice that the function also sets up a unique identifier for our LiveView sessions. That ID will come in handy later. We can expect to see this function called within the code that logs in a user. In fact, that code is within the lib/pento_web/controllers/user_session_controller:

```
auth/pento/lib/pento_web/controllers/user_session_controller.ex
# magic link login
defp create(conn, %{"user" => %{"token" => token} = user_params}, info) do
  case Accounts.login_user_by_magic_link(token) do
    {:ok, user, tokens_to_disconnect} ->
      UserAuth.disconnect_sessions(tokens_to_disconnect)

      conn
      |> put_flash(:info, info)
      |> UserAuth.log_in_user(user, user_params)

    _ ->
      conn
      |> put_flash(:error, "The link is invalid or it has expired.")
      |> redirect(to: ~p"/users/log-in")
  end
end
```

Short and sweet. This controller handles the magic link authentication flow. The controller checks for a magic token in the parameters and calls the Accounts.login_user_by_magic_link/1 function to validate it. If the token is valid, the user is logged in. If not, we redirect to the login page with an error message. Let's look at how this magic link login process works in detail:

```
auth/pento/lib/pento/accounts.ex
def login_user_by_magic_link(token) do
  {:ok, query} = UserToken.verify_magic_link_token_query(token)

  case Repo.one(query) do
    # Prevent session fixation attacks by disallowing magic links
```

```elixir
    # for unconfirmed users with password
    {%User{confirmed_at: nil, hashed_password: hash}, _token}
      when not is_nil(hash) ->
      raise """
      magic link log in is not allowed for unconfirmed users with a
      password set!

      This cannot happen with the default implementation, which indicates
      that you might have adapted the code to a different use case. Please
      make sure to read the "Mixing magic link and password registration"
      section of `mix help phx.gen.auth`.
      """

    {%User{confirmed_at: nil} = user, _token} ->
      user
      |> User.confirm_changeset()
      |> update_user_and_delete_all_tokens()

    {user, token} ->
      Repo.delete!(token)
      {:ok, user, []}

    nil ->
      {:error, :not_found}
  end
end
```

This function handles three different cases for magic link authentication: confirmed users, unconfirmed users without passwords, and the security case where an unconfirmed user has a password set. Once the magic link is validated, we'll execute the log_in_user/3 function implemented by the UserAuth module, passing our connection:

auth/pento/lib/pento_web/user_auth.ex
```elixir
def log_in_user(conn, user, params \\ %{}) do
  token = Accounts.generate_user_session_token(user)
  user_return_to = get_session(conn, :user_return_to)
  remember_me = get_session(conn, :user_remember_me)

  conn
  |> renew_session()
  |> put_token_in_session(token)
  |> maybe_write_remember_me_cookie(token, params, remember_me)
  |> redirect(to: user_return_to || signed_in_path(conn))
end
```

We build a token and grab our redirect path from the session. Then we renew the session for security's sake. We then add the token to the session and create a remember_me cookie if the user has selected that option and, finally, redirect the user. This beautiful code weaves a plain English narrative for us. Later, you'll learn how to use this token to identify the authenticated user in a live view.

With those out of the way, let's look at the plugs that will let us use all of the infrastructure we've generated. We're ready to tweak our router to make sure users are logged in before visiting certain routes. With this, we'll have put together all of the pieces of the generated authentication code.

Authenticate the Live View

Let's integrate our wrong_live view with the authentication infrastructure. This quick test will let us make sure our infrastructure is working. Then we'll show you how to customize the auth behavior of your live views with the help of a shared live session. We'll talk about the security requirements of using live sessions and illustrate the need to secure your live views in the router *and* when the live view mounts.

We'll start in the router by putting our live route behind authentication.

Protect Sensitive Routes

When we ran the generator earlier, a scope was added to our router containing the set of routes that require a logged-in user. The scope pipes requests to such routes through two pipelines—the browser pipeline, which establishes the policy for web requests from browsers, and the generated UserAuth.require_authenticated_user/2 function plug, which ensures that a current user is present or else redirects to the sign-in page.

To authenticate our wrong_live view, we'll delete the live view route from its spot beneath the "/" route beneath PageController browser and move it into the one with UserSettings, like this:

```
auth/pento/lib/pento_web/router.ex
scope "/", PentoWeb do
  pipe_through([:browser, :require_authenticated_user])

  live_session :require_authenticated_user,
    on_mount: [{PentoWeb.UserAuth, :require_authenticated}] do
    live("/users/settings", UserLive.Settings, :edit)
    live("/users/settings/confirm-email/:token", UserLive.Settings, :confirm_email)
    live("/guess", WrongLive)
  end

  post("/users/update-password", UserSessionController, :update_password)
end
```

This code shows the two authentication concerns LiveView apps have to manage. First, notice the pipe_through function makes sure any HTTP requests go through the browser pipeline and also calls the plug require_authenticated_user. Believe it or not, that's all we have to do to restrict the HTTP route to logged-in users.

We have only one additional step—the :on_mount step. We'll talk about that one later. For now, let's take our generated authentication code for a spin.

Test Drive the Live View

Start up your web server with mix phx.server and point your browser to localhost:4000/guess. The plug fires and redirects you to the login page, as shown here:

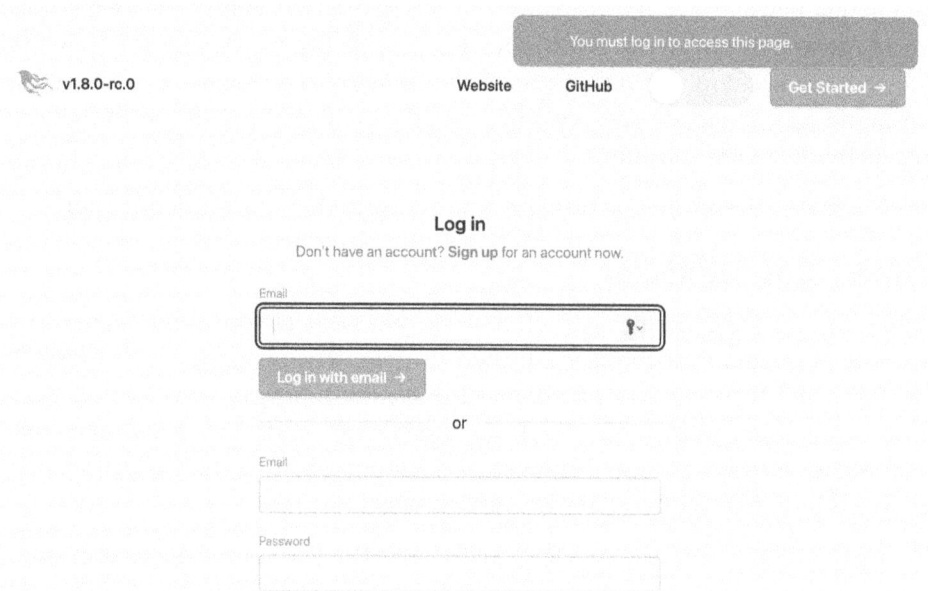

You might see a slightly different version number than ours, but the major details should be the same. You can click Sign up to go to the registration form, shown in the next image:

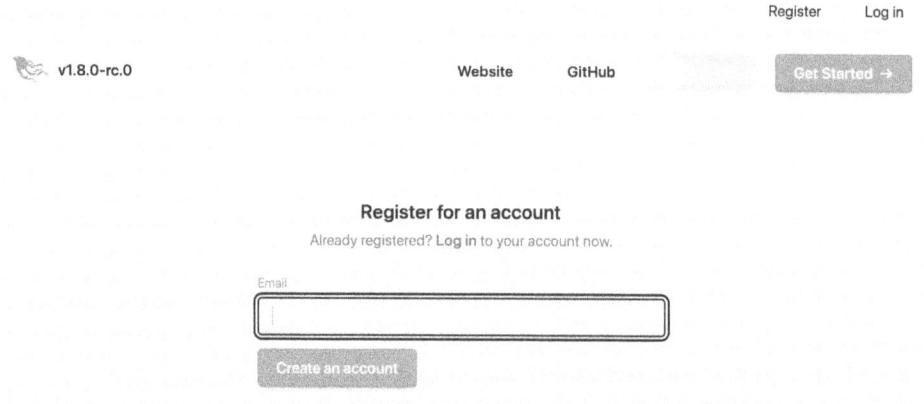

After submitting your email address, Phoenix 1.8 sends you a magic link. You can view the email in the development mailbox at localhost:4000/dev/mailbox, as seen here:

Click the magic link in the email, and Phoenix will take you to a confirmation page where the authentication process completes, as shown in the next image:

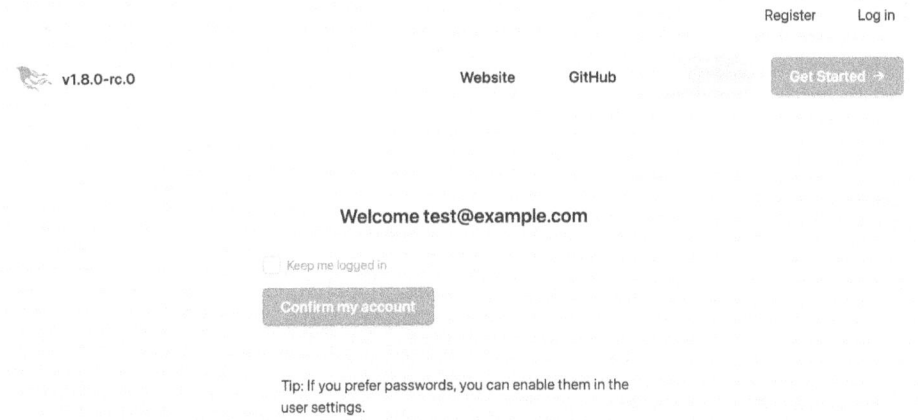

Once authentication is confirmed, you're automatically logged in and can access protected areas of the application, as you can see in the screenshot on the next page.

The logged-in user now appears in the title bar. We can build onto this layout to customize the authentication behavior of a single live view, or a group of live views, with the help of some LiveView authentication features.

In the remainder of this chapter, we'll dig into those features to make our live view authentication even more secure.

Group Live Views in a Live Session

Live sessions help us with two concerns: they provide common layouts and close an important security loophole. You'll use live sessions to group together similar live routes with shared layouts and auth logic.

When we do so, we'll need to also use on_mount to make sure our live views are secure. We'll dig into that in a bit. First, let's implement our first live session grouping.

Specify a Common Layout

Live sessions let us optimize how LiveView navigates between views that share a common layout. Remember, layouts are templates, and ours is in lib/pento_web/components/layouts/root.html.heex.

Open up that file now and you'll see this:

```
<!-- lib/pento_web/components/layouts/root.html.heex -->
<!DOCTYPE html>
<html lang="en" style="scrollbar-gutter: stable;">
  <head>
    <meta charset="utf-8" />
    <meta name="viewport" content="width=device-width, initial-scale=1" />
    <meta name="csrf-token" content={get_csrf_token()} />
    <.live_title suffix=" · Phoenix Framework">
      { assigns[:page_title] || "Pento" }
    </.live_title>
    <link phx-track-static rel="stylesheet" href={~p"/assets/app.css"} />
    <script defer phx-track-static type="text/javascript"
            src={~p"/assets/app.js"}>
    </script>
  </head>
```

```
  <body class="bg-white antialiased">
    <ul>
      ...menu code...
    </ul>
    { @inner_content }
  </body>
</html>
```

The heading of this layout has some common metadata (branding) in the title. The body has the menu code we saw earlier followed by custom content. Any individual live views that use this layout will have their own template rendered in place of the { @inner_content } expression. You could easily imagine customizing this layout, or adding another layout for a specific live view or live views, with some additional content. Different layouts might have special requirements based on what the authenticated user is allowed to do. For example, an admin layout may have a menu with some links for admins that a regular user shouldn't see.

Wouldn't it be great if we could group similar live views together when those live views need to share a layout file? We can do exactly that with the help of the live_session macro. This feature allows us to logically group routes together based on the permissions we'd like to grant to an authenticated user. This live session grouping can then share auth logic between live views in the group and allow them to safely share a layout. We'll take a look at how that works later on in this chapter.

With that background, let's explicitly add our layout to the live session we used for WrongLive:

```
# /lib/pento_web/router.ex
scope "/", PentoWeb do
  pipe_through [:browser, :require_authenticated_user]

  live_session :require_authenticated_user,
    root_layout: {PentoWeb.Layouts, :root},
    on_mount: [{PentoWeb.UserAuth, :require_authenticated}] do

    live "/users/settings", UserLive.Settings, :edit
    live "/users/settings/confirm_email/:token",
        UserLive.Settings, :confirm_email
    live "/guess", WrongLive
  end
end
```

Note that these routes would share the default root layout specified here even if we *didn't* add the root_layout: specification. This is just an example to demonstrate how you can customize the layout for a set of routes in a shared live session. You could easily imagine wanting to create a distinct layout for a given group of live routes.

This code ties the code for /users/settings routes and /guess together with a common policy and a common layout. Specifically, the code enables the following:

- Allows any routes in this live_session group to support a live_redirect from the client with navigation purely over the existing WebSocket connection. With a live_redirect, a new HTTP request won't be sent to the server to mount a new live view. This efficiently cuts down on web traffic and on the data that is sent down to the client over the WebSocket since the shared root layout won't be re-rendered during the live_redirect.
- Allows us to define shared LiveView life cycle callbacks in which we can perform additional authorization work or set up auth-related live view state.

Let's talk about this second piece of functionality now.

Protect Live Views When They Mount

Requests to LiveView applications arrive through Live routes within a live_session block over the existing WebSocket, *without* any new HTTP requests. Skipping the regular HTTP request means we're *also* skipping the plug pipeline. So in the example above, if we live redirect from the "/user/settings" live view to the "/guess" live view, we *won't* re-invoke the :require_authenticated_user plug. This represents a security loophole. We should always protect regular routes with pipe_through in the router, including live routes which originate as HTTP GET requests. *And* we should implement the same authentication and authorization logic when a live view mounts to ensure that if a live view is live redirected from a *different* live view in the same live session, it's also protected.

We can do this with the help of the on_mount callback. We'll see this approach in action in the next section, when we use the on_mount callback to access and authenticate the user from the session. Along the way, you'll see how LiveView uses the authentication service we generated to identify the signed-in user.

Access Session Data in the Live View

In Phoenix 1.8, accessing user data in live views is much simpler thanks to the new scopes system. Instead of manually handling session tokens, we leverage the on_mount callback that automatically provides the current user's scope.

Our session has both a token and a live view socket ID, but Phoenix 1.8 handles the token-to-user lookup automatically through the scopes system. When a live view mounts within a properly configured live_session, the on_mount callback automatically assigns the current user's scope to socket.assigns.current_scope.

This magic happens through the mount_current_scope/2 function:

auth/pento/lib/pento_web/user_auth.ex
```elixir
defp mount_current_scope(socket, session) do
  Phoenix.Component.assign_new(socket, :current_scope, fn ->
    user =
      if user_token = session["user_token"] do
        Accounts.get_user_by_session_token(user_token)
      end

    Scope.for_user(user)
  end)
end
```

This function uses assign_new/3 to efficiently assign the scope only when needed, looking up the user by session token and wrapping it in a scope struct.

Here's how we can access the user in our live view:

```elixir
# lib/pento_web/live/wrong_live.ex
def mount(_params, _session, socket) do
  # current_scope is automatically available thanks to on_mount callback
  user = socket.assigns.current_scope.user
  {
    :ok,
    assign(
      socket,
      score: 0,
      message: "Guess a number.",
      current_user: user
    )
  }
end
```

In the preceding code, we access the user directly from the scope that was automatically assigned by the on_mount callback. The scope contains all the user information we need, eliminating the need for manual token lookups. To make sure things are working, let's render the user information. We can do so by accessing the values of the @current_user assignment in the markup returned by the render/1 function:

auth/pento/lib/pento_web/live/wrong_live.ex
```elixir
def render(assigns) do
  ~H"""
  <main class="px-4 py-20 sm:px-6 lg:px-8">
  <h1 class="mb-4 text-4xl font-extrabold">Your score: {@score}</h1>
  <h2>
    {@message}
  </h2>
  <br />
  <h2>
```

```
    <%= for n <- 1..10 do %>
      <.link
        class="btn btn-secondary"
        phx-click="guess"
        phx-value-number={n}
      >
        {n}
      </.link>
    <% end %>
  </h2>
  <h2>
    {@current_user.email}
  </h2>
</main>
"""
```
end

Now, if you refresh the page at /guess, you'll see the user information:

bruce@example.com

The user information slides into place, just like we planned it! We demonstrated how Phoenix 1.8's scopes system seamlessly integrates authentication with LiveView, providing a clean and secure way to access user data.

Here's the thing, though. When we navigate to a live view from within another view from the same live session, the resulting live redirect uses the existing WebSocket connection to mount the new live view *without* calling on the plug pipeline. This could represent a security loophole if not handled properly.

Fortunately, Phoenix 1.8's scopes system solves this elegantly through the on_mount life cycle hook. The LiveView framework exposes this on_mount life cycle hook that fires before the live view mounts, and we can tell every live view in our live session to use the same on_mount hook. This ensures that authentication and authorization logic is consistently applied across all live views in a session, whether they're accessed via direct HTTP requests or live redirects.

The on_mount hook is the perfect place to isolate reusable auth logic that can be shared among live views in a live session, and Phoenix 1.8's scopes system makes this both secure and convenient.

Our application can customize what happens with these hooks. Here's the on_mount function generated by phx.gen.auth:

auth/pento/lib/pento_web/user_auth.ex
```
def on_mount(:require_authenticated, _params, session, socket) do
  socket = mount_current_scope(socket, session)

  if socket.assigns.current_scope && socket.assigns.current_scope.user do
    {:cont, socket}
  else
    socket =
      socket
      |> Phoenix.LiveView.put_flash(
        :error, "You must log in to access this page.")
      |> Phoenix.LiveView.redirect(to: ~p"/users/log-in")

    {:halt, socket}
  end
end
```

This code implements the on_mount callback with four arguments. The first is the activity we want to match. This will come into play when we tell our live session to invoke this specific version of the on_mount function for all of the live views grouped there. With the different versions of the on_mount function provided by the auth generator, we can execute code that adds the current scope to the socket with :mount_current_scope, make sure the user is authenticated with :require_authenticated, or perform a redirect using :redirect_if_user_is_authenticated. We're looking at the callback to authenticate the user. The other arguments given to this function are the same ones in the mount/3 function—params, session, and socket.‘

In the callback, we mount the user's scope by adding it to socket.assigns.current_scope. The scope contains the user information and can be extended with additional authorization data. If we get a valid scope back, we continue. Otherwise, we present an error message in the flash, redirect to /users/log-in, and halt. Since we have access to this generated code, we can teach any live views that are grouped within a live session to fire this callback before the live view itself mounts. In fact, the shared live session that we placed our "/guess" route within earlier is already configured to use this on_mount callback. Here's a refresher:

auth/pento/lib/pento_web/router.ex
```
scope "/", PentoWeb do
  pipe_through([:browser, :require_authenticated_user])

  live_session :require_authenticated_user,
    on_mount: [{PentoWeb.UserAuth, :require_authenticated}] do
    live("/users/settings", UserLive.Settings, :edit)
    live("/users/settings/confirm-email/:token", UserLive.Settings, :confirm_email)
    live("/guess", WrongLive)
  end

  post("/users/update-password", UserSessionController, :update_password)
end
```

Whenever a live view live-redirects to the "/guess" route or any other route in that live session, the given live view will invoke an on_mount callback of PentoWeb.UserAuth.on_mount/4 with a first argument of :require_authenticated, and our auth logic will execute. With this in place, we can simplify the WrongLive's own mount function so that it looks like this:

```
auth/pento/lib/pento_web/live/wrong_live.ex
def mount(_params, _session, socket) do
  # current_scope is automatically available thanks to on_mount callback
  user = socket.assigns.current_scope.user
  {
    :ok,
    assign(
      socket,
      score: 0,
      message: "Guess a number.",
      current_user: user
    )
  }
end
```

We no longer need to manually assign user information from the session here. The on_mount callback automatically provides the current_scope containing the user information, so by the time this live view module's mount/3 function is invoked, the socket assigns already contains the scope with all necessary user data. Now our live view is secure, whether you navigate to it directly by pointing your browser at /guess or get live-redirected there from another view in the same live session. The on_mount callback teams up perfectly with live sessions and Phoenix 1.8's scopes system to provide a clean, secure, and reusable API for authenticating your live views.

This is a brief look at how we can combine live sessions and LiveView callbacks to bulletproof our live views, making them highly secure and capable of sophisticated authorization logic. In chapters to come, we'll learn how to kick bad actors out of an active live view process, and we'll build complex authorization logic into our application neatly with the help of the tools we've introduced here.

It's been a long and intense chapter, so it's time to wrap up.

Your Turn

Rather than using libraries for authentication, a good strategy is to generate your code with the phx.gen.auth code generator. The code that this generator creates checks all of the must-have boxes for an authentication service, especially satisfying the OWASP standards, and saves us the tedious work of building out authentication ourselves. When you're building your own Phoenix LiveView apps in the wild, you'll reach for this generator to quickly add a tried and tested authentication solution to your web app.

Once you install and run the generator, you'll be able to maintain the code as if it were your own. Phoenix 1.8's generator provides modern authentication features, including magic link authentication by default, a comprehensive scopes system for secure data access, and streamlined LiveView integration. The code comes with a context for long-term persistence of users and session tokens, magic link generation, and a solution for adding authenticated tokens representing users to a session. The generator creates live views and controllers to handle registration, magic link login, confirming users, and optional password management, as well as plugs and scopes that you'll use throughout your application to apply authentication and authorization policies.

You saw exactly how Phoenix uses plugs to respond to web requests by constructing pipelines of small functions, each of which applies some transformation to a common connection struct. Later, you'll see that this is the same pattern individual live views will use to respond to both initial web requests and user interactions with a live view page. You also saw how LiveView allows you to group live routes together in a shared session, making it easy for live views to share a layout and to implement shared authentication and authorization logic.

With all of this under your belt, it's time to put what you've learned into practice.

Give It a Try

These problems deal with small tweaks to the existing generated code:

- Phoenix 1.8 uses magic links by default, which means email delivery is already integrated. Try configuring a real email service (like SendGrid or Mailgun) instead of the development mailbox. Visit /dev/mailbox to see how magic link emails are formatted.

- Add a migration and a field to give the User schema a username field, and display that username instead of the email address when a user logs in. Did you require the username to be unique? How does this interact with the magic link authentication flow?

- If a logged-in user visits the / route, make them redirect to the /guess route. Use the scopes system to detect if a user is authenticated.

- Explore the new scopes system: modify the Scope.ex file to include additional user information (like roles or preferences) and access this data in your live views.

This more advanced problem gives you a chance to understand how to optimize your authorization code with Phoenix 1.8's scopes system:

- In the PentoWeb.UserAuth.on_mount/4 callback, explore how the assign_new/3 function is used to efficiently assign the :current_scope to socket assigns. The assign_new/3[10] function only assigns a value if the given key isn't already present in socket.assigns. This is useful to ensure that code you've written to populate a given socket assigns key doesn't execute unnecessarily in these situations:
  - When the live view first mounts in its disconnected state if the plug pipeline has already populated the given key in the Plug.Conn struct.
  - If the live view is being redirected to itself and its socket assigns already contains the given key.

You'll notice that the generated mount_current_scope/2 function uses the assign_new/3 function to assign the :current_scope. When a live view first mounts in its disconnected state via the initial HTTP request, the socket provided to on_mount contains the same assignments as the Plug.Conn struct. So during that first disconnected mount, socket.assigns will already contain a key of :current_scope. Using assign_new/3 here lets us take advantage of that existing assignment and avoid making unnecessary database calls for scope information that's already available.

Next Time

After a long chapter of Phoenix configuration, you may want a break from the detailed concepts. With the authentication chapter behind us, we're ready to play. In the next chapter, we're going to start building out the specific functionality of our application. We'll begin with a product management system—we want to be able to persist a list of products and provide simple admin pages to maintain them. Let's keep it rolling!

---

10. https://hexdocs.pm/phoenix_live_view/Phoenix.Component.html#assign_new/3

CHAPTER 3

Generators: Contexts and Schemas

So far, we've focused our efforts on briefly building some intuition for how Phoenix LiveView works and building an authentication layer. While we did create our own custom live view to explore LiveView interactions, we haven't yet written any serious LiveView code. In this chapter, that changes.

The next two chapters will build a product catalog into our application. Rather than write the code by hand, we'll use the Phoenix generators to build the bulk of what we need.

In the previous chapter, we took our first test drive through the Phoenix code generators with mix phx.gen.auth for authentication code. That generator created Phoenix 1.8's enhanced authentication system with magic links for password-less authentication and user scopes for secure data access. In this chapter, we'll generate a slice of application including live views, an API context, the related database code, and supporting plumbing for all of the previous code. We'll also see how the generated code seamlessly integrates with Phoenix 1.8's scope-based authentication system.

You might wonder why we're planning to generate code in a book dedicated to teaching you to write your own LiveView code. We do so because Phoenix's Live generator is a powerful tool that will increase your productivity as a LiveView developer and your understanding of idiomatic Phoenix patterns. With just one command, you can generate a full CRUD feature for a given resource, with all of the seamless real-time interactions that LiveView provides. You'll reach for the Phoenix Live generator whenever you need to build a basic CRUD feature in LiveView, saving yourself the time and effort of implementing this common functionality. Beyond that, the generated code provides a strong, organized foundation on which to build additional features when you do need to go beyond CRUD.

The Phoenix Live generator is just one more way that Phoenix empowers developers to be highly productive, while bringing the real-time capabilities of LiveView to the table to meet the increasingly interactive demands of the modern web. While you won't use the Phoenix Live generator every time you build a LiveView application, you will reach for it when building common, foundational web app functionality. This helps you cut down on coding time, making it a valuable tool in your toolbox.

Let's make a brief plan. First, we'll run the generator. Some of the code we generate will be back-end database code, and some will be front-end code. In this chapter, we'll focus on the back-end code, and in the next chapter we'll take a deep dive into the generated front-end code, including the code in the generated live views. The Phoenix generators will separate back-end code into two layers. The schema layer describes the Elixir entities that map to our individual database tables. It provides functions for interacting with those database tables. The API layer, called a context, provides the interface through which we'll interact with the schema, and therefore the database.

The generated code was built and shaped by experts, and we believe it reflects one of the best ways to build LiveView applications. In these two chapters, we'll trace through the execution of our generated code and show you why it represents the best way to build and organize LiveView. When you're done, you'll know how to leverage the powerful generator tool to create full-fledged CRUD features, you'll have a strong understanding of how that generated code ties together, and you'll start to appreciate the best practices for organizing LiveView code.

These two chapters will be demanding—but fun. It's time to get to work.

Get to Know the Phoenix Live Generator

The `mix phx.gen.live` script is a utility that generates code supporting full CRUD functionality for a given resource. This includes the back-end schema and context code as well as the front-end code, including routes, LiveView, and templates. With Phoenix 1.8, the generator has been enhanced to produce even more modern and accessible code, including DaisyUI integration for improved styling and better integration with the enhanced authentication system. As this is our second pass through generated code, it's worth discussing just what's so great about this generated code in the first place. To do that, we'll address the elephant in the room—the not-uncommon skepticism of code generators.

Let's be honest. Code generators have a checkered past. The potential land mines are many. In some environments, generated code is so difficult to understand that application developers can't make reliable changes. In others, generated code doesn't follow the best practices for a given ecosystem or is too simplistic to serve as a meaningful foundation for custom, non-generated code.

Furthermore, in Elixir, code generation isn't as essential to our productivity as it is in some other languages. This is in part because Elixir supports macros. Since macros are code that writes code, macros often replace code that must be generated in other environments. In fact, we'll see that our generated code will take advantage of macros to pull in key pieces of both back-end and front-end functionality.

Code generators are still critical in one area, though: the creation of generic application code. No macro can satisfy the needs of a generic application, so sometimes the best approach is to generate the tedious, simple code as a foundation. Then the developer can rely on that foundation to build the rest of their application.

Foundations only work if they're right, and the Phoenix team worked hard to make sure the abstractions within the generated code are right and that the encapsulated ideas are accessible. The whole Phoenix team placed serious emphasis on refactoring the generated code, bit by bit, until it was right.

So, the Phoenix Live generator provides us with a quick and easy way to build CRUD features, taking over the often tedious and repetitive work of building out this common functionality. It does so in a way that adheres to common practices for organizing Phoenix code in general and LiveView code specifically, making it easy for developers to plan, generate, and customize a quick base. The Phoenix Live generator is just one of many reasons why Phoenix and LiveView developers can be so highly productive.

Now that you understand what the Phoenix Live generator is and what it does for you at a high level, we're ready to get started.

Run the Phoenix Live Generator

We'll use the Phoenix Live generator to create a feature for managing products. If you're familiar with web development with Phoenix or even other languages, you know many web libraries and frameworks have a concept called a *resource*. In common terms, a resource is a collection of like entities. Product will be our resource.

Running the generator will give us all of the code needed to support the CRUD interactions for this resource. The generated front-end code, including the live views, will reside in lib/pento_web. Back-end code, on the other hand, will live in lib/pento. It will deal with database interactions via the schema and provide an API through which to manage those interactions, called the context.

When we're done, we'll have a schema for a Product, a Catalog context, along with live views for managing a product. As this figure demonstrates, all of these pieces of generated code will work together to make up the CRUD interactions for the Product resource.

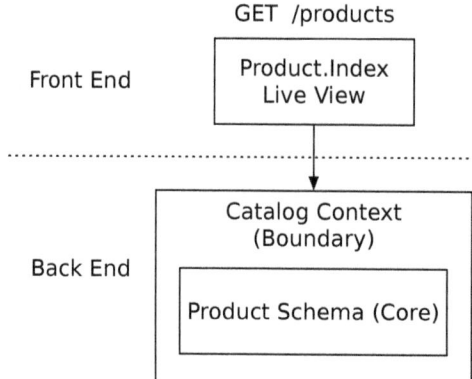

At a high level, you can see that an HTTP request, one for the /products route for example, will be routed to and handled by a live view. These are the front-end concerns. The live view will in turn rely on the context, which wraps the schema, to interact with product records in the database. Together, the context and schema make up the back-end concerns. We'll learn more about the context and schema and how they work in the following sections.

Let's fire up the generator!

Learn How to Use the Generator

When we generate the code for our resource, we'll need to specify both a context and a schema. We'll also need to tell Phoenix which fields to support for the resource's corresponding database table. To learn exactly how to structure the generator command, we'll use the generator tool's help functionality. As with most Elixir tooling, the documentation and help is excellent.

The first way to get help for a tool is to use it without required options. Run the generator without options, like this:

```
$ mix phx.gen.live
...compiling...
** (Mix) Invalid arguments

mix phx.gen.html, phx.gen.json, phx.gen.live, and phx.gen.context
expect a context module name, followed by singular and plural names
of the generated resource, ending with any number of attributes.
For example:

    mix phx.gen.html Accounts User users name:string
    mix phx.gen.json Accounts User users name:string
    mix phx.gen.live Accounts User users name:string
    mix phx.gen.context Accounts User users name:string

The context serves as the API boundary for the given resource.
Multiple resources may belong to a context and a resource may be
split over distinct contexts (such as Accounts.User and Payments.User).
----------
```

The command to run the Phoenix Live generator is `mix phx.gen.live`. Since we executed the command without any options, it provides some help for us. Specifically, it offers us some examples of how to use Phoenix generators more generally. The third example down on the indented list of examples illustrates how to use the `mix phx.gen.live` command to generate a hypothetical Accounts context and User schema. Let's dig into this example so that we can understand how to structure our own generator command for the Product resource.

Here's the example from the help output:

```
mix phx.gen.live Accounts User users name:string
```

The first argument given to `mix phx.gen.live` is the *context*—here called Accounts. The second argument, User, is the name of the *resource* and *schema*, while the attributes that follow are the names and types of the fields our schema will support. The generator will take these arguments and use it to generate an Accounts context and a User schema that maps the provided fields to database columns. Let's use the guidance provided by this example to write our own generator command for the Product resource now.

Generate a Resource

Run the generator again, this time filling in the blanks for the context, resource, and fields.

We construct the generator command such that it will generate a Catalog context with a schema for Product, corresponding to a products database table. A product will have name, description, unit_price, and SKU fields, as shown on the next page.

```
[pento] → mix phx.gen.live Catalog Product products name:string \
description:string unit_price:float sku:integer:unique
* creating lib/pento_web/live/product_live/show.ex
* creating lib/pento_web/live/product_live/index.ex
* creating lib/pento_web/live/product_live/form.ex
* creating test/pento_web/live/product_live_test.exs
* creating lib/pento/catalog/product.ex
* creating priv/repo/migrations/20250724132712_create_products.exs
* creating lib/pento/catalog.ex
* injecting lib/pento/catalog.ex
* creating test/pento/catalog_test.exs
* injecting test/pento/catalog_test.exs
* creating test/support/fixtures/catalog_fixtures.ex
* injecting test/support/fixtures/catalog_fixtures.ex

Add the live routes to your browser scope in lib/pento_web/router.ex:

    live "/products", ProductLive.Index, :index
    live "/products/new", ProductLive.Form, :new
    live "/products/:id", ProductLive.Show, :show
    live "/products/:id/edit", ProductLive.Form, :edit

Ensure the routes are defined in a block that sets the :current_scope assign.
-----
```

Notice the significant improvements in Phoenix 1.8's generator output. First, it creates a dedicated ProductLive.Form component for handling new and edit operations rather than cramming these responsibilities into the Index component. This separation of concerns makes the code more maintainable and follows better LiveView patterns.

Second, and most importantly, Phoenix 1.8 reminds us to ensure routes are defined in a scope-aware block. This is because Phoenix 1.8's enhanced authentication system integrates deeply with user scopes, automatically ensuring data isolation and security at every level of the application.

Phoenix generated a bunch of files and left some instructions for us. Let's add these routes to router.ex, like this:

```
generators/pento/lib/pento_web/router.ex
# Product routes (Phoenix 1.8 generator output)
live "/products", ProductLive.Index, :index
live "/products/new", ProductLive.Form, :new
live "/products/:id", ProductLive.Show, :show
live "/products/:id/edit", ProductLive.Form, :edit
```

Add the new routes to the browser scope that pipes requests through the :require_authenticated_user plug and within the live_session block. Notice that Phoenix 1.8 routes new and edit operations to ProductLive.Form rather than ProductLive.Index, providing better separation of concerns.

This will ensure that only logged-in users can see the products pages. In Phoenix 1.8, this authentication system integrates seamlessly with the enhanced scope system, automatically ensuring that users can only access data within their proper scope boundaries. The live_session block with on_mount: [{PentoWeb.UserAuth, :require_authenticated}] automatically sets up the scope context for all routes within it. We'll also be able to redirect to other views within this block without forcing a page reload. These details will become important later on in this book.

As you saw in Chapter 1, Get to Know LiveView, on page 1, for live views these routes tie URL patterns to the module that implements them. Let's look at one of these routes in more detail.

```
live "/products/new", ProductLive.Index, :new
```

The live macro instructs Phoenix that this request will start a live view, and we pass three arguments. You've seen the first two in action. The "/products/new" argument is the URL pattern our route will match, and ProductLive.Index is the module that implements the live view. The :new argument is the *live action*. As you'll see later, Phoenix will put the :new live action into the socket when it starts the live view. We'll take a closer look at this macro in the next chapter. Let's shift our attention to verifying our new generated code with tests.

Verify the Generated Code

The Phoenix team has done a good job generating tests alongside generated code. We'll rely on tests for our generated code to keep things running smoothly and manage regressions. In Chapter 10, Test Your Live Views, on page 303, we'll cover testing in more detail. For now, let's see if our tests are working. Run them:

```
[pento] → mix test
Compiling 11 files (.ex)
Generated pento app
... ...more... ...
  1) test Index saves new product (PentoWeb.ProductLiveTest)
     test/pento_web/live/product_live_test.exs:26
     ** (MatchError) no match of right hand side value:
     {:error, {:redirect, %{to: "/users/log_in",
     flash: %{"error" => "You must log in to access this page."}}}}
     code: {:ok, index_live, _html} = live(conn, ~p"/products")
     stacktrace:
       test/pento_web/live/product_live_test.exs:27: (test)
... ...more... ...
Finished in 0.3 seconds (0.1s async, 0.1s sync)
142 tests, 6 failures
```

Let's run our tests to see if our new generated code works:

```
[pento] → mix test
..................................................
..................................................
..............
Finished in 0.3 seconds (0.1s async, 0.1s sync)
122 tests, 0 failures

Randomized with seed 829064
```

Remarkable! All tests pass immediately. This is a significant improvement from earlier Phoenix versions. Phoenix 1.8's generator automatically creates authentication-ready tests, eliminating the manual authentication setup that was previously required.

Let's examine how Phoenix 1.8 achieves this automatic authentication. Looking at the generated test file shows us the key:

generators/pento/test/pento_web/live/product_live_test.exs
```
setup :register_and_log_in_user

defp create_product(%{scope: scope}) do
  product = product_fixture(scope)

  %{product: product}
end
```

The `setup :register_and_log_in_user` line automatically handles authentication for all tests in this module. This function, provided by phx.gen.auth, creates a user and logs them in, setting up the proper scope context for every test. This means that every test automatically has an authenticated user with an associated scope, ready to work with scope-aware data operations.

But there's more to this automatic authentication than meets the eye. Phoenix 1.8's scope system fundamentally changes how we think about data access and testing.

Understanding Scope-Aware Fixtures

The Phoenix 1.8 generator doesn't just create tests; it creates *scope-aware* tests that reflect the secure, multi-tenant nature of modern applications. Let's examine the create_product/1 helper function more closely:

generators/pento/test/pento_web/live/product_live_test.exs
```
setup :register_and_log_in_user

defp create_product(%{scope: scope}) do
  product = product_fixture(scope)

  %{product: product}
end
```

Notice how the create_product/1 function expects a scope parameter and passes it to product_fixture(scope). This isn't just a convenience—it's a fundamental shift in how Phoenix handles data isolation.

Let's look at the generated fixture to understand what's happening:

```
generators/pento/test/support/fixtures/catalog_fixtures.ex
def product_fixture(scope, attrs \\ %{}) do
  attrs =
    Enum.into(attrs, %{
      description: "some description",
      name: "some name",
      sku: unique_product_sku(),
      unit_price: 120.5
    })

  {:ok, product} = Pento.Catalog.create_product(scope, attrs)
  product
end
```

The product_fixture/2 function takes a scope as its first parameter and passes it directly to the context function Pento.Catalog.create_product(scope, attrs). This pattern ensures that every piece of test data is automatically associated with the correct user scope.

The Job of Scopes in Testing

Scopes serve several critical jobs in Phoenix 1.8's testing architecture:

Data isolation: Each test user operates within their own data sandbox. When a test creates a product, that product belongs exclusively to the test user's scope. This prevents test pollution where one test's data affects another test's results.

Security verification: By running tests within scopes, we automatically verify that our application's security boundaries work correctly. If a test passes, we know that the scope system is properly isolating that user's data.

Realistic testing: Tests now mirror production, where users can only access their own data; our tests are more trustworthy indicators of real-world behavior.

Simplified setup: The automatic scope setup eliminates the tedious work of manually associating test data with specific users. Every piece of test data is automatically scoped to the test user.

This scope-aware testing pattern extends throughout the entire application. Every context function, every database query, and every LiveView interaction respects scope boundaries, creating a comprehensive security and isolation model that's built into the fabric of Phoenix 1.8 applications.

Now it's time to shift our attention to the back end—the context and schema. Let's look at the back-end code the generator created and how that code works together to support the CRUD features for products.

Understand the Generated Core

In *Designing Elixir Systems with OTP [IT19]*, we separate the concerns for each resource into two layers, the *boundary* and the *core*. Our generated back-end code is also separated in this way. The Catalog context represents the boundary layer—it is the API through which external input can make its way into the application.

The Product schema, on the other hand, represents the application's core. The generated migrations are also part of the core. The core is the home of code that is certain and predictable—code that will always behave the same way given the same inputs. The core is responsible for managing and interacting with the database. You'll use code in the core to create and maintain database tables and prepare database transactions and queries. Later, you'll see how LiveView uses some of this code, through the API provided by the context, to manage product records. Before we get to that, though, it's important to understand how the core handles these responsibilities and how the context and core work together to expose an API for database interactions to the rest of the application.

> **Context vs. Boundary**
>
>  A Phoenix Context is a module in your Phoenix application that provides an API for a service or resource. It is responsible for managing uncertainty, external interfaces, and process machinery. The context implements the *boundary layer* of your application. In this book, we'll refer to the context to denote such a module, and the boundary to describe the role that a context plays in your application's architecture.

Let's walk through the generated core code—the migration file and the Product schema. Then we'll take a deep dive into the Catalog context.

The Product Migration

We don't need to understand the whole user interface before we put our back-end code to work, but we do need to tweak the database so it supports our new products table. Fortunately, the generator created a migration file for us to do exactly that.

Open up the migration in a file that looks something like pento/priv/repo/migrations/20240515172308_create_products.exs. The filename, including the timestamp, was generated for us when we ran our generator command, so yours won't match exactly, because the timestamp was built into the filename.

The migration file defines a database table, products, and a set of fields for that table. The generator took the table name and the field name and type specifications from the generator command and used them to inform the content of this file.

generators/pento/priv/repo/migrations/20250724132712_create_products.exs
```elixir
defmodule Pento.Repo.Migrations.CreateProducts do
  use Ecto.Migration

  def change do
    create table(:products) do
      add :name, :string
      add :description, :string
      add :unit_price, :float
      add :sku, :integer
      add :user_id, references(:users, type: :id, on_delete: :delete_all)

      timestamps(type: :utc_datetime)
    end

    create unique_index(:products, [:sku])
  end
end
```

Migration files allow us to build key changes to the database into code. Executing the files makes these changes to your database. Since these files need to be executed in a specific order, the filename should begin with a timestamp. You can, and likely will, build your own custom migration files and customize generated migration files. Luckily for us, however, the migration file that the generator command built already has exactly what we need to create the products table. All we need to do is execute the file.

Run the migration now by opening up your terminal and firing off the Mix command:

```
[pento] → mix ecto.migrate
Compiling 6 files (.ex)
Generated pento app

09:27:43.643 [info] == Running 20250724132712
  Pento.Repo.Migrations.CreateProducts.change/0 forward

09:27:43.644 [info] create table products

09:27:43.650 [info] create index products_sku_index

09:27:43.651 [info] == Migrated 20250724132712 in 0.0s
```

Notice the [info] messages. As we expected, running the migration via mix ecto.migrate created the products database table.

Now that we have a shiny new table, let's turn our attention to the schema.

The Product Schema

Think of schemas as maps between two kinds of data. On the database side is the products table we generated with our migration. On the Elixir side, the Product schema knows how to translate between the products database table and the Pento.Catalog.Product Elixir struct. We don't have to write all of that translation code. Ecto will do that for us in the Product schema module.

The generator created that module and placed it in the lib/pento/catalog/product.ex file. Crack it open now.

```
generators/pento/lib/pento/catalog/product.ex
schema "products" do
  field :name, :string
  field :description, :string
  field :unit_price, :float
  field :sku, :integer
  field :user_id, :id
  timestamps(type: :utc_datetime)
end
```

Notice the use Ecto.Schema expression. The use macro injects code from the specified module into the current module. Here, the generated code is giving the Product schema access to the functionality implemented in the Ecto.Schema module. This includes access to the schema/1 function.

The schema/1 function creates an Elixir struct that weaves in fields from a database table. The generator knew what fields to specify here based on the field name and types that we gave the mix phx.gen.live command. The timestamps function means our code will also have :inserted_at and updated_at timestamps.

We'll begin by examining the public API of our Product schema with the help of the exports function in IEx, like this:

```
iex> alias Pento.Catalog.Product
iex> exports Product
__changeset__/0      __schema__/1         __schema__/2         __struct__/0
__struct__/1         changeset/2
```

When you look at the public functions with exports Product, you can see the __struct__ function. We didn't create that __struct__/1 function, but our schema macro did. You also see a few other functions Ecto created for us. We'll use structs to represent database rows in Elixir form.

Let's take a closer look at the Product struct:

```
iex> Product.__struct__
%Pento.Catalog.Product{
  __meta__: #Ecto.Schema.Metadata<:built, "products">,
  description: nil,
  id: nil,
  inserted_at: nil,
  name: nil,
  sku: nil,
  unit_price: nil,
  updated_at: nil
}
```

Let's use struct/2, the close cousin of _struct_/1, to create a new Product struct in IEx:

```
iex> struct Product
%Pento.Catalog.Product{...}
```

We build a struct using the embedded function. For convenience, Elixir allows us to eliminate parentheses when our intentions are clear. Often, developers use this technique in IEx to save keystrokes in the overall flow of exploration or debugging. Parens or not? The choice is yours.

Next, let's use struct/2 to pass in some data:

```
iex> struct(Product, name: "Exploding Ninja Cows")
%Pento.Catalog.Product{
  ...
  id: nil,
  name: "Exploding Ninja Cows",
  ...
}
```

The _struct_/1 function works like the struct/2 function. Moving on, the schema macro is not the only aspect of the Product module that helps us interact with the products database table. The Product schema has a generated changeset/x function, much like the ones you saw in phx.gen.auth generated code. We'll use it to prepare unsafe input for interactions with the database. You've had a taste. Let's take a more detailed look at Ecto changesets.

Changesets

Maintaining database integrity is the sacred duty of every application developer, according to the rules of our business. To keep data correct, we need to check every piece of data that our application creates or updates. Rules for data integrity together form change *policies* that need to be implemented in code.

Schemas are not limited to a single change policy. For example, admins may be able to make changes that other users can't, while users may not be able to change their email addresses without validation. In Ecto, *changesets* allow us to implement any number of change *policies*. The Product schema has access to Ecto's changeset functionality, thanks to the call to import Ecto.Changeset in the Pento.Catalog.Product module. The import function allows us to use the imported module's functions without using the fully qualified name.

Here's what our changeset looks like:

```
generators/pento/lib/pento/catalog/product.ex
@doc false
def changeset(product, attrs, user_scope) do
  product
  |> cast(attrs, [:name, :description, :unit_price, :sku])
  |> validate_required([:name, :description, :unit_price, :sku])
  |> unique_constraint(:sku)
  |> validate_number(:unit_price, greater_than: 0.0)
  |> put_change(:user_id, user_scope.user.id)
end
```

This changeset implements the change policy for new records and updates alike. The piped syntax tells a beautiful story. The pipeline starts with the Product struct we want to change. The Ecto.Changeset.cast/4 function filters the user data we pass into params. Our changeset allows the :name, :description, :unit_price, and :sku fields. Other fields are rejected.

The cast/4 function also takes input data, usually as maps with atom keys and string values, and transforms them into the right types.

The next part of our change policy is to validate the data according to the rules. Ecto supports a long list of validations.[1] Our changeset requires all of our attributes to be present and the SKU to be unique.

The result of our changeset function is a changeset struct. We'll try to interact with our database with changesets to keep both our database and our database administrators happy.

Test Drive the Schema

Now that we've run our migration and taken a closer look at the Product schema, let's open up IEx and see what we can do with our changeset.

First, alias the Product schema if you've not already done so. Then initialize an empty Product struct:

---

1. https://hexdocs.pm/ecto/Ecto.Changeset.html#module-validations-and-constraints

```
iex> alias Pento.Catalog.Product
Pento.Catalog.Product

iex> product = %Product{}
%Pento.Catalog.Product{__meta__: ..., description: nil...}
```

Now establish a map of valid Product attributes:

```
iex> attrs = %{
      name: "Pentominoes",
      sku: 123456,
      unit_price: 5.00,
      description: "A super fun game!"
    }
%{
  description: "A super fun game!",
  name: "Pentominoes",
  sku: 123456,
  unit_price: 5.0
}
```

Next, execute the Product.changeset/2 function to create a valid Product changeset:

```
iex> Product.changeset(product, attrs)
#Ecto.Changeset<
  action: nil,
  changes: %{
    description: "A super fun game!",
    name: "Pentominoes",
    sku: 123456,
    unit_price: 5.0
  },
  errors: [],
  data: #Pento.Catalog.Product<>,
  valid?: true
```

We can take this valid changeset and insert it into our database with a call to the Pento.Repo.insert/2 function:

```
iex> alias Pento.Repo
Pento.Repo
iex> Product.changeset(product, attrs) |> Repo.insert()
[debug] QUERY OK source="products"  ...
INSERT INTO "products" ("name","description","unit_price","sku",
"inserted_at","updated_at") VALUES ($1,$2,$3,$4,$5,$6) RETURNING "id"
["Pentominoes", "A super fun game!", 5.0, 123456,
~U[2024-12-09 12:07:37Z], ~U[2024-12-09 12:07:37Z]]...

{:ok,
 %Pento.Catalog.Product{
    __meta__: #Ecto.Schema.Metadata<:loaded, "products">,
    id: 1,
    name: "Pentominoes",
```

```
    description: "A super fun game!",
    unit_price: 5.0,
    sku: 123456,
    inserted_at: ~U[2024-12-09 12:07:37Z],
    updated_at: ~U[2024-12-09 12:07:37Z]
  ]}
```

The database logging shows us the actual SQL inserts, and the console shows the result. What happens if we create a changeset with a map of attributes that won't pass our validations? Let's find out:

```
iex> invalid_attrs = %{name: "Not a valid game"}
%{name: "Not a valid game"}
iex> Product.changeset(product, invalid_attrs)
#Ecto.Changeset<
  action: nil,
  changes: %{name: "Not a valid game"},
  errors: [
    description: {"can't be blank", [validation: :required]},
    unit_price: {"can't be blank", [validation: :required]},
    sku: {"can't be blank", [validation: :required]}
  ],
  data: #Pento.Catalog.Product<>,
  valid?: false
```

Nice! Our changeset has an attribute of valid?: false, and an :errors key that describes the problem in a generic way we can present to users. Later, Ecto will use the valid? flag to keep bad data out of our database, and Phoenix forms will use the error messages to present validation errors to the user.

Our generated schema already does so much for us, but we can build on it to customize our changeset validations. The schema also integrates seamlessly with Phoenix 1.8's scope system, ensuring that data access is properly controlled at the database level. Let's add an additional validation to the changeset to validate that a product's price is greater than 0.

Add a new validation rule within lib/pento/catalog/product.ex, like this:

generators/pento/lib/pento/catalog/product.ex
```
|> validate_number(:unit_price, greater_than: 0.0)
```

Now, let's see what happens when we create a changeset with an attribute map that contains an invalid :unit_price:

```
iex> recompile()
iex> invalid_price_attrs = %{
    name: "Pentominoes",
    sku: 123456,
    unit_price: 0.00,
    description: "A super fun game!"}
```

```
%{
  description: "A super fun game!",
  name: "Pentominoes",
  sku: 123456,
  unit_price: 0.0
}
iex> Product.changeset(product, invalid_price_attrs)
#Ecto.Changeset<
  action: nil,
  changes: %{
    description: "A super fun game!",
    name: "Pentominoes",
    sku: 123456,
    unit_price: 0.0
  },
  errors: [
    unit_price: {"must be greater than %{number}",
     [validation: :number, kind: :greater_than, number: 0.0]}
  ],
  data: #Pento.Catalog.Product<>,
  valid?: false
```

Perfect! Our changeset's `valid?` flag is false, and the `errors` list describes the `unit_price` error.

Our application code won't work on the `Pento.Catalog.Product` schema directly. Instead, any interactions with it will be through the API, our `Catalog` context. This structure lets us protect the functional core, making sure that data is valid and correct *before* it gets to our database.

Now that we have a working schema, let's put it through its paces using the `Catalog` context.

Understand the Generated Boundary

We've spent a little time in the functional core, the land of certainty and beauty. We've seen that our schema and changeset code is predictable and certain—it behaves the same way given the same inputs, every time. In this section, we'll shift away from the core and into the places where the uncertain world intrudes on our beautiful assumptions. We've come to the Phoenix context.

Contexts represent the boundary for an application. As with all boundaries, it defines the point where our single purpose code meets the world outside. That means contexts are APIs responsible for taking unsanitized, unvalidated data and transforming it to work within the core or rejecting it before it reaches the core. In Phoenix 1.8, contexts also integrate with the enhanced scope system to ensure that all boundary interactions respect user access controls and data isolation requirements.

The boundary code isn't just an API layer. It's the place we try to hold *all* uncertainty. Our context has at least these responsibilities:

Access external services
  The context allows a single point of access for external services.

Abstract away tedious details
  The context abstracts away tedious, inconvenient concepts.

Handle uncertainty
  The context handles uncertainty, often by using result tuples.

Present a single, common API
  The context provides a single access point for a family of services.

Based on what you're doing in your code, the boundary may have other responsibilities as well. Boundaries might handle process machinery. They might also transform correct outputs to work as inputs to other services. Our generated Phoenix context doesn't have those issues, though. Let's dig a little deeper into the context we've generated.

Access External Services

External services will always be accessed from the context. Accessing external services may result in failure, and managing this unpredictability is squarely the responsibility of the context.

Our application's database is an external service, and the Catalog context provides the service of *database access*. This access is enacted using Ecto code. Just like the rest of our application, Ecto code can be divided into core and boundary concerns. Ecto code that deals with the certain and predictable work of building queries and preparing database transactions belongs in the core. That's why, for example, we found the changeset code that sets up database transactions in the Product schema. Executing database requests, on the other hand, is unpredictable—it could always fail. Ecto implements the Repo module to do this work, and any such code that calls on the Repo module belongs in the context module, our application's boundary layer. In Phoenix 1.8, this database access is enhanced with automatic scope filtering, ensuring that users can only access data within their authorized scope boundaries.

Here are a few functions from the context module. Notice that each of them use the Repo module, so we know they're in the right place. More importantly, notice that each function takes a %Scope{} parameter as its first argument—this is the revolutionary change in Phoenix 1.8.

```
generators/pento/lib/pento/catalog.ex
def list_products(%Scope{} = scope) do
  Repo.all(from product in Product,
    where: product.user_id == ^scope.user.id)
end

def get_product!(%Scope{} = scope, id) do
  Repo.get_by!(Product, id: id, user_id: scope.user.id)
end
```

We can get one product, or a list of them. Here's another one:

```
def delete_product(%Scope{} = scope, %Product{} = product) do
  true = product.user_id == scope.user.id

  with {:ok, product = %Product{}} <-
         Repo.delete(product) do
    broadcast(scope, {:deleted, product})
    {:ok, product}
  end
end
```

Each of these functions demonstrates Phoenix 1.8's scope-first approach. The list_products/1 function automatically filters products to only show those belonging to the user in the given scope. The get_product!/2 function ensures that users can only retrieve products they own. This automatic data isolation happens at the database level, making it both secure and performant.

These functions perform some of the classic CRUD operations. CRUD stands for create, read, update, and delete. We've shown only a few functions here, but you get the idea. We don't want to get too bogged down in the Ecto details. If you need more Ecto information, check out the excellent hex documentation[2] or the definitive book on Ecto, *Programming Ecto [WM19]*, for more details.

The last expression in each of these CRUD functions is some function call to Repo. Any function call to Repo can fail, so they come in one of two forms. By convention, if the function name ends in a !, it can throw an exception. Otherwise, the function will return a *result tuple*. These tuples will have either :ok or :error as their first element. That means it's up to the client of this context to handle both conditions.

If you can't do anything about an error, you should use the ! form. Otherwise, you should use the form with a result tuple.

---

2. https://hexdocs.pm/ecto/Ecto.html

Abstract Away Tedious Details

Elixir will always use Ecto to transact against the database. But the work of using Ecto to cast and validate changesets or execute common queries can be repetitive. Phoenix contexts provide an API through which we can abstract away these tedious details; our generated context is no different.

Let's walk through an example of this concept now and see how Phoenix 1.8's scope integration makes the API both simpler and more secure.

In previous Phoenix versions, creating a product required manual user association and complex security checks. With Phoenix 1.8's scope-aware context, these details are abstracted away while maintaining bulletproof security.

Instead of creating a changeset and inserting it into the database ourselves, we can leverage the generated Catalog context function Catalog.create_product/2:

```elixir
generators/pento/lib/pento/catalog.ex
def create_product(%Scope{} = scope, attrs \\ %{}) do
  with {:ok, product = %Product{}} <-
         %Product{}
         |> Product.changeset(attrs, scope)
         |> Repo.insert() do
    broadcast(scope, {:created, product})
    {:ok, product}
  end
end
```

Notice that this function takes a scope as its first parameter. This might seem like it's adding complexity, but it's actually eliminating it. The scope parameter handles all user association, security verification, and data isolation automatically.

Let's see this in action. When working with Phoenix 1.8 in a live view or controller, the scope is automatically available from the authentication system, making usage incredibly clean:

```elixir
# In a live view or controller, scope is available from the socket/conn
def handle_event("create_product", product_params, socket) do
  case Catalog.create_product(socket.assigns.current_scope, product_params) do
    {:ok, product} ->
      # Product automatically belongs to the current user
      {:noreply, put_flash(socket, :info, "Product created!")}
    {:error, changeset} ->
      {:noreply, assign(socket, :changeset, changeset)}
  end
end
```

The beauty of this approach is that we never have to think about user association or security. Here's what the scope system ensures:

- The product is automatically associated with the correct user.
- Only the owning user can access their products.
- All database queries are automatically scoped for security.
- Cross-user data access is impossible.

This represents a fundamental evolution in Phoenix application architecture, where security and multi-tenancy are built into the foundation rather than being added as an afterthought.

Present a Single, Common API

A tried and true approach of good software design is to funnel all code for related tasks through a common, unified API. Our schema has features that other services will need, but we don't want external services to call our schema directly. Instead, we'll wrap our Product.changeset/2 API in a simple function.

```
generators/pento/lib/pento/catalog.ex
def change_product(%Scope{} = scope, %Product{} = product, attrs \\ %{}) do
  true = product.user_id == scope.user.id

  Product.changeset(product, attrs, scope)
end
```

This code may seem pointless because it's a one-line function that calls an existing function implemented elsewhere. Still, the extra effort is worth it because now our clients won't have to call functions in our schema layer directly. That's the core; we want all external access to go through a single, common API.

Now we can move on to the sticky topic of managing uncertainty.

Handle Uncertainty

One of the most important duties of the context is to translate unverified user input into data that's safe and consistent with the rules of our database. As you've seen, our tool for doing so is the changeset. Let's see how our context works in these instances:

```
generators/pento/lib/pento/catalog.ex
def create_product(%Scope{} = scope, attrs \\ %{}) do
  with {:ok, product = %Product{}} <-
         %Product{}
         |> Product.changeset(attrs, scope)
         |> Repo.insert() do
    broadcast(scope, {:created, product})
```

```elixir
      {:ok, product}
    end
end

def update_product(%Scope{} = scope, %Product{} = product, attrs) do
  true = product.user_id == scope.user.id

  with {:ok, product = %Product{}} <-
         product
         |> Product.changeset(attrs, scope)
         |> Repo.update() do
    broadcast(scope, {:updated, product})
    {:ok, product}
  end
end
```

This code uses the changeset/2 function in the Product schema to build a changeset that we try to save. If the changeset isn't valid, the database transaction executed via the call to Repo.insert/1 or Repo.update/1 will ignore it and return the changeset with errors. If the changeset *is* valid, the database will process the request. This type of uncertainty belongs in our context. We don't know *what* will be returned by our call to the Repo module, but it's the context's job to manage this uncertainty and orchestrate any downstream code that depends on these outcomes.

Now that you understand how to use the context to interact with our application's database, let's put that knowledge to use.

Use the Context to Seed the Database

As we continue to develop our web application and add more features in the coming chapters, it'll be helpful to have a quick and easy way to insert a set of records into the database. We'll create some seed data to populate our database, and we'll use our context to do it.

Open up priv/repo/seeds.exs and key this in:

generators/pento/priv/repo/seeds.exs
```elixir
alias Pento.{Accounts, Catalog}

# Create a seed user for development
{:ok, user} = Accounts.register_user(%{
  email: "seed@example.com",
  password: "password123password123"
})

# Get the scope for this user
scope = Accounts.get_scope_for_user(user.id)

# Create sample products using the scope-aware context
products = [
```

```
  %{
    name: "Chess",
    description: "The classic strategy game",
    unit_price: 10.00,
    sku: 5678910
  },
  %{
    name: "Checkers",
    description: "A classic board game",
    unit_price: 8.00,
    sku: 1234567
  },
  %{
    name: "Backgammon",
    description: "An ancient strategy game",
    unit_price: 15.00,
    sku: 9876543
  }
]
Enum.each(products, fn product_attrs ->
  {:ok, product} = Catalog.create_product(scope, product_attrs)
  IO.puts("Created product: #{product.name}")
end)
```

Now execute it:

```
[debug] QUERY OK source="products" db=2.2ms decode=0.3ms queue=7.6ms idle=0ms
INSERT INTO "products" ("name","description","unit_price","sku",
"inserted_at","updated_at")
VALUES ($1,$2,$3,$4,$5,$6) RETURNING "id"
["Chess", "The classic strategy game", 10.0, 5678910,
~U[2024-12-09 12:20:35Z], ~U[2024-12-09 12:20:35Z]]
 ↳ Enum."-each/2-lists^foreach/1-0-"/2, at: lib/enum.ex:987
[debug] QUERY OK source="products" db=0.4ms queue=0.4ms idle=7.6ms
INSERT INTO "products" ("name","description","unit_price","sku",
"inserted_at","updated_at")
...
 ↳ Enum."-each/2-lists^foreach/1-0-"/2, at: lib/enum.ex:987
```

Nice! The log shows each new row as Ecto inserts it. For bigger seed files, we could make this code more efficient by using batch commands, such as Repo.insert_all/2. For these few records, that optimization isn't worth our time.

After looking at these layers, you might ask yourself, Where should new code go? The next section has some advice for you as you organize your project.

Boundary, Core, or Script?

As you add new functions, you can think about them in this way: any function that deals with process machinery (think input/output) or uncertainty will go in the *boundary*, or context. Functions that have certainty and support the boundary go in the *core*. Scripts that support operational tasks, such as running tests, migrations, or seeds, live outside the lib codebase altogether. Let's dive a little deeper.

The Context API Is With-Land

As you saw in Chapter 2, Phoenix and Authentication, on page 31, the context module is the API for a service. Now you know that the context module acts as the application's boundary layer. Boundary layers handle uncertainty. This is why one of the responsibilities of the context is to manage database interactions—database requests can fail.

In Elixir, we can use with statements to manage code flow that contains uncertainty. The with/1 function allows us to compose a series of function calls while providing an option to execute if a given function's return doesn't match a corresponding expectation. Reach for with/1 when you can't pipe your code cleanly.

So, you can think of the boundary as *with-land*—a place where you want to leverage the with/1 function, rather than the pipe operator, to compose code that deals with uncertainty. You might chafe a bit at this advice. Many Elixir developers fall in love with the language based on the beautiful idea of composing with pipes, but the pipe operator often falls short of our needs in the context, or boundary layer. Let's take a look at why this is.

We'll start by looking at an appropriate usage of the pipe operator in our application's core. Here's what a pipe that builds a query might look like:

```
defmodule Catalog.Product.Query do
  ...
  def base_product_query, do: Product
  def cheaper_than(query, price), do: from p in query, where...
  def cheap_product_skus(price)
    base_product_query()
    |> cheaper_than(price)
    |> skus
  end
  ...
end
```

Don't worry about how the individual functions work. Just know they build queries or transform them. If we've verified that price is correct, this code shouldn't fail. In other words, the behavior of this code is certain. Pipes work great under these conditions.

When the outcome of a given step in a pipeline *isn't* certain, however, pipes are *not* the right choice. Let's look at what an *inappropriate* usage of the pipe operator in our application's boundary layer, the context, might look like.

Consider the following code:

```elixir
# this is a bad idea!
defmodule Pento.Catalog do
  alias Catalog.Coupon.Validator
  alias Catalog.Coupon

  defp validate_code(code) do
    {:ok, code} = Validator.validate_code(code)
    code
  end

  defp calculate_new_total(code, purchase_total) do
    # will return an :ok, *or* an :error tuple
    Coupon.calculate_new_total(code, purchase_total)
  end

  def apply_coupon_code(code, purchase_total) do
    code
    |> validate_code
    |> calculate_new_total(purchase_total)
  end
end
```

This fictional code takes an input, validates it (which can fail), and then performs an operation—Coupon.calculate_new_total/2 (which can *also* fail). The Catalog.calculate_new_total/2 function takes in the result of calling the validation function, validate_code/1, as a first argument. But the Catalog.validate_code/1 function can fail! This means that Catalog.calculate_new_total/2 won't work reliably. Whenever Catalog.validate_code/1 fails to return the :ok tuple, our code will blow up. In fact, the result tuple we abstract away in the calculate_new_total/2 function is a hint that something might go wrong. The pipeline we built can handle the :ok case but not the error case. Furthermore, the Catalog.calculate_new_total/2 can also fail. It's responsible for performing an operation with two pieces of outside input—the coupon code and the current purchase total. Given this external input, the function (not pictured here) will return an :ok tuple if the input is valid and can be operated on and an :error tuple if not.

Instead of this code, we need to compose such statements with Elixir's with/1 function.[3] Here's what a with example might look like:

```elixir
defmodule Pento.Catalog do
  alias Catalog.Coupon.Validator
  alias Catalog.Coupon

  defp validate_code(code) do
    # will return an :ok, *or* an :error tuple
    Validator.validate_code(code)
  end

  defp calculate_new_total(code, purchase_total) do
    # will return an :ok, *or* an :error tuple
    Coupon.calculate_new_total(code, purchase_total)
  end

  def apply_coupon_code(code, purchase_total) do
    with {:ok, code} <- validate_coupon(code),
         {:ok, new_total} <- calculate_new_total(code, purchase_total) do
      new_total
    else
      {:error, reason} ->
        IO.puts "Error applying coupon: #{reason}"
      _ ->
        IO.puts "Unknown error applying coupon."
    end
  end
end
```

Some Elixir programmers are frustrated when they encounter code that uses with because it's more verbose than piped code. The truth is that code with uncertainty *needs to be* more verbose because it *must* deal with failure.

If you find yourself mired in too much with, remember that with code properly belongs in the application's boundary layer, the context. Use with in boundary code; use the pipe operator, |>, in core code, and seek to move as much code as possible *from the boundary to the core!*

The Core Is Pipe-Land

The core has functions that support the boundary API. We'll learn to shape core code from scratch later. For now, know that core code is *predictable* and *reliable* enough that we can compose our functions together with pipes. Let's look at a few examples.

---

3. https://elixirschool.com/en/lessons/basics/control-structures/#with

Though executing queries might fail, building queries is completely predictable. If you're building code to compose complex queries, you'll put that code in the *core*. So, you can remember this rule:

> Build a query in the *core* and execute it in the *boundary*.

Schemas don't interact with the database. Instead, think of them as road maps that describe how to tie one *Elixir module* to a *database table*. The schema doesn't connect to the database; it just has the data that answers key questions about how to do so:

- What's the name of the table?
- What are the fields the schema supports?
- What are the relationships between tables?

Once you've debugged your code, the outcomes of schema definitions are *certain*. Put them in the core.

Working with data that comes from the database is *predictable and certain*, so code that constructs or validates database transactions can go in the core.

Operations Code

We've looked at boundary and core code. Sometimes you need code to support common development, deployment, or testing tasks. Rather than compiling such operations code, Elixir places it in scripts. Migrations, other mix tasks, and code to add data to your database fit this model. Put such code in /priv. If it deals with the database, the code will reside in /priv/repo. Mix configuration will go in mix.exs. Configuration of your main environments goes in /config. In general, .exs scripts simply go where they are most convenient.

We've been working for a whole chapter, and we're still not done with the generated code! That's okay. It's time for a much needed break.

Your Turn

Generating code is a useful technique for creating an early foundation you can freely customize. You'll use it when developing your own Phoenix LiveView apps anytime you need to quickly build the CRUD functionality that so often forms the basis of more complex, custom features.

The Phoenix Live generator has a layering system, and the back-end layers include core and boundary code. In the core, the schema contains information to define a struct that ties Elixir data to fields in a database. Each struct represents a row of the database. Changesets implement change policies for those rows.

Phoenix contexts represent the boundary layer of your application, with important responsibilities for protecting the core. Each context presents a common API for some problem domain, one that abstracts away tedious details. Contexts wrap services and handle unverified user input.

Now you get to put some of these ideas into practice.

Give It a Try

You'll have more of an opportunity to get your hands dirty with the exercises at the end of the next chapter. Until then, these tasks will give you some practice with writing core and boundary code.

- Create another changeset in the Product schema that only changes the unit_price field and only allows for a price decrease from the current price.
- Then create a context function called markdown_product/2 that takes in an argument of the product and the amount by which the price should decrease. This function should use the new changeset you created to update the product with the newly decreased price.

Next Time

In the next chapter, we'll cover the front-end generated code we've not yet touched. Don't stop now—we're just getting started!

CHAPTER 4

Generators: Live Views and Templates

In the last chapter, we generated a context and live views for a service that will let us enter products into a user interface and save them into a database. Then we started a careful exploration of the *context*, the application's boundary layer, along with the schema, our functional core. In this chapter, we're going to shift to an examination of the front-end code that the Phoenix Live generator built.

By taking a deep dive through the generated front-end code, you'll understand how LiveView works to support the CRUD functionality for the Product resource in Phoenix 1.8's streamlined architecture. You'll experience how Phoenix 1.8 has simplified LiveView code organization by eliminating modal-based forms in favor of dedicated pages, and you'll see how the integration with DaisyUI provides professional styling out of the box. You'll be prepared to build custom LiveView functionality on top of this strong, simplified foundation.

Phoenix 1.8 represents a significant evolution in how LiveView applications are generated. Gone are the complex modal dialogs and form components of earlier versions. Instead, you'll discover a cleaner, more accessible approach where each CRUD operation has its own dedicated page with consistent navigation patterns. The generated code integrates seamlessly with the authentication and scope system from the previous chapter, and the DaisyUI styling provides a modern, professional appearance with built-in dark mode support.

Before we dive in, let's make a plan.

First, we'll start with the routes and use them to understand the views that our generator has made available to the user. Then we'll take inventory of the files that the generator created. We'll look at these files and what each one does.

Finally, we'll walk through the main details of a live view and show you how things work in Phoenix 1.8's simplified architecture. Along the way, you'll pick up key concepts about how Phoenix 1.8 has streamlined LiveView development. We'll demonstrate how LiveView builds and handles routes for dedicated pages rather than modal overlays. We'll explore the clean navigation patterns between pages and how the new ProductLive.Form component handles both creation and editing on separate pages. We'll illustrate how LiveView's life cycle manages the presentation and state of each dedicated view and show you how the simplified architecture makes LiveView code easier to understand and maintain.

When you're through, you won't *only* know about this generated code. You'll understand how experts weave typical LiveView applications together and how well-structured code is layered. You'll be prepared to write your own LiveView applications, the right way.

Application Inventory

So far, we've spent all of our time on the back-end service that manages products in our catalog. We were lucky because we could focus our exploration on a single API, the Catalog context.

In the live view, we're not so lucky. We have nearly a dozen files that we need to worry about. It would be nice to start with a common interface for our user-facing features.

In turns out we *do* have such an interface, but it's not an Elixir API. Instead, it's a list of the routes a user can access. That's right. The routes in lib/pento_web/router.ex are an interface, and we can use it to understand the capabilities of the generated code.

Let's take a look at the LiveView routes we generated in the last chapter now.

Route the Live Views

The router tells us all of the things a user can *do* with products. It represents a high-level overview of how each piece of CRUD functionality is backed by LiveView. Let's look at the routes we added to our application's router after we ran the generator in the previous chapter. We'll break down how Phoenix routes requests to a live view and how LiveView operates on those requests. Take a look at the generated product routes here:

```
generate_web/pento/lib/pento_web/router.ex
# Product routes (Phoenix 1.8 generator output)
live "/products", ProductLive.Index, :index
live "/products/new", ProductLive.Form, :new
live "/products/:id", ProductLive.Show, :show
live "/products/:id/edit", ProductLive.Form, :edit
```

That's exactly the API we're looking for. This list of routes describes all of the ways a user can interact with products in our application. Each of these routes starts with a macro defining the type of request, followed by three options. All of our routes are live routes, defined with the live macro. We'll take a brief look at where this function comes from. Then we'll talk about what it does for us.

The live/4 macro function is implemented by the Phoenix.LiveView.Router module. It is made available inside the router thanks to this line:

generate_web/pento/lib/pento_web/router.ex
```
use PentoWeb, :router
```

Here, we see another example of Phoenix's reliance on macros to share code—even the generated code takes this approach! The use macro injects the PentoWeb.router/0 function into the current module. If we look at that module now, we see that it in turn imports the Phoenix.LiveView.Router module.

generate_web/pento/lib/pento_web.ex
```
def router do
  quote do
    use Phoenix.Router, helpers: false

    # Import common connection and controller functions to use in pipelines
    import Plug.Conn
    import Phoenix.Controller
    import Phoenix.LiveView.Router
  end
end
```

For a closer look at exactly how use, and macros in general, work in Elixir, check out Chris McCord's *Metaprogramming Elixir [McC15]*.

For our purposes, it's enough to understand that the live/4 macro function is available in our application's router by way of the Phoenix.LiveView.Router module. Let's move on to discuss what this function does.

The live macro generates a route that ties a URL pattern to a given LiveView module. So when a user visits the URL in the browser, the LiveView process starts up and renders a template for the client.

The first argument to a live route is the URL pattern. This pattern defines what the URL looks like. Notice the colons. These represent *named parameters*. For example, if the user types the URL products/7, the router will match the pattern "/products/:id" and prepare this map of params to be made available to the corresponding live view:

```
%{"id" => "7"}
```

The second argument to a live route is the LiveView module implementing our code. Phoenix 1.8 has simplified this architecture significantly. Looking at the routes, you'll notice that we now have three distinct LiveView modules that each handle specific responsibilities: ProductLive.Index for listing products, ProductLive.Show for displaying a single product, and ProductLive.Form for both creating and editing products. This clean separation makes the code much easier to understand and maintain.

The final argument to live/4 is called the *live action*. The action allows a live view to understand which specific operation it should perform.

Looking at these routes, you can see how Phoenix 1.8 has streamlined the architecture. The ProductLive.Index view handles only the :index action—displaying the list of products. When users want to create a new product, they navigate to a dedicated page handled by ProductLive.Form with the :new action. Similarly, editing a product takes users to the same ProductLive.Form component but with the :edit action and the product ID in the URL.

This approach eliminates the complexity of modal dialogs and pop-up windows that existed in earlier Phoenix versions. Instead, each operation gets its own clean URL and dedicated page, making the application more accessible, easier to bookmark, and simpler to understand. The ProductLive.Show view handles only the :show action, providing a clean, focused display of a single product with clear navigation to edit or return to the index.

If this seems like a lot of detail right now, don't worry. We'll break it down later on in this chapter. For now, it's enough to understand that a single live view can handle multiple page states, and therefore multiple features, with the help of live actions.

With that first pass behind us, let's take a second look at the output from the generator and familiarize ourselves with the generated files.

Explore the Generated Files

Before we dive into the generated LiveView code, let's briefly review the files that the Phoenix Live generator created. This will help us navigate around the code in the next few sections.

When we ran the mix phx.gen.live command, the code generator told us exactly which files it created. It's been a while, so here they are again. This is the portion of output from the generator describing the front-end files, though they're shown here in a different order:

```
* creating lib/pento_web/live/product_live/show.ex (with embedded render/1)
* creating lib/pento_web/live/product_live/show.html.heex (fallback template)
* creating lib/pento_web/live/product_live/index.ex (with embedded render/1)
* creating lib/pento_web/live/product_live/index.html.heex (fallback template)
* creating lib/pento_web/live/product_live/form.ex (with embedded render/1)
* creating lib/pento_web/live/product_live/form.html.heex (fallback template)
* creating test/pento_web/live/product_live_test.exs
```

That's a clean, streamlined set of files! Let's break down what Phoenix 1.8 generates.

The show.ex file implements the LiveView module for displaying a single product. In Phoenix 1.8, it includes an embedded render/1 function that defines the HTML markup directly within the module rather than using a separate template file. Similarly, index.ex implements a list of products with its own embedded render/1 function.

The form.ex file implements Phoenix 1.8's new approach to form handling. Instead of the complex live component approach used in earlier versions, Phoenix 1.8 generates a dedicated live view for form operations. This ProductLive.Form module handles both creating new products and editing existing ones but does so on dedicated pages rather than in modal dialogs. This approach is simpler to understand, more accessible, and easier to customize.

The product_live_test.exs implements tests. We'll get to them later on in Chapter 10, Test Your Live Views, on page 303.

> **Phoenix 1.8 Template Precedence**
>
> While Phoenix 1.8 still generates .html.heex template files alongside the LiveView modules, when a render/1 function is present in the LiveView module, it takes precedence over the separate template file. This embedded approach keeps the view logic and markup colocated, making it easier to understand the complete behavior of a LiveView in a single file. The generated template files serve as a fallback and can be useful for complex UIs where you might want to extract the markup to a separate file.

The LiveView programming model has two main workflows. The mount/render workflow establishes custom data in the socket and then renders the entire web page the first time. It serves the purpose of rendering a page for search engine optimization and also renders all static portions of the page once and for all. This workflow uses primarily the mount/3 (or alternatively the initial handle_params/3) and render/1 functions. Skip handle_params/3 for now. We'll dive into that function later.

The change management workflow deals with events. Within it, handlers receive events, update the socket, and then render the result. This workflow primarily uses handlers such as handle_event/3 and render/1. You saw both of these flows in action when you built your simple guessing game live view in Chapter 1, Get to Know LiveView, on page 1, and now we'll cover them in more detail.

We'll begin with the mount/render workflow for our Product Index feature. Then we'll explore how Phoenix 1.8's dedicated page approach simplifies the architecture by giving each operation (index, show, new, edit) its own focused live view with clear responsibilities and straightforward navigation patterns.

Mount and Render the Product Index

The mount/render workflow describes the process in which a live view sets its initial state and renders it, along with some markup, for the client. This workflow is responsible for creating the entire initial page. This initial rendering pass is what a search engine sees when it indexes your application. The best way to understand the mount/render workflow is to see it in action. The Product Index feature is our entry point into this workflow. We'll play around with adding specific data to that live view's socket to tweak what's rendered.

The easiest way to put data into the socket is via the mount/3 function. Open up lib/pento_web/live/product_live/index.ex and look at the live view's mount/3 function:

```
alias Pento.Catalog

def mount(_params, _session, socket) do
  {:ok, stream(socket, :products, Catalog.list_products())}
end
```

You saw the Catalog.list_products/0 function in the previous chapter. It was created for us by the generator and returns the list of all products from the database. Something new is here that you haven't seen before, though, and that's the stream/4 function.[1] To understand streams, let's first consider a question. If Catalog.list_products/0 returns *all* of the products in the database, what happens in our live view when that list is very large? Our live view would have to keep the whole collection of products in its socket forever. Storing all of that data server-side, in the socket, could get expensive, which could cause our live view to slow down. Streams are the solution to that problem. Streams let us manage large collections *without* keeping them all in the socket after they're consumed by the user interface. Let's break down how this works.

---

1. https://hexdocs.pm/phoenix_live_view/Phoenix.LiveView.html#stream/4

When we call stream(socket, :products, Catalog.list_products()), a new key of :streams is added to the socket assigns, which is available in the template as @streams. Under the :streams key, you'll find a map with a key of :products pointing to the list of all products. That data can be accessed in the template with @streams.products. When the template is rendered, the data stored in the @streams assigned will be detached from the socket and stored client-side, in the DOM itself. Later, when we take advantage of the LiveView streams API to update or delete data stored in @streams.products, LiveView will enact those changes on the data stored *client-side*. This keeps our live views running quickly and efficiently. We don't have to store large datasets on the server, and we don't have to send large payloads between the client and the server to maintain those datasets. You'll continue to see streams in action throughout this book.

Turning our attention back to our own mount/3 function, let's update this mount/3 function to add an additional key of :greeting to the socket assigns. We'll do so building a small pipeline of calls to the assign/3 function, like this:

generate_web/pento/lib/pento_web/live/product_live/index.ex
```
{:ok,
 socket
 |> assign(:page_title, "Listing Products")
 |> assign(:greeting, "Welcome to Pento!")
 |> stream(:products, Catalog.list_products(socket.assigns.current_scope))}
```

This call to the Phoenix.LiveView.assign/3 function adds a key/value pair to the socket struct's map of :assigns. As you'll remember from Chapter 2, Phoenix and Authentication, on page 31, the :assigns map is where the socket struct holds state. Our live view's template can access any key/value pair placed in the socket's :assigns via the @ macro. For example, you can now access the value of the :greeting key in this live view's corresponding template with @greeting. Go ahead and do that now.

Since Phoenix 1.8 uses embedded render/1 functions, we'll add the greeting directly to the render/1 function in lib/pento_web/live/product_live/index.ex. In the render/1 function's HEEx template, add a header that renders the value of the @greeting assignment, like this:

generate_web/pento/lib/pento_web/live/product_live/index.ex
```
<h1 class="text-2xl font-bold">{@greeting}</h1>
```

Now, start up the Phoenix server by executing the mix phx.server command in your terminal and point your browser at localhost:4000/products. You should see the Product Index page render with your greeting!

| | Website | GitHub | |

Welcome to Pento!

Listing Products   New Product

Name	Description	Unit price	Sku		
Chess	The classic strategy game	10.0	5678910	Edit	Delete
Checkers	A classic board game	8.0	1234567	Edit	Delete
Backgammon	An ancient strategy game	15.0	9876543	Edit	Delete

The greeting shows exactly like we expected it to. Now, it's a good time to take a detailed look at how the LiveView framework leverages Elixir's behaviours to enact the mount/render workflow.

Understand LiveView Behaviours

Let's peel back the onion one layer. Live views are called *behaviours*. (Remember, we spell them the proper British way, following the lead of Joe Armstrong and the rest of the Swedish team that created OTP.) Think of consuming a behaviour as the opposite of using a library. When you use a library, your program is in control and it calls library functions.

Live views don't work like that. Your code is not in control. In a sense, a behaviour is a *plugin*, a module that provides a service. The LiveView behaviour has common user interface architecture, and our modules provide customizations that establish, render, and change data. Let's dive deeper.

The behaviour runs a specified application and calls your code according to a contract. The LiveView contract defines several callbacks.[2] The contract specifies which callback functions are available, whether they are optional, where the code should be located, and when LiveView will call it.

When we talk about the LiveView life cycle, we're talking about specific callbacks defined in the behaviour. These callbacks include the mount/3 function

---

2. https://hexdocs.pm/phoenix_live_view/Phoenix.LiveView.html#callbacks

to set up data in the socket, the render/1 function to return data to the client, the handle_* functions to change the socket, and so on.

When we say that mount/3 happens before render/1 in a live view, we don't mean mount/3 actually calls render/1. We mean the *behaviour* calls mount/3, and then render/1. Similarly, when we say render/1 uses the data from mount/3, we don't mean mount/3 directly passes data directly to render/1. We mean mount/3 sets data so functions like render/1 can later make use of it. Conceptually, you can look at a simple interaction as a pipeline:

```
socket |> mount() |> render() |> handle_event() |> render()
```

This code won't really run. Phoenix has hundreds of lines of boilerplate between each of these piped functions. The number and order of the arguments don't even match. This code snippet is merely a useful way of thinking about the LiveView callbacks and the order that they fire. With that caveat in mind, it's time to take a closer look at how LiveView's behaviour works, starting with a live route and ending with the first render.

Route to the Product Index

The entry point of the mount/render life cycle is the route. When you point your browser at the /products route, the router will match the URL pattern to the code that will execute the request and extract any parameters. Next, the live view will start up. If you care about the details, the live view is actually an OTP GenServer. If this doesn't mean anything to you, don't be concerned. You only need to know what the different parts of the behaviour do.

The first call that the LiveView behaviour will make to our code is the mount/3 function. Its job is to *set up* the initial data in the live view. Next, the live view will do the initial *render*. In Phoenix 1.8, the generated LiveView modules include explicit render/1 functions with embedded HEEx templates, keeping the view logic and markup colocated in a single file. The ProductLive.Index live view has an embedded render/1 function that defines its template directly within the module.

If you'd rather not think about the behaviour, that's ok. You can think about it in simplistic terms instead. The diagram at the top of the next page shows what's happening.

This flow represents a common pattern in Elixir and Phoenix programming that you'll see again and again as you work in LiveView. When the LiveView process starts up, the live view builds a preliminary socket with some of the internal data Phoenix will need. In the mount function, we combine that preliminary socket, the URL params, and any session data to *construct* the initial

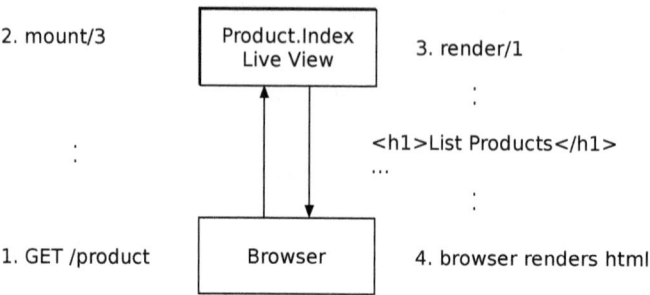

application data our live view needs. Later, when we start to respond to user events, handlers will *reduce* over that data, transforming it based on the needs of the application. Over time, events will continue to transform the socket, one event at a time. Whenever the socket changes, Phoenix will send the socket through render/1 to *convert* the socket state into markup for the user. Keep this "construct, reduce, convert" pattern in mind as we dive deeper into LiveView. It will help you understand how LiveView manages the state of your single-page app and will prepare you to write clean, organized LiveView code in the coming chapters.

Now that you know what will happen after the router matches a route, let's open up the code in our live view and trace through it line by line.

Establish Product Index State

The job of the ProductLive.Index live view is to provide a user interface to manage all actions that deal with lists of products. Regardless of the URL pattern we match to get there, each path takes us first to the mount/3 function:

```
generate_web/pento/lib/pento_web/live/product_live/index.ex
@impl true
def mount(_params, _session, socket) do
  Catalog.subscribe_products(socket.assigns.current_scope)

  {:ok,
   socket
   |> assign(:page_title, "Listing Products")
   |> assign(:greeting, "Welcome to Pento!")
   |> stream(:products, Catalog.list_products(socket.assigns.current_scope))}
end
```

You already know that a live view revolves around its state. The mount/3 function sets up the initial state, in this case a stream of products in the socket assigns. Here, it does so with the help of the list_products() function within the Catalog context. This adds a key of :streams to socket assigns, which in turn points to a struct that contains a key of :products. The value of *that* key is the list of products returned by Catalog.list_products.

With that, you can see how the generated back-end code we explored in the previous chapter—specifically the Catalog.list_products function—supports the CRUD interactions on the front end.

Now that the product list has been added to :streams in the socket assigns in the mount/3 function, let's examine the socket assigns now. Add the following snippet to your index.html.eex template:

```
<!== lib/pento_web/live/product_live/index.ex render/1 function -->
<pre><%= inspect assigns, pretty: true %></pre>
```

Run your server and point your browser to /products, and you should see something like this:

```
%{
  ...some private stuff...,
  assigns: %{
    live_action: :index,

    streams: %{
  __changed__: MapSet.new([:products]), ...
  ...
    products: %Phoenix.LiveView.LiveStream{
      name: :products,
      dom_id: #Function<3.76265957/1 in Phoenix.LiveView.LiveStream.new/4>,
      ref: "0",
      inserts: [
        {"products-1", -1,%...Product{...name: "Pentominoes",...}, nil},
        {"products-2", -1,%...Product{...name: "Candy Smush",...}, nil},
        {"products-3", -1,%...Product{...name: "Chess",...}, nil},
        {"products-4", -1, %...Product{...name: "Tic Tac Toe",...}, nil},
        {"products-5", -1, %...Product{...name: "Table Tennis",...}, nil}
      ],
      deletes: [],
      reset?: false,
      consumable?: false
    }
    ...other keys...
  }
}
```

Notice the :assigns key contains a top-level key of :streams that in turn contains a :products key. That key doesn't *quite* point to a list of products. Instead, it holds a value of a Phoenix.LiveView.LiveStream struct. That struct contains all the info that LiveView needs to render the stream data in the template and continue to maintain that data client-side. LiveView knows to *insert* the list of products into the DOM by looking under streams.products.inserts. Later on, you may tell LiveView to update or remove certain products from the DOM by using server-side functions that will put certain instructions in socket.streams.products.inserts or socket.streams.products.deletes.

This behavior reveals a common theme. Again and again you'll see that you don't have to tell LiveView *how* to do something. Instead, you just have to tell it *what* to do. Here, you don't have to write client-side code to pull data out of socket.streams.products.inserts or socket.streams.products.deletes and make UI changes accordingly. Instead, you call functions like stream/4 to tell LiveView *what* changes to make, and the framework handles the rest.

Once LiveView takes the data in streams.products and adds it to the DOM, that data is removed from the socket. With just a handful of products in our database, this isn't necessarily a huge win. But if you have dozens, hundreds, or even thousands of products to work with, you can imagine the performance pitfalls that streams help us avoid.

Now our LiveView's index state is complete and ready to be rendered! Our Phoenix 1.8 live view implements an embedded render/1 function that contains the HEEx template directly within the LiveView module. It's time to discuss the template.

Render Product Index State

Before we take a closer look at how the template renders the products in socket assigns, let's look at just how these HEEx templates function in a LiveView application.

LiveView's built-in templates use the .heex extension. HEEx is similar to EEx but with two main differences. First, it's designed to minimize the amount of data sent down to the client over the WebSocket connection. Second, it has some structure and typing information to make sure that the combination of HTML and LiveView tags is correct. So, HEEx templates make sure the initial HTML is correct and that LiveView *only* updates portions of the template impacted by any state changes.

If you've ever worked with a web-scripting language before, HEEx will probably look familiar to you. The job of the embedded render/1 function's HEEx template is simple. It has text and substitution strings in the form of eex tags, and it renders some components.

Most of the file is pure text—usually HTML—that will be rendered one time upon the first render. The rest of the template has embedded Elixir substitutions.

These come in the form of EEx substitutions and components. When the eex compiler encounters Elixir code within the <%= %> tags (notice the =), the compiler will compute the code and leave the result in place of the embedded Elixir. When the eex compiler encounters the <% %> tags, any Elixir code between them will be computed, but nothing will be rendered in their place. The same kind of transformation happens when the HEEx templates encounter <. > tags. This syntax forms something called a function component (we'll get to those details later on). This text and the substitutions make up the entire page, and most of a page is typically text.

LiveView makes the data stored within socket.assigns available for computations in HEEx templates. When that data changes, the HEEx template is reevaluated, and the live view will keep track of any differences from one evaluation to the next. By processing templates in this way, LiveView only needs to re-render the parts of the template that have actually changed based on changes in socket assigns. In this way, HEEx templates are highly efficient.

After the first invocation of mount/3, the only thing added to socket.assigns is the :streams key, containing the list of products. Let's take a look at how we'll render those products. Generally speaking, our template has three different sections:

```
...heading...
...product list...
...modal form...
```

This general skeleton outlines roughly what's happening in our embedded render/1 template. Let's break each of those sections down.

Use Components to Render HTML

A component implements each of the three major sections on the page. Phoenix components are functions with some additional capabilities to allow them to work well with markup. Components let us wrap up reuseable markup and provide some compile-time structure so the compiler can check some of our HTML work.

The first section is a header component that renders a heading and a link. Take a look at the implementation:

generate_web/pento/lib/pento_web/live/product_live/index.ex
```
<.header>
  Listing Products
  <:actions>
    <.button variant="primary" navigate={~p"/products/new"}>
      <.icon name="hero-plus" /> New Product
```

```
      </.button>
    </:actions>
</.header>
```

Look at this `<.header>` ... syntax as a *function call* to the header component. Our header renders some custom content in the form of the title text and a section of *actions* that contain a button linking to the New Product route. The header component renders this content with the help of a feature called *slots*. Let's take a look at the implementation of the header component now, so you can see how it renders this custom content.

Examine the Generated Code

The header component was created for us when we generated our LiveView application. If you look inside the file deps/phoenix/priv/templates/phx.gen.live/core_components.ex, you'll find an eex template that Phoenix uses when you run the generator mix phx.gen.live. You'll find this code:

```
defmodule <%= @web_namespace %>.CoreComponents do
  ...
  def header(assigns) do
    ~H"""
    ...
    """
  end
  ...
end
```

The generator uses this template to generate the file lib/pento_web/components/core_components.ex. The rules are simple. EEx processes any interpolations inside `<%= %>` blocks. Because generated code might also have `<%= %>` blocks, these are escaped to `<%%= %>` blocks in the template and unescaped after EEx processes substitutions. Here's the generated CoreComponents module with the header/1 definition:

generate_web/pento/lib/pento_web/components/core_components.ex
```
def header(assigns) do
  ~H"""
  <header class={[
    @actions != [] && "flex items-center justify-between gap-6",
    "pb-4",
    @class
  ]}>
    <div>
      <h1 class="text-lg font-semibold leading-8">
        {render_slot(@inner_block)}
      </h1>
      <p :if={@subtitle != []} class="text-sm text-base-content/70">
```

```
      {render_slot(@subtitle)}
    </p>
  </div>
  <div class="flex-none">{render_slot(@actions)}</div>
</header>
"""
```
end

So the header component is really just a function that takes in an argument of some assigns and returns some HEEx markup. This is called a *function component*. We call on the header/1 function in our template like this:

```
<.header>
  Listing Products
  ...
</.header>
```

Here, we haven't called header/1 with any arguments, so the assigns passed to the header/1 function component is empty. If we did want to make some data available to the function component, we could pass it in like this:

```
<.header class="bold" >
  Listing Products
  ...
</.header>
```

Then we could access the @class assignment in the HEEx markup returned by our function component:

```
def header(assigns) do
  ~H"""
    <%= @class %>
  """
end
```

The generated header/1 function component doesn't need to be called with any assigns though, so we won't worry too much about how this works for now. Let's move on to examining the important part of the header/1 function component implementation.

The header/1 function component implements three slots for rendering custom content—the *inner block*, *subtitle*, and *actions* slots. The inner block slot is the default slot—any content in between the opening and closing <.header> tags that *isn't* encapsulated in a named slot like the <:actions> content becomes the value of the @inner_block assignment. The function component renders the @inner_block assignment like this:

```
<%= render_slot(@inner_block) %>
```

Our <.header> function invocation in the index template doesn't make use of the <:subtitle> slot, so the header/1 function component has nothing to render when it calls <%= render_slot(@subtitle) %>. But it does make use of the actions slot like this:

```
<:actions>
  <.link patch={~p"/products/new"}>
    <.button>New Product</.button>
  </.link>
</:actions>
```

So, inside the header/1 function, the @actions assignment contains the markup that was placed in between the opening and closing <:actions> tags. That content actually calls on *another* function component, the .link/1 helper, to render a button, but more on that later. Putting it all together, the header/1 function component renders the contents of the actions slot like this:

```
<%= render_slot(@actions) %>
```

While we're here, you should be aware of interpolation of HTML attribute values. When you need interpolated Elixir for HTML attribute values, use the {} characters instead of the traditional <%= %> interpolation. You can see that in action in the class attribute of the header HTML element:

```
<header
  class={[@actions != [] && "flex items-center justify-between gap-6",
        @class]}>
```

This special interpolation syntax is because HEEx templates don't just provide interpolation services—they also provide some type protection. You might wonder where programmers specify this type data. Check just above the def header(...) to see the definition of typed attributes and slots in action:

```
generate_web/pento/lib/pento_web/components/core_components.ex
attr :class, :string, default: nil

slot :inner_block, required: true
slot :subtitle
slot :actions
```

From these instructions, we know the header component has a class attribute of type string that isn't required and defaults to nil. This means that the header/1 function can be invoked with a class="some string" attribute that will then be made available to the function's assigns. We can also see the three slot definitions and learn that only the inner_block is required.

Render the Header Component

Now that you know the implementation behind the code, let's look back at that header/1 component:

```
generate_web/pento/lib/pento_web/live/product_live/index.ex
<.header>
  Listing Products
  <:actions>
    <.button variant="primary" navigate={~p"/products/new"}>
      <.icon name="hero-plus" /> New Product
    </.button>
  </:actions>
</.header>
```

Everything between the <.header>...</.header> tags becomes the contents of the default slot called inner_block. Meanwhile, the content between the <:actions> slot tags becomes the value of the @actions assignment in the function component. We only specify a single action, a link component. That link has a patch attribute specifying a route. The link also has its own inner_block, a button with the text New Product. In this way, function component calls are nested to compose a simple UI.

That's pretty dense code! We won't walk you through every one of the definitions of every component, but you know how to find them now. We'll take a much deeper dive into components in later chapters. For now, it's enough for you to have a high-level understanding of how function components are used to wrap up some reuseable markup, with the help of slots to dynamically render custom content. Let's move on to the next section of the product page, the product list.

Render a List of Products as a Table

The heading represents code that uses a component to simplify one block of HTML. Some components are more interesting. The product list is a specialized bit of code that builds a table. Each table has headers and a variable list of customizable rows. Each row must then render a variable list of custom columns. Let's see how the view uses a component to render a table:

```
generate_web/pento/lib/pento_web/live/product_live/index.ex
<.table
  id="products"
  rows={@streams.products}
  row_click={fn {_id, product} ->
    JS.navigate(~p"/products/#{product}")
  end}
>
```

```
    <:col :let={{_id, product}} label="Name">{product.name}</:col>
    <:col
      :let={{_id, product}}
      label="Description">{product.description}
    </:col>
    <:col
      :let={{_id, product}}
      label="Unit price">{product.unit_price}
    </:col>
    <:col :let={{_id, product}} label="Sku">{product.sku}</:col>
    <:action :let={{_id, product}}>
      <div class="sr-only">
        <.link navigate={~p"/products/#{product}"}>Show</.link>
      </div>
      <.link navigate={~p"/products/#{product}/edit"}>Edit</.link>
    </:action>
    <:action :let={{id, product}}>
      <.link
        phx-click={
          JS.push("delete", value: %{id: product.id})
          |> hide("##{id}")
        }
        data-confirm="Are you sure?"
      >
        Delete
      </.link>
    </:action>
</.table>
```

The table is a component with attributes for id, rows, and row_click. You can expect to find a function component, table/1, implemented in our app's generated code. The rows attribute has a list of items, and each one will be used to produce a row. We don't have to know the details yet, but when a user clicks a row, it will call JS.navigate with the route to show a product.

To render a row, each table will use two repeated slots—the :col slot and the :actions slot. The :col slot will implement a new column each time it's invoked, so our table will have four columns, one each for name, description, price, and SKU. The table/1 function component also renders a table row for each member of the @rows assignment, with a value for each column.

Notice the :let attribute attached to each <:col> slot. Under the hood, the table/1 function component iterates over the list of items in the @rows assignment and renders a table cell for each row/column combination. It yields each element in the @rows list back up to the index template and sets it equal to the product variable via the let assignment. So, all of the :col slots will fire for each product. That means if there are five products, the slot will fire 20 times:

four columns each for five different products. Two action slots will also fire for each row, one to provide an edit link and one to provide a delete link.

Don't worry about the details of how the table/1 function component renders row data for each column just yet. We'll go into greater detail on component slots in Chapter 6, Function Components, on page 173. At this time, all you need to know is that the Phoenix Live generator provided us with a table/1 function component that is used here to render the list of products into a table.

Navigation to Dedicated Form Pages

Phoenix 1.8 has eliminated the complexity of modal components in favor of clean, dedicated pages for form operations. Instead of overlaying forms on top of existing pages, users navigate to separate URLs for creating and editing products.

Let's examine how this works. When a user clicks a New Product link from the index page, they navigate to /products/new, which is handled by the ProductLive.Form module with the :new action. Similarly, when they click Edit on a product, they go to /products/:id/edit, handled by the same ProductLive.Form module but with the :edit action.

This approach offers several advantages over the previous modal-based system:

- *Better accessibility:* Screen readers and keyboard navigation work more naturally with dedicated pages.
- *Bookmarkable URLs:* Users can bookmark or share direct links to form pages.
- *Cleaner state management:* Each page has its own focused responsibility.
- *Easier testing:* Each page can be tested independently.
- *Simplified code:* No need to manage modal visibility state or complex JavaScript interactions.

The ProductLive.Form module is a full live view that handles both creation and editing scenarios, determining its behavior based on the live action and the presence of a product ID in the parameters.

Put those components aside for a moment. For now, let's think about changes on a page. LiveView updates only the bits of the page that change. That means after the first render, LiveView will re-render each row *only when its values change*. That means if one product changes, only the row for that table will change!

You've finally seen the entire mount/render workflow in action. First, we set up the socket using mount/3, and then we render it via the explicit render/1 function.

That seems like a workflow that's almost the same as a traditional web app, and it is. LiveView really shines when we use it for scenarios that *change* our socket through the use of params and event handlers. We're ready to dive into the change management workflow.

Handle Change for the Product Edit

The ProductLive.Index live view will also support the Product Edit and Product New features. Clicking on an edit or new link will fire an event and trigger a whole new workflow. In it, our code will use handlers to respond to the event by changing socket state. Then LiveView will render any changes on the page. In this way, a single live view can easily handle multiple pieces of CRUD functionality. Let's see how it works with an edit click.

Route to the Product Edit

Let's trace the code that fires when you point your browser at the /products/:id/edit route, starting with the route definition.

When we ran the generator, LiveView gave us some routes to paste into our router.ex file. One of them was the route to edit a product:

```
live "/products/:id/edit", ProductLive.Index, :edit
```

Assuming we're logged in, this route maps the /products/:id/edit route to the same ProductLive.Index live view that we examined earlier, this time with a live action of :edit. By specifying the :edit live action in the route definition, LiveView adds a key of :live_action to the live view's socket assigns and the :edit value we supplied in the route.

To take advantage of this live action to change the live view's state, we'll hook into a slightly different LiveView life cycle than we saw for mount/render.

When we navigate to the Product Index route, /products, the LiveView life cycle that kicks off first calls the mount/3 life cycle function, followed by render/1. If, however, we want to access and use the live action from socket assigns, we must do so in the handle_params/3 life cycle function. This callback, if it's implemented, fires right after mount/3. So our adjusted LiveView life cycle looks something like this:

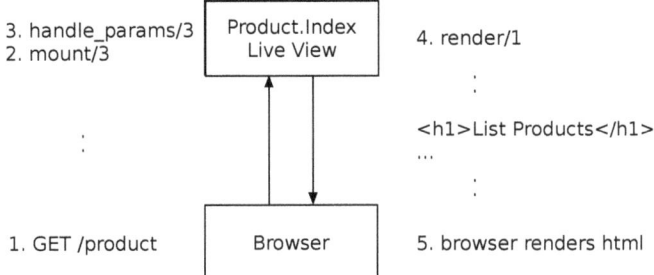

Before we take a closer look at handle_params/3, it's important to understand that users can navigate to the Product Edit view two different ways. The user can point their browser at /products/1/edit. This fires an old-school HTTP request. The user can also follow the edit links generated for one of the products in the Product Index template. Rather than forcing a whole new page load, these links will use the change management workflow. This powerful concept will let the user click a link and see changes on the page without experiencing a page reload! We'll walk through that flow next.

Navigate with a Live Patch

Open up the render/1 function in lib/pento_web/live/product_live/index.ex and look at the markup. Remember, our HEEx template has an :action slot for each product in @streams.products. One of those actions renders the Edit link with this link component:

```
<.link patch={~p"/products/#{product}/edit"}>Edit</.link>
```

Before we talk about what patch navigation is and how it works, let's consider the ~p, or p sigil,[3] and understand how it constructs the URL to which we want to navigate. The ~p comes to us from the Phoenix framework; it's not specific to LiveView. It generates a router path and verifies it. So if you use ~p and provide a route that does not exist in your router.ex, you'll get a compiler warning. In addition to verifying the route, the ~p will construct routes for you by generating a slug based on the provided, interpolated struct. So, while a product in the preceding template snippet is a full Pento.Catalog.Product struct, the ~p function will use the Phoenix.Param protocol to return the following route: /products/1/edit, where the ID of the given product is 1.

You can see this in action for yourself. Open up an interactive terminal session with iex -S mix and try out the code on the next page.

---

3. https://hexdocs.pm/phoenix/Phoenix.VerifiedRoutes.html#sigil_p/2

```
iex> product = Pento.Catalog.Product.__struct__(id: 42)
%Pento.Catalog.Product{... id: 42, name: nil, ...}
iex> i
Term
  %Pento.Catalog.Product{...}
Data type
  Pento.Catalog.Product
...
Implemented protocols
  ... Phoenix.Param, ...
iex> Phoenix.Param.to_param product
"42"
```

This gives you a sense of what Phoenix uses under the hood when computing URL parameters using ~p.

Now that you understand how the route provided to the patch attribute of the .link component was constructed, let's discuss how patch navigation works. The call to the link component that we showed you earlier will result in the following HTML:

```
<a  href="/products/1/edit"
    data-phx-link="patch"
    data-phx-link-state="push">
  Edit
</a>
```

If you open the element inspector in your browser and inspect any of the edit links on the /products page, you should see exactly that.

Calling the link function component with a patch attribute adds the data-phx-link="patch" to the resulting HTML. This special link, called a live patch, will "patch" the current live view. Unlike traditional links, the href attribute here is merely a fallback. It will take over if no LiveView JavaScript is present. With a live patch, clicking the link *will* change the URL in the browser bar, courtesy of a JavaScript feature called *push state navigation*. But it *won't* send a web request to reload the page. Instead, clicking this link will kick off LiveView's change management workflow—the handle_params/3 function will be invoked for the linked live view, followed by the render/1 function.

So when you click the edit link on the product index template, you'll navigate to a dedicated edit page:

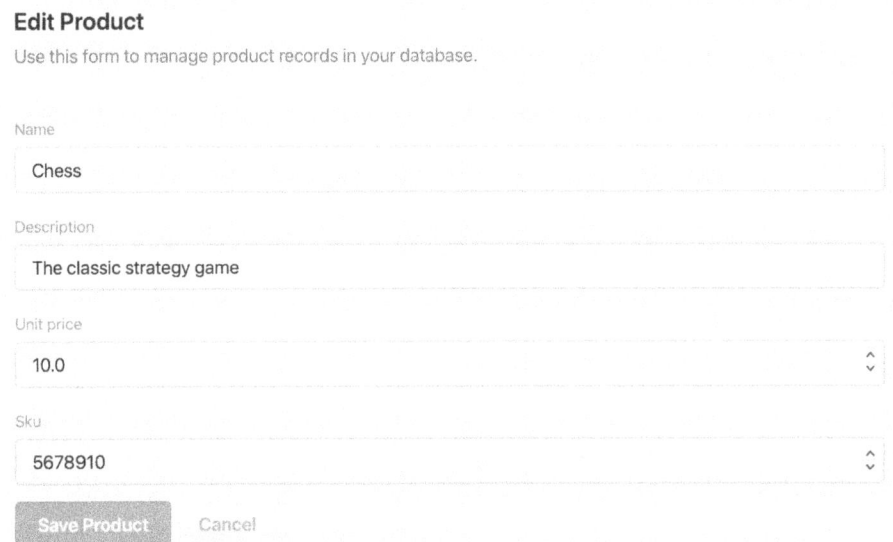

You'll see the URL changes to /products/1/edit and the entire page content updates to show the focused editing interface! This clean page transition maintains all the benefits of LiveView's real-time features while providing a much cleaner, more accessible user experience.

In Phoenix 1.8, clicking the edit link navigates to the ProductLive.Form live view, which is a completely separate LiveView module dedicated to form operations. This navigation triggers the full mount/handle_params/render life cycle for the ProductLive.Form module. Whether you click the edit link from the index page or directly navigate your browser to /products/1/edit, you're accessing the same dedicated form live view.

The ProductLive.Form module's handle_params/3 function is responsible for determining whether it's handling a :new or :edit action and setting up the appropriate state. This approach is much cleaner than the previous modal-based system because each live view has a single, focused responsibility.

It's time to take a closer look at how the handle_params/3 function works to set the edit product state.

ProductLive.Form: Dedicated Form Handling

Phoenix 1.8's dedicated form approach simplifies state management significantly. When a user navigates to an edit URL, the ProductLive.Form live view handles the request with clear, focused responsibility.

The workflow begins when the user clicks the edit link or navigates directly to /products/1/edit. Phoenix then calls the ProductLive.Form module's mount/3 function, which immediately delegates to apply_action/3 to handle the specific live action and parameters:

```
generate_web/pento/lib/pento_web/live/product_live/form.ex
defp apply_action(socket, :edit, %{"id" => id}) do
  product = Catalog.get_product!(socket.assigns.current_scope, id)

  socket
  |> assign(:page_title, "Edit Product")
  |> assign(:product, product)
  |> assign(:form,
    to_form(Catalog.change_product(socket.assigns.current_scope, product)))
end
```

Phoenix 1.8 has simplified this pattern significantly. Instead of the complex handle_params/3 life cycle used in earlier versions, the form live view uses a straightforward mount/3 → apply_action/3 pattern. The apply_action/3 helper function handles setting up the socket based on the live action (:new or :edit) and parameters. This approach is much cleaner and easier to understand, with each action getting its own focused function clause.

The beauty of Phoenix 1.8's approach is its simplicity and separation of concerns. When a user clicks an edit link, they navigate to a completely separate live view (ProductLive.Form) rather than changing state within the same view. This eliminates the complex state management that was required in earlier versions and provides several benefits:

- *Clearer mental model:* Each page has one clear purpose.
- *Simpler state management:* No need to track which mode a view is in.
- *Better URL structure:* Each operation has its own clean, bookmarkable URL.
- *Easier testing:* Each live view can be tested independently.
- *Improved accessibility:* Screen readers and keyboard navigation work naturally.

The apply_action/3 function uses pattern matching to handle different scenarios. For editing, it loads the existing product from the database using the ID from the URL parameters, sets an appropriate page title, and creates a form changeset. For new products, it creates a fresh product struct with the current user's ID and sets up the form accordingly.

This approach scales beautifully because each LiveView module has a single, focused responsibility. As your application grows more complex, you don't end up with monolithic live views trying to handle multiple different page states. Instead, you have clean, focused modules that are easy to understand, maintain, and extend.

Now let's turn our attention to some additional CRUD interactions and take a closer look at how LiveView streams allow us to manage those interactions efficiently.

Manage Data with Streams

We briefly discussed streams earlier on in this chapter. Streams are how LiveView manages collections of data on the client-side, rather than on the server-side. We added a key of :products to socket.assigns.streams by calling stream/4 in our mount function. Then, in the template, we iterated over those products by calling on @streams.products. This tells LiveView to remove the products collection from socket assigns and instead store that information client-side, by inserting it into the DOM. Subsequent interactions with that data, for example when a user deletes a product, will also be handled client-side. Let's take a look at that flow now.

In the index template, you'll see the following markup for creating a delete button:

```
<.link
  phx-click={JS.push("delete", value: %{id: product.id}) |> hide("##{id}")}
  data-confirm="Are you sure?"
>
  Delete
</.link>
```

The call to JS.push will send an event with the name "delete", and a payload of %{id: product.id} to the server. Our corresponding event handler looks like this:

generate_web/pento/lib/pento_web/live/product_live/index.ex
```
@impl true
def handle_event("delete", %{"id" => id}, socket) do
  product = Catalog.get_product!(socket.assigns.current_scope, id)
  {:ok, _} = Catalog.delete_product(socket.assigns.current_scope, product)

  {:noreply, stream_delete(socket, :products, product)}
end
```

Here, we fetch the product from the database and destroy it. Then we tell LiveView to remove the product from the collection of products in the products stream stored client-side with stream_delete(socket, :products, product). This will result in a socket assigns that looks something like this:

```
streams: %{
__changed__: MapSet.new([:products]), ...
...
  products: %Phoenix.LiveView.LiveStream{
    name: :products,
    dom_id: #Function<3.76265957/1 in Phoenix.LiveView.LiveStream.new/4>,
    ref: "0",
    inserts: [],
    deletes: [
      {"products-1", -1,%...Product{...name: "Pentominoes",...}, nil}
    ],
    reset?: false,
    consumable?: false
  }
  ...other keys...
}
```

Remember that any updates to socket assigns will cause LiveView to re-render the template. When the template re-renders with this new socket assigns, the LiveView client-side code will know to remove the product in the @streams.products.deletes list from the collection of products rendereed on the page via our iteration over @streams.products.

Once again, we didn't have to tell LiveView *how* to remove data from the template. Instead, we just told it *what* to remove with our call to stream_delete. This approach isn't just nice and declarative, it's also efficient. LiveView doesn't have to re-fetch a long list of products and store it in the socket again. Nor do we have to write tedious code to remove a specific product from a server-side list of products ourselves.

The LiveView streams API provides a similar function to add or update a member of a data collection. Let's take a look at the generated event handler that's invoked when the user submits the form for a new or updated product:

```
generate_web/pento/lib/pento_web/live/product_live/index.ex
@impl true
def handle_info({type, %Pento.Catalog.Product{}}, socket)
    when type in [:created, :updated, :deleted] do
  {:noreply,
    stream(socket, :products,
        Catalog.list_products(socket.assigns.current_scope), reset: true)}
end
```

Don't worry about the details of how the form is submitted or how it triggers this function for now, we'll revisit this later on in this chapter. For now, notice the call to stream_insert. This tells LiveView that when the template is re-rendered, it should add or update the product referenced in @streams.products.inserts. This update will be performed directly in the DOM.

Now, let's shift our attention to rendering and take a closer look at how LiveView will handle the edit product state.

Render Product Edit State

Let's look at the way LiveView renders the index template with the new :live_action and @streams.products keys from socket assigns. Remember, we're still in the ProductLive.Index live view, so we'll look at the render function:

generate_web/pento/lib/pento_web/live/product_live/index.ex
```
<.table
  id="products"
  rows={@streams.products}
  row_click={fn {_id, product} ->
    JS.navigate(~p"/products/#{product}")
  end}
>
  <:col :let={{_id, product}} label="Name">{product.name}</:col>
  <:col
    :let={{_id, product}}
    label="Description">{product.description}
  </:col>
  <:col
    :let={{_id, product}}
    label="Unit price">{product.unit_price}
  </:col>
  <:col :let={{_id, product}} label="Sku">{product.sku}</:col>
  <:action :let={{_id, product}}>
    <div class="sr-only">
      <.link navigate={~p"/products/#{product}"}>Show</.link>
    </div>
    <.link navigate={~p"/products/#{product}/edit"}>Edit</.link>
  </:action>
  <:action :let={{id, product}}>
    <.link
      phx-click={
        JS.push("delete", value: %{id: product.id})
        |> hide("##{id}")
      }
      data-confirm="Are you sure?"
    >
      Delete
    </.link>
  </:action>
</.table>
```

The ProductLive.Index template in Phoenix 1.8 is refreshingly simple and focused. Unlike earlier versions that included complex modal components and form state management, the index template has a single, clear responsibility: displaying the list of products.

When a user clicks the edit link next to a given product, they navigate to a completely separate page handled by ProductLive.Form. This clean navigation approach eliminates the need for the following:

- Modal state management within the index view.
- Complex conditional rendering based on live actions.
- JavaScript-based modal show/hide logic.
- Nested live components within the same view.

The index template's simplicity is one of Phoenix 1.8's major improvements. By removing the modal complexity, the code becomes much easier to understand, test, and maintain. Each live view has a clear, focused purpose, and the user experience is more accessible since each operation has its own dedicated URL.

Manage JavaScript in the Component

If you want to see the tedious details of the modal dialog, you can check out its definition in all its glory in the lib/pento_web/components/core_components.ex file. It's a function component with some attr and slot directives to establish the allowed inputs to the component.

Keep in mind that the modal function produces a dialog that works completely via JavaScript. The component makes use of JavaScript to close the dialog, and you can tailor the code if you want to.

The modal dialog has an x button to close it. The code that renders the button is HTML with JavaScript utilities to manage that transition:

```
<div class="absolute top-6 right-5">
  <button
    phx-click={JS.exec("data-cancel", to: "##{@id}")}
    type="button"
    class="-m-3 flex-none p-3 opacity-20 hover:opacity-40"
    aria-label={gettext("close")}
  >
    <.icon name="hero-x-mark-solid" class="h-5 w-5" />
  </button>
</div>
```

Most of these details are tedious HTML and CSS concerns. The code displays a x icon wrapped in a button wrapped in a div. Focus on the phx-click attribute for a moment. We compute it with JS.exec("data-cancel", to: "##{@id}"). The actual script, defined on the modal component, looks like this:

```
def hide_modal(js \\ %JS{}, id) do
  js
  |> JS.hide(
    to: "##{id}-bg",
    transition: {"transition-all transform ease-in duration-200",
      "opacity-100", "opacity-0"}
  )
  |> hide("##{id}-container")
  |> JS.hide(to: "##{id}", transition: {"block", "block", "hidden"})
  |> JS.remove_class("overflow-hidden", to: "body")
  |> JS.pop_focus()
end
```

This code demonstrates the sophisticated JavaScript capabilities that Phoenix LiveView provides through the JS module. However, Phoenix 1.8 has moved beyond modal-based interfaces entirely, adopting a cleaner page-based approach that provides better accessibility and user experience.

In Phoenix 1.8, instead of managing complex modal state and JavaScript transitions, forms simply navigate between dedicated pages. When a user clicks Edit on a product, they navigate directly to /products/1/edit—a clean, bookmarkable URL with its own dedicated live view.

This architectural shift eliminates the need for complex modal management while providing users with a more familiar web navigation experience. Let's explore how Phoenix 1.8's dedicated form live views work.

Phoenix 1.8's Dedicated Form Live View

Phoenix 1.8 has revolutionized form handling by replacing the complex live component pattern with dedicated LiveView modules. Instead of embedding form components within other views, Phoenix 1.8 generates ProductLive.Form as a stand-alone live view that handles both creating and editing products.

This approach offers significant advantages:

- *Simplified architecture:* Each form operation gets its own dedicated page with a clean URL structure (/products/new, /products/1/edit).
- *Clearer separation of concerns:* The form live view has a single, focused responsibility without needing to coordinate with a parent view.
- *Better user experience:* Users can bookmark form pages, use browser navigation naturally, and screen readers work more effectively.
- *Easier testing:* Form functionality can be tested in isolation without complex setup.

ProductLive.Form Structure

The ProductLive.Form module follows the standard LiveView pattern with mount/3, render/1, and event handlers. Unlike the old live component approach, it doesn't need complex update/2 callbacks or coordination with parent views.

The form determines its behavior based on the live action and URL parameters. The apply_action/3 function we saw earlier handles this setup:

- *For :new action:* Creates a fresh product struct with the current user's ID.
- *For :edit action:* Loads the existing product from the database using the ID parameter.

Both scenarios create an Ecto changeset using Catalog.change_product/2 and store it in the socket assigns as a form. This approach is much simpler than the old live component pattern because there's no need for complex update/2 callbacks or coordination with parent views.

The Phoenix 1.8 approach leverages the standard LiveView life cycle without the additional complexity layers that live components introduced. The form live view manages its own state independently, receiving initial data through URL parameters and maintaining that state through its own event handlers.

Phoenix 1.8 Form Rendering

Phoenix 1.8's form rendering is much more straightforward than the old live component approach. The ProductLive.Form module renders its form using the standard .form function component with modern input components that provide excellent DaisyUI styling out of the box.

The form in Phoenix 1.8 uses the @form assign which contains the changeset created during the apply_action/3 call. Here's how the form is structured:

1. *Form component:* Uses the .form function component with phx-change="validate" and phx-submit="save" events.
2. *Input components:* Each field uses the .input component with automatic error handling and DaisyUI styling.
3. *Event handling:* Events are sent directly to the ProductLive.Form live view (no need for phx-target or @myself).
4. *Cancel navigation:* Provides clean navigation back to the appropriate page using navigate attributes.

The Phoenix 1.8 approach eliminates several complexities from the old system:

- *No phx-target complexity:* Events go directly to the current live view.

- *No @myself references:* Simplified event routing.
- *Better styling:* DaisyUI integration provides professional appearance.
- *Cleaner templates:* More readable HEEx markup without nested component complexity.

The form validation happens in real time as users type, and submission handling is managed through straightforward event handlers within the same LiveView module.

ProductLive.Form Event Handling

Phoenix 1.8's form event handling is straightforward and follows standard LiveView patterns. The ProductLive.Form module handles two main events:

1. *"validate":* Triggered by phx-change when users type in form fields.
2. *"save":* Triggered by phx-submit when users submit the form.

The validation event provides real-time feedback as users interact with the form, while the save event processes the final form submission. Both events work directly with the form's changeset to provide immediate feedback and smooth user experience.

The save operation uses pattern matching on the live action to determine whether to create a new product or update an existing one, calling the appropriate Catalog function with the current scope for proper authentication and data isolation.

```
generate_web/pento/lib/pento_web/live/product_live/form.ex
defp save_product(socket, :edit, product_params) do
  case Catalog.update_product(socket.assigns.current_scope,
                              socket.assigns.product,
                              product_params) do
    {:ok, product} ->
      {:noreply,
       socket
       |> put_flash(:info, "Product updated successfully")
       |> push_navigate(
         to: return_path(socket.assigns.current_scope,
                         socket.assigns.return_to, product)
       )}
    {:error, %Ecto.Changeset{} = changeset} ->
      {:noreply, assign(socket, form: to_form(changeset))}
  end
end
```

There are two function heads for save_product/3, one that fires when the action is "edit" and one that fires when the action is "new." The function shown here is the "edit" version. We update the product with a call to Catalog.update_product/2. If the update is not successful, we add the changeset with the errors to the socket, allowing the template to re-render and display those errors. But what about when the update is successful? Before we break down this code, let's think about what we *want* to happen here at a high level. We want a few things to occur:

- Show a flash message saying the update was successful.
- Navigate back to the /products index page, which should now show a list of products that contains the updated product.

We achieve the flash message and redirect like this:

```
:noreply,
  socket
  |> put_flash(:info, "Product updated successfully")
  |> push_patch(to: socket.assigns.patch)}
```

Instead of having form components send messages to parent live views, Phoenix 1.8 uses a much cleaner approach called Phoenix PubSub. We'll talk more about PubSub in Chapter 9, Build a Distributed Dashboard, on page 281. Think of PubSub as a notification mechanism across processes.

When a product is created, updated, or deleted in the ProductLive.Form, the operation triggers a PubSub broadcast through the Catalog context. The ProductLive.Index view subscribes to these product events during its mount/3 function with Catalog.subscribe_products/1.

This is the handle_info/2 function we saw earlier that handles these PubSub messages:

```
generate_web/pento/lib/pento_web/live/product_live/index.ex
@impl true
def handle_info({type, %Pento.Catalog.Product{}}, socket)
    when type in [:created, :updated, :deleted] do
  {:noreply,
    stream(socket, :products,
           Catalog.list_products(socket.assigns.current_scope), reset: true)}
end
```

The beauty of this approach is that it works automatically across completely separate LiveView processes. The form live view and index live view don't need to know about each other—they communicate through the clean PubSub interface. This makes the system more robust and easier to understand.

Here are some benefits of Phoenix 1.8's PubSub approach:

- *Decoupled architecture:* LiveViews don't directly reference each other.
- *Automatic updates:* Index pages update automatically when forms save.
- *Multiuser support:* All connected users see updates in real time.
- *Simpler testing:* Each live view can be tested independently.

With that much under our belt, let's take a deeper dive into the push_patch/2 function and its client-side counterpart.

Live Navigation with Patching

The push_patch/2 function and its client-slide counterpart, JS.patch/1, annotate the socket for navigation within the current live view. In other words, you're doing a kind of redirect to the current live view without reloading the live view. When this happens, the current live view process and existing WebSocket connection are reused, and the mount/3 function is not invoked but the handle_params/3 function is.

Recall the code that invokes the form component in the index template:

```
<.live_component
    module={PentoWeb.ProductLive.FormComponent}
    id={@product.id || :new}
    title={@page_title}
    action={@live_action}
    product={@product}
    patch={~p"/products"}
/>
```

You can see that we set patch equal to the /products route. This means that when a product is successfully edited, we're redirecting to the *same* Index route we were already on. Thanks to the handle_info/2 function we implemented previously, that page will already have inserted the new or updated product into the stream of products in the socket. So, the page will display the updated list or products.

Putting it all together, you see how the ProductLive.Index live view renders the form component throughout the entire life-span of our form. When the Index live view renders the HTML in index.html.heex, it first invokes the component with the live_component function, including the options with the product and the other data the form will need. Once the form's own life cycle starts, it fires update/2 to set up the socket with the data the form will need, including the changeset. When the user submits the form, the handle_event/3 calls a live redirect to re-render the page with fresh state for the Index view. Then the live_action changes, so the index.html.heex template no longer renders it.

This is a good stopping point. Now, you can put some of what you've learned into practice.

Your Turn

By tracing through the ProductLive.Index live view, you've seen the major pieces of the LiveView framework—the route, the live view module, the optional view template, and the helpers, component modules and component templates that support the parent view.

The entry point of the LiveView life cycle is the route. The route matches a URL onto a LiveView module and sets a live action. The live view puts data in the socket using mount/3 and handle_params/3 and then renders that data in a template with the same name as the live view. The mount/render and change management workflows make it easy to reason about state management and help you find a home for *all* of your CRUD code across just *two* live views.

When live views become too complex or repetitive, you can break off components. A function component compartmentalizes markup, while a live component compartmentalizes state, HTML markup, and event processing for a small part of a live view. The generators built two different components: a function component to handle a modal window and a live component to process a form.

All of this code demonstrates that LiveView provides an elegant system you can use to handle the complex interactions of a single-page app. LiveView empowers you to build highly interactive, real-time features in a way that is organized and easy to maintain. You could easily imagine adding custom features on top of the generated CRUD functionality, or applying the lessons of the generated code to your own hand-rolled live views.

Now that you're starting to see the beauty of LiveView as a single-page app system, it's time to get your hands dirty.

Give It a Try

These three problems are different in nature. You'll accomplish three tasks. The first, most straightforward one, is to trace through the ProductLive.Show live view.

Trace Through a Live View

Start from the Index page's implementation of the link to the product show page and work your way through the route, mount/3, handle_params/3, and render/1 life cycle. Answer these questions:

- Which route gets invoked when you click the link on the Index page to view a given product?
- What data does ProductLive.Show.mount/3 add to the socket?
- How does the ProductLive.Show live view use the handle_params/3 callback?
- How does the ProductLive.Show template render the Product Edit form and what events does that form support?

When you're done, display your own message on the page by adding some content to the ProductLive.Show live view's socket.assigns and then rendering it in the template.

Generate Your Own Live View

This final, more complex, task will ask you to combine everything you've learned in this and the previous chapter. You'll run the Phoenix Live generator again to create a new set of CRUD features for a resource, FAQ, or frequently asked questions. This feature will allow users of our gaming site to submit questions, answer them, and up-vote them. Each FAQ should have fields for a question, an answer, and a vote count.

Devise your generator command and run it. Then fire up the Phoenix server and interact with your generated FAQ CRUD features! Can you create a new question? Can you answer it? Trace some of the generated code pathways that support this functionality.

Next Time

In the next part of this book, we're ready to move away from generated code and roll our own live view from scratch. The following chapter will take a deep dive into working with LiveView forms and explore how changesets model changes to data in our live views, with and without database persistence. We'll finish with a look at an exciting and powerful LiveView feature—reactive file uploads. When we're done, you'll have built a new custom live view, you'll have gained a solid understanding of how changesets and forms work together in LiveView, and you'll be prepared to build interactive forms that meet a variety of user requirements. Let's go!

Part II

LiveView Composition

In Part II, you'll move away from generated code and start building your own live views from scratch. We'll dive into how LiveView lets you compose layers that manage change. We'll begin with a look at forms and show you how to organize code for the changesets that model change in your live views. Then we'll build a custom LiveView feature with components. Components allow programmers to partition and share views, including both presentation and event processing. First, we'll use a function component to share common presentation code while building a widget to collect demographic data from customers. Then we'll extend that work with a live component so the widget component can manage events.

CHAPTER 5

Forms and Changesets

On the web, many user interactions are basic, such as typing a URL or clicking a link. But sometimes, users need more sophisticated interactions. HTML provides forms to represent complex data. In single-page apps, form interactions go beyond one-time submissions with a single response. Any user interaction could lead to immediate changes on a page. Today's users expect immediate feedback with clear error messages. Changing a country form field, for example, might impact available options in a state or province field. LiveView meets this need perfectly, giving us the opportunity to make adjustments to a page in real time as the user fills out a form piece by piece.

Let's look at how these forms relate to the generated code you've seen so far.

The past few chapters focused on generated code, specifically database-backed live views. These generated web pages let users type data into Phoenix forms to change data in your database through Ecto-backed context and schema layers. Ecto changesets provide the connective tissue to weave these two disparate worlds together. In fact, Phoenix forms *are* representations of changesets in the user interface. This chapter will take a deeper dive into forms and changesets. You'll see how to compose LiveView code specifically, and Phoenix code generally, to manage change.

Model Change with Changesets

Before we get too deep into this topic, let's think about the role that forms and changesets play in our application.

First, consider Ecto changesets. Changesets are policies for changing data, and they play these roles:

- Changesets *cast unstructured user data* into a known, structured form—most commonly, an Ecto database schema—ensuring data *safety*.

- Changesets *capture differences* between safe, consistent data and a proposed change, allowing *efficiency*.

- Changesets *validate data* using known consistent rules, ensuring data *consistency*.

- Changesets provide a *contract* for communicating error states and valid states, ensuring a *common interface for change*.

In Chapter 3, Generators: Contexts and Schemas, on page 71, you saw changesets in action in the Product.changeset/2 function:

```
generators/pento/lib/pento/catalog/product.ex
@doc false
def changeset(product, attrs, user_scope) do
  product
  |> cast(attrs, [:name, :description, :unit_price, :sku])
  |> validate_required([:name, :description, :unit_price, :sku])
  |> unique_constraint(:sku)
  |> validate_number(:unit_price, greater_than: 0.0)
  |> put_change(:user_id, user_scope.user.id)
end
```

The changeset/2 function captures differences between the structured product and the unstructured attrs.

Then, with cast/4, the changeset trims the attributes to a known field list and converts to the correct types, ensuring safety by guaranteeing that you don't let any unknown or invalid attributes into your database.

Finally, the validate_required/2, unique_constraint/2, and validate_number/2 functions validate the inbound data, ensuring consistency.

The result is a data structure with known states and error message formats, ensuring interface compatibility.

Consequently, the forms in the ProductLive views knew exactly how to behave—validating form input and presenting errors in accordance with the changeset's rules in real time as the users typed. We didn't have to change the generated code much at all.

In this chapter, we're going to shift off of the well-worn path of generated, database-backed changesets. You'll learn how versatile changesets can be when it comes to modeling changes to data, with or without a database. You'll build a custom, schemaless changeset for data that *isn't* backed by a database table. Then we'll switch from schemaless changesets to an embedded schema without database backing to achieve an API nearly identical to the database-backed one you see in product.ex, and you'll use that changeset in a form within a live view. Along the way, we'll explore some of the niceties LiveView provides for working with forms.

Finally, we'll work with an exciting and powerful LiveView feature—live uploads. You'll use this feature to build an image uploader in LiveView. When we're done, you'll have built a custom live view, worked extensively with Ecto changesets, and seen the full power of LiveView forms.

Let's get started.

Model Change with Embedded Schemas

We've used changesets to model changes to data that is persisted in our database, but we can easily imagine scenarios in which we want to present the user with the ability to input data that *isn't* persisted. Consider the following examples:

- A guest checkout experience in which a user inputs their billing and shipping info without saving it.
- A gaming UI in which a user provides a temporary username for the lifespan of the game.
- A search form in which input is validated but not saved.

All of these scenarios require presenting some interface to the user for collecting input, validating that input, and managing the results of that validation. This is exactly what changesets and forms did for us in our ProductLive views. Luckily for us, we can continue to use changesets in this way, even without schema-backed modules and data persistence.

In this section, we'll show you how to use schemaless changesets and embedded schemas to model data that you won't save in your database. You'll build a new live view that uses embedded schemas to allow users to send promo codes for game purchases to their friends. Then we'll take a look at some of the tools that LiveView provides for working with forms. Let's dive in.

Build Database-Free Schemas from Structs

Simply put, you can use changesets with basic Elixir structs or maps—you don't need to use Ecto schemas to generate those structs. But when you do use changesets with plain structs, your code needs to provide the type information Ecto would normally handle.

That might sound confusing at first, but after a quick example, you'll get the hang of it. All you need to do is call Ecto.Changeset.cast/4. For the first argument, you'll pass a tuple containing your struct and a map of your struct's attribute types, and you're off to the races.

Let's take a look at a brief example. Then we'll outline a use case for embedded schemas in our Pento app and build it out together.

Open up IEx and key in this simple module definition for a game player:

```
[pento] → iex -S mix
iex> defmodule Player do
      defstruct [:username, :age]
     end
```

It's a plain old module with a `defstruct` directive. Now create a new empty struct:

```
iex> player = %Player{}
```

We have a struct, and we've done nothing Ecto-specific. We want to use a changeset to cast and validate the data in our struct. Let's think about how we can give the changeset enough information to do its job.

A typical changeset pipeline combines data, a cast, and validations. To successfully judge whether a change is consistent, the provided data *must* include information about both the changes and the type. So far, we've passed schema-backed structs as a first argument to `Ecto.Changeset.cast/4`. Such structs are produced by modules, like `Catalog.Product`, that implement a `schema/1` function containing information about the struct's allowed types. We don't have a schema struct though, so let's dig deeper. Get `help` for the `Changeset.cast/4` function:

```
iex> h Ecto.Changeset.cast/4

def cast(data, params, permitted, opts \\ [])

Applies the given params...

The given data may be either a changeset, a schema struct, or a {data, types}
tuple. ...
```

The "or" phrase in this sentence is the key: "The given data may be either a changeset, a schema struct, or a {data, types}." We can start with a changeset or a schema struct, both of which embed data and type information. *Or* we can start with a two-tuple that explicitly contains the data as the first element and provides type information as the second. Now, let's follow that advice and build a tuple with both a `player` struct and a map of `types`, like this:

```
iex> types = %{username: :string, age: :integer}
%{username: :string, age: :integer}
iex> attrs = %{username: "player1", age: 20}
%{username: "player1", age: 20}
```

```
iex> changeset = {player, types} \
   |> Ecto.Changeset.cast(attrs, Map.keys(types))
#Ecto.Changeset<changes: %{age: 20, ...}, ...,valid?: true>
```

Brilliant! This bit of code can create a changeset. With schemaless changesets, you don't have to have established fields or type data at compile time. This great flexibility would be useful if we needed to build dynamic forms with user-defined fields, but we're working with a fixed Player struct with known fields and types. Given these constraints, Ecto provides a better solution than schemaless changesets.

Ecto's *embedded schemas* combine both types and field information without requiring database backing. Here's the same player, tweaked to use embedded schemas:

```
iex> defmodule Player do
...>   use Ecto.Schema
...>   @primary_key false
...>   embedded_schema do
...>     field :user_name, :string
...>     field :age, :integer
...>   end
...> end
{:module, Player, ...}

iex> %Player{}
%Player{user_name: nil, age: nil}
```

We define our schema just as we would any other Ecto schema. The only differences are the use of @primary_key false to disable the unneeded id field and the use of embedded_schema instead of schema. Now, our schema clearly defines each field along with its associated type.

Now we can build changesets and validations just as we would with any other schema. We take the same Ecto.Changeset.cast/3 function. We'll need some proposed changes and valid fields for our cast, in addition to our player struct we previously built:

```
iex> import Ecto.Changeset
Ecto.Changeset
iex> changes = %{age: 16, name: "Mario"}
%{name: "Mario", age: 16}
iex> allowed_fields = [:user_name, :age]
[:user_name, :age]
```

With all of the setup out of the way, we can build a changeset with cast just as we do in our product.ex schema:

```
iex> changeset = cast(player, changes, allowed_fields)
#Ecto.Changeset<
  action: nil,
  changes: %{age: 16},
  errors: [],
  data: #Player<>,
  valid?: true
```

And we're left with a valid changeset. We can even run validations using the same syntax as before by passing the fresh changeset into an existing validation:

```
iex> validate_number(changeset, :age, greater_than: 16)
#Ecto.Changeset<
  action: nil,
  changes: %{age: 16},
  errors: [
    age: {"must be greater than %{number}",
     [validation: :number, kind: :greater_than, number: 16]}
  ],
  data: #Player<>,
  valid?: false
```

Perfect. This changeset behaves just like the generated Product one. Though our schema isn't database backed, the API is otherwise exactly the same! That fact will come in handy when it's time to build a live view with a form.

With our quick experimentation out of the way, we can shift to our editor to write some code. Let's see what an embedded schema looks like in a live view.

Use Embedded Schemas in LiveView

To celebrate the one week anniversary of our wildly successful game company, we're offering a special promotion. Any registered user can log in and visit the /promo page. There, they can submit the email address of a friend and our app will email a promo code to that person, providing 10% off of their first game purchase.

We'll need to provide a form for the promo recipient's email, but we *won't* be storing this email in our database. We don't have that person's permission to persist their personal data, so we'll use an embedded schema to cast and validate the form input. That way, the email layer will only send promotional emails to valid email addresses. Let's make a plan.

We'll need a new /promo live view with a form backed by an embedded schema. The form will collect a name and email for a lucky 10% off promo recipient. Changeset functions are purely functional, so we'll build a model and some changeset functions in a tiny core. You'll notice that once we've coded up the embedded schema, the live view will work exactly the same way it always has, displaying any errors for invalid changesets and enabling the submit button for valid ones.

We'll start in the core. The `Promo.Recipient` core module will—you guessed it—model the data for a promo recipient. It will have a converter to produce the changeset that works with the live view's form. Then we'll build a context module, called `Promo`, to provide an interface for interacting with `Promo.Recipient` changesets. The context is the boundary layer between our predictable core and the outside world. It is the home of code that deals with uncertainty. It will be responsible for receiving the uncertain form input from the user and translating it into predictable changesets. The context will also interact with potentially unreliable external services—in this case the code that sends the promotional emails. We won't write any email-sending code. We'll keep our focus on changesets in LiveView and create a tiny stub instead.

Once we have the back end wired up, we'll define a live view, `PromoLive`, that will manage the user interface for our feature. We'll provide users with a form through which they can input the promo recipient's name and email. That form will apply and display any recipient validations we define in our changeset, and the live view will manage the state of the page in response to invalid inputs or valid form submissions.

Let's get started!

The Promo Boundary and Core

First up, we'll build the core of the promo feature. Create a file, lib/pento/promo/recipient.ex, and key in the following:

```
forms/pento/lib/pento/promo/recipient.ex
defmodule Pento.Promo.Recipient do
  use Ecto.Schema
  import Ecto.Changeset

  embedded_schema do
    field :first_name, :string
    field :email, :string
  end
end
```

Our module is simple so far. We announce our intention to consume Ecto's `Schema` API and import the `Changeset` functions. Then we disable our primary key since our live view won't make use of an `:id` field.

Next, we define our fields and their types with the `embedded_schema` block. Run `iex -S mix`, and you can see that we're on the right track:

```
iex>alias Pento.Promo.Recipient
Pento.Promo.Recipient
iex> user = %Recipient{}
%Pento.Promo.Recipient{first_name: nil, email: nil}
```

So far, so good. The embedded_schema directive is defining our module's struct, just as it should. Next, we'll flesh out the changeset/2 function. We'll use the one in lib/pento/catalog/product.ex as a guide.

forms/pento/lib/pento/promo/recipient.ex
```
def changeset(recipient, attrs) do
  recipient
  |> cast(attrs, [:first_name, :email])
  |> validate_required([:first_name, :email])
  |> validate_format(:email, ~r/@/)
end
```

Our changeset/2 function takes in a first argument of any Promo.Recipient struct, pattern matched using the __MODULE__ macro, which evaluates to the name of the current module. It takes in a second argument of an attrs map. We validate the presence of the :first_name and :email attributes and then validate the format of :email. Notice we're pulling type data for the changeset from a module attribute rather than a full Ecto schema. Now we can create recipient changesets, like this:

```
iex> recompile
Compiling 1 file (.ex)
:ok
iex> valid = %{first_name: "Mario", email: "super@example.com"}
%{email: "super@example.com", first_name: "Mario"}
iex> changeset = Recipient.changeset(user, valid)
#Ecto.Changeset<
  action: nil,
  changes: %{email: "super@example.com", first_name: "Mario"},
  errors: [],
  data: #Pento.Promo.Recipient<>,
  valid?: true
```

Excellent. Our changeset flawlessly implements our validations for valid data. While we're at it, let's explore the data structure. Use the i command to get IEx info about the term:

```
i changeset
Term
  #Ecto.Changeset<..., valid?: true, ...>
Data type
  Ecto.Changeset
Description
  This is a struct. Structs are maps with a __struct__ key.
```

```
Reference modules
  Ecto.Changeset, Map
Implemented protocols
  IEx.Info, Inspect, Jason.Encoder, Phoenix.HTML.FormData, Phoenix.Param, ...
```

Look down at the implemented protocols. These are contracts. Notice that Recipient supports Phoenix.HTML.FormData. That means we can pass changesets to to_form/1 to build a form struct, like this:

```
Phoenix.HTML.FormData.to_form changeset, []
%Phoenix.HTML.Form{
  source: #Ecto.Changeset<
    ...
    changes: %{email: "super@example.com", first_name: "Mario"},
    valid?: true,
    ...
  >,
  impl: Phoenix.HTML.FormData.Ecto.Changeset,
  params: %{"email" => "super@example.com", "first_name" => "Mario"},
}
```

We're using an elixir *protocol*. A protocol is a type-based contract. Since the FormData protocol implements Ecto.Changeset, we can use changesets to build forms.

Next, let's see what happens if we try to create a changeset with an attribute of an invalid type:

```
iex> invalid = %{email: "joe@email.com", first_name: 1234}
%{email: "joe@email.com", first_name: 1234}
iex> Recipient.changeset user, invalid
#Ecto.Changeset<
  action: nil,
  changes: %{email: "joe@email.com"},
  errors: [first_name: {"is invalid", [type: :string, validation: :cast]}],
  data: #Pento.Promo.Recipient<>,
  valid?: false
```

Ecto.Changeset.cast/4 relies on the types provided in the embedded_struct to identify the invalid type and provide a descriptive error.

Next, try a changeset that breaks one of the custom validation rules:

```
iex> bad_email = %{email: "joe's email", first_name: "Joe"}
%{email: "joe's email", first_name: "Joe"}
iex> Recipient.changeset user, bad_email
#Ecto.Changeset<
  action: nil,
  changes: %{email: "joe's email", first_name: "Joe"},
  errors: [email: {"has invalid format", [validation: :format]}],
  data: #Pento.Promo.Recipient<>,
  valid?: false
```

This function successfully captures our change policy in code, and the returned changeset tells the user exactly what's wrong.

Now that our changeset is up and running, let's quickly build out the Promo context that will present the interface for interacting with the changeset. Create a file, lib/pento/promo.ex, and add in the following:

forms/pento/lib/pento/promo.ex
```elixir
defmodule Pento.Promo do
  alias Pento.Promo.Recipient

  def change_recipient(%Recipient{} = recipient, attrs \\ %{}) do
    Recipient.changeset(recipient, attrs)
  end

  def send_promo(recipient, attrs) do
    recipient
    |> change_recipient(attrs)
    |> Ecto.Changeset.apply_action(:update)
  end
end
```

This context is a beautifully concise boundary for our service. The change_recipient/2 function returns a recipient changeset, and send_promo/2 is a placeholder for sending a promotional email. You'll get a chance to implement this feature in the chapter exercises. Other than the internal tweaks we made inside Recipient.changeset/2, building the context layer with an embedded schema looks identical to building an Ecto-backed one. When all is said and done, in the view layer, embedded schemas and database-backed ones will look identical.

The Promo Live View

This live view will have the feel of a typical live view with a form. By this time, the development flow will look familiar to you. First, we'll create a simple route and wire it to the live view. Next, we'll use our Promo context to produce an embedded schema and add it to the socket within a mount/3 function. We'll render a form with this changeset and apply changes to the changeset by handling events from the form.

This section will move quickly since you already know the underlying concepts. Create a file, lib/pento_web/live/promo_live.ex, and fill in the following:

forms/pento/lib/pento_web/live/promo_live.ex
```elixir
defmodule PentoWeb.PromoLive do
  use PentoWeb, :live_view
  alias Pento.Promo
  alias Pento.Promo.Recipient
end
```

We pull in the LiveView behaviour and alias our modules for later use. Since we're simply returning the socket, we don't need a mount/3. Our code will pick up the default one, which looks like this:

```
def mount(_params, _session, socket) do
  {:ok, socket}
end
```

Next, we need something to render. Let's use an implicit render/1. Create a template file, starting with some promotional markup:

forms/pento/lib/pento_web/live/promo_live.html.heex
```
<.header>
  Send Your Promo Code to a Friend
  <:subtitle>
    Use this form to send a 10% off promo code for their first game purchase!
  </:subtitle>
</.header>
```

We use the generated CoreComponents.header/1 function component we first saw in the ProductLive.Index live view. In IEx, you can see basic help for it, describing the slots and attributes exposed by the component:

```
h PentoWeb.CoreComponents.header

  def header(assigns)

Renders a header with title.

## Attributes

  • class (:string) - Defaults to nil.
## Slots

  • inner_block (required)
  • subtitle
  • actions
```

Our code makes use of the inner block to specify the title and uses the subtitle slot to display some subtitle text. We leave off the actions slot and class attribute. Now, let's define a live route and fire up the server. In the router, add the following route behind authentication:

forms/pento/lib/pento_web/router.ex
```
live "/promo", PromoLive
```

Note that we've put our new route in the same live session as the original /guess route. This means they will share a root layout and share the on_mount callback, PentoWeb.UserAuth.on_mount/4, that validates the presence of the current user.

Start up the server, log in, and point your browser at /promo. You should see the following:

> **Send Your Promo Code to a Friend**
> Use this form to send a 10% off promo code for their first game purchase!

Everything is going according to plan. With the live view up and running, we're ready to build out the form for a promo recipient. We'll use mount/3 to store a recipient struct and a form struct in the socket:

forms/pento/lib/pento_web/live/promo_live.ex
```
def mount(_params, _session, socket) do
  {:ok,
   socket
   |> assign_recipient()
   |> clear_form()}
end

def assign_recipient(socket) do
  socket
  |> assign(:recipient, %Recipient{})
end
```

The assign_recipient/1 reducer function we call within mount/3 is straightforward. We add an empty recipient struct to socket assigns. We'll use this empty recipient struct to build the form struct that we'll render in the template. That happens in the next reducer function, clear_form/1, shown here:

forms/pento/lib/pento_web/live/promo_live.ex
```
def clear_form(socket) do
  changeset =
    socket.assigns.recipient
    |> Promo.change_recipient()

  socket |> assign_form(changeset)
end
```

Here, we take the recipient struct from socket assigns, use it to generate a new empty embedded schema with a call to Promo.change_recipient/1, and then use *that* changeset to build a new form struct with the help of the assign_form/1 reducer, which you can see here:

forms/pento/lib/pento_web/live/promo_live.ex
```
def assign_form(socket, changeset) do
  assign(socket, :form, to_form(changeset))
end
```

Let's talk about this form struct now.

The Phoenix.Component.to_form/2 function takes in some params or a changeset and returns a Phoenix.HTML.Form.[1] The Phoenix.HTML.Form struct is designed to be provided to calls to the .simple_form function component in your live view templates. The form struct, used on the front end when you render your form, is analogous to how we use changesets on the back end. It provides better change tracking, more efficiency since you no longer have to store changesets in memory, and some additional conveniences for working with forms that we'll see as we continue on in this chapter.

You'll notice that, remarkably, the embedded schema can be used in our form exactly like database-backed ones. Now that we've created a form from our changeset and added it to socket assigns, let's render it in our template:

```
<div>
  <.simple_form
    for={@form}
    id="promo-form"
    phx-change="validate"
    phx-submit="save"
  >
    <.input field={@form[:first_name]} type="text" label="First Name" />
    <.input
      field={@form[:email]}
      type="email"
      label="Email"
    />
    <:actions>
      <.button phx-disable-with="Sending...">Send Promo</.button>
    </:actions>
  </.simple_form>
</div>
```

Here we're using the same simple_form function component you saw in the generated ProductLive.Index live view. We specify the attributes, including the form we put in the socket assigns. Under the hood, the simple_form component makes use of the existing .form function component from Phoenix, and that one in turn is built on top of the Phoenix.HTML.Form.form_for/4 function. That means our component returns a form for the given @form struct, with the specified LiveView bindings and any other attributes you provide.

Our code specifies the content of the default inner_block slot inside the <.simple_form> tags. We put two types of tags here: input fields and actions. The *actions* define the behavior associated with our form. We have just one action, the submit button bound to the phx-submit event. The input fields define the

---

1. https://hexdocs.pm/phoenix_html/3.3.0/Phoenix.HTML.Form.html

> **Elixir Interpolation in HEEx**
>
>
> We've touched on some interesting syntax for interpolations inside attribute definitions. In the PromoLive template, the for attribute is assigned to values interpolated using curly braces, like this {}, instead of the <%= %> EEx tags you might be used to. This is because HEEx, unlike EEx, isn't just responsible for evaluating and templating Elixir expressions into your HTML. It also parses and validates the HTML itself. So you can't use the traditional EEx tags *inside* HTML tags in a HEEx template. Beginning with LiveView version 1.0 and Phoenix version 1.7.17, you can optionally use curly braces for interpolation instead of EEx interpolations everywhere.

data for our form in the form of input components. Each one is a composite component defined in the CoreComponents.input/1 function, such as:

```
def input(assigns) do
  ~H"""
  ...
    <.label for={@id}><%= @label %></.label>
    <input type={@type} name={@name} ... />
    <.error :for={msg <- @errors}><%= msg %></.error>
  ...
  """
end
```

Some of the tedious detail has been stripped out, but you get the idea. Inputs render a HEEx template with three individual tags: a label, an HTML input control, and an error tag. That means our form is composed of the outer form definition, a series of input forms, and an action slot with a submit button.

With our updated template in place, if you point your browser at /promo, you should see this:

First Name

Email

Send Promo

Furthermore, our usage of the simple_form/1 function component illustrates a running theme in LiveView: the framework handles the tedious parts, like constructing and rendering form markup, and the hard parts, like sending events from the client to the server. Our job as application developers is to tell LiveView the "what" and the "when," but not the "how." In other words, we tell LiveView what to render: the specific input fields and action buttons for our promo form. And we tell LiveView when to fire certain events: when the user changes or submits the form. We *don't* tell LiveView how to render form markup or how to send events between the client and the server.

With the user interface complete and the mount/render workflow complete, we can shift our attention to the change management workflow. Before we do, we need to think about which events LiveView will send in response to user interactions with our form. Our form implements two LiveView bindings, phx-change and phx-submit. We'll address the phx-disable-with binding on the submit button later. Let's build the handler for the phx-change event first. LiveView will send a "validate" event each time the form changes and include the form params in the event metadata. So we'll implement a handle_event/3 function for this event that builds a new changeset from the params, validates it, and adds it to the socket:

```
forms/pento/lib/pento_web/live/promo_live.ex
def handle_event(
      "validate",
      %{"recipient" => recipient_params},
      %{assigns: %{recipient: recipient}} = socket
    ) do
  changeset =
    recipient
    |> Promo.change_recipient(recipient_params)
    |> Map.put(:action, :validate)

  {:noreply, assign_form(socket, changeset)}
end
```

This code should look familiar to you; it's almost exactly what the generated ProductLive.FormComponent did. The Promo.change_recipient/2 context function creates a new changeset using the recipient from state and the params from the form change event. Then we use Map.put(:action, :validate) to add the validate action to the changeset, a signal that instructs Phoenix to display errors. Phoenix otherwise will *not* display the changeset's errors. When you think about it, this approach makes sense. Not all invalid changesets should show errors on the page. For example, the empty form for the new changeset *shouldn't* show any errors, because the user hasn't provided any input yet. So the Phoenix form_for function needs to be told when to display a changeset's errors.

If the changeset's :action is empty, then no errors are set on the form object—even if the changeset is invalid and has a nonempty :errors value.

Finally, the assign_form/2 reducer adds a new form for the changeset to the socket, triggering render/1 and displaying any errors. The new form is created using the validated changeset, like this:

forms/pento/lib/pento_web/live/promo_live.ex
```
def assign_form(socket, changeset) do
  assign(socket, :form, to_form(changeset))
end
```

A pattern is emerging here—we use changesets on the back end to represent the state of our changing data. Then we convert those changesets to form structs for representation in the user interface on the front end. This new form struct, since it's based on a changeset that's been validated and may contain errors, now contains the information that Phoenix needs to display those errors on the front end.

Let's take a look at the form tag that displays the errors now. Remember, each input component has a label, an input control, and an error tag, like this:

```
def input(assigns) do
  ~H"""
  <.label for={@id}><%= @label %></.label>
  <input type={@type} name={@name} ... />
  <.error :for={msg <- @errors}><%= msg %></.error>
  """
end
```

The .error function component displays the form's errors for a given field on a @form, which wraps our changeset. When the changeset's action is :validate, the .error component ensures that we display *only* feedback for form fields that have received input, preventing the page from displaying errors for form fields that the user has yet to edit. Let's take a look at this error/1 function component now:

```
def error(assigns) do
  ~H"""
  <p class=...>
    <.icon name="hero-exclamation-circle-mini" .../>
    <%= render_slot(@inner_block) %>
  </p>
  """
end
```

This function does nothing more than show an error icon and the contents of the slot inside a paragraph tag. Let's look again at the code that invokes it:

```
<.error :for={msg <- @errors}><%= msg %></.error>
```

This error/1 function component uses the :for directive to iteratively invoke the component for every msg in @errors. If there are no errors, we won't see the error tag at all.

To try it out, point your browser at /promo and fill out the form with a name and an invalid email. As you can see in this image, the UI updates to display the validation errors:

First Name

Joe

Email

joe.com

has invalid format

That was surprisingly easy! We built a simple and powerful live view with a reactive form that displays any errors in real time. The live view calls on the context to create a changeset, renders it in a form, validates it on form change, and then re-renders the template after each form event. We get reactive form validations for free, without writing any JavaScript or HTML. We let Ecto changesets handle the data validation rules and we let the LiveView framework handle the client-server communication for triggering validation events and displaying the results.

As you might imagine, the phx-submit event works pretty much the same way. The "save" event fires when the user submits the form. We can implement a handle_event/3 function that uses the (stubbed out) context function, Promo.send_promo/2, to respond to this event. The context function should create and validate a changeset. If the changeset is in fact valid, we can pipe it to some helper function or service that handles the details of sending promotional emails. If the changeset is not valid, we can return an error tuple. Then we can update the UI with a success or failure message accordingly. As an exercise, you can take on building out this flow.

Now you've seen that while changesets are packaged with the Ecto library, they're not tightly coupled to the database. Embedded schemas let you tie back-end services to Phoenix forms anytime you require validation and security, whether or not your application needs to access a full relational database.

Before we move on to our last LiveView form feature, the live uploader, let's take a quick look at some additional LiveView form bindings.

LiveView Form Bindings

You already know that LiveView uses annotations called bindings to tie live views to events using platform JavaScript. This chapter demonstrated the use of two form bindings: phx-submit for submitting a form and phx-change for form validations.

LiveView also offers bindings to control how often and under what circumstances LiveView JavaScript emits form events. These bindings can disable form submission and *debounce*, or slow down, form change events. These bindings help you provide sane user experiences on the front end and ensure less unnecessary load on the back end.

Let's take a brief look at these bindings and how they work.

Submit and Disable a Form

By default, binding phx-submit events causes three things to occur on the client:

- The form's inputs are set to readonly.
- The submit button is disabled.
- The "phx-submit-loading" CSS class is applied to the form.

While the form is being submitted, no further form submissions can occur, since LiveView JavaScript disables the submit button. Our code uses the phx-disable-with binding to configure the text of a disabled submit button. Let's try it out now.

Normally, our form submission happens so quickly that you won't notice this disabled form state and updated submit button text. LiveView's client-side library ships with a helper for just this situation. The enableLatencySim(milliseconds) is a latency simulator that allows us to slow down LiveView's lightning-fast development environment behavior. Let's tell LiveView to simulate one second of latency by pasting the following into our browser's JavaScript console:

```
liveSocket.enableLatencySim(1000)
```

Now, point your browser at /promo and submit the form. You should see the disabled form with our new button text, as shown at the top of the facing page.

Nice! The blue line at the top of the page shows the progress. You can now disable the simulated latency with the following:

```
liveSocket.disableLatencySim()
```

[Form screenshot showing First Name "Chris", Email "chris@example.com", and a disabled "Sending..." button]

Once again, the LiveView framework handles the details for us—doing the work of disabling the form submit button and applying the new button text.

Next up, we'll take a look at a couple of bindings to control rapidly repeating form events.

Rate Limit Form Events

LiveView makes it easy to rate limit events on the client with the `phx-debounce` and `phx-throttle` LiveView bindings. You'll use `phx-debounce` when you want to rate limit form events, like `phx-change`, for a single field.

By default, our promo form will send a `phx-change` event *every time* the form changes. As soon as a user starts typing into the email input field, LiveView JavaScript will start sending events to the server. These events trigger the event handler for the "validate" event, which validates the changeset and renders any errors.

Let's think through what this means for the user.

If a user visits /promo and types even just one letter into the email field, then the error message describing an invalid email will immediately appear.

This somewhat aggressive validation forces both the client and the server to process a lot of information quickly. Let's fix this by giving our users a chance to type the entire email into the field before validating it. We can do so with the help of `phx-debounce`. The `phx-debounce` binding let's you specify an integer time-out value or a value of `blur`. Use an integer to delay the event by the specified number of milliseconds. Use `blur` to have LiveView JavaScript emit the event when the user finishes and tabs away from the field.

Let's use debounce to delay the firing of the `phx-change` event until a user has blurred the email input field. Update the email input form field so that it looks like this:

```
<.input field={@form[:email]} type="email"
    label="Email" phx-debounce="blur" />
```

Now, if you visit /promo and type just one letter into the email field, the error message won't appear prematurely. Notice this invalid email address without an error message:

Send Your Promo Code to a Friend

Use this form to send a 10% off promo code for their first game purchase!

First Name

    sophie

Email

    sophie@

Send Promo

If you blur away from the email input field, however, you'll see the error message.

Now you know almost everything that you can do with forms in LiveView. Before we go, we'll look at one more LiveView form feature you'll need to master—live uploads.

Live Uploads

The LiveView framework supports the most common features single-page apps must offer their users, including multipart uploads. LiveView gives us highly interactive file uploads, right out of the box.

In this section, you'll add a product image upload feature to your application. You'll also use LiveView to display upload progress and feedback while editing and saving uploaded files. When we're done, you'll have all the tools you need to handle complex forms, even those that require file uploads.

Let's plan our approach to the problem. We'll be using Phoenix 1.8's dedicated ProductLive.Form live view, which handles both product creation and editing on separate pages. Here are the individual steps we need to take.

- Extend our database and schema for Products to allow images in a new migration and in our Product schema.
- Establish an upload configuration for images in our ProductLive.Form live view socket in the mount/3 function.
- Render the components to allow uploads, track upload progress, and handle upload errors in the ProductLive.Form render/1 function.
- Handle the new uploaded form data when the user saves.

In the remainder of this chapter, we'll be adding code to the application core and LiveView front end in the dedicated Form live view. The Product schema is a fairly typical one, and most of the image validation will occur elsewhere. In Phoenix 1.8, both the New Product and Edit Product functionality are handled by the same ProductLive.Form live view, but on dedicated pages rather than in modal overlays. This module provides one centralized place to maintain our product form while giving each operation its own clean URL. Changes to this LiveView will let users upload an image for new products and existing ones as well. All of this code will go fairly quickly because we won't have to worry about any custom JavaScript. Let's start at the top of the list with the migration and schema code.

Persist Product Images

We'll start in the back end by updating the products table and Product schema to store an attribute, image_upload, pointing to the location of the uploaded file. Once we have our back end wired up, we'll be able to update our live view's form to accommodate file uploads.

We'll start at the database layer by generating a migration to add a field, :image_upload, to the products table.

First, generate your migration file:

```
[pento] → mix ecto.gen.migration add_image_to_products
* creating priv/repo/migrations/20240517144807_add_image_to_products.exs
```

This creates a migration file for us, priv/repo/migrations/20240517144807_add_image_to_products.exs. Open up that file now and key in the contents to the change function:

forms/pento/priv/repo/migrations/20250726191532_add_image_to_products.exs
```
defmodule Pento.Repo.Migrations.AddImageToProducts do
  use Ecto.Migration

  def change do
    alter table(:products) do
      add :image_upload, :string
    end
  end
end
```

The preceding code will add the new database field when we run the migration. Let's do that now:

```
[pento] → mix ecto.migrate
08:49:40.286 [info] == Running 20241211134812
  Pento.Repo.Migrations.AddImageToProducts.change/0 forward
08:49:40.286 [info] alter table products
08:49:40.287 [info] == Migrated 20241211134812 in 0.0s
```

This migration added a new column, :image_upload, of type :string, to the products table, but our schema still needs attention.

Update the corresponding Product schema by adding the new :image_upload field to the schema function, like this:

forms/pento/lib/pento/catalog/product.ex
```
field :image_upload, :string
```

Remember, the changeset cast/4 function must explicitly whitelist new fields, so make sure you add the :image_upload attribute:

forms/pento/lib/pento/catalog/product.ex
```
|> cast(attrs, [:name, :description, :unit_price, :sku, :image_upload])
```

We don't need to add any validations for a product's image upload. We simply add :image_upload to cast/4 and that's it.

Now that the changeset has an :image_upload attribute, we can save product records that know their image upload location. With that in place, we can make an image upload field available in the ProductLive.Form live view's form. We're one step closer to giving users the ability to save products with images.

Nothing's left to do in the schema, so let's turn our attention to the Form live view, where the majority of our work will happen.

Enable File Uploads with allow_upload/3

Usually, when you're working with file uploads on a form, they're processed independently from the other fields on the form. The @product assignment we added to the Form live view's socket assigns will continue to track all of the product fields—name, description, and the like. However, file upload configuration and the status of all uploads for the form will be tracked in a separate assignment, @uploads. Let's set up that :uploads key now.

To enable uploads for our live view, we need to call the allow_upload/3 function with an argument of the socket. This will put the data into socket assigns that the LiveView framework will then use to perform file uploads. In Phoenix 1.8's dedicated Form live view, we'll call allow_upload/3 when the live view first starts up and establishes its initial state in the mount/3 function.

The allow_upload/3 function is a reducer that takes in an argument of the socket, the upload name, and the upload options. It returns an annotated socket that contains the :uploads key populated accordingly. Supported options include file types, file size, number of files per upload name, and more. Let's see it in action:

forms/pento/lib/pento_web/live/product_live/form.ex
```
|> allow_upload(:image,
  accept: ~w(.jpg .jpeg .png),
  max_entries: 1,
  max_file_size: 9_000_000,
  auto_upload: true
)
```

In allow_upload/3, we pipe in a socket and specify a name for our upload, :image. This function will add the uploads key to the socket with the configuration, progress, and path information for each upload. We provide some options, including the maximum number of permitted files, the permitted file types, and an auto_upload setting of true. Setting this option tells LiveView to begin uploading the file as soon as a user attaches it to the form rather than waiting until the form is submitted.

Since we're working with a dedicated Form live view in Phoenix 1.8, the form assignment is handled through the standard LiveView apply_action/3 pattern that we set up in the mount function:

forms/pento/lib/pento_web/live/product_live/form.ex
```
defp assign_form(socket, changeset) do
  assign(socket, :form, to_form(changeset))
end
```

It's a simple one-liner. With the allow_update/3 enabled, we can take a look at what our socket assigns looks like after allow_upload/3 is invoked:

```
%{
  uploads: %{
    __phoenix_refs_to_names__: %{"phx-FlZ_j-hPIdCQuQGG" => :image},
    image: #Phoenix.LiveView.UploadConfig<
      accept: ".jpg,.jpeg,.png",
      auto_upload?: true,
      entries: [],
      errors: [],
      max_entries: 1,
      max_file_size: 9000000,
      name: :image,
      ...
    >
  },
  product: %Pento.Catalog.Product{...},
}
```

The socket now contains an :uploads map that specifies configuration for each upload field your live view allows. We allowed uploads for an upload called :image. So our map contains a key of :image pointing to a value of the configuration constructed using the options we gave allow_upload/3. This means that we can add a file upload field called :image to our form, and LiveView will track the progress of files uploaded via the field within socket.assigns.uploads.image.

Notice that the upload configuration contains the options we passed to allow_upload/3: the accepted file types list and the auto upload setting, among other things.

It also has an attribute called :entries, which points to an empty list. When a user uploads a file for the :image form field, LiveView will automatically update this list with data about the upload. Here's what an entry looks like:

```
%Phoenix.LiveView.UploadEntry{
    progress: 66,
    preflighted?: true,
    upload_config: :image,
    upload_ref: "phx-FzvII24GtrtIvQLm",
    ref: "1",
    uuid: "f6781ab0-f062-4a89-b441-f5861544d2b5",
    valid?: true,
    done?: false,
    cancelled?: false,
    client_name: "tic-tac-toe.jpg",
    client_type: "image/jpeg",
    client_last_modified: 1655835404000
  }
```

Similarly, the :errors list starts out empty and will be automatically populated by LiveView with any errors that result from an invalid upload entry. In this way, the LiveView framework does the work of performing the file upload and tracking its state for you. We'll see both of these attributes in action later on in this chapter.

In the future, if we wanted to add something like a hero_image, we could do that too, because you can call allow_upload/3 multiple times with different upload names. That way, Phoenix allows any number of file uploads in a given live view. Now that we've allowed uploads in our Form live view, we're ready to update the template with the file upload form field.

Render the File Upload Field

You'll use the function component live_file_input/2 to generate the HTML for a file upload form field. First, add the input control. We'll give the user two ways to upload an image: via a drag-and-drop functionality or by clicking a choose file button. Add a div within the <.form> inner block with the attribute phx-drop-target={ @uploads.image.ref } and the file input, like this:

```
forms/pento/lib/pento_web/live/product_live/form.ex
<div phx-drop-target={@uploads.image.ref}
    class="border-2 border-dashed border-gray-300 rounded-lg p-6">
  <label for={@uploads.image.ref} class="block text-sm font-medium">
  Product Image
  </label>
  <.live_file_input upload={@uploads.image} />
</div>
```

This adds a drag-and-drop container to our form, where the phx-drop-target HTML attribute points to the @uploads.image.ref socket assignment. This is the ID that LiveView JavaScript uses to identify the file upload form field and tie it to the correct key in socket.assigns.uploads.

Inside the drop zone, we placed a <.label > component and a <.live_file_input /> component to render our input control and a component function to render our choose file button with a label. Let's take a closer look at how this works.

Remember, socket.assigns has a map of uploads. Here, we provide @uploads.image to live_file_input/2 to create a form field with the right configuration and tie that form field to the correct part of socket state. This means that LiveView will update socket.assigns.uploads.image with any new entries or errors that occur when a user uploads a file via this form input.

The live view can present upload progress by displaying data from the @uploads.image.entries and @uploads.image.errors. LiveView will handle all of the details of uploading the file and updating socket assigns @uploads.image entries and errors for us. All we have to do is render the data that's stored in the socket.

Now if you point your browser at /products/new, you should see the file upload field displayed like this:

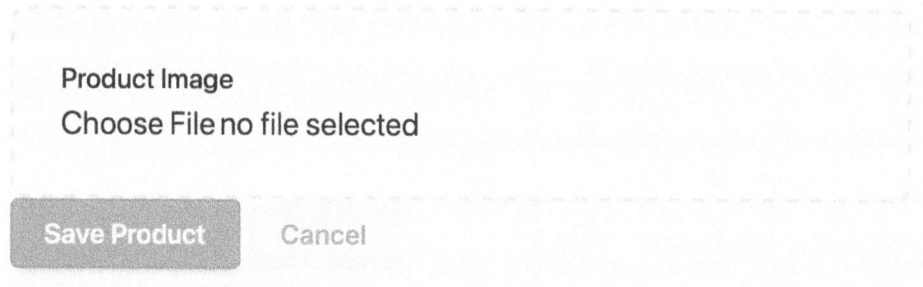

And if you inspect the element, you'll see that the live_file_input/2 function generated the appropriate HTML:

```
<input
  id="phx-FzvNu1Y0VXwmYgek"
  type="file"
  name="image"
  accept=".jpg,.jpeg,.png"
  data-phx-hook="Phoenix.LiveFileUpload"
  data-phx-update="ignore"
  data-phx-upload-ref="phx-FzvNu1Y0VXwmYgek"
  data-phx-active-refs=""
  data-phx-done-refs="" data-phx-preflighted-refs="">
```

It shows a type="file" and a name="image", just as it should. You can also verify the accept attribute, thanks to the options we passed to allow_upload/3.

As with other form interactions, LiveView automatically handles the client-server communication for us. Depending on the auto_upload setting, LiveView will upload the file when the user attaches the file or when the user submits the form. Since we specified an auto_upload setting of true, LiveView will start uploading the file as soon as it's attached. All we have to do is implement an event handler to respond to the file upload progress event. Let's do that now.

Present Upload Progress, Previews, and Errors

LiveView will update the @uploads struct in socket assigns when a user attaches a file to the form (if we set auto_upload: true) or when the user submits the form. When these events happen, LiveView will update any upload previews, progress bars, and error messages on the page. All we need to do is write a few functions to translate the potential error atoms to strings and present them. The rest is handled automatically.

Let's drop in some code to track progress and show a preview. Add the following code *below* the closing </.simple_form> tag. We don't want the image preview, upload progress, and error messages to be part of our form's inner block. Upload data is tracked separately from our form params, and adding upload data and interactions inside the form will cause some unexpected behavior.

```
forms/pento/lib/pento_web/live/product_live/form.ex
<div :for={entry <- @uploads.image.entries}>
  <div class="bg-blue-100 border border-blue-400 text-blue-700
              px-4 py-3 rounded">
    <%= entry.client_name %> - <%= entry.progress %>%
  </div>
</div>
```

We iterate over the entries in the @uploads.image.entries assignment and render a progress bar and an image preview for each one. Remember that, while we specified max_entries: 1 in our allow_upload call, you *can* allow multiple entries for each upload you allow in your live view. So, @upload.image stores uploaded files in the :entries list. That means we need to iterate over this list to access our upload entry.

The progress-rendering code uses a standard HTML progress indicator, plugging in image.progress as the value attribute. We don't have to worry about animating that control. LiveView does it all for us. We also add a preview for the entry with a call to the <.live_img_preview> component. We don't need to do anything else to make it work.

With that, you can edit a product in the browser. When you attach a file to the form, you should see a progress bar and an image preview that looks like this:

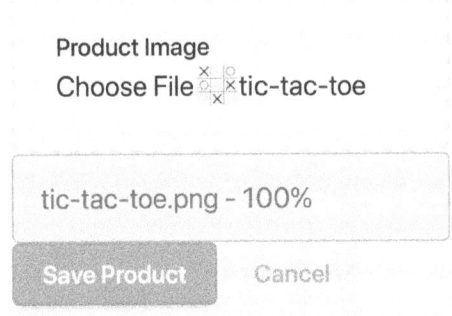

We can render any upload entry errors in a similar manner. Inside the same for loop over the @uploads.image.entries assignment, add the following code:

```
forms/pento/lib/pento_web/live/product_live/form.ex
<div :for={err <- upload_errors(@uploads.image)}
     class="bg-red-100 border border-red-400 text-red-700
            px-4 py-3 rounded">
  Upload error: <%= upload_error_to_string(err) %>
</div>
<div :for={entry <- @uploads.image.entries}>
  <div :for={_err <- upload_errors(@uploads.image, entry)}
       class="bg-red-100 border border-red-400 text-red-700
              px-4 py-3 rounded">
    <%= upload_image_error(@uploads, entry) %>
  </div>
</div>
```

We call the LiveView helper function, upload_errors/2, to extract any errors for each upload entry. We iterate over those errors and display them. Let's see this feature in action. Use the drag-and-drop functionality to drag over a file that's not of one of the accepted types. You should see a Not Accepted error message.

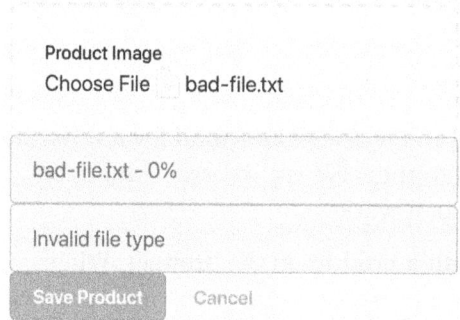

Now that we have a working upload form input, all that remains is to upload the image to a place our user can use it and make sure that information is reflected in our database.

Save the Image

Before we get too far, let's look at how the handle_event/3 callback works for the save event:

```
forms/pento/lib/pento_web/live/product_live/form.ex
def handle_event("save", %{"product" => product_params}, socket) do
  product_params = params_with_image(socket, product_params)
  save_product(socket, socket.assigns.live_action, product_params)
end
```

The event handler calls the save_product/3 helper function, which uses pattern matching to implement a version to handle when the :action assignment is :edit and when it's :new. Take a look at the :edit version of the save_product/3 function here:

generate_web/pento/lib/pento_web/live/product_live/form.ex
```elixir
defp save_product(socket, :edit, product_params) do
  case Catalog.update_product(socket.assigns.current_scope,
                              socket.assigns.product,
                              product_params) do
    {:ok, product} ->
      {:noreply,
        socket
        |> put_flash(:info, "Product updated successfully")
        |> push_navigate(
          to: return_path(socket.assigns.current_scope,
                          socket.assigns.return_to, product)
        )}
    {:error, %Ecto.Changeset{} = changeset} ->
      {:noreply, assign(socket, form: to_form(changeset))}
  end
end
```

We need to update this code to work with the image upload data stored in socket.assigns.uploads. Remember, our image data and our product data are not together in the socket. We'll build a function to save the image upload and add the saved image data to the product params. That way, we can use those params in Catalog.update_product/2 such that a product will be saved along with the image upload path.

Define a function, params_with_image/2. It will need to consume any uploaded images, save them, and then return a list of product parameters including the image_upload path to the user. Here's that function:

forms/pento/lib/pento_web/live/product_live/form.ex
```elixir
def params_with_image(socket, params) do
  path =
    socket
    |> consume_uploaded_entries(:image, &upload_static_file/2)
    |> List.first()
  Map.put(params, "image_upload", path)
end
```

We use a LiveView function called consume_uploaded_entries/3 to iterate through the list of entries in socket.assigns.uploads.image.entries and process each one with a custom callback function, upload_static_file/2. The call to consume_uploaded_entries/3 returns a list of upload results based on the return value of our custom upload_static_file/2 function. Since we know there was only one entry in socket.assigns.uploads.image.entries, we know the return of consume_uploaded_entries will be a list with one item. So we use List.first to grab that result and add it to the product params under a key of "image_upload".

Now we need to write our custom callback function:

forms/pento/lib/pento_web/live/product_live/form.ex
```elixir
defp upload_static_file(%{path: path}, _entry) do
  # Plug in your production image file persistence implementation here!
  filename = Path.basename(path)
  dest = Path.join("priv/static/images", filename)
  File.cp!(path, dest)

  {:ok, ~p"/images/#{filename}"}
end
```

This function is where you'd manage any custom persistence concerns like cloud storage. We're just going to copy it to a static directory for now. Make sure that directory exists with a mkdir priv/static/images command from your shell! The consume_uploaded_entries/3 function will call the custom upload_static_file callback with metadata about each of the uploads we consume. We pick off the path, pull out the filename from the end of the path, and then copy that file to our destination. Then we use Phoenix to verify the route with a ~p sigil with the filename. The custom callback must return the {:ok, result} tuple. In our case, result is the path to which we have uploaded the file.

Now we're ready to plug our custom code into the save_product helper functions. Since we've delegated most of the hard work to two other functions, save_product/3 remains relatively concise. The beauty of Phoenix 1.8's dedicated Form live view is that we can handle image uploads directly in the same live view without the complexity of component message passing. Here's the save event handler that processes uploaded images:

forms/pento/lib/pento_web/live/product_live/form.ex
```elixir
defp save_product(socket, :edit, product_params) do
  case Catalog.update_product(socket.assigns.current_scope,
                              socket.assigns.product,
                              product_params) do
    {:ok, product} ->
      {:noreply,
       socket
       |> put_flash(:info, "Product updated successfully")
       |> push_navigate(
         to: return_path(socket.assigns.current_scope,
                         socket.assigns.return_to, product)
       )}

    {:error, %Ecto.Changeset{} = changeset} ->
```

```
      {:noreply, assign_form(socket, changeset)}
    end
end

defp save_product(socket, :new, product_params) do
  case Catalog.create_product(
    socket.assigns.current_scope, product_params) do
    {:ok, product} ->
      {:noreply,
       socket
       |> put_flash(:info, "Product created successfully")
       |> push_navigate(
         to: return_path(socket.assigns.current_scope,
                         socket.assigns.return_to, product)
       )}
    {:error, %Ecto.Changeset{} = changeset} ->
      {:noreply, assign_form(socket, changeset)}
  end
end
```

The only difference in this implementation and the previous is the call to params_with_image. We simply transform parameters without an image to parameters with one. This happens in a straightforward event handler without the complexity of component message passing or @myself targets.

We can modify the function for the :new action in the same way. Here are the lines that change:

```
# lib/pento_web/live/product_live/form.ex
defp save_product(socket, :new, params) do
    product_params = params_with_image(socket, params)

    case Catalog.create_product(product_params) do
      ...
end
```

Now we can save data for individual file uploads. We can verify our new feature with a few lines in IEx. Upload a product image in the browser and then open up a console with iex -S mix and query for the product you just updated with an image. You should see something like this:

```
[
  ...
  %Pento.Catalog.Product{
    name: "Tic-Tac-Toe",
  },
  %Pento.Catalog.Product{
    name: "Table Tennis",
  },
  %Pento.Catalog.Product{
```

```
    id: 14,
    description: "Right in the face",
    name: "Pie Fight",
    sku: 935,
    unit_price: 12.0,
    image_upload: "/images/live_view_upload-1674145592-493939070126-1",
    inserted_at: ~N[2023-01-19 16:26:39],
    updated_at: ~N[2023-01-19 16:26:39]
  }
]
```

You can see the image upload has happened because we have an entry in the database with a populated image_upload field—but we didn't do all of this work to simply show a string in the database. Let's present it on the page.

Display Image Uploads

Open up lib/pento_web/live/product_live/show.html.heex and add the following markup after the list of schema fields to display the uploaded image or an alternative default image:

```
<div>
  <img
    alt="product image" width="200"
    src={@product.image_upload}
  >
</div>
```

Perfect. Now you can test drive this fine new machine. Visit /products/1/edit and upload a file. Once you submit the form, you'll see the show page render the newly uploaded image, as shown here:

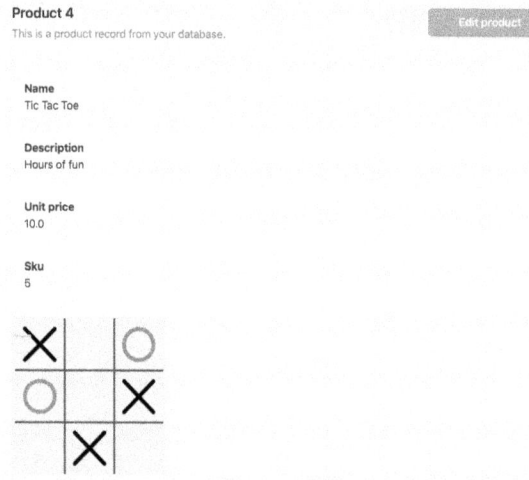

You did it! Yet again, the LiveView framework handled all of the details of the client-server communication that makes the page interactive. LiveView performed the file upload for you and made responding to upload events easy and customizable. All you needed to do was tell the live view which uploads to track and what to do with uploaded files. Then you added the file upload form field to the page with the view helper, and LiveView handled the rest!

LiveView file uploads can do more. LiveView makes it easy to cancel an upload, upload multiple files for a given upload config, upload files directly from the client to a cloud provider, and more. Check out the LiveView file upload documentation[2] for details.

We've covered a lot of ground in this chapter, so it's time to wrap up.

Your Turn

LiveView supports custom integration of forms to back-end code with embedded schemas. To do so, you need only replace the first argument to Changeset.cast/4 with a two-tuple holding both data and type information. This type of code is ideal for implementing form scenarios requiring validation, but without the typical database back end.

Whether you're working with database-backed or database-free changesets, LiveView provides features to manage change through forms. LiveView's full-fledged form functionality also let's us throttle events for a smoother user experience and better performance on the back end.

In addition to these powerful, flexible form features, LiveView enables reactive file uploads right out of the box. Without writing any JavaScript, or even any custom HTML, you can build interactive file upload forms directly into your live view. LiveView handles the details of client-server communication and upload state management, leaving you on the hook for writing a very small amount of custom code to specify how your uploads should behave and how uploaded files should be saved. This is the pattern we see again and again in LiveView—the framework handles the communication and state management details of our SPA, and we can focus on writing application-specific code to support our features.

Now, take the time to put these ideas into practice.

---

2. https://hexdocs.pm/phoenix_live_view/uploads.html#content

Give It a Try

These exercises will help you master a few different principles. First, you'll work with changesets in a traditional database-backed form. Then you'll tackle an exercise to use embedded schemas on your own. Finally, you'll get to customize file uploads.

Add a Custom Validation

This simple task will give you a chance to practice working with changesets in LiveView.

First, add a custom validation to the Product schema's changeset that validates that :sku is a six-digit number.

Then visit /products/new and try to create a new product with an invalid SKU.

What happens when you start typing into the SKU field? What happens if you submit the form with an invalid SKU? Can you trace through the code flow for each of these scenarios and identify when and how the template is updated to display the validation error?

Implement a Notifier

This task will give you experience with the Swoosh mail delivery service. You'll implement the Pento.Promo.send_promo/2 function.

First, look for a model that delivers email. Phoenix generated an email notifier module when you ran the mix phx.gen.auth command in Chapter 2, Phoenix and Authentication, on page 31. Open up lib/pento/accounts/user_notifier.ex. Find the deliver/2 function and the deliver_confirmation_instructions/2 function.

Next, add a Pento.Accounts.UserNotifier.deliver_promotion/2 notification function and call that function from the Pento.Promo.send_promo/2 function.

Use Embedded Schemas

This third, more complex, exercise requires you to build out a new live view, backed by an embedded schema, from scratch.

Define a new route associating the path /search with a live view called PentoWeb.SearchLive. This live view should present a user with a search form allowing them to search products by SKU, and only by SKU. Assuming that all product SKU have at least seven digits, ensure that the form validates the SKU input and displays errors when provided with an invalid SKU. Use an embedded schema to build this form and enact these validations.

Customize Your File Uploader

This last task provides a deeper dive into the LiveView file upload feature. Earlier, we tried to drag and drop a file of an invalid type and saw an error message displayed. Now, you need to provide your user with a way to cancel any stuck errored uploads so that they can try again. Implement an upload cancel feature using the info at hexdocs.[3] A few helpful things to keep in mind:

- Make sure you add the phx-target={@myself} attribute to your cancel button so that the event targets the form component and not the parent live view.
- Remember to use the {} interpolation syntax for the phx-value-ref HTML attribute of your button.
- Use a <.button> component to render your cancel button.

Finally, if you have an Amazon S3 account, upload your image to S3 instead of saving it to the priv/static/images directory.

Next Time

In the next chapter, we'll build on what you've learned about forms to construct a layered live view that manages the state of a multistage form. We'll create a user survey feature that asks users to rate our games. Along the way, we'll take a deep dive into LiveView components. You'll learn how to compose LiveView pipelines for elegant state management and design your own set of LiveView layers to handle complex user interactions. Let's get going!

---

3. https://hexdocs.pm/phoenix_live_view/Phoenix.LiveView.html#cancel_upload/3

CHAPTER 6

Function Components

At every level of difficulty, writing good code depends on breaking complex problems into simpler ones. As yet, we haven't built any very complex live views. That changes in this chapter. We'll use the tools we've explored so far to build a complex live view with a multistage form, and you'll build your own components from scratch to help you manage this complexity. We'll begin building a simple survey tool, one that collects both demographic and rating information.

Along the way, we'll focus specifically on use cases that require components, both live and function. In this chapter, you'll create your own stateless function component that you'll layer into a parent live view. Function components allow the extraction of common *rendering* code. You'll use them to wrap up reusable markup. We'll start by building a multistage form in which the state of the survey changes to progressively reveal more and more questions depending on the user's input. In the following chapter, we'll take our survey to the next level. We'll show you how user interfaces interact with state and events and take a deep dive into live components that encapsulate not just markup but also behavior.

While the survey itself is simple, it represents the most complex functionality you'll have seen so far. When you're done building it, you'll be able to orchestrate a set of LiveView components to cleanly handle even the most complex interactive, real-time features in your Phoenix app.

Back in Chapter 3, Generators: Contexts and Schemas, on page 71, we promised that you'd be programming LiveView like a professional. That means that we'll take our time, building our survey feature from the ground up, starting with the schema and context our survey live view will need. This will give you another opportunity to practice good code organization, and it's in line with how you'll build live views on your own in the future.

It's going to be an exciting two chapters, so let's get started.

The Survey

Great companies know what their customers think, and Pento should be no different. We'd like to build a survey tool. We want to be able to track what our customers think about us over time, and our data scientists want to be able to slice and dice those results by several important demographics.

A sure way to irritate our customers is to ask the same demographic questions each time, so we'll ask demographic questions *once*. Then we can ask a few short product review questions multiple times and track those responses over time.

To satisfy these requirements, we'll build a survey feature that asks a user to fill out a survey to review our products. The survey will consist of a *demographics* section in which we ask a user to fill out a few basic questions about themselves. Then we'll ask the user to rate each product on a scale of one to five stars. Logged-in users will be able to visit /survey and fill out the survey.

Our survey will be dynamic. First, it will prompt the user to fill out the demographics section. Only when that section has been successfully completed will we reveal the product rating sections. Here's how it'll work.

- When no demographic exists for the user, we'll show just the demographic portion of the survey, like this:

- When the demographic portion of the survey is complete, we'll show demographic details and the product ratings portion of the survey, as shown here:

- For any product ratings that are complete, we'll display rating details:

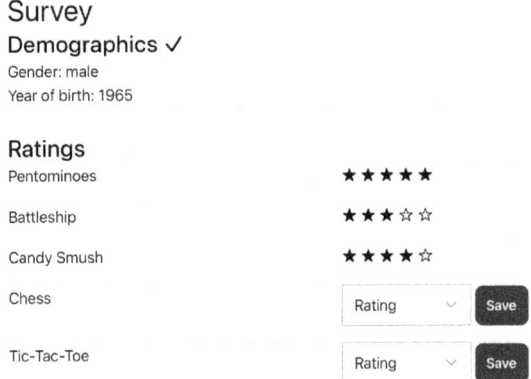

When all ratings are complete, we'll show the completed survey:

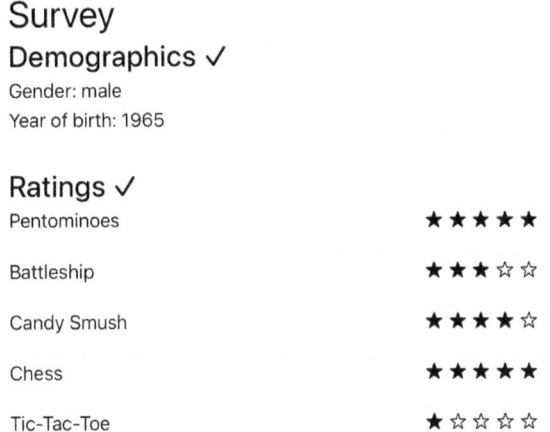

The dynamic nature of the survey gently guides the user through a multipage form and shows them exactly what they need to see, exactly when they need to see it. This approach adds complexity to our application, but you'll see that LiveView gives us the tools we need to manage this complexity with ease.

We'll begin by building the back-end context and schemas that support the survey. Then we'll move onto the front end. We'll set up the live view and use a component to compartmentalize the demographic portion of the survey's markup and behavior. When we're done, you'll have a firm understanding of when to reach for function components and when to reach for live components.

With a plan placed firmly in our pocket, let's take another major look at the main feature we need to use—components.

Organize Your Live View with Components

Let's think through the design considerations for our survey. We may eventually want to display the survey in several different places on the site. You can imagine, for example, wanting to place *just* the product rating portion of the survey on the show page for a given product or *just* the demographic details portion on some sort of user profile page. And, as we've seen, the dynamic nature of the survey represents a decent amount of complexity.

Both of these considerations push us toward components. Having a dedicated place to put the code related to each portion of our survey will allow us to share these concepts across the site. Also, as we've said before, great software is built in layers, and components are ideal layers for LiveView because they help us compartmentalize the markup of our survey sections and the state of each of those sections. LiveView components are the perfect fit to meet the requirements of reusability and complex state management.

Let's take a closer look at what a component is under the hood and how it fits into a live view.

Components Isolate Markup, Events, and State

When you're building applications with pure HTML, it's relatively easy to share code. HTML is a string, so composing with plain HTML templates is straightforward. Live views are different. A single live view combines the ideas of state management, HTML rendering, and event handling. We need a more sophisticated strategy to compose code with LiveView beyond the typical ideas of helpers and templates, which can't do much more than wrap up sections of HTML. That leaves a void.

Function components step neatly into that void. You've already seen that a component is a way to build live views in layers. Each layer maintains its own markup and state. In the case of live, or stateful, components, the component can also respond to its own events. Components therefore allow us to break down *all* of the functionality of LiveView into smaller sections that are composable and reusable.

Now that you understand a bit more about how components fit into the LiveView framework, let's look closely at how they operate.

Components Share the Parent LiveView Process

Components run in the same LiveView process as the parent live view in which they are rendered. That means the parent live view manages the overall state of the survey and each LiveView component manages its markup and handles the state for the individual part of the view it represents.

> **OTP, LiveView, and Components**
>
>  Components run in the same OTP server as their parent, sharing common state and a single supervisor. That means error and failure handling all happen at the level of the parent live view. So a crash in a component will crash the parent live view as well, and that's typically what we want.

For our survey feature, a parent live view will manage the state changes related to the overall survey. Individual components will handle the markup details and manage the state of the individual survey sections—the demographics section and the product ratings sections.

Now that you have a little more background on what components are and how they function, we can get to work. We're going to generate a context to build the base model—one that will let us manage the surveys.

Then we'll build a front end that leverages components to let our users do what we want. Let's get rolling.

Build the Survey Context

Before we can create the live view and components that represent the survey feature, we need to build out the back-end services that will support them. We'll design a Survey context, with schemas for Demographic and Rating. Then we'll be able to use the Survey context in our live view.

We'll take a slightly different approach to building the context and schemas than the one you saw in the previous chapters. We'll still rely on code generation, this time reaching for the phx.gen.context generator to build *just* a context and schemas rather than the Phoenix Live generator that *also* creates live views and routes. This is because we'll be creating our own custom live view and components to handle the survey functionality later on. We're building a LiveView front end with specific behaviors and features that the Phoenix Live generator won't accommodate.

We'll begin by running the generator, and then do a little customization on top of the generated code to get our data into the correct shape. When we're done with this section, you'll know how to strategically deploy the Phoenix Context generator to build the foundation of a custom feature set, you'll be comfortable adding your own code on top of the generated code, and you'll be prepared to use your new context in LiveView to build out the dynamic, interactive survey.

Generate and Customize the Context

Type this command to generate the context:

```
[pento] → mix phx.gen.context Survey Demographic demographics gender:string \
          year_of_birth:integer
* creating lib/pento/survey/demographic.ex
* creating priv/repo/migrations/20250728134555_create_demographics.exs
* creating lib/pento/survey.ex
* creating test/pento/survey_test.exs
* creating test/support/fixtures/survey_fixtures.ex
...
```

Notice the constraint on user_id. Recall that constraints are enforced by the database. Let's see what the migration looks like:

stateless_components/pento/priv/repo/migrations/20250728134555_create_demographics.exs
```elixir
defmodule Pento.Repo.Migrations.CreateDemographics do
  use Ecto.Migration

  def change do
    create table(:demographics) do
      add :gender, :string
      add :year_of_birth, :integer
      add :user_id, references(:users, type: :id, on_delete: :delete_all)

      timestamps(type: :utc_datetime)
    end

    create unique_index(:demographics, [:user_id])
  end
end
```

You've seen everything in this migration before, but we should emphasize a point. This short script tells the Phoenix Context generator to make a demographics database table with the provided columns, a Demographic schema module for interacting with that database table, and a Survey context to present an API through which to interact with the Demographic core. The references(:users, on_delete: :nothing) field builds a referential constraint, to be enforced by the database. Additionally, the create unique_index(:demographics, [:user_id]) index makes sure one user_id will be present per demographic. Remember, the role of constraints is to enforce consistency at the database level. It's up to you, the programmer, to present a nice user interface to the user. We do so in the changeset:

stateless_components/pento/lib/pento/survey/demographic.ex
```elixir
|> unique_constraint(:user_id)
```

Next, generate the Rating schema, like this:

```
[pento] → mix phx.gen.context Survey Rating ratings stars:integer
The Pento.Survey context currently has 6 functions and 1 file
in its directory.

  * It's okay to have multiple resources in the same context
    as long as they are closely related. But if a context
    grows too large, consider breaking it apart.

  * If they are not closely related, another context probably works better.

The fact two entities are related in the database does not mean
they belong to the same context.

If you are not sure, prefer creating a new context over adding
to the existing one.

Would you like to proceed? [Yn] Y

...
Y
...
* creating lib/pento/survey/rating.ex
* creating priv/repo/migrations/20250728135254_create_ratings.exs
...
```

Phoenix warns us that we're putting our Rating schema in the same Survey context as the Demographic schema. Since we believe these concepts are closely related, that's exactly what we want to do. So we specify Y to continue.

Once again, we're creating a referential constraint. We'll do the same thing we did for demographics. The migration will define a database constraint to keep our database integrity pure, and the changeset will provide enough information to keep our users happy.

We'll want to ensure that a user rates a given product just once, so open up the generated ratings migration and add a unique index on the user_id and product_id fields, like this:

stateless_components/pento/priv/repo/migrations/20250728135254_create_ratings.exs
```
create unique_index(:ratings, [:user_id, :product_id])
```

The first two indexes came with the migration. We added the last one, an Ecto unique_index that will allow only one rating per [:user_id, :product_id] combination.

Now we'll add that unique constraint to the Rating changeset that we promised:

stateless_components/pento/lib/pento/survey/rating.ex
```
|> unique_constraint([:user_id, :product_id])
```

While we're here in the Rating schema, let's make a few other changes. First, we'll update the schema to reflect that ratings belong to both users and products. That way, we'll have access to user and product fields as well as the existing user_id and product_id fields on our Rating struct. Add a belongs_to association for both User and Product, like this:

stateless_components/pento/lib/pento/survey/rating.ex
```
schema "ratings" do
  field :stars, :integer
  belongs_to :user, User
  belongs_to :product, Product

  timestamps(type: :utc_datetime)
end
```

Remember to add an alias for Pento.Catalog.Product and Pento.Accounts.User to your Pento.Survey.Rating module while you're there.

Next up, let's update the changeset to cast and require the :user_id and :product_id attributes. Finally, validate :stars as an integer between 1 and 5, like this:

stateless_components/pento/lib/pento/survey/rating.ex
```
@doc false
def changeset(rating, attrs, user_scope) do
  rating
  |> cast(attrs, [:stars, :product_id])
  |> validate_required([:stars, :product_id])
  |> validate_inclusion(:stars, 1..5)
  |> put_change(:user_id, user_scope.user.id)
  |> unique_constraint([:user_id, :product_id])
end
```

Excellent. We take advantage of the built-in validate_inclusion/3 Ecto changeset validation, passing the field and the range of possible values.

We've told the Rating schema that ratings belong to a product. Now we need to add the inverse of this relationship to the Product schemas. Open up the Product schema and add these changes to specify that a product has many ratings:

stateless_components/pento/lib/pento/catalog/product.ex
```
has_many :ratings, Pento.Survey.Rating
```

We alias the new Rating schema and make use of it in the has_many relationship. This will give us the ability to ask a given product for its ratings by calling product.ratings. We'll take advantage of this capability later on. Let's move on for now to the Demographic schema.

First, update the Demographic schema to use the belongs_to macro for the User association:

```
stateless_components/pento/lib/pento/survey/demographic.ex
schema "demographics" do
  field :gender, :string
  field :year_of_birth, :integer
  belongs_to :user, User

  timestamps(type: :utc_datetime)
end
```

Perfect. It works the same way that it did in the Rating schema. Now, update the Demographic schema's changeset/2 function to cast and require the user_id field, add a constraint for the unique user_id index, and add some custom validations for demographic gender and year of birth.

```
stateless_components/pento/lib/pento/survey/demographic.ex
@doc false
def changeset(demographic, attrs, user_scope) do
  demographic
  |> cast(attrs, [:gender, :year_of_birth])
  |> validate_required([:gender, :year_of_birth])
  |> validate_inclusion( :gender, ["male", "female", "other", "prefer not to say"])
  |> validate_inclusion(:year_of_birth, 1900..2010)
  |> unique_constraint(:user_id)
  |> put_change(:user_id, user_scope.user.id)
end
```

Easy enough. We have one more task to handle since we've changed the validation rules, but the code that generates our test fixtures doesn't know that. Within the file test/support/fixtures/survey_fixtures.ex, we'll import the fixtures we need and tweak the attributes. Since there's a relationship to Product, we need to import the fixture now:

```
stateless_components/pento/test/support/fixtures/survey_fixtures.ex
import Pento.CatalogFixtures
```

Next, demographics will need a user ID, a valid gender, and a valid birth year:

```
stateless_components/pento/test/support/fixtures/survey_fixtures.ex
def demographic_fixture(scope, attrs \\ %{}) do
  attrs =
    Enum.into(attrs, %{
      gender: "male",
      year_of_birth: 1990
    })

  {:ok, demographic} = Pento.Survey.create_demographic(scope, attrs)
  demographic
end
```

Ratings, in turn, will need a valid user ID and product ID, in addition to a valid star count:

```
stateless_components/pento/test/support/fixtures/survey_fixtures.ex
def rating_fixture(scope, attrs \\ %{}) do
  product = product_fixture()

  attrs =
    Enum.into(attrs, %{
      stars: 4,
      product_id: product.id
    })

  {:ok, rating} = Pento.Survey.create_rating(scope, attrs)
  rating
end
```

These changes make use of the user_fixture/0 and the product_fixture/0 functions the generators built for us earlier. We also have some data built into generated tests. Open up test/pento/survey_test.exs and correct the generated invalid data. Start with the demographic describe block, making all of these changes. We'll show only the impacted areas:

```
stateless_components/pento/test/pento/survey_test.exs
describe "demographics" do
  alias Pento.Survey.Demographic

  import Pento.AccountsFixtures, only: [user_scope_fixture: 0]
  import Pento.SurveyFixtures

  @invalid_attrs %{gender: nil, year_of_birth: nil}
```

We add the fixture to our existing import. Then we tweak the update_attributes and valid_attr maps and update the associated assertions. Do the same for the ratings describe block, like this:

```
stateless_components/pento/test/pento/survey_test.exs
describe "ratings" do
  alias Pento.Survey.Rating

  import Pento.AccountsFixtures, only: [user_scope_fixture: 0]
  import Pento.SurveyFixtures

  @invalid_attrs %{stars: nil}
```

We repeat the same process within the ratings. Now, reset the database to run all migrations and populate seed data:

```
[pento] → mix ecto.reset
09:55:44.536 [info] == Running 20250722114420
  Pento.Repo.Migrations.CreateUsersAuthTables.change/0 forward
...
09:55:44.570 [info] == Running 20250728134555 Pento.Repo.Migrations.
```

```
    CreateDemographics.change/0 forward
09:55:44.570 [info] create table demographics
09:55:44.572 [info] == Running 20250728135254
    Pento.Repo.Migrations.CreateRatings.change/0 forward
09:55:44.572 [info] create table ratings
...
Created product: Chess
Created product: Checkers
Created product: Backgammon
```

The mix ecto.reset command drops the database, re-creates it, runs all migrations, and executes the seed file to populate sample data. This gives us a clean database with our new survey tables and sample products to work with.

And run the tests:

```
[pento] → mix test
..... ...
Finished in 0.4 seconds (0.2s async, 0.2s sync)
158 tests, 0 failures
```

Excellent. We have an up-to-date database and a working Survey context, and it's all verified with working tests. Now we can take it for a test drive.

Explore the Generated Context and Schema

Let's fire up IEx and play around with creating some demographics and ratings using the generated Survey context, which provides the API for the CRUD interactions of these schemas. This will familiarize you with the usage of our generated and customized context so that you'll be prepared to leverage it in our live views.

We'll create a user with the help of the Accounts context:

```
iex> alias Pento.Accounts
Pento.Accounts
iex>  user_attrs = %{email: "cassandra@grox.io", password: "Tr0yW1llF8ll"}
%{email: "cassandra@grox.io", password: "Tr0yW1llF8ll"}
iex> {:ok, user} = Accounts.register_user(user_attrs)
...
{:ok,
 #Pento.Accounts.User<email: "cassandra@grox.io",id: 1,...>}
```

We added a user, and now we can create a demographic for them:

```
iex> alias Pento.Survey
Pento.Survey
iex> demo_attrs = %{
      user_id: user.id,
```

```
        gender: "prefer not to say",
        year_of_birth: 1989
    }
%{gender: "prefer not to say", user_id: 1, year_of_birth: 1989}
iex> Survey.create_demographic(demo_attrs)
...
{:ok,
 %Pento.Survey.Demographic{gender: "prefer not to say",id: 1,user_id: 1,...}
}
```

Nice. Now, assuming you have a product in your database from the seeding exercise we did in Chapter 3, Generators: Contexts and Schemas, on page 71, you can create a rating for the new user and the product with an ID of 1. Go back to your IEx session and add in this:

```
iex> pid = Pento.Catalog.list_products |> hd |> Map.get(:id)
...
1
iex> rating_attrs = %{user_id: user.id, product_id: pid, stars: 5}
%{user_id: user.id, product_id: 1, stars: 5}
iex> Survey.create_rating(rating_attrs)
{:ok,%Pento.Survey.Rating{id: 1,product_id: 1,stars: 5,user_id: 1}}
```

Easy enough. Now, let's exercise the rating constraints. Try creating another rating for the same user and product like this:

```
iex> Survey.create_rating(%{user_id: user.id, product_id: 1, stars: 1})
[debug] QUERY ERROR db=4.5ms queue=0.5ms idle=1952.2ms...
{:error, #Ecto.Changeset<...
    errors: [
      product_id: {"has already been taken",
        [constraint: :unique, constraint_name: "index_ratings_on_user_product"]}
    ],
    ...
    valid?: false
>}
```

It's not valid, and the message tells us exactly why. The database is doing its job by keeping bad data out of the database. Our changeset is also doing its job by providing nice data the user interface can later show.

We've seen the basic functionality of the Survey context in action. Let's shift our attention to working with the core.

Organize the Application Core and Boundary

In previous chapters, we didn't need to execute queries that were more complex than the CRUD-supporting ones provided by generated code. Our survey feature is different, however. To support the survey functionality, we'll need to execute some custom queries. In this section, you'll learn how to compose and execute complex database queries with Ecto, and you'll see how this work fits into the organized core and boundary layers of an application. Then you'll be ready to use your custom queries in the survey live view.

Ecto query composition, as you already know, is certain and predictable. It belongs in your application's core. But where exactly in the core should you put code that dynamically constructs complex queries?

Queries are a bit like functions. It's fine to express short ones inline, much like anonymous functions, within the scope of a module like a context. Sometimes, however, it's important to provide a first-class function to express and name more complex queries. These functions belong in their very own dedicated query builder modules in the application core. Before we build any such modules though, let's discuss the queries that our survey feature will need to use.

We'll need the following individual queries to support the survey feature:

- The demographic section of our survey will need a query to return the demographic for a given user.
- The ratings section of the survey will rely on a query to return all products, with preloaded ratings for a given user.

Let's begin with the first query.

Query for User Demographics

We need to define a module that will implement the function for querying a user's demographic record. This module will live in the application core, and since it's responsible for demographic queries, we'll name it Survey.Demographic.Query:

```
stateless_components/pento/lib/pento/survey/demographic/query.ex
defmodule Pento.Survey.Demographic.Query do
  import Ecto.Query
  alias Pento.Survey.Demographic

  def base do
    from(d in Demographic)
  end

  def for_user(query, %{user: user}) do
    where(query, [d], d.user_id == ^user.id)
  end
end
```

With the base/0 function, we name the concept of a base query and we provide one common way to build the foundation for all Demographic queries. This type of function is the *constructor* for our Demographic.Query module. We'll rely on it to create an initial query for demographics. You'll also notice the use of the ^ here. This safely interpolates variables into your Ecto queries.

Next, we'll build our *reducer*. These are not specifically functions that we can use in Enum.reduce/2. Instead, they're functions that take some type along with additional arguments and apply those additional arguments to return the same type. In our case, our classic reducer takes a user and transforms the initial query with an additional where clause. By building code in this way, we create elements that pipe together cleanly. This reducer pattern should look familiar to you from our examination of Phoenix request handling in Chapter 2, Phoenix and Authentication, on page 31. It's no different from the manner in which a pipeline of plugs operates on a connection.

Now, we can make the query available in the context.

```
stateless_components/pento/lib/pento/survey.ex
@doc """
Gets a demographic for the given user scope.

Returns nil if no demographic exists for the user.
"""
def get_demographic_by_user(%Scope{} = scope) do
  Repo.one(
    from demographic in Demographic,
    where: demographic.user_id == ^scope.user.id
  )
end
```

We always wrap calls to the query builder in the relevant context. The Survey context pipes the constructed query into a call to Repo.one/1. While we're in there, you might notice the call to alias Pento.Survey.Rating in the middle of the module. It will work there just fine, but we'll move that line to the top of the file with the other alias directives. Now we can test drive the new query and context wrapper in IEx:

```
iex> recompile
iex> Survey.get_demographic_by_user(user)
...
%Pento.Survey.Demographic{gender: "prefer not to say", id: 1,user_id: 1...}
```

Let's apply the same approach to our product ratings query.

Query for Product Ratings

We'll begin by implementing another dedicated querying module in the application's core—Pento.Catalog.Product.Query:

```
stateless_components/pento/lib/pento/catalog/product/query.ex
defmodule Pento.Catalog.Product.Query do
  import Ecto.Query
  alias Pento.Catalog.Product
  alias Pento.Survey.Rating.Query, as: RatingQuery
```

We import and alias the modules we need and build a constructor to start any query pipeline.

Next, we need to build the foundation for any query. The Ecto.Query API supports a protocol called Queryable. In fact, all queries are queryable. Let's open up IEx and examine what our API might look like.

```
iex> import Ecto.Query
Ecto.Query
iex> from(p in Product)
#Ecto.Query<from p0 in Pento.Catalog.Product>
iex> i
#Ecto.Query<from p0 in Pento.Catalog.Product>
iex(19)> i
Term
  #Ecto.Query<from p0 in Pento.Catalog.Product>
Data type
  Ecto.Query
Description
  This is a struct. Structs are maps with a __struct__ key.
Reference modules
  Ecto.Query, Map
Implemented protocols
  Ecto.Queryable, IEx.Info, Inspect, ...
```

So queries are queryable. from(Product) is one simple option. Here's another one:

```
iex>  i Product
Term
  Pento.Catalog.Product
...
Implemented protocols
  Ecto.Queryable, IEx.Info, Inspect, ...
```

Ecto schemas are also queryable! We can use that, as shown on the next page.

```
stateless_components/pento/lib/pento/catalog/product/query.ex
def base, do: Product
```

Rather than make the user guess our intentions for our API, we're explicit. The base/0 function establishes the simplest possible query, one that returns all products. Once again, it makes sense to put this base query in a reusable function. Beyond naming the concept explicitly, which is a good practice in its own right, this approach saves us a lot of potential future work. If we ever need to change the base query for our whole application, we can do so in one place. For example, some future requirement might require us to filter out archived products or remove products marked as deleted, or the like.

Next up, we create a reducer function that takes in a query and returns an annotated query to preload user ratings for the desired products.

```
stateless_components/pento/lib/pento/catalog/product/query.ex
def with_user_ratings(query, user) do
  ratings_query = RatingQuery.preload_user(user)
  from(p in query, preload: [ratings: ^ratings_query])
end
```

In the with_user_ratings/2 reducer, we execute the Ecto preload/2 function to fetch user ratings. Remember, Ecto is explicit. If you want it to load relationships, you need to ask for them. We execute the preload/2 function with a query for ratings belonging to the given user. That logic is in turn wrapped up in another query builder module responsible for rating query logic, Survey.Rating.Query:

```
stateless_components/pento/lib/pento/survey/rating/query.ex
defmodule Pento.Survey.Rating.Query do
  import Ecto.Query
  alias Pento.Survey.Rating

  def preload_user(user) do
    from(r in Rating, where: r.user_id == ^user.id)
  end
end
```

Next, we consume our reducer function in the Catalog context. Remember that the context module functions as the boundary layer of the Phoenix application. It handles the uncertainty of executing database interactions. So we call on our new query function on the context, piping it into a call to Repo.all/2 to execute the query, like this:

```
stateless_components/pento/lib/pento/catalog.ex
def list_products_with_user_rating(user) do
  Pento.Catalog.Product.Query.base()
  |> Pento.Catalog.Product.Query.with_user_ratings(user)
  |> Repo.all()
end
```

Our function accepts a user, calls with_user_ratings/2, and pipes it straight to Repo.all/1. The function will return a list of all products, each with any user ratings. Let's see it in action:

```
iex> alias Pento.{Survey, Accounts, Catalog}
iex> user = Accounts.get_user!(1)
iex> Survey.create_rating(%{user_id: user.id, product_id: 1, stars: 5})
...
iex> Catalog.list_products_with_user_rating(user)
[
  %Pento.Catalog.Product{
    description: "The classic strategy game",name: "Chess", ...
    ratings: [%Pento.Survey.Rating{id: 1,product_id: 1,stars: 5,user_id: 1}]
  },
  %Pento.Catalog.Product{
    description: "The game of Xs and Os",name: "Tic-Tac-Toe",ratings: []
  },...
]
```

And it works! We alias what we need, create a rating, get a user, and then fetch our products. Notice that the products include the preloaded ratings belonging to the given user.

Now that we have a handle on the core functionality of our survey, let's build some LiveView.

Build the Survey Live View

It's time to focus on the survey live view. We know in broad strokes what it will look like. Users will be asked to fill out their demographic information, followed by a rating for each of our products. We're going to approach the survey feature from the outside in. We'll build a common menu first and a route to fit inside it. Then we'll mount and render the initial live view.

Establishing the initial state of the survey live view in the mount/render workflow will give you yet another opportunity to see the reducer pattern in action. You've seen plug pipelines iteratively transform a connection struct, and you've written query builders that do the same for Ecto queries. In this section, you'll see that live view applies this same exact pattern to create and update the state of a live view for our users by reducing over the common data structure of the socket struct. You'll build your own live view reducer pipeline and use it in the mount/3 function. Along the way, you'll get a look at one of the tools that LiveView provides to improve performance during the mount/render workflow, the assign_new/3 function.

Let's get started by tidying up some menus.

Establish a Menu in a Layout

Web applications usually have some common elements across the whole application, some elements shared across a block of pages, and some elements unique to a page. In Phoenix, those layouts are the root layout, the app layout, and LiveView templates. Let's see how those are configured.

Phoenix LiveView applications have two important layouts. The outermost *root layout* typically has the common HTML for many live views, including the html, head, and body tags. It's defined in lib/pento_web/components/layouts/root.html.heex. This code has common elements across many live views that you might not want to change. Therefore, we'll specify root layouts in the router pipeline. Open up our router in lib/pento_web/router.ex and look at the browser pipeline:

```
pipeline :browser do
  ...
  plug :put_root_layout, {PentoWeb.Layouts, :root}
  ...
end
```

This line of code was added by the generator when we first generated our Phoenix LiveView app. Remember, each plug is a reducer that transforms the socket. This one makes the root layout available to any routes that are piped through the :browser pipeline. The root layout is a template like any other in Phoenix, and it contains some menu HTML that's placed at the top of each page. When we generated our authentication code, the generator placed a menu in a list element inside lib/pento_web/components/root.html.heex. If you log in and point your browser at /, you'll see this menu:

>   jose@example.com   Settings   Log out

If you navigate to any other page, you'll see the menu present there too. Let's add a few links so logged-in users can access our coming survey pages:

```
stateless_components/pento/lib/pento_web/components/layouts/root.html.heex
<ul class="menu menu-horizontal w-full relative z-10 flex items-center
  gap-4 px-4 sm:px-6 lg:px-8 justify-end">
  <%= if @current_scope do %>
    <li>
      <.link href={~p"/products"}>Products</.link>
    </li>
    <li>
      <.link href={~p"/survey"}>Survey</.link>
    </li>
    <li>
      {@current_scope.user.email}
```

```
      </li>
      <li>
        <.link href={~p"/users/settings"}>Settings</.link>
      </li>
      <li>
        <.link href={~p"/users/log-out"} method="delete">Log out</.link>
      </li>
    <% else %>
      <li>
        <.link href={~p"/users/register"}>Register</.link>
      </li>
      <li>
        <.link href={~p"/users/log-in"}>Log in</.link>
      </li>
    <% end %>
</ul>
```

You can see the menu code with some Tailwind styles and some code based on the @current_user set by our router, along with some additional links. You might notice a compile warning because our router doesn't yet support the /survey path. Simply ignore it for now because we'll add it shortly. Next, the <%= @inner_content %> will inject the second type of layout, our *application layout*. This is where we'll see a bit of Phoenix code we can delete—back to that in minute.

To allow web pages with different layouts, LiveView lets you specify the layout when you define a live view module and use the LiveView behaviour. If you look at the top of the page in lib/pento_web/live/product_live/index.ex, you'll see a use directive:

```
use PentoWeb, :live_view
```

The preceding code doesn't specify the layout option, but it could. Open up the pento_web.ex file to view the liveview/1 function:

```
def live_view do
  quote do
    use Phoenix.LiveView,
      layout: {PentoWeb.Layouts, :app}

    unquote(html_helpers())
  end
end
```

This code injects the use Phoenix.LiveView code and passes a layout. Notice this one is the app layout. So, the root layout is rendered first, and it in turn renders the app layout in its inner_content block.

Open up the app layout function component, defined in lib/pento_web/components/layouts.ex. Phoenix 1.8 uses function components for layouts instead of separate template files. You can see the current app layout navigation menu with DaisyUI styling by pointing your browser to the /products route:

Phoenix Framework v1.8.0-rc.0

The app layout includes modern features like dark mode support through DaisyUI. We'll simplify this navigation for our book application by replacing the Phoenix branding links with our application-specific navigation.

Update the app layout function component like this:

```
# lib/pento_web/components/layouts.ex
def app(assigns) do
  ~H"""
  <header class="navbar px-4 sm:px-6 lg:px-8">
    <div class="flex-1">
      <a href="/" class="flex-1 flex items-center gap-2">
        <span class="text-xl font-bold">Pento</span>
      </a>
    </div>
    <div class="flex-none">
      <ul class="flex flex-column px-1 space-x-4 items-center">
        <li>
          <.link
            navigate={~p"/products"}
            class="btn btn-ghost">Products
          </.link>
        </li>
        <li>
          <.link navigate={~p"/survey"} class="btn btn-ghost">Survey</.link>
        </li>
        <li>
          <.theme_toggle />
        </li>
      </ul>
    </div>
  </header>

  <main class="px-4 py-20 sm:px-6 lg:px-8">
    <div class="mx-auto max-w-2xl space-y-4">
      {render_slot(@inner_block)}
    </div>
  </main>

  <.flash_group flash={@flash} />
  """
end
```

We've replaced the Phoenix branding with our Pento application name and simplified the navigation to include only our essential routes: Products and Survey. Notice we kept the theme_toggle component, which provides users with system/light/dark theme switching using DaisyUI's theme system. The navigation uses DaisyUI's btn btn-ghost classes for consistent styling. This is the app layout navigation with the light/dark theme:

Phoenix Framework v1.8.0-rc.0

Let's talk about how the Phoenix 1.8 layout system works for our live views. The root layout provides the HTML foundation and user authentication menu, while the app layout function component wraps our LiveView content with application-specific navigation.

DaisyUI provides theming capabilities with theme state persisted in localStorage. DaisyUI handles all the CSS variable switching automatically, giving users a smooth theme transition experience.

Here, you see the contents of the template for this particular live view rendered—in this case, the Product Index template. Let's talk through how this works. Check out the following code at the bottom of the app function component in the layouts module:

```
<header...>
  ...
</header>
<main ...>
  <div ...>
    <.flash ... />
    ...
    <%= @inner_content %>
  </div>
</main>
```

Remember, LiveView renders the root layout first, rendering an <%= @inner_content %> block inside the body tags. Then the app layout is rendered, which displays the markup in the header tag, followed by another call to render <%= @inner_content %>. This in turn renders the template for the current live view.

That's a lot of explanation but not much code. Once again, LiveView, and Phoenix, handle the nitty-gritty details for us. We don't have to tell LiveView how to render a series of templates. We just tell it *what* markup to render in those templates. The code won't work yet because we don't have a working /survey route or corresponding live view—let's fix that now.

Define the Survey Route

Our first job is to establish a route. The survey will live at /survey, and it should work only for authenticated users. We'll tie the route to the yet-to-be-written SurveyLive live view with the :index live action, like this:

stateless_components/pento/lib/pento_web/router.ex
```
live "/survey", SurveyLive, :index
```

Note that once again we've added our new route in the same live session block so that this view shares a root layout and some authentication logic, via the on_mount callback, with the other routes in the block. Also notice that this live session block is within a scope that leverages the [:browser, :require_authenticated_user] pipeline. This means that HTTP requests to our new route will flow through the full browser pipeline and then the require_authenticated_user plug before matching our route. We don't want unauthenticated users to be able to fill out this survey—we need to be able to identify the current user to associate them to the survey data.

Recall that the require_authenticated_user/2 is one of the function plugs we generated earlier on in Chapter 2, Phoenix and Authentication, on page 31. As a result, anyone who tries to visit /survey without first logging in will be redirected to the log-in page. Once again, we're seeing our generated authentication layer used to protect a live view route.

With our route established, it's time to define the SurveyLive live view.

Mount the Survey Live View

First, create a file, lib/pento_web/live/survey_live.ex, and define the SurveyLive module. Next up, we'll define the mount/3 function. The mount/3 function builds the initial state for SurveyLive. Let's think about that initial state. We know we'll need to use the current user to build the demographic and rating portions of our survey, so we want to store that user in the live view's state. This way, we can make it available to the demographic and ratings components later on. Luckily for us, the UserAuth.on_mount/4 function will do the hard work for us. When mounting any of the live views in our live session, it will verify the presence of the current user and add it to the socket.assigns.user key. So when this live view mounts, the socket assigns already contains the :current_user key. That means we can code a very simple SurveyLive.mount/3 function, like this:

```
stateless_components/pento/lib/pento_web/live/survey_live.ex
defmodule PentoWeb.SurveyLive do
  use PentoWeb, :live_view

  alias Pento.{Survey, Catalog}
  alias PentoWeb.DemographicLive.Show
  alias __MODULE__.Component

  @impl true
  def mount(_params, _session, socket) do
    socket =
      socket
      |> assign_demographic()
      |> assign_products()

    {:ok, socket}
  end

  defp assign_demographic(socket) do
    demographic = Survey.get_demographic_by_user(socket.assigns.current_scope)
    assign(socket, :demographic, demographic)
  end

  defp assign_products(socket) do
    products = Catalog.list_products(socket.assigns.current_scope)
    assign(socket, :products, products)
  end
end
```

We pick up the standard default mount, returning the socket unchanged. This code is simpler than it might have otherwise been because of the live session code. Before our mount fires, the on_mount function will fire, loading a user. Here's the code that looks up the user from the database:

```
stateless_components/pento/lib/pento_web/user_auth.ex
defp mount_current_scope(socket, session) do
  Phoenix.Component.assign_new(socket, :current_scope, fn ->
    user =
      if user_token = session["user_token"] do
        Accounts.get_user_by_session_token(user_token)
      end

    Scope.for_user(user)
  end)
end
```

The code checks the session for a user token. If one exists, we use assign_new/3 to look up a new user *if none exists in the socket*. When the live view is first mounted when a user navigates directly to that page in the browser, a plain HTTP request fires. At this time, LiveView makes the Plug.Conn data available to the mounting live view in socket.assigns. So, for this first invocation of the on_mount callback, socket.assigns already contains a current user. By using assign_new here, we take advantage of this fact and make sure that we only make a database request to look up the user for the token if we don't already have a current user in the socket.

If no valid token exists, we erase the current_user in the socket.

With on_mount handling auth and adding :current_user to socket.assigns, SurveyLive is free to implement a trivial mount/3 function. It's time to render.

Render the Template

After our on_mount callback runs, and PentoWeb.SurveyLive.mount/3 finishes, the live view will render. We don't provide a render/1 function; instead we're using a template—lib/pento_web/live/survey_live.html.heex. We'll plug in a simple stub until we're ready for more:

```
<!-- lib/pento_web/live/survey_live.html.heex -->
<section>
  <h2>Survey</h2>
</section>
```

Reload your browser and you'll see the bare-bones template shown here:

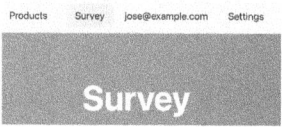

It's not much, but we've confirmed a good bit of our infrastructure, and the rest of the exercise will move quickly. We have the basic framework for our survey UI in place. Now, let's take a step back and explore function components.

Build a Simple Function Component

As you've already seen, a function component is a function that takes in an assigns argument and returns a HEEx template. You can define these functions in any LiveView module or module that uses the Phoenix.Component behaviour. Rather than passing arguments as we do when we call typical Elixir functions, these components use a style that's a bit closer to HTML than Elixir, like this:

```
<ComponentModule.function_component attr1="value1" attr2={1+2} >
  slot contents
</ComponentModule.function_component>
```

You've seen code like this code before, but let's review with a bit more detail. This function component is a simple function called ComponentModule.function_component/1 with an argument of a hard-coded string value and another argument of an interpolated value. This invocation has one default slot called inner_block that we specify between the tags. Alternatively, you can call function_component/1 functions with <.component_function ...>. The leading . tells the ~H template to invoke a function component. You can use this shorter invocation in the template for the live view module in which the function component is defined or if you've aliased the function component module into that live view.

The preceding argument-passing style allows HEEx to name arguments and specify some type information. Now let's look at the corresponding function definition:

```
defmodule ComponentModule do
  use Phoenix.Component

  attr :attr1, :string, default: nil
  attr :attr2, :integer
  slot :inner_block, required: true
  def function_component(assigns) do
    ~H"""
    <p><%= render_slot(@inner_block) %></p>
    """
  end
end
```

First, we define the attributes and the slot. The code uses the attr macro to define attributes and the slot macro to define the space between our tags as a slot. By defining attributes, we get compile-time warnings if the function component is called without required attributes or with attributes of the wrong type. This declarative approach helps us build function components that are easy to use, even for developers new to the application who are unfamiliar with the definition of a given component. By defining slots, we can tell HEEx how to render specific pieces of content placed in between opening and closing component tags when the function component is invoked. The :inner_block slot is the default slot. Call on a function component with opening and closing tags, like this:

```
<ComponentModule.function_component attr1="value1" attr2={1+2} >
  <!-- ... -->
</ComponentModule.function_component>
```

The content between the opening and closing tags becomes the value of the @inner_block assignment. Then, in our function definition, we can render that content inside the specified markup by calling render_slot(@inner_block).

Moving on, the function itself is a simple Elixir function taking a map called assigns as the lone argument. Say we invoke the function component like this: .function_component attr1="value1" attr2={1+2}>. LiveView calls the function_component function with an assigns argument that looks like this: %{attr1: "value1", attr2: 3}. Each key/value pair is derived from the attributes given to your function invocation.

Finally, executing the code renders this output, thanks to our call to render_slot/2:

```
<p>slot contents</p>
```

This example shows how the declaration, invocation, and results of a function component fit together. Now, let's use that style to build our first custom function component. Function components are implemented in modules that use the Phoenix.Component behaviour, which also gives us a convenient syntax for rendering function components. First, we'll build and render a simple function component. Then we'll customize it further.

Define a Function Component

Define a module in lib/pento_web/live/survey_live/component.ex that looks like this:

```
stateless_components/pento/lib/pento_web/live/survey_live/component.ex
defmodule PentoWeb.SurveyLive.Component do
  use Phoenix.Component

  attr :content, :string, required: true
  slot :inner_block, required: true

  def hero(assigns) do
    ~H"""
    <div class="hero bg-gradient-to-r from-blue-500 to-purple-600 text-white">
      <div class="hero-content text-center py-16">
        <div class="max-w-md">
          <h1 class="mb-5 text-5xl font-bold"><%= @content %></h1>
          <div class="mb-5 text-lg">
            <%= render_slot(@inner_block) %>
          </div>
        </div>
      </div>
    </div>
    """
  end
end
```

Our module calls use Phoenix.Component to gain access to the ~H sigil for rendering HEEx templates and the macros for managing attributes and slots. Our simple module implements a function called hero/1. We'll call it with HTML-style attributes we'll pass in when we invoke the function. Let's do that next.

Use the Component

Now we make use of the function component. Alias the component in SurveyLive by adding this line to the top your module: alias PentoWeb.SurveyLive.Component.

stateless_components/pento/lib/pento_web/live/survey_live.ex
```
alias __MODULE__.Component
```

With the alias added, we can call on the new function component from the SurveyLive template:

stateless_components/pento/lib/pento_web/live/survey_live.html.heex
```
<Component.hero content="Survey">
  Please fill out our survey
</Component.hero>
```

The component rendering syntax is eloquent and easy to read. It follows the pattern <ComponentName.function_name assigns>.

Here, we pass an assigns that contains %{content: "Survey", inner_block: "Please fill out our survey"}. So the assigns that the hero/1 function is called with will contain the @content assignment and the @inner_block assignment. Now if you point your browser at /survey, you should see the new component rendered:

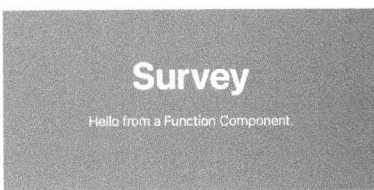

Before we move on, let's see the compile-time HEEx validations provided by the attr and slot macros in action. Here's what happens if you try to call on our function component with a content attribute of an invalid type:

```
<Component.hero content={123} >
attribute "content" in component
PentoWeb.SurveyLive.Component.hero/1 must be a :string,
got: 123 Elixir
View Problem (⌥F8)   No quick fixes available
```

And here's what happens if you try to call on our function component without any inner_block content:

```
missing required slot "inner_block" for component
PentoWeb.SurveyLive.Component.hero/1 Elixir
View Problem (⌥F8)   No quick fixes available
<Component.hero content="Survey" />
```

The Elixir Language Server extension in VS Code provides us with these helpful warnings.

If you don't use VS Code, fear not! The Phoenix server logs will display similar warnings, like this one in the case of our first error example:

```
warning: attribute "content" in component PentoWeb.SurveyLive.Component.hero/1
must be a :string, got: 123
  lib/pento_web/live/survey_live.html.heex:1: (file)
```

> **Function Components as Tiny Helpers**
>
> If you need a component to handle markup issues like lists or the like, without the need to process events or states, a function component is a good way to go. Function components allow you to wrap up reusable bits of markup and styling that you can render again and again across your application. CSS frameworks also have specific markup requirements for onscreen elements like menus that need only input parameters. These kinds of problems are perfect for function components. They participate well in LiveView's change tracking because they'll update and re-render as needed, whenever the parent live view changes.

Now we'll take a closer look at how LiveView renders the @inner_block and other contents in assigns. We'll start by examining exactly what data is present in the assigns argument given to our function. Add this markup to the bottom of your Component.hero/1 function:

```
<pre>
  <%= inspect(assigns, pretty: true) %>
</pre>
```

Now check out your browser. You'll see a data structure like this:

```
%{
  __changed__: nil,
  content: "Survey",
  inner_block: [%{
    __slot__: :inner_block,
    inner_block: #Function<...>}]
}
```

As expected, you can see the content attribute. You can also see the __changed__ key. LiveView uses this key to track the exact changes on the page! That means even with your code layered into components, LiveView will only refresh changed parts of the page. Let's shift our attention to the inner block.

Notice the list of maps in inner_block. Our page invokes the inner_block only once, so there's only one in this list. Each slot map has a slot name and a function to render it. We don't have to guess what the function does. Let's call it—change the <pre> block on the page to extract and inspect the results of the inner_block/2 anonymous function:

```
<pre>
  <%= inspect(assigns, pretty: true) %>
  <% %{ inner_block: [%{inner_block: block_fn}]} = assigns %>
  <%= inspect(block_fn.(assigns.__changed__, assigns), pretty: true) %>
</pre>
```

We do a pattern match to grab the inner block function from the assigns and also call the function with the component changes from assigns.__changed__ and the assigns map itself. You'll see something like this, formatted for clarity:

```
%Phoenix.LiveView.Rendered{
  static: ["\n  Please fill out our survey\n"],
  dynamic: #Function<4.6220252/1 in PentoWeb.SurveyLive.render/1>,
  fingerprint: 31772444813748785948940385709943669798,
  root: nil,
  caller: :not_available}
```

We see the results of rendering our slot along with some additional data LiveView needs. In this way, LiveView users can easily invoke inner slots and place those values wherever on the page they want. LiveView simply calls the function, leaving rendered content behind wherever the user needs to display the slot contents.

This simple example shows how useful function components can be to wrap up commonly used bits of markup. You can imagine using function components to build reusable elements like lists, buttons, and more. With slots, your single-purpose function components can become even more dynamic, rendering whatever inner content you specify. In fact, many such helper components are generated for you when you use the Phoenix Live generator, and they're made available in the PentoWeb.CoreComponents module. We've even used some of these generated function components in earlier chapters—for example, when we rendered a table of products on the index page with the help of the table/1 function component.

Now that you have a pretty good handle on working with function components, let's turn our attention back to the survey UI. We'll start with the demographic portion of our survey. We'll use a function component to display the details of a saved demographic record. Then we'll render that component from the SurveyLive template if such a record exists. In the next chapter, we'll build out a stateful live component to contain the form for a new demographic when one doesn't exist.

Build the Demographic Show Function Component

Recall that our final survey UI will support the following behavior. When the demographic portion of the survey is complete, we'll show demographic details and the product ratings portion of the survey. This image shows the UI we're going to build:

In this section, you'll build a function component that will show the demographic details if a demographic for the given user exists. We'll start by implementing this function component in DemographicLive.Show.details/1. Then we'll return to the parent live view, SurveyLive, which will query for the user's demographic record and store it in state. Finally, we'll call on our function component from within the SurveyLive template, passing it an assigns that includes the current user and the demographic struct.

We've got our plan. Let's dive in.

Define the Function Component

First up, let's define our function component module. Create a new file, lib/pento_web/live/demographic_live/show.ex, and fill it out like this:

```
stateless_components/pento/lib/pento_web/live/demographic_live/show.ex
defmodule PentoWeb.DemographicLive.Show do
  use Phoenix.Component
  alias PentoWeb.CoreComponents
end
```

This module looks like most LiveView modules, with a slight difference. The use Phoenix.Component gives us access to the Phoenix.Component API. We also import the Phoenix.HTML module, which we'll later use to access some Phoenix.HTML functions to help us render Unicode characters and a few other modules we'll need.

Now, add a function called details/1. Because that function is a component, it will need to return a ~H HEEx sigil with the contents we want, like this:

```
def details(assigns) do
  ~H"""
  <div>
    <h2 class="font-medium text-2xl">
      Demographics {raw("&#x2713;")}
    </h2>
    <ul>
      <li>Gender: {@demographic.gender}</li>
      <li>
        Year of birth: {@demographic.year_of_birth}
      </li>
    </ul>
  </div>
  """
end
```

Our function component is short and sweet. We have a header that includes the Unicode characters for a checkmark symbol to give the user a visual indicator that they've completed the Demographics portion of the survey. Then we have a simple list that displays the demographic details. We also added a call to the attr macro to specify that our function component expects to be called with a required demographic attribute of type Pento.Survey.Demographic. Once again, we can see this validation in action. Take a look at what happens if you try to pass in demographic={nil} to your function component call in the template:

KeyError at GET /survey

key :gender not found in: nil

If you are using the dot syntax, such as map.field, make sure
the left-hand side of the dot is a map

lib/pento_web/live/demographic_live/show.ex

```
10    def details(assigns) do
11      ~H"""
12      <h2>Demographics ✅</h2>
13      <CoreComponents.table id="demographics" rows={[@dem
14        <:col :let={demographic} label="Gender">
15          <%= demographic.gender %>
16        </:col>
17        <:col :let={demographic} label="Year of Birth">
18          <%= demographic.year_of_birth %>
19        </:col>
20      </CoreComponents.table>
```

The function was expecting to be called with an assigns argument where the :demographic key points to a value that is a Demographic struct, and it errors if that doesn't happen.

Great! Now we're ready to render our component from the SurveyLive template.

Render the Demographic Show Function Component

We're ready to render our function component from the parent live view. The SurveyLive template will call on our function component with the demographic record for the current user. Our SurveyLive view doesn't have the user's associated demographic though. Let's get that set up now.

Open up lib/pento_web/live/survey_live.ex. First, add the aliases we'll need:

```
stateless_components/pento/lib/pento_web/live/survey_live.ex
alias Pento.{Survey, Catalog}
alias PentoWeb.DemographicLive.Show
alias __MODULE__.Component
```

Then update the mount/3 function to set a key of :demographic in the socket assigns using a new reducer, as shown here:

```
stateless_components/pento/lib/pento_web/live/survey_live.ex
@impl true
def mount(_params, _session, socket) do
  socket =
    socket
    |> assign_demographic()
    |> assign_products()

  {:ok, socket}
end
```

```
stateless_components/pento/lib/pento_web/live/survey_live.ex
def mount(_params, _session, socket) do
  socket =
    socket
    |> assign_demographic()
    |> assign_products()

  {:ok, socket}
end

defp assign_demographic(socket) do
  demographic = Survey.get_demographic_by_user(socket.assigns.current_scope)
  assign(socket, :demographic, demographic)
end
```

Here, we use our boundary function, Survey.get_demographic_by_user/1, to fetch the demographic for the current user. If there is such a record, it will return a demographic struct representing that record. Otherwise, it will return nil. So the :demographic key in socket assigns *could* be set to a demographic struct, or it could be set to nil.

With that in place, let's render our function component. If a demographic struct is present in the assigns, then we want to render the function component to display its details. If not, then we want to render the form for the new demographic. We'll add some conditional logic to the SurveyLive template, shown here:

```
stateless_components/pento/lib/pento_web/live/survey_live.html.heex
<div class="container mx-auto px-4 py-8 max-w-4xl">
  <%= if @demographic do %>
    <Show.details demographic={@demographic} />
  <% else %>
    <h3>Demographic form coming soon...</h3>
  <% end %>
</div>
```

Now if you point your browser at /survey, you should see our form placeholder text displayed, as you can see in this screenshot:

Let's take our logic for another test drive. Open up IEx and manually create a demographic record for your user, like this:

```
iex> alias Pento.Accounts
iex> alias Pento.Survey
iex> email = "your_logged_in_email" # use logged in user's email here
iex> user = Accounts.get_user_by_email(email)
iex> attrs = %{gender: "male", year_of_birth: 2020, user_id: user.id}
iex> Survey.create_demographic(attrs)
```

If you refresh the /survey page, you should see our function component render the demographic details, just like in this image:

Before we wrap up, we're going to dive even deeper into some function component functionality. We'll use the <.table> component provided in the generated PentoWeb.CoreComponents module to render demographic details in a table. We'll look under the hood at how this function component dynamically and agnostically renders any provided collection in a table. When we're done, you'll have the understanding you need to build these kinds of dynamic function components on your own.

Using Dynamic Function Components

You've seen the <.table> function component in action once before when we generated the Product Index template. In that template, the <.table> component displays a table of product data. Now we'll use that same component to render demographic details in a table that looks like this:

Open up the DemographicShow.details/1 function and add a new alias, alias PentoWeb.CoreComponents. Then update our function's HEEx markup to call on the <CoreComponents.table> function component with a rows attribute set equal to a list that contains our one @demographic struct. The table component is meant for rendering a table with rows populated from a list of items. In our case, we want to render one single demographic's details, so our list of rows has just the one item.

```
# stateless_components/pento/lib/pento_web/live/demographic_live/show.ex
attr :demographic, :map, required: true

def details(assigns) do
  ~H"""
  <h2>Demographics ✓</h2>
  <CoreComponents.table id="demographics" rows={[@demographic]}>
    <:col :let={demographic} label="Gender">
      <%= demographic.gender %>
    </:col>
    <:col :let={demographic} label="Year of Birth">
      <%= demographic.year_of_birth %>
    </:col>
  </CoreComponents.table>
  """
end
```

Now we'll take a look under the hood of the <.table> component to understand how it works, starting with the use of the <:col> slot to create table columns. The collection of :col slots becomes available in the table/1 function component as the @col assignment. The function component iterates over the collection in @col and renders a table heading element for each column, displaying the value of the Label attribute, like this:

```
# lib/pento_web/components/core_components.ex
def table(assigns) do
  ~H"""
  # ...
  <thead class="text-sm text-left leading-6 text-zinc-500">
    <tr>
      <th :for={col <- @col} class="p-0 pr-6 pb-4 font-normal">
        <%= col[:label] %>
      </th>
      # ...
  """
end
```

The function component also renders a table row for each member of the @rows assignment. Here's a simplified version of that code:

```
# lib/pento_web/components/core_components.ex
def table(assigns) do
  ~H"""
  # ...
  <tbody ...
    class="relative divide-y
           divide-zinc-100
           border-t
           border-zinc-200
           text-sm
```

```
              leading-6
              text-zinc-700">
  <tr :for={row <- @rows}
      id={@row_id && @row_id.(row)}
      class="group hover:bg-zinc-50">
    # ...
  """
end
```

The :for directive embedded in the <tr> element iterates over all of the items in the @rows assignment and renders a <tr> element for each one, setting the row variable equal to each item in the @rows list. The @rows assignment contains our demographic list (which, remember, just has one element in it), so at each step through the iteration, row is set equal to an individual demographic struct. Turn your attention back to our HEEx template for a moment and take a look at how each <:col> slot is invoked, like this one for example:

```
# lib/pento_web/live/demographic_live/show.ex
<:col :let={demographic} label="Gender">
  <%= demographic.gender %>
</:col>
```

Notice the let attribute attached to each <:col> slot. Under the hood, the table/1 function component iterates over the list of items in the @rows assignment and renders a table cell for each row/column combination. It yields each element in the @rows list back up to the index template and sets it equal to the demographic variable via the let assignment. This allows us to pass the individual demographic from the @rows iteration back up to the caller—the HEEx template in our DemographicShow.details/1 function. This way, we can call demographic.gender to render the gender of the demographic :col slot. Here's a simplified version of the relevant snippet of code from within the table/1 function component:

```
# lib/pento_web/components/core_components.ex
def table(assigns) do
  ~H"""
  <tbody class="relative divide-y divide-zinc-100 border-t border-zinc-200
      text-sm leading-6 text-zinc-700">
    <tr :for={row <- @rows} class="relative group hover:bg-zinc-50">
    <td :for={col <- @col}>
        <%= render_slot(col, row) %>
    </td>
    # ..
  """
end
```

The render_slot/2 function is called here with two arguments. The first is the col variable, which represents the content between the opening and closing <:col> tags of the given column we're iterating over. This is the content that's rendered when calling render_slot. The second argument we give is the row variable. Since @rows contains a list of demographics, row points to an individual demographic struct at each step through the iteration. Here's where the :let comes in. When we call render_slot/2 with a second argument, whatever we pass as that argument gets set equal to the value of the :let variable declared in the caller. Our template sets :let={demographic}. So inside the opening and closing <:col> slot tags in the index template, the demographic variable is set equal to each demographic from the @rows iteration. In this way, each column slot's content is rendered for each demographic in the list. So all of the :col slots will fire for each demographic.

Revisiting our table in the browser, you'll notice that the value of the Gender column is in bold. See it again here:

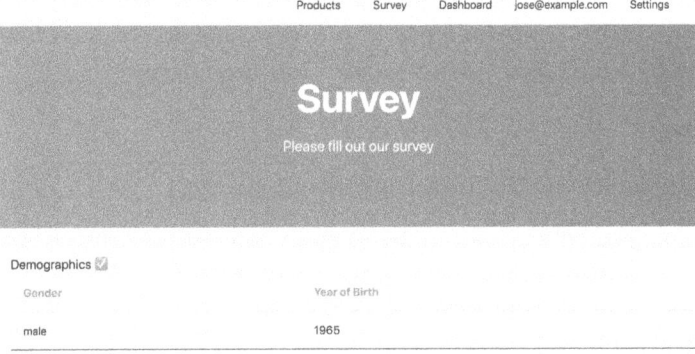

This is because the table function component defined in CoreComponents adds a class of "font-semibold" to the <td> element content for the first column. As an extra challenge to familiarize yourself with CoreComponents code, open up the CoreComponents module and find the line of code in the table function definition that applies this class.

Phew! That was a lot of detail. Take some time to read through the code in the table/1 function component more closely on your own. You can use the combined tools of slots and the let attribute to build your own dynamic function components that can render any kind of data. In the meantime, you can keep your new table rendering in place or revert back to the simple list from the earlier example. We don't necessarily need the full power of a table to render the details for just one demographic, but it was a useful lens through which to examine a common pattern you'll see in function components.

At this point we've created the beginnings of our survey UI by layering together a parent live view and a child function component. In the next chapter, we'll explore stateful, or live, components and build a live component for this form and the remainder of the forms that will make up our survey UI.

Your Turn

The art of building software is the art of breaking down one complex problem into several simple ones, and that means layering. LiveView provides two kinds of components for this purpose: function components and live components. Function components encapsulate common *rendering* code and allow you to compose such code into layers.

In this chapter, you built a simple hero function component, and you rendered it from a parent live view. You made that function component dynamic by teaching it to render slot content. With that under your belt, you built the demographic details function component to start composing our layered survey UI. You also set up the application core and boundary layer for our user survey feature, and you'll put it to further use in the next chapter. Now it's your turn to put what you've learned into practice.

Give It a Try

These problems let you build your own components.

- Function components provide a great way of sharing common user interface blocks. Build a component to render an HTML title, with a heading and a configurable message. Render this component multiple times with different messages on the same page in your SurveyLive live view. What are the strengths and limitations of this approach?

- Build a function component that renders an HTML list item. Then build a component that uses this list item component to render a whole HTML list in the SurveyLive live view. Can you configure your components to render any given list of items? Although this composable list exercise is somewhat simplified, can you think of some scenarios in which this component-based approach will help you build live views in a layered, organized, and reusable way?

- Update the table function component in CoreComponents to contain a new attribute you can use to style the first column of the table however you like. This way, the first element in the column doesn't have to be bold. Or, build your own custom function component to display demographic details in some other format.

Next Time

Live components allow shared rendering just as function ones do, and they also support *events that manage state*. In the next chapter, we'll build a live demographic form component and teach it to respond to user input. Then we'll move on to the product ratings functionality of our survey. When we're done with the survey feature, you'll have learned how a set of components can be composed to manage the state and behavior of a single-page flow.

CHAPTER 7

Live Components

In the previous chapter, we began building an interactive survey feature by creating the back-end core and boundary functionality, along with a live view and function component, to make up the beginnings of our UI. In this chapter, we'll build *live components* to manage demographics and ratings. Our live component will manage its own state in its own life cycle. We'll compose an interactive survey with it layer by layer.

Along the way, you'll learn how live components work. You've seen this concept briefly within the forms we generated. The function components you built in the previous chapter render static markup, such as HTML. Those components don't have their own state, and users can't modify the state through events. Live components are different. They have their own state, can process their own events, and even have their own life cycle. You'll use them to build fully interactive parts of a page, such as counters, timers, data-backed forms, and the like. Our live components will be tiny forms that permit our users to rate products.

You'll explore for yourself how these communicate with their parent live view, you'll continue to see how components allow you to build clean and organized code that adheres to the single responsibility principle, and you'll implement component composition logic that allows you to manage even complex state for your single-page applications.

Before we dig into live components, a word of caution. Live components are a powerful tool, and you'll find that experienced LiveView developers reach for them less frequently than you might expect—and for good reasons. The main downside to live components is that they make it harder to understand where state is definitively managed. When you build a live component, you now have state in both the parent live view and in the live component itself. That means you can have multiple copies of the same state in multiple places, and keeping those in sync can be tricky. Further, messages between the parent live view and a live component can get complicated over time as nested pages evolve. If you find yourself passing a lot of data back and forth between a parent and a live component, or if your component doesn't really need its own event handling, you might be better off with a simple function component. That said, when you need a component that manages its own interactive state—such as a form or a timer—live components are exactly the right tool for the job. If you do use live components, make sure each piece of state has one definitive source of truth, and manage all state from that single place.

Build the Live Demographic Form Component

Let's put together a plan before we get started. We'll begin by implementing a live component module to house our demographic form. We'll use the available LiveView and LiveComponent life cycle callbacks to establish the state of our form component. Then we'll render the form markup using the same simple_form/1 function component you saw in earlier chapters. Finally, we'll teach our form component to respond to user input and save demographic data for the user.

Define the Live Component

First up, create a new file, lib/pento_web/live/demographic_live/form.ex, and define the form component module, like this:

```
defmodule PentoWeb.DemographicLive.Form do
  use PentoWeb, :live_component
  alias Pento.Survey
  alias Pento.Survey.Demographic
end
```

This is simple enough to begin with. We implement a module that uses the :live_component behaviour to create a live component. Then we add a few aliases that we'll take advantage of in a bit.

We'll use LiveView's simple_form/1 function to construct the demographic form. This function requires a form wrapping a changeset, so we'll need to store one in our component's state. Like full live views, live components first have one workflow to establish the initial page and then a change management workflow to modify and render the component state. As we did in our live views, we'll use CRC to think about how to organize our code. For the initial mount/render workflow, we don't need a reducer. The flow looks like this:

```
inputs |> construct() |> convert()
```

construct() refers to a function that establishes the initial state in the form of a socket and convert() is transforms all of that socket data to HTML. In the constructor, the component life cycle comes into play. For our component, the update callback will act as our constructor, and the render callback will act as our converter. Why the update function and not the mount function? The answer to that question lies in understanding the live component life cycle.

When we render a live component, LiveView starts the component in the parent view's process and calls these callbacks in order:

mount/1
> The argument is the socket, and we use this callback to set initial state. This callback is invoked only once, when the component is first rendered from the parent live view. You'll use this function to do one-time setup.

update/2
> The two arguments are the assigns argument given to live_component/3 and the socket. By default, it merges the assigns argument into the socket.assigns established in mount/1. You'll use this callback to add additional content to the socket *each time live_component/3 is called*.

render/1
> The argument is socket.assigns. It works like a render in any other live view.

Live components will always follow this three-step process when they're first mounted and rendered. Then, when the component updates in response to changes in the parent live view, only the update/2 and render/1 callbacks fire. Since these updates skip the mount/1 callback, the update/2 function is the safest place to establish the component's initial state.

We'll use the update/2 callback as our constructor to add a Demographic changeset to socket.assigns so we can render it in a form on the template. For a converter, we'll let the implicit render/1 function render a HEEx template that matches the name of our live component.

Let's get ready to set the initial state of our live component now. Our demographic *belongs to* a user, and we'll need access to that user to construct a demographic changeset. Recall that we're planning to render our form live component from the SurveyLive template defined in lib/pento_web/live/survey_live.html.heex, as shown on the next page.

```
<%= if @demographic do %>
  <DemographicLive.Show.details demographic={@demographic} />
<% else %>
  <h2>Demographic Form coming soon!</h2>
<% end %>
```

The SurveyLive socket assigns already contains a @current_user assignment, so we'll make sure to pass it into our live component. The DemographicLive.Form.update/2 function can then safely rely on a current user.

With that assumption in mind, we can implement an update/2 function to build a Demographic struct and a form struct, like this:

```
stateful_components/pento/lib/pento_web/live/demographic_live/form.ex
@impl true
def update(assigns, socket) do
  socket =
    socket
    |> assign(assigns)
    |> assign_demographic()
    |> clear_form()

  {:ok, socket}
end
```

This code uses the same technique we used in our SurveyLive.mount/3 function. We build a couple of single-purpose reducers to add the demographic and empty form to our socket.assigns and string them into a nice pipeline. By this point, the reducer functions should look familiar. Here's the first one, assign_demographic/1:

```
stateful_components/pento/lib/pento_web/live/demographic_live/form.ex
defp assign_demographic( %{assigns: %{current_scope: current_scope}} = socket) do
  assign(socket, :demographic, %Demographic{user_id: current_scope.user.id})
end
```

It creates a demographic struct with the current user's ID, ensuring the validation in our Survey context will pass.

And here are two functions to add forms to our socket—one for an empty, or clear, form and one for a form with a validated changeset:

```
stateful_components/pento/lib/pento_web/live/demographic_live/form.ex
defp assign_form(socket, changeset) do
  assign(socket, :form, to_form(changeset))
end

defp clear_form(%{assigns: %{demographic: demographic}} = socket) do
  current_scope = socket.assigns.current_scope
  changeset = Survey.change_demographic(current_scope, demographic)
  assign_form(socket, changeset)
end
```

For the assign_form/2 function, we convert an existing changeset to a form. For the clear_form/1 function, we take the empty demographic from the socket, wrap that in a changeset, and then add that to the socket with assign_form/2. Once the update/2 function finishes, the component renders the template. Let's define that template now to render the demographic form for our shiny new changeset.

Render the Demographic Form

You've seen what a LiveView form looks like. We won't bore you with the details. For now, add this to lib/pento_web/live/demographic_live/form.html.heex:

```
stateful_components/pento/lib/pento_web/live/demographic_live/form.html.heex
<.form
  for={@form}
  phx-submit="save"
  id={@id}
  phx-target={@myself}>

  <.input
    field={@form[:gender]}
    type="select"
    label="Gender"
    options={["female", "male", "other", "prefer not to say"]} />
  <.input
    field={@form[:year_of_birth]}
    type="select"
    label="Year of Birth"
    options={Enum.reverse(1920..2025)} />
  <div>
    <.button phx-disable-with="Saving...">Save</.button>
  </div>
</.form>
```

Notice that our form is contained within a root <div> element. All live components require a single root element in their HTML templates. Also notice that we're using the <.simple_form> component defined in the CoreComponents module. Let's dig briefly into our form rendering code.

Our update/2 function added the form struct to our socket assigns, and we access it with @form in our call to simple_form/1. The simple_form/1 function takes in the form struct, has an id, and applies the phx-submit LiveView binding for saving the form. Our form has labels, fields, and error tags for each field we want the user to populate. Finally, there's a submit tag with a phx-disable_with function—a little nicety that LiveView provides to handle multiple submits.

We're ready to put it all together by rendering the form component from the SurveyLive template in pento/lib/pento_web/live/survey_live.html.heex.

First, we need to alias our LiveComponent modules in survey_live.ex:

```
stateful_components/pento/lib/pento_web/live/survey_live.ex
alias PentoWeb.DemographicLive.{Show, Form}
```

Then render the component from the template using the live_component/1[1] function component, like this:

```
stateful_components/pento/lib/pento_web/live/survey_live.html.heex
<.live_component module={Form}
      id="demographic-form"
      current_scope={@current_scope} />
```

The live_component/1 function is a function component made available to us by the LiveView framework. It takes in an argument of some assigns and returns a HEEx template that renders the given component within the parent live view. When using live_component/1 to render a live component, you must specify an assigns of module, pointing to the name of the live component module to mount and render, and an assigns of id, which LiveView will use to keep track of the component. Notice that we pass the current_scope to the component so it can access the current user for creating demographic records.

Now log in as a user that doesn't have an associated demographic record, or simply temporarily tweak the if statement to render if !@demographic. Then visit /survey to see our survey page with the demographic form, as shown here:

Survey

Gender

female

Year of Birth

2023

Save

If you try to submit the form, you'll find the live view crashes, but maybe not for the reason you thought. Look at the logs:

```
[error] GenServer #PID<0.1159.0> terminating
** (UndefinedFunctionError) function PentoWeb.SurveyLive.handle_event/3 is
   undefined or private
```

Did you catch the problem? We did get an undefined handle_event/3, but we got it for the parent SurveyLive view, *not* our component! While we *could* send the event to SurveyLive, that's not in the spirit of using components. Components are responsible for wrapping up markup, state, *and* events. Let's keep our code clean and respect the *single responsibility principle*.

---

1. https://hexdocs.pm/phoenix_live_view/Phoenix.LiveView.Helpers.html#live_component/1

The `DemographicLive.Form` should handle both the state for the survey's demographic section and the events to manage that state. To fix this, add the following `phx-target` attribute to your form in the `lib/pento_web/live/demographic_live/form.html.heex` template:

```
<.simple_form
    for={@form}
    phx-submit="save"
    id={@id}
    phx-target={@myself}  <!-- add this line -->
  <!-- ... -->
</.simple_form>
```

The `@myself` assignment is made available in our component by LiveView, for free, and it always refers to the current component. This will ensure that any events sent by LiveView bindings on this element will go to the current component rather than the parent live view.

Now that we can send events to our demo form, it's time to add some handlers.

Manage Component State

First, we'll briefly revisit the live component life cycle that we'll take advantage of to manage component state. Then we'll implement the event handlers we need to respond to our form events.

Consider the update_many/1 Callback

Whenever `live_component/1` is first invoked, the component will call `mount/1`, `update/2`, and `render/1`. Sometimes these callbacks aren't enough. You might need an additional callback called `update_many/1` to prevent a potentially serious N + 1 performance problem. For the mount/render workflow, LiveView calls `update_many/1`, then `mount/1`, followed by `update/2`, and finally `render/1`. The change management workflow *drops* the `mount/1` but maintains `update_many/1`, then `update/2`, and finally `render/1`.

We won't take advantage of `update_many/1` in our component, but it's worth discussing what it can do for us. This function lets LiveView load all components of the same type at once, potentially saving many extra database queries. To understand how this works, we'll look at an example.

Let's say you're rendering a list of product detail components. You might accomplish this by iterating over a list of product IDs in the parent live view and calling `live_component/3` to render each product detail component with a given product ID. Each component in our scenario is responsible for taking the product ID, using it to query for a product from the database, and rendering some markup that displays the product info. Now imagine that update_many/1 doesn't exist. This means you're rendering a product detail component once for each product ID in the list. So 20 product IDs would mean 20 components and 20 queries—each product detail component would need to issue its own query for the product with the given ID.

With update_many/1, you can specify a way to load *all* components of the same type *at once*, while issuing a single query for all of the products in the list of product IDs. You should reach for this approach whenever you find yourself in such a situation.

Because our component doesn't render any lists or child components, we can safely move forward without implementing update_many/1. We're ready to teach our live component how to handle events.

Handle the Save Event

We're already sending events to our component when the form is saved. Now we need to implement a handle_event/3 function for that "save" event. Here's how it will work.

First, we'll build our handle_event/3 function head that matches the "save" event. The event will receive a socket and the parameters from the form.

Next, we'll make a reducer to save the form and return the saved socket.

Finally, we'll call our reducer in handle_event/3. In this way, our handler will stay skinny, and we'll have another single-purpose function to add to our module.

Let's start with the handler. We define a function head that pattern matches the "save" event and simply logs the result, like this:

```
# pento/lib/pento_web/live/demographic_live/form.ex
def handle_event("save", %{"demographic" => demographic_params}, socket) do
  IO.puts("Handling 'save' event and saving demographic record...")
  IO.inspect(demographic_params)
  {:noreply, socket}
end
```

Now, if we visit /survey, fill out the demographics form, and hit Save, we should see the following log statements:

```
Handling 'save' event and saving demographic record...
%{"gender" => "female", "year_of_birth" => "1989"}
```

Perfect! Thanks to the phx-target={@myself} attribute, our component is receiving the event. But we have one problem: our form params don't include the "user_id", and the Survey.create_demographic function we plan to call in our reducer expects to receive a complete scope and demographic params. We can fix this with a simple helper function to get the ID of the current user from the scope assignment and add it to the params map:

```
stateful_components/pento/lib/pento_web/live/demographic_live/form.ex
defp params_with_user_id(params, socket) do
  user_id = socket.assigns.current_scope.user.id
  Map.put(params, "user_id", user_id)
end
```

We call on this function in the event handler to construct the complete params to pass to our reducer, like this:

```
def handle_event("save", %{"demographic" => demographic_params}, socket) do
  params = params_with_user_id(demographic_params, socket)
  # ...
end
```

Now, we can build our reducer to save the event:

```
stateful_components/pento/lib/pento_web/live/demographic_live/form.ex
defp save_demographic(socket, demographic_params) do
  current_scope = socket.assigns.current_scope
  case Survey.create_demographic(current_scope, demographic_params) do
    {:ok, demographic} ->
      send(self(), {:created_demographic, demographic})
      socket

    {:error, %Ecto.Changeset{} = changeset} ->
      assign_form(socket, changeset)
  end
end
```

Our component is responsible for managing the state of the demographic form and saving the demographic record. We lean on the context function, Survey.create_demographic/1, to do the heavy lifting. We need to handle both the success and error cases, and we do so. We save the implementation of the :ok case for later and simply put the form back in the socket in the event of an :error. That way, the error tags in our form can tell our user exactly what to do to fix the form data.

Now we need to call the reducer in the handler. Key in the handle_event/3 function shown on the next page into your DemographicLive.Form:

```
stateful_components/pento/lib/pento_web/live/demographic_live/form.ex
@impl true
def handle_event("save", %{"demographic" => demographic_params}, socket) do
  params = params_with_user_id(demographic_params, socket)
  socket = save_demographic(socket, params)
  {:noreply, socket}
end
```

We plug in the reducer, and we're off to the races. Our implementation is almost complete. We're left with one final question: What should our reducer do if the save succeeds? We'll look at that problem next.

Send a Message to the Parent

At a high level, when the form saves successfully, we should *stop* rendering the form and instead render the demographic's details. This sounds like a job for the SurveyLive view! After all, SurveyLive is responsible for managing the overall survey state.

If the SurveyLive is going to stop showing the demographic form and instead show the completed demographic details, we'll need some way for the form component to tell SurveyLive that it's time to do so. We need to send a message from the child component to the parent live view.

It turns out that it's easy to do so with plain old Elixir message passing via the send function.

Remember, our component is running in the parent's process, and they share a PID. So we can use the component's own PID to send a message to the parent. Then we can implement a handler in the parent live view that receives that message.

Our live view is a plain old GenServer,[2] so it implements its own behaviour with its own callbacks. handle_info/2[3] is the GenServer callback function for receiving generic Elixir messages. Update save_demographic/2 to send a message to the parent on success:

```
stateful_components/pento/lib/pento_web/live/demographic_live/form.ex
defp save_demographic(socket, demographic_params) do
  current_scope = socket.assigns.current_scope
  case Survey.create_demographic(current_scope, demographic_params) do
    {:ok, demographic} ->
      send(self(), {:created_demographic, demographic})
      socket
```

---

2. https://hexdocs.pm/elixir/1.14/GenServer.html
3. https://hexdocs.pm/elixir/1.14/GenServer.html#c:handle_info/2

```
    {:error, %Ecto.Changeset{} = changeset} ->
      assign_form(socket, changeset)
  end
end
```

Now we'll implement handle_info/2 to teach the SurveyLive view how to respond to our message.

stateful_components/pento/lib/pento_web/live/survey_live.ex
```
@impl true
def handle_info({:created_demographic, demographic}, socket) do
  socket = handle_demographic_created(socket, demographic)
  {:noreply, socket}
end
```

The function head of handle_info/2 matches our message—a tuple with the message name and a payload containing the saved demographic—and receives the socket. As usual, we want skinny handlers, so we call the handle_demographic_created/2 reducer to do the work. Now we need to decide exactly what work to do in the handle_demographic_created/2 function.

We'll want to notify the user that the save was successful and store the new demographic in the socket. Let's implement those new features in handle_demographic_create/2, like this:

stateful_components/pento/lib/pento_web/live/survey_live.ex
```
defp handle_demographic_created(socket, demographic) do
  socket
  |> put_flash(:info, "Demographic created successfully")
  |> assign(:demographic, demographic)
end
```

We pipe our socket through functions to store a flash message and add the :demographic assign key to our socket. The SurveyLive live view will re-render, this time with the :demographic key in socket assigns set to a valid demographic struct. Now when the conditional logic in the SurveyLive template runs, the check for the @demographic assignment will evaluate as true. So we invoke the DemographicLive.Show.details function component to display the demographic details instead of displaying the form.

To display the flash message, we need to add a flash component to our template:

stateful_components/pento/lib/pento_web/live/survey_live.html.heex
```
<Layouts.flash_group flash={@flash} />
```

Let's see it in action. Log in as a user that doesn't yet have an associated demographic record. Then point your browser at /survey and submit the demographic form. You should see the flash message, and you'll also see the form replaced with the demographic details.

Great! With that, we've beautifully composed a set of layered components to support the beginnings of our survey UI. Each piece of the puzzle is simple and sweet—the SurveyLive live view conditionally renders either a child function component to display the demographic details or a child live component to display the interactive form. The SurveyLive view's state runs the show—the presence or absence of a demographic in socket assigns tells the child components how to behave, and each child component has just one job to do. In this way, we can break down even complex view logic into simple components.

Our survey UI has a solid foundation. We're ready to build out the ratings flow.

Build the Ratings Components

We're going to do very much the same thing we did with demographics—let the SurveyLive view orchestrate the state and appearance of the overall survey and devise a set of components to handle the state of the individual product ratings.

We'll have the SurveyLive template implement some logic to display product rating components only if the demographic form is complete and the demographic record exists. If there's an existing demographic, we'll render a ratings index component that will iterate over the products and render the rating details or rating forms accordingly.

Again, here's roughly what a user will see if they've not yet entered demographic data:

Notice we present a form for demographic data but no product ratings.

And this is what a user will see after completing the demographic form:

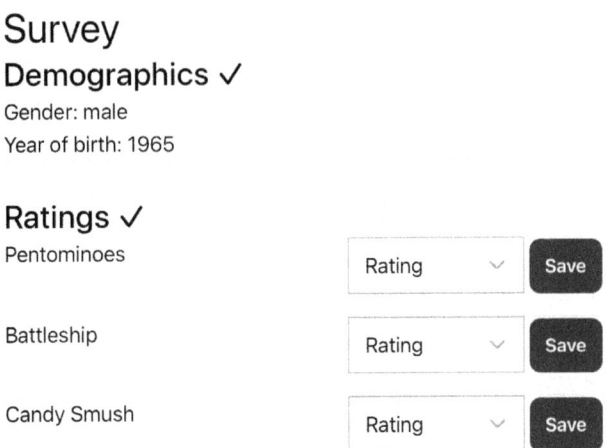

Our code doesn't give the user a chance to enter any product rating data until they've given us demographics. After that, they can rate a product.

That means our live view will have a lot to manage. But by organizing our code with components, we'll avoid needless complexity.

We'll create a Ratings Index function component to hold the whole list of ratings, a Ratings Show function component to show a completed rating, and a Rating form live component to manage the form for a single rating. In this way, we'll maintain a nice separation of concerns. The SurveyLive will manage the state of the overall survey UI, implementing logic that dictates whether to show the ratings index component or the demographic form. The ratings index component will manage the state of product ratings, implementing logic that dictates whether to show rating details or rating forms.

Let's begin with a ratings index component that the SurveyLive template can render.

List Ratings

We'll build a ratings index component that will be responsible for orchestrating the state of *all* of the product ratings in our survey. This component will iterate over the products and determine whether to render the rating details if a rating by the user exists, or the rating form if it doesn't. The responsibility for rendering rating details will be handled by a stateless *rating show* function component and the responsibility for rendering and managing a rating form will be handled by a stateful *rating form* live component.

Meanwhile, SurveyLive will continue to be responsible for managing the overall state and appearance of the survey page. Only if the demographic record exists for the user will the SurveyLive view render the ratings index component, and the ratings index component will receive the list of product ratings to render from the parent live view.

In this way, we keep our code organized and easy to maintain because it's adherent to the single responsibility principle—each component has one job to do. By layering these components within the parent SurveyLive view, we're able to compose a series of small, manageable pieces into one interactive feature—the user survey page.

We'll begin by implementing the RatingsLive.Index function component. Then we'll move on to the rating show component, followed by the rating form component. Let's get started.

Build the Ratings Index Component

The ratings portion of the survey UI will have three parts—an index to make a list of products and check for rating completion, a show to handle product star ratings, and a form to collect new ratings for a given product. Our RatingsLive.Index will be a stateless component that implements the logic to orchestrate these three parts. It can be stateless because it doesn't need to respond to any events from the user. All it needs to do is iterate over the list of products and show a rating or a form accordingly. Let's implement it now.

Create a file, lib/pento_web/live/rating_live/index.ex, and key in the following component definition:

```elixir
defmodule PentoWeb.RatingLive.Index do
  use Phoenix.Component
  alias PentoWeb.RatingLive
end
```

The entry point of module will be the product_list/1 function. This is the function component that we'll call on from the parent live view to render the list of products. The function will take in an assigns argument containing the list of products and the current user. It will return a HEEx template with a heading and product rating details. Our component will be short because we're only handling a few of the critical details now:

```elixir
# stateful_components/pento/lib/pento_web/live/rating_live/index.ex
attr :products, :list, required: true
attr :current_scope, :map, required: true

def product_list(assigns) do
  ~H"""
  <.heading products={@products} current_scope={@current_scope} />
  <div class="divide-y">
    <.product_rating
      :for={{product, index} <- Enum.with_index(@products)}
      product={product}
      index={index}
      current_scope={@current_scope} />
  </div>
  """
end
```

We first express our component API with the help of the attr macro. Our component needs to be called with the current user and the product list. Then we use the heading/1 component (that we'll define in a bit) to show a heading and a check if the ratings are complete. Next, we have an outer div with the Tailwind classes to build a two-column listing. Tailwind will display the divs row by row. Finally, we use the :for directive to loop over the products and render the product_rating/1 component for each one. That component will build two divs, one for the product name and the other for the product rating. Let's build these functions, starting with heading/1:

```
stateful_components/pento/lib/pento_web/live/rating_live/index.ex
attr :products, :list, required: true
attr :current_scope, :map, required: true

def heading(assigns) do
  ~H"""
  <h2 class="flex justify-between">
    Ratings
    <%= if ratings_complete?(@products, @current_scope) do %>
      ✓
    <% end %>
  </h2>
  """
end
```

The heading/1 function satisfies a single purpose. It renders an <h2> element that encapsulates some text along with a helper function that checks to see if *all* of the products have a rating by the current user. If so, we render the Unicode for a checkmark to indicate to the user that all of the ratings forms have been completed. Before we implement this ratings_complete? helper function, we'll cover how we're planning to render the index component with a list of products.

Later, when we render this index component from the SurveyLive template, we'll use the SurveyLive view to query for the list of products with ratings by the current user preloaded. Then we'll pass that list of products down into the index component. So, we can assume that each product in the @products list has its ratings list populated *only* with the rating by the current user. With that in mind, we can implement the ratings_complete?/1 function to iterate over the list of products and return true if there's a rating for every product. Build that function now:

```
stateful_components/pento/lib/pento_web/live/rating_live/index.ex
def ratings_complete?(products, current_scope) do
  Enum.all?(products, fn product ->
    Enum.any?(product.ratings, &(&1.user_id == current_scope.user.id))
  end)
end
```

A rating for a product is complete if the product's list of ratings is not empty. Now, if a user has completed all of the product ratings, they'll see the Ratings header with this nice checkmark next to it, as shown at the top of the next page.

With the heading/1 function component out of the way, let's turn our attention to product_rating/1. That one will use a product with ratings, a current_user, and a product index to build a list, like this:

Demographics

Gender	Year of Birth
female	2025

Ratings

Chess
★ ★ ★ ★ ★

Checkers
★ ★ ★ ☆ ☆

Backgammon
★ ★ ☆ ☆ ☆

```elixir
# lib/pento_web/live/rating_live/index.ex
def product_rating(assigns) do
  ~H"""
    <div><%= @product.name %></div>
    <%= if rating = List.first(@product.ratings) do %>
      <RatingLive.Show.stars rating={rating} />
    <% else %>
      <div>
        <h3><%= @product.name %> rating form coming soon!</h3>
      </div>
    <% end %>
  """
end
```

The template will render the rating details if a rating exists (with the yet-to-be-built Show.stars/1 component) or a form for that rating if not. Notice that we use List.first/1 to get the rating. This is safe here because, as we mentioned earlier, each product in the @products list has its ratings preloaded and filtered to contain only the rating by the current user. So the ratings list will either be empty (no rating yet) or contain exactly one rating (the current user's rating). Nesting components in this manner lets the reader of the code deal with a tiny bit of complexity at a time. We'll dig into this logic more when we're ready to implement these final two components. With the index component out of the way, we're finally ready to weave it into our SurveyLive template.

Render the Component

The next code we'll write shows how the presentation of our view can change based on the contents of the socket. The SurveyLive view will use the state of the overall survey to control what is shown to the user on the page. Specifically, this template will determine what to show based on whether a demographic exists.

In SurveyLive, we query for a demographic and store the results of that query in the socket. If a demographic exists, and the socket assigns a key of :demographic points to something that is truthy, then the template renders the demographic show component along with a call to the RatingLive.Index.product_list/1 function component to add the product ratings to our view. Otherwise, we'll want to render our form for a new demographic.

Let's build out this logic now. First, make sure you've added the PentoWeb.RatingLive alias to lib/pento_web/live/survey_live.ex. Then open up the SurveyLive template and look for the DemographicLive.Show.details/1 function call. Beneath it, add the call to the RatingLive.Index.product_list/1 function, shown here:

stateful_components/pento/lib/pento_web/live/survey_live.html.heex
```
<hr />
<br/>
<RatingLive.Index.product_list
  products={@products}
  current_scope={@current_scope} />
```

Perfect. Now our view renders the component that will present ratings underneath a divider line. Notice that we pass current_scope instead of current_user, following Phoenix 1.8's authentication patterns. To make this work, we need to pass the list of products to the RatingLive.Index.product_list/1 function component so that the component can iterate over them to render a rating (or a form) for each one. In the SurveyLive template, we pass the list, @products, to our component, but we haven't added it to the live view socket yet. Let's fix that now.

Update the mount/3 function of SurveyLive to query for products and their associated rating by the given user and put them in assigns.

stateful_components/pento/lib/pento_web/live/survey_live.ex
```
@impl true
def mount(_params, _session, socket) do
  socket =
    socket
    |> assign_demographic()
    |> assign_products()

  {:ok, socket}
end
```

We're up to our old tricks, building another reducer called assign_products/1 to do the work:

```
stateful_components/pento/lib/pento_web/live/survey_live.ex
defp assign_products(socket) do
  user = socket.assigns.current_scope.user
  products = Catalog.list_products_with_user_rating(user)
  assign(socket, :products, products)
end
```

We use our Catalog context and the assign/2 function to drop the requisite key/value pair into our socket. Notice that we're using the Catalog.list_products_with_user_rating/1 boundary function we defined in the previous chapter, passing current_scope.user to extract the user from Phoenix 1.8's scope structure. This returns a list of products where each product has preloaded only those ratings by the current user.

Now that we're rendering our RatingLive.Index.product_list/1 function component with the product list, let's build the stateless function component that will show the existing rating for a product.

Show a Rating

We're getting closer to the goal of showing ratings, step by step. Remember, we'll show the ratings that exist and forms for ratings otherwise. Let's cover the case for ratings that exist first. We'll define a stateless component to show a rating. Then we'll render that component from within the HEEx template returned by RatingLive.Index.product_rating/1. Let's get started.

Build the Rating Show Component

Create a file, lib/pento_web/live/rating_live/show.ex, and key this in:

```
stateful_components/pento/lib/pento_web/live/rating_live/show.ex
attr :rating, :map, required: true

  def stars(assigns) do
    filled = filled_stars(assigns.rating.stars)
    unfilled = unfilled_stars(assigns.rating.stars)
    all_stars = Enum.concat(filled, unfilled)
    star_display = Enum.join(all_stars, " ")

    assigns = assign(assigns, :star_display, star_display)

    ~H"""
    <div>
      <%= raw(@star_display) %>
    </div>
    """
  end

  def filled_stars(stars) do
    List.duplicate("★", stars)
```

```
end

def unfilled_stars(stars) do
  List.duplicate("☆", 5 - stars)
end
```

We're defining a module that uses the Phoenix.Component behaviour and the Phoenix.HTML behaviour, since we'll once again need support for the Phoenix.HTML.raw/1 function to render the Unicode star character. Tack an end on there and we're ready to move on to the stars/1 function. We'll call this function from within the HEEx template returned by RatingLive.Index.product_rating/1 with an assigns that includes the given product's rating by the current user. The stars/1 function will operate on this rating and use some helper functions to construct a list of filled and unfilled Unicode star characters. We'll construct that list using a simple pipeline and then render it in a HEEx template, like this:

stateful_components/pento/lib/pento_web/live/rating_live/show.ex
```
attr :rating, :map, required: true

  def stars(assigns) do
  filled = filled_stars(assigns.rating.stars)
  unfilled = unfilled_stars(assigns.rating.stars)
  all_stars = Enum.concat(filled, unfilled)
  star_display = Enum.join(all_stars, " ")

  assigns = assign(assigns, :star_display, star_display)

  ~H"""
  <div>
    <%= raw(@star_display) %>
  </div>
  """
end
```

The filled_stars/1 and unfilled_stars/1 helper functions are interesting. Take a look a them here:

stateful_components/pento/lib/pento_web/live/rating_live/show.ex
```
def filled_stars(stars) do
  List.duplicate("★", stars)
end

def unfilled_stars(stars) do
  List.duplicate("☆", 5 - stars)
end
```

Examining our pipeline in the stars/1 function, we can see that we call on filled_stars/1 to produce a list of filled-in, or checked, star Unicode characters corresponding to the number of stars that the product rating has. Then we pipe that into a call to Enum.concat/2 with a second argument of the output from unfilled_stars/1. This second helper function produces a list of empty, or not checked, star characters for the remaining number of stars. For example, if the number of stars in the rating is 3, our pipeline of helper functions will create a list of three checked stars and two unchecked stars. Our pipeline concatenates the two lists together and joins them into a string of HTML that we can render in the template. Make sure to alias the module in rating_live/index.ex like this:

```
alias PentoWeb.RatingLive.Show
```

We have everything we need to display a completed rating, so it's time to roll several components up together.

Render the Component

We're ready to implement the next phase of our plan. The RatingLive.Index.product_list/1 function component iterates over the list of products in the @products assigns and calls on product_rating/1 with each one. In product_rating/1, if a rating is present, we display it. Add in the call to our new Show.stars/1 component now:

```
# lib/pento_web/live/rating_live/index.ex
alias RatingLive.Show
# ...
def product_rating(assigns) do
  ~H"""
  <div><%= @product.name %></div>
  <%= if rating = List.first(@product.ratings) do %>
    <Show.stars rating={rating} />
  <% else %>
    <h3><%= @product.name %> rating form coming soon!</h3>
  <% end %>
  """
end
```

It's a straightforward if statement. If a rating exists, we render the function component by calling on it with the rating assigns. If not, we need to render the form. This is a chance for you to explore. See if you can open up the console and add a product rating by hand using our context functions. Then visit /survey in the browser to see your product rating displayed. When you're ready to move on, we'll build that rating form.

Show the Rating Form

Our rating form will display the form and manage its state, validating and saving the rating. We'll need to pass a product and user for our rating associations and also the product's index in the parent LiveView's socket.assigns.products list. We'll use this index later on to update SurveyLive state efficiently.

Build the Rating Form Component

The live component will need to use update/2 to stash our rating and form struct in the socket. Create a new file, lib/pento_web/live/rating_live/form.ex, and define a component, PentoWeb.RatingLive.Form. Then key in this update function:

stateful_components/pento/lib/pento_web/live/rating_live/form.ex
```elixir
def update(assigns, socket) do
  {:ok,
   socket
   |> assign(assigns)
   |> assign_rating()
   |> assign_form()}
end
```

These reducer functions will add the necessary keys to our socket.assigns. They'll drop in any assigns our parent sends, add a new Rating struct with the user ID properly initialized, and, finally, establish a form for the new rating.

Here's a closer look at our *add rating* and *add changeset* reducers:

stateful_components/pento/lib/pento_web/live/rating_live/form.ex
```elixir
def assign_rating(socket) do
  rating = %Rating{user_id: socket.assigns.current_scope.user.id}
  assign(socket, :rating, rating)
end

def assign_form(socket, changeset \\ nil) do
  form =
    case changeset do
      nil ->
        current_scope = socket.assigns.current_scope
        rating = socket.assigns.rating
        to_form(Survey.change_rating(current_scope, rating))
      changeset -> to_form(changeset)
    end

  assign(socket, :form, form)
end
```

Notice how the assign_rating/1 function initializes the %Rating{} struct with the user_id from current_scope.user.id. This is essential for Phoenix 1.8, as our Survey context's change_rating/3 function validates that the rating belongs to the current user with the validation rating.user_id == scope.user.id. The assign_form/2 function uses Survey.change_rating/3, which requires both the scope and the rating as parameters, following Phoenix 1.8's authentication patterns.

Before we render, we need to make a few tweaks to our core components.

Prepare to Render

With our socket established, we're ready to render. For the rating input, we'll use the existing select input type with custom options that display star characters. This approach leverages Phoenix's built-in form components while providing an intuitive star-based interface.

Let's look at the rating form that will use this input next. As usual, we'll choose a template to keep our markup code neatly compartmentalized. Create the file lib/pento_web/live/rating_live/form.html.heex and add the product rating form shown here:

```
stateful_components/pento/lib/pento_web/live/rating_live/form.html.heex
<div>
  <.form
    for={@form}
    phx-submit="save"
    phx-target={@myself}
    id={"rating-form-#{@id}"}>
    <div class="flex items-center gap-2">
      <.input
        field={@form[:stars]}
        type="select"
        prompt={RatingLive.Show.unfilled_stars(0) |> Enum.join()}
        options={[
          "★★★★★": 5,
          "★★★★": 4,
          "★★★": 3,
          "★★": 2,
          "★": 1
        ]}
      />
      <.button type="submit">Save</.button>
    </div>
    <input
      type="hidden"
      name={@form[:user_id].name}
      value={@form[:user_id].value} />
    <input type="hidden"
      name={@form[:product_id].name}
      value={@form[:product_id].value} />
  </.form>
</div>
```

We bind one event to the form, a phx-submit to send a "save" event. We target our form component to receive events by setting phx-target to @myself, and we tack on an id. Note that we've set a dynamic HTML ID of the live component ID, stored in socket assigns as @id. This is because the product rating form will appear multiple times on the page, once for each product, and we need to ensure that each form gets a unique ID. You'll see how we set the id assigns for the component when we render it.

Our form has a stars field that uses a select drop-down with star-based options. Each option displays the appropriate number of star characters (★) corresponding to the rating value: "★" for 1, "★★" for 2, and so on up to "★★★★★" for 5. The form uses the RatingLive.Show.unfilled_stars(0) function to generate five empty stars as the prompt, demonstrating code reuse between the display and form components. Users select their rating by choosing the visual representation that matches their desired star count along with hidden fields for the user and product relationships.

We'll come back to the events later. For now, let's fold our work into the RatingLive.Index.product_rating/1 function component.

Render the Component

The RatingLive.Index.product_rating/1 function component should render the rating form component if no rating for the given product and user exists. Let's do that now.

```
stateful_components/pento/lib/pento_web/live/rating_live/index.ex
attr :product, :map, required: true
attr :index, :integer, required: true
attr :current_scope, :map, required: true

def product_rating(assigns) do
  ~H"""
  <div class="py-0">
    <div><%= @product.name %></div>
    <%= if rating = List.first(@product.ratings) do %>
      <RatingLive.Show.stars rating={rating} />
    <% else %>
      <.live_component
        module={RatingLive.Form}
        id={"rating-form-#{@product.id}"}
        product={@product}
        index={@index}
        current_scope={@current_scope} />
    <% end %>
  </div>
  """
end
```

Here, we call on the component with the live_component/1 function, passing the user and product into the component as assigns, along with the product's index in the @products assignment. We add an :id, so our rating form is a live component. Since we'll only have one rating per component, our id with an embedded product.id should be unique.

It's been a while since we've looked at things in the browser, but now, if you point your browser at /survey, you should see something like this:

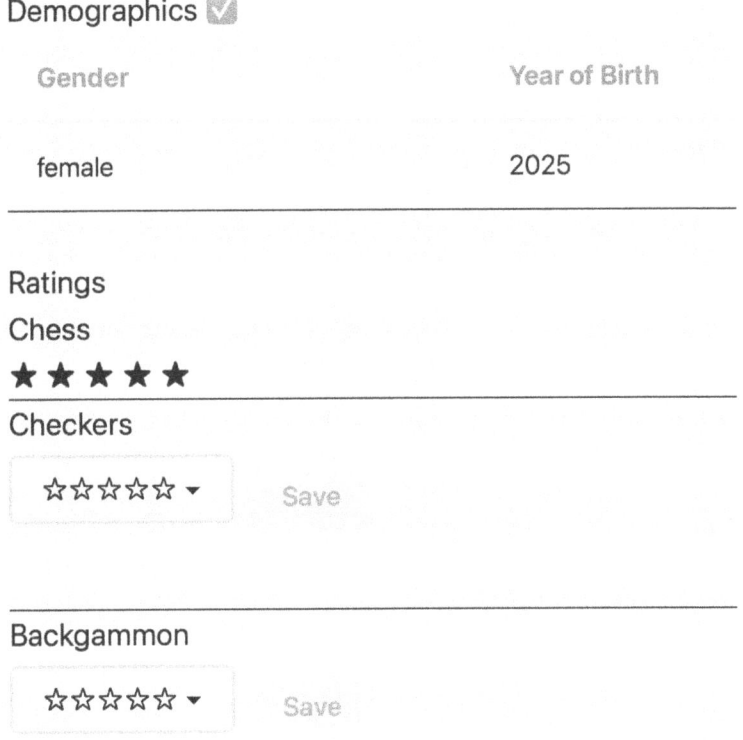

Handle Component Events

You know the drill by now. We've bound an event to save our form, so we should teach our component how to handle that event. We need a handle_event/2 function head for the "save" event. Add it in like this:

stateful_components/pento/lib/pento_web/live/rating_live/form.ex
```elixir
def handle_event("save", %{"rating" => rating_params}, socket) do
  save_rating(socket, rating_params)
end
```

And here's the reducer:

```
stateful_components/pento/lib/pento_web/live/rating_live/form.ex
def save_rating(socket, rating_params) do
  case Survey.create_rating(
         socket.assigns.current_scope,
         rating_params
         |> Map.put("product_id", socket.assigns.product.id)
       ) do
    {:ok, rating} ->
      product = %{socket.assigns.product | ratings: [rating]}
      send(self(), {:created_rating, product, socket.assigns.index})
      {:noreply, socket}

    {:error, changeset} ->
      {:noreply, assign_form(socket, changeset)}
  end
end
```

Just as we did in the demographic form component, we attempted to save the form. On failure, we assign a new form with the returned changeset. This will re-render the template, and the simple_form function component will display the @form's errors, derived from that changeset. On success, we send a message to the parent live view to do the heavy lifting for us.

Notice how we only need to pass the product_id from socket assigns to the rating parameters since the improved Rating.changeset/3 function now properly casts both :stars and :product_id fields while automatically setting the :user_id from the scope. This provides cleaner separation of concerns between the form component and the changeset validation logic. Then, as all handlers must do, we return the {:noreply, socket} tuple.

Update the Rating Index

Here's what should happen when the rating is saved. The RatingLive.Index.product_rating/1 function should no longer render the form for that product. Instead, the survey should display the saved rating. This kind of state change is squarely the responsibility of the SurveyLive. Our message will serve to notify the parent live view to change.

Here's the interesting bit. All the parent needs to do is update the socket. The RatingLive.Index.product_rating/1 function already renders the right thing based on the contents of the assigns that it receives from the parent, SurveyLive. All we need to do is implement a handler to deal with the created rating message.

```
stateful_components/pento/lib/pento_web/live/survey_live.ex
def handle_info({:created_rating, product, product_index}, socket) do
  socket = handle_rating_created(socket, product, product_index)
```

```
  {:noreply, socket}
end
```

We use a handle_info, just as we did before with the demographic. Now our reducer can take the appropriate action. Notice that the message we match has a message name, an updated product, *and* its index in the :products list. We can use that information to update the product list without going back to the database. We'll implement the following reducer to do this work:

stateful_components/pento/lib/pento_web/live/survey_live.ex
```
defp handle_rating_created(socket, product, product_index) do
  current_products = socket.assigns.products
  products = List.replace_at(current_products, product_index, product)

  socket
  |> put_flash(:info, "Rating created successfully")
  |> assign(:products, products)
end
```

The handle_rating_created/3 reducer adds a flash message and updates the product in place in the product list using List.replace_at/3 for efficient list updating. This causes the template to re-render, passing this updated product list to RatingLive.Index.product_list/1. That function component in turn renders RatingLive.Index.product_rating/1, which knows what to do with a product that does contain a rating by the given user—it will render that rating's details instead of a rating form.

Notice the lovely layering. In the parent live view layer, all we need to do is manage the list of products and ratings. All of the form handling and rating or demographic details go elsewhere.

The end result of a submitted rating is an updated product list and a flash message. Submit a rating; the screenshot at the top of the next page shows what happens.

This code layering system has a tremendous amount of power. Live components are complex because they have to be. Still, the LiveView structure lets us deal with only a small bit of complexity at a time. That's the power of live components.

Your Turn

Though every component renders some state represented by assigns, only live components can *modify* that state. In this chapter, you built your first live component and you layered live and function components into an elegant and easy-to-maintain UI.

[Screenshot of the survey form showing Demographics section with Gender "female" and Year of Birth "2025", a Ratings section with Chess rated 5 stars, and Checkers and Backgammon with unrated stars and Save buttons. A "Rating created successfully" flash message appears at the top.]

With our set of function and live components, we've built out a fully interactive survey feature in a way that is sane, organized, and easy to maintain. By breaking out the specific responsibilities of the survey page into discrete components, we keep our code adherent to the single responsibility principle. LiveView then allows us to layer those components, composing them into one single-page flow orchestrated by the parent live view, `SurveyLive`. In this way, LiveView let's us build complex interactive features quickly and easily.

Now that you have a fully functioning set of components, it's your chance to put what you've learned into practice.

Give It a Try

These problems will let you extend what we've already done.

- Save a rating on `phx-change` rather than `phx-submit`. What are the pros and cons to this approach?
- Show validation errors when the user selects no rating.
- Live components are often tied to back-end database services—our `DemographicLive.Form` is backed by the `Survey` context, which wraps interactions with the `Demographic` schema. Add a field to the `Demographic` schema and corresponding database table to track the education level of a user,

allowing them to choose from High School, Bachelor's Degree, Graduate Degree, Other, or Prefer Not to Say. Then update your LiveView code to support this field in the demographic form.

- Build a component that toggles a button showing either + expand or - contract and then marks a corresponding div as hidden or visible. Under what circumstances would you use a CSS style with display: none versus rendering/removing the whole div? Hint: think about how many bytes LiveView would need to move and when it would move them.

- Bonus: Consider the downside of implementing a common JS interaction—like showing and hiding an element—with a live component. With a live component, you're making a round-trip to the server to do something you could easily do purely on the client-side. Check out the docs on LiveView's JS Commands[4] and use them to refactor your live component into a stateless one. Use JS Commands to implement the show/hide functionality without round-tripping to the server.

Next Time

Now we have a set of components for collecting survey data, but nowhere to aggregate that data. In the next chapter, we'll review many of the techniques you've seen in the first part of this book as we build an admin dashboard that allows us to view survey results and more. Since this dashboard is built with LiveView, it will be more interactive than typical dashboards. Along the way, you'll get even more experience building live components to handle complex user interactions.

---

4. https://hexdocs.pm/phoenix_live_view/Phoenix.LiveView.JS.html#module-client-utility-commands

Part III

Extend LiveView

In Part III, we'll build another custom LiveView feature that we'll extend with Phoenix PubSub-backed capabilities to support real-time interactions. We'll use LiveView communication mechanisms, along with PubSub, to build an admin dashboard that reflects the state of not only the page but also the application at large. We'll wrap up with a look at LiveView testing to ensure that our admin dashboard is well tested.

CHAPTER 8

Build an Interactive Dashboard

In the previous part, we completed a survey tool our company will use to collect data from our customers. In the next two chapters, we're going to build an interactive dashboard that tracks real-time data, including survey data, as it flows into our system. This chapter will focus on building the dashboard, and the next will integrate real-time data feeds into that dashboard. Interactive views presenting data synchronized in real time is a perfect LiveView use case—you'll see how you can extend a custom live view with the help of Phoenix PubSub to support such synchronization.

Many dashboards fall into one of two traps. Some are afterthoughts, seemingly slapped together at the last moment. These views are often casualties of a time crunch. Others have lots of interactive bells and whistles, but they lack the impact they might otherwise have because the dashboard shows content that lags behind the needs of the organization. LiveView can help solve both of these common problems by making it easy to quickly put together components that snap seamlessly into LiveView's overall architecture.

In this chapter, you'll discover how easy it can be to build a dashboard that does what your users need but also fits into the quick development-cycle times most organizations require. When you're done, you'll have more experience writing core and boundary functions in Phoenix and more experience composing live views with components. You'll also be able to use libraries that leverage SVG to render graphics and wrap them into APIs that are easy to consume.

Let's make a plan.

The Plan

Our interactive dashboard will show the health of our products with a glance. It will have several different elements on the page. A survey component will display survey results for each product and its average star rating. In the next chapter, we'll add a real-time list of users, and we'll supercharge our survey results chart by enabling it to update in real time as new results come in.

Here's a rough mock-up of what our users say they want:

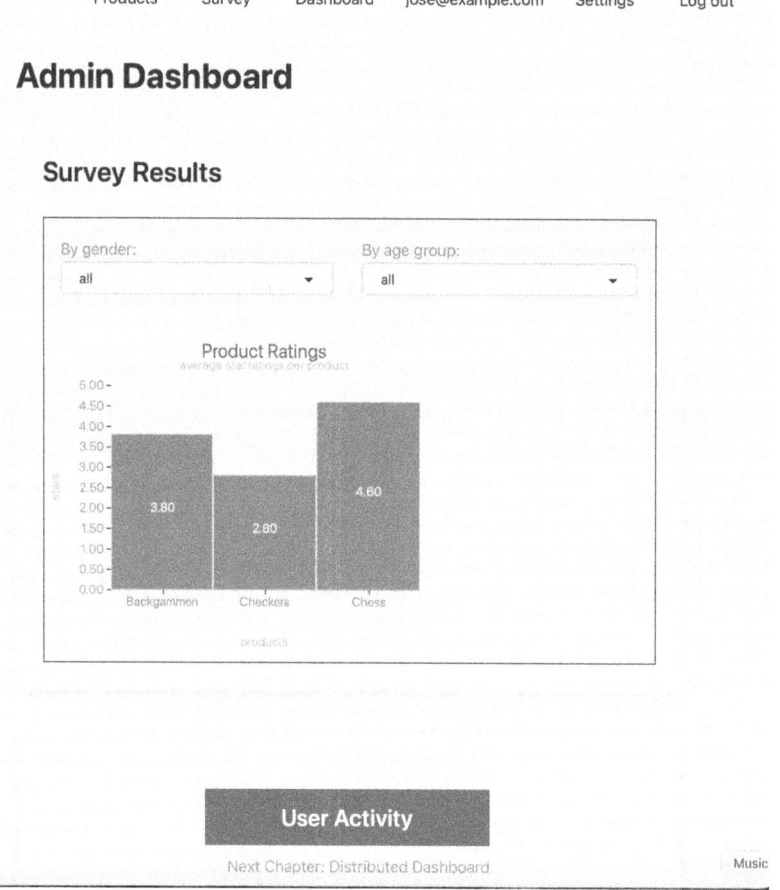

In this chapter, we'll focus on building the interactive survey results chart portion of our dashboard. Tracking customer satisfaction is critical for a game company's marketing, so the survey results chart will show the average survey star rating for each product. To assist our marketing efforts, we'll let our users visualize star ratings across demographic groups.

The dashboard will be its own live view. We'll delegate the responsibilities of presenting survey data to a component.

We'll start by leveraging the CRC pattern to define a core module that composes the queries we need and a context in which to execute them.

Then we'll wrap that much in a live view with a survey results component and use an SVG graphics charting library to display data on the page.

Finally, we'll make our chart interactive by providing a simple form that lets the user filter survey data by demographics.

To wrap up, we'll use the common _using_ macro to make our chart helper functions easier to use.

We'll need three things to kick things off. We'll define the view in the Admin.DashboardLive live view. Then we'll wire that view to a live route. Finally, we'll delegate the survey data on the page to a live component called Admin.SurveyResultsLive.

Let's start things off with the live view.

Define the Admin.DashboardLive Live View

The dashboard we're building will represent each major section of the page as a *component*. That means the socket of the live view itself will be pretty empty—instead, the socket of each component will hold the data that the component is responsible for rendering.

Create a new file, pento_web/live/admin/dashboard_live.ex, and key in the live view definition with this mount/3 function:

```
defmodule PentoWeb.Admin.DashboardLive do
  use PentoWeb, :live_view

  def mount(_params, _session, socket) do
    {:ok,
      socket
      |> assign(:survey_results_component_id, "survey-results")}
  end
end
```

Our live view is simple so far—it only holds a very small piece of data in socket assigns, the :survey_results_component_id (more on how we'll use that later on).

Now, let's add this code to connect our route in router.ex:

interactive_dashboard/pento/lib/pento_web/router.ex
```
live "/admin/dashboard", Admin.DashboardLive
```

This route is for browser users who are logged in, so make sure to place this route in the "/" scope with the pipe_through that specifies both the browser and require_authenticated_user pipelines. We'll get all of the benefits of the browser pipeline in router.ex and the require_authenticated_user plug we created in Chapter 2, Phoenix and Authentication, on page 31. We also ensure that our live view is authenticated whenever it's live redirected to, thanks to the live_session's on_mount callback. We should add the new feature to our menu:

interactive_dashboard/pento/lib/pento_web/components/layouts/root.html.heex
```
<li>
  <.link href={~p"/admin/dashboard"}>Dashboard</.link>
</li>
```

Let's take a step back and think about our authorization needs here. We've placed our route behind authentication so that only a logged-in user can visit it either directly in the browser or through a live redirect. But we want this page to be accessible *only* to admins. If you think about it, our Products routes should be available only to admins as well. Our app doesn't currently have a concept of admin users—we won't build that out together but will leave it as an exercise for you. But you can imagine that if our app *did* store awareness of which users are admins, then we might want to do the following:

- Create a new plug that authorizes admin users and redirects if the user is not an admin.

- Create a new live_session block with a *different* on_mount callback that authorizes admin users and redirects if the user is not an admin. You might even implement another version of UserAuth.on_mount/4 that pattern matches on a first argument of :admin to achieve this.

You have all of the tools you need to solve that issue without our help. For now, we can start with just enough of a template to test out our new view. Create the file live/admin/dashboard_live.html.heex and add a simple header, like this:

```
<section class="row">
  <h1 class="font-heavy text-3xl">Admin Dashboard</h1>
</section>
```

Not much is in there for now, but we do have a header to show whether the code is working or not. Now, you can start your server and point your browser to /admin/dashboard to see the sparse, but working, view:

Products   Survey   Dashboard   jose@example.com   Settings   Log out

Admin Dashboard

One of the nice things about LiveView is that you can often stand up a new page in a few minutes and then build many quick iterations from there. Now we're ready to build the Admin.SurveyResultsLive component.

Represent Dashboard Concepts with Components

We'll model each portion of our dashboard with its very own component. Let's kick things off with the Admin.SurveyResultsLive component, which will be responsible for the survey results chart that displays interactive product ratings.

Create a Component Module

We'll start by implementing a basic live component and template that don't do much. Since the component will eventually need to handle events so the user can filter by demographic data, we know we need a live component rather than a functional one. So we'll implement the component module with the :live_component behaviour and render it with an ID of :survey_results_component_id from the parent socket assigns (again, more on why the parent live view needs awareness of this ID later on). We'll render it from Admin.DashboardLive to make sure everything's working.

Create a file, lib/pento_web/live/admin/survey_results_live.ex, and add in the initial component definition:

```
defmodule PentoWeb.Admin.SurveyResultsLive do
  use PentoWeb, :live_component
end
```

We don't define a render/1, so we need a template. Let's do that next.

Build the Component Template

Start by building a section with a heading. Key this into live/admin/survey_results_live.html.heex:

```
<section class="ml-8">
  <h2 class="font-light text-2xl">Survey Results</h2>
</section>
```

It's just a section and a header with a few Tailwind styles, but that's enough for now. In the spirit of getting small wins and iterating quickly, let's stand that much up. We need to render our live component with the live_component/1 function and the :id we specified in Admin.DashboardLive.mount/3 earlier. Render the component from the admin_dashboard_live.heex template, as shown here:

```
interactive_dashboard/pento/lib/pento_web/live/admin/dashboard_live.html.heex
<div class="container mx-auto p-6">
  <h1 class="text-3xl font-bold mb-6">Admin Dashboard</h1>
  <.live_component
        module={PentoWeb.Admin.SurveyResultsLive}
        id={@survey_results_component_id} />
</div>
```

Perfect. We supply the component's module and the id from socket.assigns. Point your browser at /admin/dashboard:

Products   Survey   Dashboard   jose@example.com

Admin Dashboard

Survey Results

Excellent. Now that everything is wired up and running, we're ready to build the survey results bar chart.

Fetch Survey Results Data

To go much further, we're going to need data, so we'll switch gears from the view and focus on the back-end service. To render products and their average star ratings in a chart, the live view must be able to query for this data in the form of a list of product names and their associated average star ratings.

This will be a good time to practice good Phoenix design. You'll add a new function to the Catalog context to make requests to the database. Your context function will rely on new query functions in the core to extract exactly the data it needs. Separating these concerns will keep the codebase organized and beautiful.

Shape the Data With Ecto

The format of the data is somewhat dictated by the manner in which we'll need to feed it into our chart. We'll provide the exact details later. For now, its enough to understand that we need to fetch a list of products and average ratings as a list of tuples, as in this example:

```
[
  {"Tic-Tac-Toe", 3.4285714285714284},
  {"Table Tennis", 2.5714285714285716},
  {"Chess", 2.625}
]
```

With any luck, Ecto can return data in exactly the shape we need, but first we need to decide where the queries should go. If we make sure to validate any data before it ever reaches the query layer, the process of building a query shouldn't ever fail unless there's a bug in our code—in other words, the process is certain and predictable, exactly the kind of job that belongs in the core. So we'll create a query builder module, Pento.Catalog.Product.Query, in our application's core.

We'll need a query to fetch products with average ratings, so we'll build a few reducers in the Pento.Catalog.Product.Query module to shape a query that does just that. We'll use Ecto where clauses to select the right demographic, a join clause to pluck out the ratings for relevant users, a group_by clause to provide the average statistic, and a select clause to pluck out the tuples that match the required shape. First, we alias the modules we'll use in the query:

interactive_dashboard/pento/lib/pento/catalog/product/query.ex
```
import Ecto.Query
alias Pento.Catalog.Product
alias Pento.Survey.{Rating, Demographic}
alias Pento.Accounts.User

def base, do: Product
```

We also add the base/0 function that returns the Product module reference.

Good enough. Now we'll start to do the work. Our grand plans are a bit much to add to one giant function, but we know how to break the code down into single-purpose reducers. Take a look at the following functions:

interactive_dashboard/pento/lib/pento/catalog/product/query.ex
```
def with_average_ratings(query \\ base()) do
  query
  |> join_ratings
  |> average_ratings
end

defp join_ratings(query) do
  query
  |> join(:inner, [p], r in Rating, on: r.product_id == p.id)
end

defp average_ratings(query) do
  query
  |> group_by([p], p.id)
```

```
    |> select([p, r], {p.name, fragment("?::float", avg(r.stars))})
    |> order_by([p, r], [{:asc, p.name}])
end
```

As usual, our module starts with a constructor, base/0, and pipes that query through a set of two reducers—one that joins products on ratings and another that selects the product name and the average of its ratings' stars.

Let's see our query in action now.

Test Drive the Query

Make sure you alias `Pento.Survey.Rating` at the top of the `Catalog.Product.Query` module. Then open up IEx and execute the query as follows:

```
iex> alias Pento.Catalog.Product
Pento.Catalog.Product
iex> alias Pento.Repo
Pento.Repo
iex> Product.Query.with_average_ratings() |> Repo.all()
...
[
  {"Chess", 5.0}
  {"Table Tennis", 2.0},
  {"Tic-Tac-Toe", 1.0},
]
```

Excellent. That's the exact format that the graphics library needs, so we don't need to do any further processing. Now it's time to leave the calm, predictable world of the core for the chaotic, failure-prone world of the boundary.

Extend the Catalog Context

Where the core is calm and predictable, the boundary, or the context, is more complex because it might fail. The code in the boundary isn't *always* more complex, but it does have responsibilities that the core doesn't. The context must validate any data from external sources, usually with changesets. If a function might return an `{:ok, result}` or an `{:error, reason}` tuple, it falls on the context to do something about that failure.

Luckily, our context function doesn't have validation or error conditions to worry about, so our context function will be blissfully short and simple. Still, the new API should go in the context as a reminder that any data must be validated and errors must be handled appropriately. Define a context function in the `Catalog` module to execute the new query:

```
interactive_dashboard/pento/lib/pento/catalog.ex
def products_with_average_ratings do
  Product.Query.with_average_ratings()
  |> Repo.all()
end
```

We feed the query into Repo.all/1, and we're off to the races.

Your Turn: Verify the API in IEx

It's important to verify results as you go. Try out the new context API in IEx. Come back when you're ready to integrate the results into our live view.

Initialize the Admin.SurveyResultsLive Component State

Now our application's core contains all of the functions we need to fetch bar-chart data in our live view. In this section, we'll teach the Admin.SurveyResultsLive component to fetch this data, put it in state, and render it. Let's get going.

Add Survey Results to the Component Socket

We could add the survey result data to the parent live view's mount/1 callback, but there's a better way. The component responsible for the given portion of the dashboard should hold, render, and manage the state for that portion of the dashboard. This keeps our code clean and organized.

The component's update/2 callback will fire each time Admin.DashboardLive renders our component, so this is where we'll add survey results data to component state. Since we're going to have to add survey results each time someone interacts with our view, we'll build a reusable reducer that does the work for us. Add the following update/2 function to survey_results_live.ex:

```elixir
defmodule PentoWeb.Admin.SurveyResultsLive do
  use PentoWeb, :live_component
  alias Pento.Catalog

  def update(assigns, socket) do
    {:ok,
     socket
     |> assign(assigns)
     |> assign_products_with_average_ratings()}
  end
end
```

Our little pipeline calls two reducers, assign/2 and assign_products_with_average_ratings/1. Remember, reducers transform accumulators, and in a live view, the accumulator is the socket. That means the return value of assign/2 is a socket, and we use it to add all of the assigns keys and values that came from the live_component/1 function.

Use Custom Reducers to Initialize State

Next, we need to write that second reducer to drop our survey results into the socket. Implement this assign_products_with_average_ratings/1 function:

```
# lib/pento_web/live/admin/survey_results_live.ex
def assign_products_with_average_ratings(socket) do
  socket
  |> assign(
    :products_with_average_ratings,
    Catalog.products_with_average_ratings())
end
```

The assign_products_with_average_ratings/1 reducer function is implemented to call on our Catalog.products_with_average_ratings/0 function and add the query results to socket assigns under the :products_with_average_ratings key.

Notice how we could have dropped this code right into update/2, and it would have worked. Keep an eye out for the code that will eventually support user interactions. We can reuse this reducer function later when we build the code flow that fires when a user filters the survey data by demographic. Take this small piece of advice: use reducers over raw socket interactions in live views to maintain both your code organization and your sanity!

Your Turn: Render Intermediate Results

If you'd like, add a tiny bit of code to your template to render a list of products. Take the data from the @products_with_average_ratings assignment. Once you've verified that your code works, come back and we'll render it as a bar chart.

Render SVG Charts with Contex

Most of the time, web developers reach for JavaScript to build beautiful graphs and charts. Because our server always has an up-to-date view of the data and a convenient way to send down changes, we don't have to settle for a cumbersome workflow that splits our focus across the client-server boundary. We can render *graphics* the same way we render HTML, with server-side rendering. That means we need a dependency that can draw our charts on the server and send that chart HTML down to the client.

We'll use the Contex charting library[1] to handle our server-side SVG chart rendering. Using Contex, we'll build out charts in two steps. We'll initialize the chart's dataset first and then render the SVG chart with that dataset. We'll continue building out the elegant reducer pipeline that our component uses to establish state—adding new functions in the pipeline for each step in our chart building and rendering process. You'll see how the reducer pattern can help us build out and maintain even complex state in an organized way. Add the contex dependency to mix.exs:

```
defp deps do
  [
    ... ,
    {:contex, "~> 0.4.0"}
  ]
end
```

Now fetch the dependency with mix deps.get:

```
[pento] → mix deps.get
Resolving Hex dependencies...
...
New:
  contex 0.4.0
  nimble_strftime 0.1.1
* Getting contex (Hex package)
* Getting nimble_strftime (Hex package)
...
```

We're ready to start the server again. Let's initialize the dataset for our chart now.

Initialize the Dataset

As with many Elixir libraries, Contex works well with CRC. The accumulator is a struct called a dataset. Contex provides us with the Dataset[2] module to produce structs describing the state of the chart, with reducer functions to manipulate that data, and converter functions to convert the data to different kinds of charts. That flow should sound familiar.

You can specify your chart data as a list of maps, list of lists, or a list of tuples. Recall that we ensured that our query for products with average ratings returns a list of tuples—now you know why.

---

1. https://github.com/mindok/contex
2. https://hexdocs.pm/contex/Contex.Dataset.html

We'll begin by adding a new reducer function to the pipeline in update/2 to add a Dataset to our socket.assigns. We'll build the Dataset with the survey results already in our socket.assigns.

Define a reducer, assign_dataset/1, that adds a new dataset to socket assigns in survey_results_live.ex:

```elixir
defmodule PentoWeb.Admin.SurveyResultsLive do
  use PentoWeb, :live_component
  alias Pento.Catalog

  # ...

  def assign_dataset(
        %{assigns: %{
          products_with_average_ratings: products_with_average_ratings}
        } = socket) do
    socket
    |> assign(
      :dataset,
      make_bar_chart_dataset(products_with_average_ratings)
    )
  end

  defp make_bar_chart_dataset(data) do
    Contex.Dataset.new(data)
  end
end
```

Then invoke it in the reducer pipeline that we're building out in the update/2 function:

```elixir
defmodule PentoWeb.Admin.SurveyResultsLive do
  use PentoWeb, :live_component
  alias Pento.Catalog

  def update(assigns, socket) do
    {:ok,
     socket
     |> assign(assigns)
     |> assign_products_with_average_ratings()
     |> assign_dataset()}
  end

  # ...
```

Once again, we create simple reducers to assign data, and Elixir rewards us with the beautiful pipeline in update/2.

If you were to inspect the return of the call to Contex.Dataset.new/1, you'd see the following struct:

```
%Contex.Dataset{
  data: [
    {"Tic-Tac-Toe", 3.4285714285714284},
    {"Table Tennis", 2.5714285714285716},
    {"Chess", 2.625}
  ],
  headers: nil,
  title: nil
}
```

The first element in a Dataset is :data, pointing to the data we'd like to render in the chart.

Initialize the BarChart

We'll wrap up the code to initialize a bar chart and add it to socket state with a nice reducer function. Define a function, assign_chart/1, as shown here:

```
defmodule PentoWeb.Admin.SurveyResultsLive do
  use PentoWeb, :live_component
  alias Pento.Catalog

  # ...

  defp assign_chart(%{assigns: %{dataset: dataset}} = socket) do
    socket
    |> assign(:chart, make_bar_chart(dataset))
  end
end
```

Now we can make a reducer to initialize a BarChart with the dataset from socket assigns:

```
defp make_bar_chart(dataset) do
  Contex.BarChart.new(dataset)
end
```

Then call assign_chart/1 from the reducer pipeline we're building out in our update/2 function:

```
defmodule PentoWeb.Admin.SurveyResultsLive do
  use PentoWeb, :live_component
  alias Pento.Catalog

  def update(assigns, socket) do
    {:ok,
      socket
      |> assign(assigns)
      |> assign_products_with_average_ratings()
      |> assign_dataset()
      |> assign_chart()}
  end
```

The call to BarChart.new/1 creates a BarChart struct that describes how to plot the bar chart. The BarChart module provides a number of configurable options with defaults.[3] You can use these options to set the orientation, the colors, the padding, and more.

The BarChart.new/1 constructor will produce a map. The column_map key will have a mapping for each bar, as you can see here:

column_map: %{category_col: 0, value_cols: [1]}

The column_map tells the bar chart how to chart the data from the dataset. The first key, the category_col, has an index of 0 and serves as the *label* of our bar chart. This means it will use the element at the 0 index of each tuple in the dataset to inform the bar chart's column name. The chart has only one column in the list of value_cols, our product rating average at index 1 of the dataset tuples. A value_col specifies the *height* of a bar.

Believe it or not, now Contex has all it needs to render an SVG chart. Let's do it.

Transform the Chart to SVG

The final step of showing our survey data is to render SVG markup on the server. We'll do this step with the Contex.Plot module. You'll notice that the Plot module is a converter that takes the intermediate accumulator and converts it to an SVG chart, the same way our render/1 function translates a live view to HTML.

We add a reducer to our update/2 pipeline to build the SVG that we'll later access as we render the chart in the template, like this:

```
defmodule PentoWeb.Admin.SurveyResultsLive do
  use PentoWeb, :live_component
  alias Pento.Catalog
  alias Contex.Plot

  def update(assigns, socket) do
    {:ok,
     socket
     |> assign(assigns)
     |> assign_products_with_average_ratings()
     |> assign_dataset()
     |> assign_chart()
     |> assign_chart_svg()}
  end
  ...
end
```

---

3. https://hexdocs.pm/contex/Contex.BarChart.html#summary

```elixir
def assign_chart_svg(%{assigns: %{chart: chart}} = socket) do
  socket
  |> assign(:chart_svg, render_bar_chart(chart))
end

defp render_bar_chart(chart) do
  Plot.new(500, 400, chart)
end
```

We have no surprises here. We merely tack another reducer onto the chain. This one renders the bar chart and assigns the result to the socket. We customize our plot with some titles and labels for the x- and y-axis—add to the render_bar_chart/1 function, like this:

```elixir
# lib/pento_web/live/admin/survey_results_live.ex
defp render_bar_chart(chart) do
  Plot.new(500, 400, chart)
  |> Plot.titles(title(), subtitle())
  |> Plot.axis_labels(x_axis(), y_axis())
end

defp title do
  "Product Ratings"
end

defp subtitle do
  "average star ratings per product"
end

defp x_axis do
  "products"
end

defp y_axis do
  "stars"
end
```

We create tiny single-purpose functions to do the work of building out the rest of the chart. This code will (you guessed it) apply the title, subtitles, and axis labels to our chart. Now we're ready to transform our plot into an SVG with the help of the Plot module's to_svg/1 function:

```elixir
# lib/pento_web/live/admin/survey_results_live.ex
def render_bar_chart(chart) do
  Plot.new(500, 400, chart)
  |> Plot.titles(title(), subtitle())
  |> Plot.axis_labels(x_axis(), y_axis())
  |> Plot.to_svg()
end
```

The code in render_bar_chart/1 is a converter, and the implementation is yet another beautiful example of the CRC pattern. We take a new plot and call a couple of reducers to tack on the title and subtitles. Then we pipe the result to the Plot.to_svg/1 converter.

We're finally ready to render this chart SVG in our template.

Render the Chart in the Template

We've implemented the update/2 constructor to establish the data in the socket. The next step is to add a bit of code to our template to render our chart SVG.

Our SurveyRatingsLive template is still pretty simple. It merely needs to call the functions we've already built. Add it at the bottom of the page, just before the close-section tag:

interactive_dashboard/pento/lib/pento_web/live/admin/survey_results_live.html.heex
```
<div id="survey-results-chart" class="w-full overflow-x-auto">
  <%= @chart_svg %>
</div>
```

That's pretty thin, exactly as we like it. The template delegates the heavy Elixir to the helpers we've written. Our template renders the SVG stored in the @chart_svg assignment and wraps that much in a div.

We need to take care of one more thing before we can see our beautiful chart in the browser. We've prepared some lightweight CSS styles for you to include in your app to show off your chart to best effect. Open assets/app.css and paste in the following beneath the comment:

```css
/* This file is for your main application CSS */
.survey-component-container {
    background-color: #fefefe;
    padding: 20px;
    border: 1px solid #888;
    width: 80%;
    margin-bottom: 20px;
}

.survey-component-container label{
    padding: 10px;
}

.survey-component-container input {
    margin-right: 10px;
}

.survey-component-container select {
    margin-right: 10px;
}

.survey-component-container h4 {
    font-weight: bold;
```

```css
}
.fa.fa-star.checked {
  color: orange;
}
.fa.fa-star {
  padding: 3px;
}
.survey-component-container ul li{
  list-style: none;
}
.fa.fa-check.survey {
  color: green;
}
.exc-tick {
  stroke: grey;
}
.exc-tick text {
  fill: grey;
  stroke: none;
  font-size: 1.0rem;
}
.exc-grid {
  stroke: lightgrey;
}
.exc-legend {
  stroke: black;
}
.exc-legend text {
  fill: grey;
  font-size: 1.5rem;
  stroke: none;
}
.exc-title {
  fill: darkslategray;
  font-size: 1.5rem;
  stroke: none;
  padding-bottom: 10px;
}
.exc-subtitle {
  fill: darkgrey;
  font-size: 1rem;
  stroke: none;
}
.exc-domain {
  stroke:  rgb(207, 207, 207);
```

```css
    }
    .exc-barlabel-in {
      fill: white;
      font-size: 1.0rem;
    }
    .exc-barlabel-out {
      fill: grey;
      font-size: 0.7rem;
    }
    .float-container {
      padding: 20px;
    }
    .float-child {
      width: 33%;
      float: left;
      padding: 20px;
    }
    #survey-results-component {
      border: 1px solid;
    }
    #survey-results-chart {
      padding-right: 200px;
    }
    .survey-results-filters {
      padding-left: 2000px;
    }
    .user-activity-component, .product-sales-component{
      border: 1px solid;
      padding: 10px;
      margin-top: 30px;
      margin-bottom: 30px;
    }
    .user-activity-component h2, h3 {
      background: rebeccapurple;
      color: white;
      padding: 10px;
    }
    .user-activity-component ul, p {
      padding-left: 20px;
    }
```

That's all you need to do for now. The default Phoenix style sheets will give us most of what we need. Now is the moment we've waited for. Navigate to /admin/dashboard to see the results of all your hard work:

Admin Dashboard

Survey Results

It works! Thanks to the beauty of CRC and reducer pipelines, we were able to manage the nontrivial work of building and rendering our SVG chart in an easy-to-read and easy-to-maintain way.

Our chart is beautiful, and it's rendered on the server. The next step is to make it responsive. Let's get to work on the demographic filters.

Add Filters to Make Charts Interactive

So far, we have a beautiful server-side rendered dashboard, but we haven't done anything yet that really leverages LiveView's interactive capabilities. In this section, we change that. We'll give our users the ability to filter the survey results chart by demographic, and you'll see how we can reuse the reducers we wrote earlier to support this functionality.

In this section, we'll walk through building out a *filter by age group* feature and leave it up to you to review the code for the *filter by gender* feature.

Filter by Age Group

It's time to make the live component smarter. When it's done, it will let users filter the survey results chart by demographic data. Along the way, you'll get another chance to implement event handlers on a live component. All we need to do is build a form for various age groups and then capture a LiveView event to refresh the survey data with a query.

We'll support age filters for All, Under 18, 18 to 25, 25 to 35, and Over 35. Here's what it will look like when we're done:

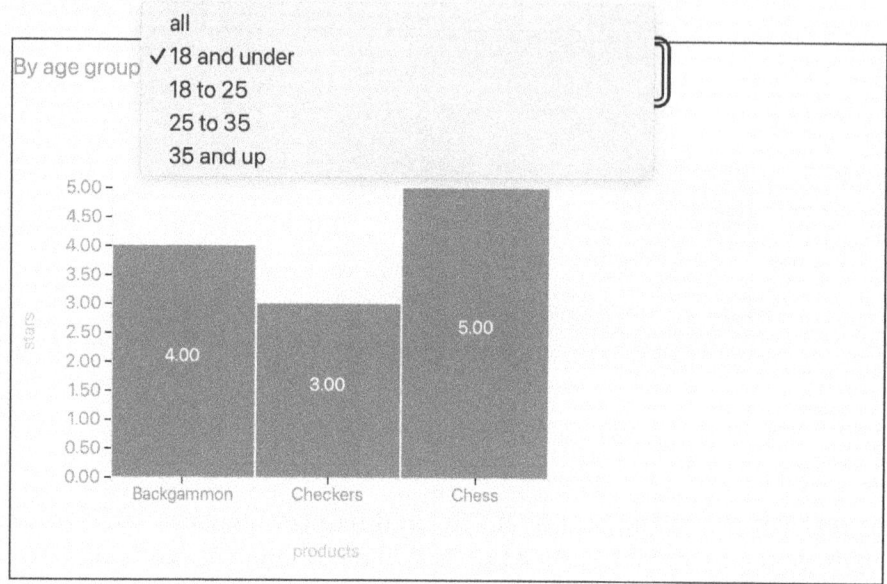

It's a simple form with a single input. We'll capture the form change event to update a query, and the survey will default to the unfiltered All when the page loads. Let's get started.

Establish Test Data

To have enough data to play with, we're going to build a simple seeds file that will generate users, random demographics for them, and random ratings. This data will let us put our interface through its paces much more easily than if we had to build out random ratings by hand. We're going to build a rating_seeds.exs script much like our seeds.exs script.

First, we need to leave a comment telling our users how to use the file and import or alias the modules our code will use.

```
interactive_dashboard/pento/priv/repo/rating_seeds.exs
# Run this script with: mix run priv/repo/rating_seeds.exs
alias Pento.{Repo, Accounts, Survey}
alias Pento.Accounts.{User, Scope}
alias Pento.Survey.{Demographic, Rating}
alias Pento.Catalog.Product
```

Our code will use context functions to create database User, Demographic, and Rating records. It will also need to make use of the schema information for Product and User data. That's a good start. Let's create some users:

interactive_dashboard/pento/priv/repo/rating_seeds.exs
```
users =
  for i <- 1..43, do:
    Accounts.register_user(%{
      email: "user#{i}@example.com",
      password: "passwordpassword"
    })
user_ids = Repo.all(User) |> Enum.map(& &1.id)
```

We create 43 users. We don't want an even number of them because we don't want the percentages to come out too clean. The exact number doesn't matter. To pass our changeset, we have to pass a valid email and a valid password. We point our email to example.com so we won't accidentally email known users. Our passwords are long enough to pass the validation. Now, we need a little setup data to use as we create demographics and ratings:

interactive_dashboard/pento/priv/repo/rating_seeds.exs
```
product_ids = Repo.all(Product) |> Enum.map(& &1.id)
genders = ["male", "female", "other", "prefer not to say"]
years = 1950..2005 |> Enum.to_list()
stars = 1..5 |> Enum.to_list()
```

We have lists we'll use in two ways. Our for comprehension will map over user and product IDs. We'll pick random elements for the other lists. This data won't be truly representative of our real-world data, but we don't care at this point. We just want tangible changing values to use for our bar charts and filters. Let's create some demographics:

interactive_dashboard/pento/priv/repo/rating_seeds.exs
```
for user_id <- user_ids do
  scope = %Scope{user: %User{id: user_id}}
  gender = Enum.random(genders)
  year_of_birth = Enum.random(years)

  Survey.create_demographic(scope, %{
    gender: gender,
    year_of_birth: year_of_birth
  })
end
```

Our comprehension covers all users in the database. We'll create demographics for each user, picking a random gender and year setting. Finally, we'll create some ratings. Add this at the end of your seed file:

```
# pento/priv/repo/rating_seeds.exs
for uid <- user_ids, pid <- product_ids do
  Survey.create_rating(%{
    user_id: uid,
    product_id: pid,
    stars: Enum.random(stars)
  })
end
```

This for comprehension will cover each possible combination with one user ID and one product ID. We create a rating with each of those values and a random number of stars.

Run the script with mix run priv/repo/rating_seeds.exs and you'll see a bunch of SQL flying by, denoting new values inserted into our database.

Load your /admin/dashboard page to satisfy yourself that there's more data, and then we can move on.

Build the Age Group Query Filters

We'll begin by building a set of query functions that will allow us to trim our survey results to match the associated age demographic. We'll need to surface an API in the boundary code and add a query to satisfy the age requirement in the core. The result will be consistent, testable, and maintainable code.

Let's add a few functions to the core in product/query.ex. First, make sure you alias Pento.Accounts.User and Pento.Survey.Demographic at the top of the Catalog.Product.Query module. Then add these functions:

```
interactive_dashboard/pento/lib/pento/catalog/product/query.ex
def join_users(query \\ base()) do
  query
  |> join(:left, [p, r], u in User, on: r.user_id == u.id)
end

def join_demographics(query \\ base()) do
  query
  |> join(:left, [p, r, u], d in Demographic, on: d.user_id == u.id)
end

def filter_by_age_group(query \\ base(), filter) do
  query
  |> apply_age_group_filter(filter)
end
```

First off, two of the reducers implement join statements. The syntax is a little confusing, so we'll break it down. The lists of variables represent the tables in the resulting join. In Ecto, it's customary to use a single letter to refer to associated tables. Our tables are p for product, r for results of surveys, u for users, and d for demographics. So the statement join(:left, [p, r, u, d], d in Demographic, on: d.user_id == u.id) means we're doing the following:

- A :left join.
- That join returns [products, results, users, and demographics].
- In that return, the id on the user is the same as the user_id on the demographic.

We also have a reducer to filter by age group. That function relies on the apply_age_group_filter/2 helper function that matches on the age group. Let's take a look at that function now.

interactive_dashboard/pento/lib/pento/catalog/product/query.ex
```
defp apply_age_group_filter(query, "18 and under") do
  birth_year = DateTime.utc_now().year - 18

  query
  |> where([p, r, u, d], d.year_of_birth >= ^birth_year)
end

defp apply_age_group_filter(query, "18 to 25") do
  birth_year_max = DateTime.utc_now().year - 18
  birth_year_min = DateTime.utc_now().year - 25

  query
  |> where(
    [p, r, u, d],
    d.year_of_birth >= ^birth_year_min and d.year_of_birth <= ^birth_year_max
  )
end

defp apply_age_group_filter(query, "25 to 35") do
  birth_year_max = DateTime.utc_now().year - 25
  birth_year_min = DateTime.utc_now().year - 35

  query
  |> where(
    [p, r, u, d],
    d.year_of_birth >= ^birth_year_min and d.year_of_birth <= ^birth_year_max
  )
end

defp apply_age_group_filter(query, "35 and up") do
  birth_year = DateTime.utc_now().year - 35

  query
  |> where([p, r, u, d], d.year_of_birth <= ^birth_year)
end

defp apply_age_group_filter(query, _filter) do
  query
end
```

Each of the demographic filters specifies an age grouping and does a quick bit of date math to date-box the demographic to the right time period. Then it's only one more short step to interpolate those dates in an Ecto clause. Notice that the default query will handle "all" and also any other input the user might add.

We can use the public functions in our Catalog boundary to further reduce the products_with_average_ratings query before executing it. Let's update the signature of our Catalog.products_with_average_ratings/0 function in catalog.ex to take an age_group_filter and apply our three reducers, like this:

```
# lib/pento/catalog.ex

def products_with_average_ratings(%{
      age_group_filter: age_group_filter
    }) do
  Product.Query.with_average_ratings()
  |> Product.Query.join_users()
  |> Product.Query.join_demographics()
  |> Product.Query.filter_by_age_group(age_group_filter)
  |> Repo.all()
end
```

This code is beautiful in its simplicity. The CRC pipeline creates a base query for the constructor. Then the reducers refine the query by joining the base to users, then to demographics, and finally filtering by age. We send the final form to the database to fetch results.

The code in the boundary simplifies things by pattern matching instead of running full validations. If a malicious user attempts to force a value we don't support, this server will crash, just as we want it to. We also accept any kind of filter, but our code will default to unfiltered code if no supported filter shows up.

Now, we're ready to consume that code in the component.

Your Turn: Test Drive the Query

Before you run the query in IEx, open up lib/pento_web/live/admin/survey_results_live.ex and comment out the call to the get_products_with_average_ratings/0 function in the assign_products_with_average_ratings/1, like this:

```
# lib/pento_web/live/admin/survey_results_live.ex

def assign_products_with_average_ratings(socket) do
  socket
  # |> assign(
  #   :products_with_average_ratings,
  #   Catalog.products_with_average_ratings())
end
```

We'll come back and make the necessary changes to this reducer's invocation of the get_products_with_average_ratings function. For now, just comment it out so that the code compiles and you can play around with your new query.

Open up IEx with iex -S mix and run the new query to filter results by age. You'll need to create a map that has the expected age filter. You should see a filtered list show up when you change between filters. Does your IEx log show the underlying SQL that's sent to the database?

Add the Age Group Filter to Component State

With a query filtered by age group in hand, it's time to weave the results into the component. Before we can change data on the page, we'll need a filter in the socket when we call update/2, a form to send the filter event, and the handlers to take advantage of it. Let's do the following to update our SurveyResultsLive component:

- Set an initial age group filter in socket assigns to "all".
- Display a drop-down menu with age group filters in the template.
- Respond to form events by calling the updated version of our Catalog.products_with_average_ratings/1 function with the age group filter from socket assigns.

Let's add a new reducer to survey_results_live.ex, called assign_age_group_filter/1:

```
defmodule PentoWeb.Admin.SurveyResultsLive do
  use PentoWeb, :live_component
  alias Pento.Catalog

  def update(assigns, socket) do
    {:ok,
      socket
      |> assign(assigns)
      |> assign_age_group_filter()
      |> assign_products_with_average_ratings()
      |> assign_dataset()
      |> assign_chart()
      |> assign_chart_svg()}
  end

  def assign_age_group_filter(socket) do
    socket
    |> assign(:age_group_filter, "all")
  end
```

The reducer pipeline is getting longer, but it's no more complex thanks to our code layering strategy. We can read our initial update/2 function like a storybook. The reducer adds the default age filter of All, and we're off to the races.

Now we'll change the assign_products_with_average_ratings/1 function in Admin.SurveyResultsLive to use the new age group filter:

```
# lib/pento_web/live/admin/survey_results_live.ex
def assign_products_with_average_ratings(
      %{assigns: %{age_group_filter: age_group_filter}} =
      socket) do
  assign(
    socket,
    :products_with_average_ratings,
    Catalog.products_with_average_ratings(
      %{age_group_filter: age_group_filter}
    )
  )
end
```

We pick up the new boundary function from Catalog and pass in the filter we set earlier. While you're at it, take a quick look at your page to make sure everything is rendering correctly.

Now we need to build the form input.

Send Age Group Filter Events

We're ready to add some event handlers to our component. We'll need a div to hold our form, like this:

```
<!-- lib/pento_web/live/admin/survey_results_live.html.heex -->
<section class="ml-8">
  <h2 class="font-light text-2xl">Survey Results</h2>
  <div id="survey-results-component">
    <div class="container">
      ...filters will go here...
    </div>
  </div>
  <div id="survey-results-chart">
    <%= @chart_svg %>
  </div>
</section>
```

Inside this div, we'll add the select input for the age group filter and default the selected value to the @age_group_filter assignment. Go ahead and add this to your template now:

```
interactive_dashboard/pento/lib/pento_web/live/admin/survey_results_live.html.heex
<div class="form-control w-full">
  <.form
    for={%{}}
    as={:age_group_filter}
```

```
      phx-change="age_group_filter"
      phx-target={@myself}
      id="age-group-form"
  >
    <label class="label">
      <span class="label-text text-sm">By age group:</span>
    </label>
    <select name="age_group_filter" id="age_group_filter"
          class="select select-bordered select-sm w-full">
      <%= for age_group <-
        ["all", "18 and under", "18 to 25", "25 to 35", "35 and up"] do %>
        <option value={age_group} selected={@age_group_filter == age_group}>
          <%= age_group %>
        </option>
      <% end %>
    </select>
  </.form>
</div>
```

LiveView works best when we surround individual form helpers with a full form. We render a drop-down menu in a form using the form/1[4] function component. Our approach here is different than what you've seen in this book so far. We don't need to track changes to data with the help of a changeset, so we didn't create one for our age group filter. As a result, we didn't create a form struct and add it to socket assigns—that is likewise not needed here. Instead, we're going with a simpler approach. We're using a form for an empty map and providing some additional instruction to teach the form how to behave. Let's take a closer look at how the form function component works with this empty struct.

Open up an IEx session with iex -S mix and key in the following:

```
iex> i %{}
Term
  %{}
...
Implemented protocols:
  Collectable, Enumerable, IEx.Info, ... Phoenix.HTML.FormData, ...

iex> i Pento.Catalog.change_product(%Pento.Catalog.Product{}, %{id: 1})
Term
  #Ecto.Changeset<...>
Implemented protocols
  IEx.Info, Inspect, Jason.Encoder, ..., Phoenix.HTML.FormData, ...
```

---

4. https://hexdocs.pm/phoenix_live_view/Phoenix.Component.html#form/1

Notice that *both* our product changeset and an empty map implement the Phoenix.HTML.FormData protocol. So when we provide the empty map to the for attribute of our form function component, the to_form/2 function is called under the hood to convert the empty struct to a Phoenix.HTML.Form struct.

In addition to providing the empty map to our form, we've added a few other attributes as well. We want the form events to target the live component itself (rather than the parent live view), so we set the phx-target attribute to @myself. The form also has the phx-change event binding, since we want to respond to the event as soon as the user selects an age group rather than forcing them to click a submit button.

To respond to this event, add a handler matching "age_group_filter" to sur-vey_results_live.ex, like this:

interactive_dashboard/pento/lib/pento_web/live/admin/survey_results_live.ex
```
# Event handler for age group filtering
def handle_event("age_group_filter", %{"age_group_filter" => age_group},
                socket) do
  {:noreply,
    socket
    |> assign_age_group_filter(age_group)
    |> assign_products_with_average_ratings()
    |> assign_dataset()
    |> assign_chart()
    |> assign_chart_svg()}
end
```

Now you can see the results of your hard work. Our event handler responds by updating the age group filter in socket assigns and then re-invoking the rest of our reducer pipeline. The reducer pipeline will operate on the new age group filter to fetch an updated list of products with average ratings and construct the SVG chart with that updated list. Then the template is re-rendered with this new state. Let's break this down step by step.

First, we update socket assigns :age_group_filter with the new age group filter from the event. We do this by implementing a new version of our assign_age_group_filter/2 function:

interactive_dashboard/pento/lib/pento_web/live/admin/survey_results_live.ex
```
def assign_age_group_filter(socket, age_group) do
  socket
  |> assign(:age_group_filter, age_group)
end
```

Then we update socket assigns :products_with_average_ratings, setting it to a re-fetched set of products for the given age group filter. We do this by once again invoking our assign_products_with_average_ratings reducer. This time it will operate on the updated :age_group_filter from socket assigns.

Lastly, we update socket assigns :dataset with a new Dataset constructed with our updated products with average ratings data. Subsequently, :chart and :chart_svg are also updated in socket assigns using the new dataset. All together, this will cause the component to re-render the chart SVG with the updated data from socket assigns.

Now, if we visit /admin/dashboard and select an age group filter from the drop-down menu, we should see the chart render again with appropriately filtered data:

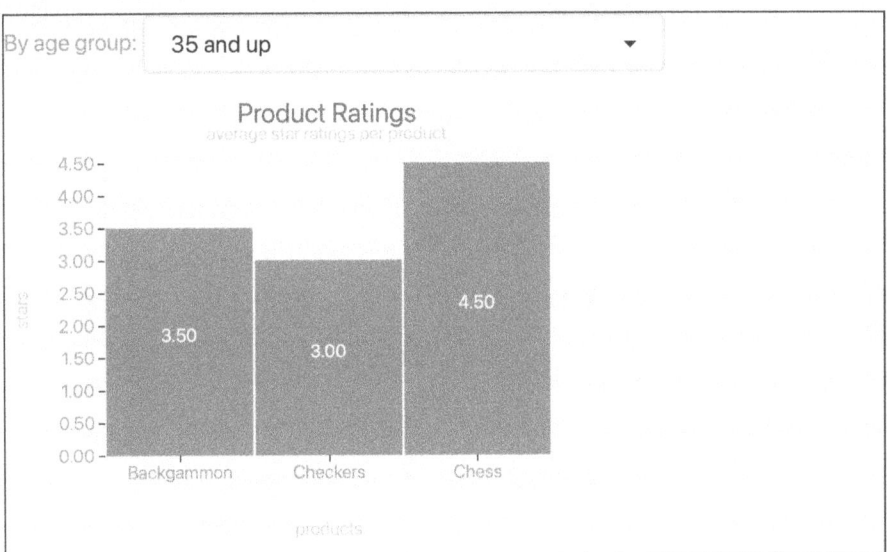

Phew! That's a *lot* of powerful capability packed into just a few lines of code. Just as we promised, our neat reducer functions proved to be highly reusable. By breaking out individual reducer functions to handle specific pieces of state, we've ensured that we can construct and reconstruct pipelines to manage even complex live view state.

This code needs to account for an important edge case before we move on. There might not be any survey results returned from our database query! If you select an age group for which no product ratings exist, you'll see the LiveView crash with the following error in the server logs:

```
[error] GenServer #PID<0.3270.0> terminating
 **(FunctionClauseError) ...
(elixir 1.10.3) lib/map_set.ex:119:
  MapSet.new_from_list(nil, [nil: []])
(elixir 1.10.3) lib/map_set.ex:95: MapSet.new/1
(contex 0.3.0) lib/chart/mapping.ex:180:
  Contex.Mapping.missing_columns/2
...
(contex 0.3.0) lib/chart/mapping.ex:139:
  Contex.Mapping.validate_mappings/3
(contex 0.3.0) lib/chart/mapping.ex:57: Contex.Mapping.new/3
(contex 0.3.0) lib/chart/barchart.ex:73: Contex.BarChart.new/2
```

As you can see, we *can't* initialize a Contex bar chart with an empty dataset. We could solve this problem a few ways. Let's solve it like this: if we get an empty results set back from our Catalog.products_with_average_ratings/1 query, then we should query for and return a list of product tuples where the first element is the product name and the second element is 0. This will allow us to render our chart with a list of products displayed on the x-axis and no values populated on the y-axis.

Assume we have the following query:

interactive_dashboard/pento/lib/pento/catalog/product/query.ex
```
def with_zero_ratings(query \\ base()) do
  query
  |> select([p], {p.name, 0})
end
```

And we have this context function:

interactive_dashboard/pento/lib/pento/catalog.ex
```
def products_with_zero_ratings do
  Product.Query.with_zero_ratings()
  |> Repo.all()
end
```

We can update our LiveView to implement the necessary logic:

```
def assign_products_with_average_ratings(
      %{assigns: %{age_group_filter: age_group_filter}} =
      socket
    ) do
  assign(
    socket,
    :products_with_average_ratings,
    get_products_with_average_ratings(%{age_group_filter: age_group_filter})
  )
end

defp get_products_with_average_ratings(filter) do
```

```
      case Catalog.products_with_average_ratings(filter) do
        [] ->
          Catalog.products_with_zero_ratings()
        products ->
          products
      end
  end
end
```

Now if we select an age group filter for which there are no results, we should see a nicely formatted empty chart:

Nice! With a few extra lines of code, we get exactly what we're looking for. We have a beautifully interactive dashboard for just a few lines of code beyond the static version. All that remains is to make this code more beautiful.

Refactor Chart Code with Macros

Our SurveyResultsLive component has a fair bit of charting support, in addition to the typical LiveComponent functions that set and change the socket. This kind of charting logic and configuration should live elsewhere so other components can take advantage of it, as well, and so that we can keep our live component module slim and focused solely on LiveView responsibilities.

Let's refactor the chart code by extracting common code into a __using__ macro. In return for these efforts, your live view logic will be clean and reusable. Here's how it works.

Refactor with __using__

At the top of every live view we've written so far, you see the call to use PentoWeb, :live_view. The use directive calls the __using__ macro on the PentoWeb module. That code in turn returns *code* that is injected into our live view modules. Open up lib/pento_web.ex and take a look:

```
def live_view do
  quote do
    use Phoenix.LiveView,
      layout: {PentoWeb.Layouts, :app}

    unquote(html_helpers())
  end
end
...
defmacro __using__(which) when is_atom(which) do
  apply(__MODULE__, which, [])
end
```

At the bottom of the file, you'll see a __using__ macro. Think of macros as Elixir code that writes and injects code. When a LiveView module calls use PentoWeb, :live_view, Elixir calls this __using__ function with a which value of :live_view. Then Phoenix calls the live_view function and returns the code listed there. The quote macro surrounds code that should be injected, so that code will add a use Phoenix.LiveView with a few options. The unquote(view_helpers()) code injects still more code, and so on.

If all of this seems a bit complicated to you, don't worry. You just need to understand that calling use with some module will make all of the functions of that module available in whichever module you're calling use.

We're going to do something similar. Future developers who want to use our charting functionality will call use PentoWeb, :chart_live to inject all of the charting configuration code our module needs. Let's do that next.

Extract Common Helpers

First, we define a module PentoWeb.BarChart that wraps up our chart rendering logic:

```
interactive_dashboard/pento/lib/pento_web/bar_chart.ex
defmodule PentoWeb.BarChart do
  alias Contex.{Dataset, BarChart, Plot}

  def make_bar_chart_dataset(data) do
    Dataset.new(data)
  end

  def make_bar_chart(dataset) do
    BarChart.new(dataset)
  end

  def render_bar_chart(chart, title, subtitle, x_axis, y_axis) do
    Plot.new(500, 400, chart)
    |> Plot.titles(title, subtitle)
    |> Plot.axis_labels(x_axis, y_axis)
    |> Plot.to_svg()
  end
end
```

We move the chart-specific functions from our LiveView to a common module. You can recognize the code that builds our dataset and bar chart and the converter that renders them. We don't make any changes at this point.

Import the Charting Module

Next up, we need code that imports the common functions. Let's think about where we want the imported code to live. PentoWeb doesn't need access to the chart helpers. Our live view does. That means we need to *inject code* that imports PentoWeb.BarChart. Luckily, we have a `quote` function that does exactly that.

Open up the `PentoWeb` module in lib/pento_web.ex and add in a function called `chart_helpers/0` that injects our import function:

```
defp chart_helpers do
  quote do
    import PentoWeb.BarChart
  end
end
```

Perfect. The `quote` macro will tell Elixir to inject the `BarChart` functions. With the implementation of the `chart_helpers` function, our application has a place to pull in common functions, aliases, and configuration related to charting.

Now, we can call that code in the traditional way with a use directive.

Inject the Code with __using__

The last job is to implement the public function that the PentoWeb's __using__ macro definition will apply via the call to use PentoWeb, :chart_live, like this:

interactive_dashboard/pento/lib/pento_web.ex
```
def chart_live do
  quote do
    use Phoenix.LiveComponent

    unquote(html_helpers())
    unquote(chart_helpers())
  end
end
```

Perfect. Now the chart_live function will work perfectly with the __using__ code, just like the use PentoWeb, :live_view expression you see at the top of each Phoenix live view. All that remains is to, um, use the macro.

Use the Macro

Go ahead and delete the refactored functions from your live view. Then add the new use directive to SurveyResultsLive component:

```
use PentoWeb, :chart_live
```

Removing make_bar_chart_dataset/1, make_bar_chart/2, and render_bar_chart/5 from the live view leaves us with this code:

interactive_dashboard/pento/lib/pento_web/live/admin/survey_results_live.ex
```
def assign_chart_svg(%{assigns: %{chart: chart}} = socket) do
  socket
  |> assign(
    :chart_svg,
    render_bar_chart(chart, title(), subtitle(), x_axis(), y_axis()))
end
```

The result is pleasing. This kind of layering shields our users from dealing with charting complexity when they're working with the data that makes those charts work. All of the code that renders a bar chart lives in PentoWeb.BarChart, while the code specific to how to render the bar chart *for the survey results component* remains in SurveyResultsLive. We could easily imagine our bar chart logic and configuration growing more complex—say, to accommodate custom color configuration, padding, orientation, and more. Now, should we want to accommodate that increased complexity, it has a logical home in the chart module.

With this new module and macro in place, you have yet another LiveView code organization tool in your kit. You can use macros to organize reusable code that keeps your live views clean and concise.

This chapter has been long, so it's time to wrap up.

Your Turn

We built a lot of new functionality in this chapter. Let's review.

You built a brand-new admin dashboard that displays survey results data with the help of the Contex library. Contex let's you render SVG charts on the server, which makes it the perfect fit for creating beautiful charts in LiveView. You took it a step further by making your survey results chart interactive. The age group filter allows your user to filter survey results by demographic info, and you once again used LiveView event handlers to manage these interactions. Finally, you did a bit of refactoring to keep your live view clean and concise with the use of macros.

At this point, you've built a number of component-backed features, and you're starting to get the hang of using the reducer pattern and the core/boundary designations to quickly and easily decide where new code belongs. You've seen how these patterns allow you to move fast and write clean, organized code. Once again, we're left with a highly interactive feature that manages complex single-page app state with very little code. On top of that, you're now prepared to use server-side-rendered SVG to visualize data in LiveView.

Before we move on to the next chapter, its your turn to get your hands dirty.

Give It a Try

The filter-by-gender code is present in the codebase. Choose the option that best reflects your confidence level.

If you're looking for an *easy* exercise, review the code to filter by gender that's already in the codebase. Take some time to walk through the code, starting in the query builder and context functions in the core and boundary and making your way up to the LiveView.

If you're looking for an *intermediate* exercise, use the same pattern that we used to build the age filter to add a gender filter to your own code.

Next Time

Now we have a working dashboard, but it doesn't react in real time to data that comes in from other parts of the system. In the next chapter, we'll use the Phoenix publish-subscribe interface to update our dashboard when new survey results come in. Then we'll add a new component to the dashboard that reports on real-time user interactions with our products. Let's keep going!

CHAPTER 9

Build a Distributed Dashboard

In the last chapter, you explored some of the capabilities, such as components, that make Phoenix LiveView the perfect fit for single-page apps like dashboards. Components help organize pages into layers, and the LiveView workflow makes quick work of adding interactive controls.

So far, the live views you've built have focused on single users interacting with browsers. Way back in the first chapter of this book, you learned that live views are effectively distributed systems. By now, you should have a better sense of why that's true. JavaScript code on browser clients triggers events that transmit data to the server, and the servers respond, often after connecting to other services like databases. We're shielded from those details because LiveView has built the complicated parts for us.

In this chapter, you'll see that live views are distributed systems not only because of the way they manage state across the client and the server but also because they're capable of reflecting the distributed state of your entire application. With the features you're about to build, you'll push LiveView and Phoenix functionality by connecting views to other events on other pages *not* triggered by the current user. Our application will be much more interactive, but we won't have to spend extraordinary effort to make it so. Rather than building the hard parts yourself, you'll rely on various Phoenix messaging frameworks. Let's talk about them now.

LiveView and Phoenix Messaging Tools

We're more than a half-way into this book, and you may be coming to appreciate the LiveView programming model. Let's revisit the LiveView flow figure that was first shown in Chapter 1, Get to Know LiveView, on page 1:

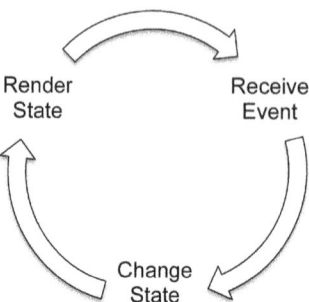

Just like this figure shows, you've expressed each view with a data model that you stored in the socket. Your code changed the data with reducers tied to event handlers, and you built a template or a render function to convert the data in the socket to HTML pages and SVG graphics.

This flow paves the way for success as we integrate other distributed elements into our Phoenix application. If you stop and think about it, it doesn't matter whether the events your live view handles are initiated by a user's mouse click on a browser page or a function that sends a message from some other area of your application. You'll use a variety of tools to send events. They'll flow through the views just as if they'd been sent by a user.

In this chapter, we're going to use several Phoenix messaging libraries to trigger other kinds of events, and we'll teach our live view to handle these events. In this way, you can build live views that are capable of reflecting the distributed state of your entire Phoenix application.

Using Phoenix.PubSub,[1] you can *publish events* to send messages to every other process that expresses interest, including live views. Meanwhile, Phoenix.Presence[2] can notify you when users interact with your site.

We're going to tie our live view to other services in our application by using the Phoenix.PubSub service, effectively making our dashboard reflect real-world updates, regardless of their source. The impact will be striking. Users will see updates in real time, with excellent responsiveness. We'll also take advantage of Phoenix Presence and integrate it into our live view for some real-time tracking of user activity around our app. Along the way, we'll introduce some new LiveView component capabilities and see how a parent live view can communicate updates to its child components.

Before we dive in, let's map out our approach to building these features.

---

1. https://hexdocs.pm/phoenix_pubsub/Phoenix.PubSub.html
2. https://hexdocs.pm/phoenix/Phoenix.Presence.html

As you recall, we've been working on a dashboard that charts survey results and allows users to interact with that chart by selecting demographics. We're going to extend this dashboard with a few new requirements.

You might have noticed that the dashboard doesn't automatically update when new results come in. The user must reload to see any newly submitted survey results. We'll fix that with with the help of Phoenix PubSub. We also want to track user engagement by displaying a real-time list of users who are viewing products. We'll do so with the help of Phoenix Presence.

We'll begin by synchronizing Admin.DashboardLive when new survey results data comes in. We'll use PubSub to send a message when a product rating is submitted, and we'll teach our admin dashboard live view to subscribe to those messages and handle them by updating the survey results chart component.

Then we'll move on to the real-time user tracking feature. We'll build a new component that leverages Presence to display a live-updating list of which users are viewing which products at a given moment in time. Similar to how we'll build our PubSub-backed feature, we'll use Presence to send messages when a user is looking at a product, and we'll teach our live view to subscribe to those messages and handle them by updating the new user list component.

Let's begin.

Track Real-Time Survey Results with PubSub

First on the agenda is automatically updating the survey results chart component when a user completes a survey. Right now, users are entering demographics and survey results through the RatingLive.FormComponent. When we handle the event for a new survey rating in the parent SurveyLive live view, we need to notify Admin.DashboardLive. The question is how.

You could try to do so with a direct message via send/2, but you'd need access to the Admin.DashboardLive PID. Even if we had access, this view could crash and the PID would change. We could give names to the Admin.DashboardLive process, but that would require more work. Fortunately, there's a better way.

Phoenix PubSub Implements the Publish/Subscribe Pattern

We're going to use Phoenix PubSub, a *publish/subscribe* implementation, to build the feature. Under the hood, a live view is just a process. Publish/subscribe is a common pattern for sending messages between processes in which messages are broadcast over a topic to dedicated subscribers listening to that topic. Let's see how it works.

Rather than sending a message directly from a sender to a receiver with send/2, you'll use a Phoenix PubSub server as an intermediary. Processes that need access to a topic announce their interest with a subscribe/1 function. Then sending processes broadcast a message through the PubSub service, over a given topic, which forwards the message to all subscribed processes.

This service is exactly what we need to pass messages between live views. Going through an intermediary is perfect for this use case. SurveyLive and Admin.DashboardLive don't need to know about each other. They need only know about a common pub/sub topic. That's good news. All we need to do is use the PubSub.broadcast/3 function to send a message over a particular topic and the PubSub.subscribe/1 function to receive a message over a particular topic.

Plan the Feature

Our Admin.DashboardLive process will use Phoenix PubSub to subscribe to a topic. This means that Admin.DashboardLive will receive messages broadcast over that topic from *anywhere else* in our application. For our new feature, we'll broadcast new Survey Results messages from the SurveyLive live view. Then we'll teach Admin.DashboardLive how to handle these messages by updating the SurveyResultsLive component with the new survey results info.

By combining LiveView's real-time functionality with PubSub's ability to pass messages across a distributed set of clients, we can seamlessly keep our live views up-to-date.

With that plan, we're ready to write some code. We'll start with a brief look at how PubSub is configured in our Phoenix application. Then we'll set up our message broadcast and subscribe workflow. Finally, we'll teach the Admin.DashboardLive how to update its SurveyResultsLive child component.

Configure Phoenix PubSub

It turns out that we don't need to do anything special to configure Phoenix PubSub. When we generated the initial application, the Phoenix application generator configured PubSub for us automatically:

```
distributed_dashboard/pento/config/config.exs
config :pento, PentoWeb.Endpoint,
  url: [host: "localhost"],
  adapter: Bandit.PhoenixAdapter,
  # ...
  pubsub_server: Pento.PubSub,
  live_view: [signing_salt: "Fg3hyca5"]
```

Remember, the endpoint is the very first function a web request encounters. Here, our app's endpoint configures a PubSub server and names it Pento.PubSub. This server is just a registered process, and in Elixir, registered processes have names. The configuration sets the default adapter, PubSub.PG2. This adapter runs on Distributed Erlang—clients across distributed nodes of our app can subscribe to a shared topic and broadcast to that shared topic because PubSub can directly exchange notifications between servers when configured to use the Phoenix.PubSub.PG2 adapter. Building on this common robust infrastructure will save us a tremendous amount of time should we ever need this capability.

As a result of this configuration, we can access the PubSub library's broadcast/3 and subscribe/1 functions through PentoWeb.Endpoint.broadcast/3 and PentoWeb.Endpoint.subscribe/1. We'll do exactly that as we incorporate message publishing and subscribing across the survey submission and survey results chart features.

Broadcast Survey Results

To make our results interactive, we need only make three tiny changes:

First, we'll need to broadcast a message over a topic when a user submits the survey within the SurveyLive view. Then we'll subscribe the Admin.DashboardLive view to that topic. Finally, we'll teach the Admin.DashboardLive view to handle messages it receives over that topic by updating the SurveyResultsLive component.

Before we proceed, we need an alias to PentoWeb.Endpoint and a broadcast topic:

```
distributed_dashboard/pento/lib/pento_web/live/survey_live.ex
use PentoWeb, :live_view

alias Pento.{Survey, Catalog}
alias PentoWeb.DemographicLive.{Show, Form}
alias PentoWeb.RatingLive
alias __MODULE__.Component
alias PentoWeb.Endpoint

@survey_results_topic "survey_results"
```

With the housekeeping out of the way, we'll broadcast our message. We send a "rating_created" message to the "survey_results" topic exactly when the SurveyLive live view receives a new rating, like this:

```
distributed_dashboard/pento/lib/pento_web/live/survey_live.ex
defp handle_rating_created(
       %{assigns: %{products: products}} = socket,
       updated_product,
       product_index
     ) do
```

```
    Endpoint.broadcast(@survey_results_topic, "rating_created", %{})
    socket
    |> put_flash(:info, "Rating submitted successfully")
    |> assign(
      :products,
      List.replace_at(products, product_index, updated_product)
    )
end
```

We alias the endpoint to access the broadcast/3 function and add a new topic as a module attribute. Later, our dashboard will subscribe to the same topic. Most of the rest of the code is the same, except this line:

`Endpoint.broadcast(@survey_results_topic, "rating_created", %{})`

The endpoint's broadcast/3 function sends the "rating_created" message over the @survey_results_topic with an empty payload. This function hands the message to an intermediary, the Pento.PubSub server, which in turn broadcasts the message with its payload to any process subscribed to the topic.

Now we're ready to subscribe our dashboard to that topic.

Subscribe to Survey Results Messages

We want to use the broadcast of this message to tell the SurveyResultsLive component to update with a fresh list of filtered product ratings. So you might want to subscribe the SurveyResultsLive component to the "survey_results" topic.

Think about it, though. When we subscribe to a topic, we do so on behalf of a process. Components don't run in their own processes—they share a process with their parent live view. In fact, components don't even implement a handle_info/2 function. That means any messages sent to the process will need to be handled by the parent live view, in this case Admin.DashboardLive. That means we'll need to do the following:

- Subscribe Admin.DashboardLive to the "survey_results" topic.
- Implement a handle_info/2 function on Admin.DashboardLive for the "rating_created" message.
- Use that function to tell the child SurveyResultsLive component to update with the latest list of ratings.

You'll be surprised at how quickly it goes. Once again, the LiveView framework handles many of the details for us and exposes easy-to-use functions that we can leverage to build this workflow.

First, in admin/dashboard_live.ex, subscribe to the topic, like this:

```elixir
defmodule PentoWeb.Admin.DashboardLive do
  use PentoWeb, :live_view
  alias PentoWeb.Endpoint
  @survey_results_topic "survey_results"

  def mount(_params, _session, socket) do
    if connected?(socket) do
      Endpoint.subscribe(@survey_results_topic)
    end

    {:ok,
      socket
      |> assign(:survey_results_component_id, "survey-results")}
  end
```

A quick note on the usage of the connected?/1 function. Remember, in the LiveView flow, mount/3 gets called twice—once when the live view first mounts and renders as a static HTML response and again when the WebSocket-connected live view process starts up. We're calling subscribe/1 *only if* the socket is connected—in the second mount/3 call.

Now when the SurveyLive live view broadcasts the "rating_created" message over this common topic, the Admin.DashboardLive will receive the message. So we need to implement a handle_info/2 callback to respond to that message.

Implement a handle_info/2 in the same file, like this:

distributed_dashboard/pento/lib/pento_web/live/admin/dashboard_live.ex
```elixir
def handle_info(%{event: "rating_created"}, socket) do
  send_update(
    SurveyResultsLive,
    id: socket.assigns.survey_results_component_id
  )
  {:noreply, socket}
end
```

We want to respond to this message by updating the SurveyResultsLive component to display the latest data. So we use the send_update/3 function to send a message from the parent live view to the child component.

Update the Component

Let's take a moment to talk about the send_update/3 function. send_update/3 asynchronously updates the component with the specified module name and ID, where that component is running in the parent live view. Remember that in the previous chapter we stored the component ID in the parent live view's socket assigns. Here's where that pays off.

Once send_update/3 is called, the component updates with any new assigns passed as the second argument to send_update/3, invoking the preload/1 and update/2 callback functions on that component. Our SurveyResultsLive component will invoke its update/2 function, causing it to fetch the updated survey results from the database, thereby including any newly submitted product ratings.

We have one problem, though. Recall that the reducer pipeline in our update/2 function hard-codes the initial state of the :gender_filter and :age_group_filter to values of "all". So, now, when our update/2 function runs *again* as a result of the Admin.DashboardLive receiving a message broadcast, we'll set the :gender_filter and :age_group_filter keys in socket assigns to "all", thereby losing whatever filter state was applied to the SurveyResultsLive's socket by user interactions.

To fix this, the assign_age_group_filter/1 and assign_gender_filter/1 reducer functions need to get a littler smarter. If the socket already has a value at either of the :age_group_filter or :gender_filter keys, then it should retain that value. Otherwise, it should set the default value to "all".

So we'll implement additional function heads for these reducers that contain this logic:

```
distributed_dashboard/pento/lib/pento_web/live/admin/survey_results_live.ex
def assign_age_group_filter(
      %{assigns: %{age_group_filter: age_group_filter}} =
        socket
    ) do
  assign(socket, :age_group_filter, age_group_filter)
end

def assign_age_group_filter(socket) do
  socket
  |> assign(:age_group_filter, "all")
end
```

That's the age_group filter. If the key/value pair is present in the socket, we match this first function head and set the value of that key in socket assigns to the existing value. Otherwise, we fall through to the next matching function and set the key to "all". Now, we can do the same thing to the gender filter:

```
distributed_dashboard/pento/lib/pento_web/live/admin/survey_results_live.ex
def assign_gender_filter(
      %{assigns: %{gender_filter: gender_filter}} = socket
    ) do
  assign(socket, :gender_filter, gender_filter)
end

def assign_gender_filter(socket) do
  assign(socket, :gender_filter, "all")
end
```

Perfect. Now when a user submits a new product rating, a message will be broadcast over PubSub and the Admin.DashboardLive view will receive that message and tell the SurveyResultsLive component to update. When that update happens, the component will reduce over the socket. Any filters in state will retain their values and the component will re-fetch products with their average ratings from the database. When the component re-renders, the users will see updated results. Putting it all together, we have something like this:

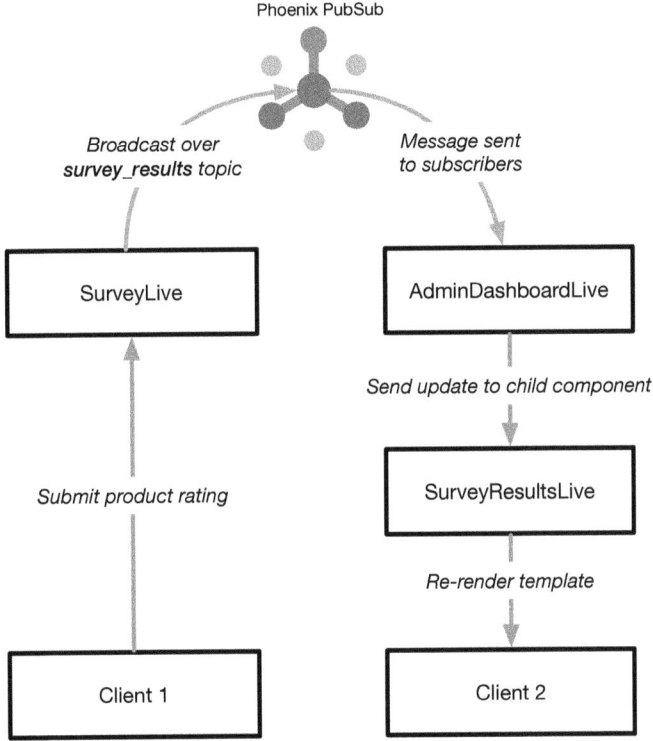

Give it a try by opening up one tab and pointing it at /admin/dashboard. Then open up another browser tab or window, register as a new user, and submit a new survey. You should see the results in the Survey Results section of the /admin/dashboard page update *without* having to refresh the page.

That's a lot of functionality all packed into, once again, just a few new lines of code. As a programmer, you get a beautiful programming model that accommodates PubSub messages the same way it handles LiveView events. Your users get connected, interactive applications that stay up-to-date when events occur anywhere in the world.

Next up, we'll build a section into our dashboard to track user activity.

Track Real-Time User Activity with Presence

Web applications are full of rich interactions. You can think of these interactions as an active conversation between the user and your app. In Phoenix, those conversations are represented and managed by processes—often implemented with channels. By gathering up a list of active processes, we can show the active conversations happening on our site. This is exactly the job of Phoenix Presence, a behaviour that provides the capabilities to track a user's conversation, or presence, within your application.

Tracking activity on a network is an easy problem to solve when everything is on one server. However, that's rarely the case. In the real world, servers are clustered together for performance and reliability, and connections between those servers sometimes fail. These problems make tracking presence by listing processes notoriously difficult.

Phoenix Presence solves these problems for us. It's built on top of Phoenix PubSub and leverages PubSub's distributed capabilities to reliably track processes across a distributed set of servers. It also uses a CRDT[3] (conflict-free replicated data type) model to ensure that presence tracking will keep working when nodes or connections on our network fail.

We'll use Presence to give us insight as users interact with our application around the world. And because Presence is backed by PubSub, the way we code the live views won't have to change at all.

When we're done, our dashboard will display a section that shows which users are viewing which products at a given moment. The list will update immediately as users visit and leave a Product Show live view, something like this:

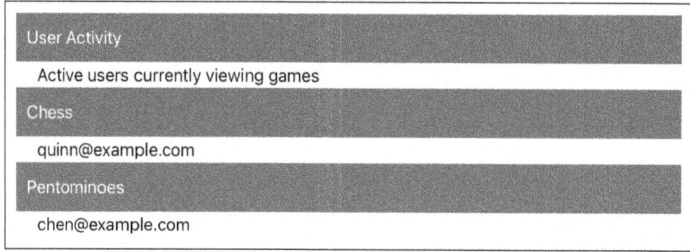

This plan may seem ambitious, but it's surprisingly easy to do. To build this feature, we'll need to build the following:

---

3. https://www.serverless.com/blog/crdt-explained-supercharge-serverless-at-edge

PentoWeb.Presence module
> This module will define our *presence model*. It will implement the Phoenix Presence behaviour, define the data structure that will track user activity, and connect it to our app's PubSub server.

UserActivityLive component
> We'll set up a live component that renders a static list of users.

handle_info/3 message handler
> A function on Admin.DashboardLive live that tells the user activity component to update based on site user activity.

We'll tie these entities together with a PubSub-backed Presence workflow. When a user visits a Product Show live view, that live view will use the Presence.track/4 function to broadcast a user activity event over a topic. We'll subscribe Admin.DashboardLive to that topic. Then our handle_info/3 function will take care of the rest, updating the user activity component, just like in our real-time survey results chart feature.

Set Up Presence

The Phoenix.Presence behaviour is an Elixir service based on OTP. It's used to notify applications via PubSub when processes or channels representing online presences come and go. Since a live view is just a process under the hood, we can use the Phoenix Presence API to track user activity within a live view. Then Presence will publish details about presences that come and go.

We'll define our own module that uses this behaviour. Let's take a look at that module definition now.

distributed_dashboard/pento/lib/pento_web/presence.ex
```
defmodule PentoWeb.Presence do
  @moduledoc """
  Provides presence tracking to channels and processes.

  See the [`Phoenix.Presence`](https://hexdocs.pm/phoenix/Phoenix.Presence.html)
  docs for more details.
  """
  use Phoenix.Presence,
    otp_app: :pento,
    pubsub_server: Pento.PubSub
end
```

The PentoWeb.Presence module defines our *presence model*. A presence model is the data structure that tracks information about active users on our site and the functions that process changes in that model. So far, there's not much happening, but let's call out the details.

First, we use the Presence behaviour. As you've already seen, that behaviour calls the __using__ macro on the Phoenix.Presence module. Notice the arguments we pass in. You might recognize Pento.PubSub as the publish/subscribe server for our application, while the otp_app: :pento key/value pair specifies the OTP application that holds our app's configuration.

Right now, the module is sparse. As our needs grow, we'll have functions to track new users. We need to do one more thing to make sure our application can use this new Presence module. We have to add the PentoWeb.Presence module to our application's children, so that the Presence process starts up when our app starts up, as part of our application's supervision tree. Open up lib/pento/application.ex and add the module to the list of children defined in the start function, like this:

```
distributed_dashboard/pento/lib/pento/application.ex
def start(_type, _args) do
  children = [
    PentoWeb.Telemetry,
    Pento.Repo,
    {DNSCluster,
     query: Application.get_env(:pento, :dns_cluster_query) || :ignore},
    {Phoenix.PubSub, name: Pento.PubSub},
    PentoWeb.Presence,

    # Start the Finch HTTP client for sending emails
    {Finch, name: Pento.Finch},
    # Start a worker by calling: Pento.Worker.start_link(arg)
    # {Pento.Worker, arg},
    # Start to serve requests, typically the last entry
    PentoWeb.Endpoint
  ]
```

Note that you'll want to make sure to start the presence process after your application's PubSub process starts up.

Let's move on to new user tracking now.

Track User Activity

To track presence, we need to answer a couple of basic questions. First, who is the user? We'll need to determine exactly which data we'll use to track the user's identity. The second question is when are they present? We'll need to pick the right point in time to hook in our presence model. Let's answer the first question first. In Chapter 2, Phoenix and Authentication, on page 31, the authentication service we generated placed a user_token in the session when a user logged in. We can use that token to fetch a user_id. As for *when* the user is considered to be present, we want to track which users are viewing which products. So the user becomes present when they're looking at the product page in ProductLive.Show.

Recall that our /products/:id product show route is defined in our router *inside* a shared live session block, like this:

```
live_session :default, on_mount: PentoWeb.UserAuth do
  # ...
  live "/products/:id", ProductLive.Show, :show
  # ...
end
```

The UserAuth module implements an on_mount/4 callback that populates the socket with a :current_scope assignment. So the ProductLive.Show live view already has the current scope (and user) in its socket assigns! Okay, let's use that current scope data now.

The handle_params/3 callback fires right after mount/3. We can use it to track the user's presence for the specified product ID. Also, remember handle_params/3 will fire twice for a new page: once when the initial page loads and once when the page's WebSocket connection is established. If the :live_action is :show and the socket is connected, then we'll perform our user tracking, like this:

distributed_dashboard/pento/lib/pento_web/live/product_live/show.ex
```
alias Pento.Catalog
alias PentoWeb.Presence

@impl true
def render(assigns) do
  ~H"""
  <Layouts.app flash={@flash} current_scope={@current_scope}>
    <.header>
      Product {@product.id}
      <:subtitle>This is a product record from your database.</:subtitle>
      <:actions>
        <.button navigate={~p"/products"}>
          <.icon name="hero-arrow-left" />
        </.button>
        <.button
          variant="primary"
          navigate={~p"/products/#{@product}/edit?return_to=show"}
        >
          <.icon name="hero-pencil-square" /> Edit product
        </.button>
      </:actions>
    </.header>

    <.list>
      <:item title="Name">{@product.name}</:item>
      <:item title="Description">{@product.description}</:item>
```

```
      <:item title="Unit price">{@product.unit_price}</:item>
      <:item title="Sku">{@product.sku}</:item>
    </.list>

    <div>
      <img
        alt="product image" width="200"
        src={@product.image_upload}
      />
    </div>
  </Layouts.app>
  """
end

@impl true
def mount(_params, _session, socket) do
  {:ok, socket}
end

@impl true
def handle_params(%{"id" => id}, _, socket) do
  product = Catalog.get_product!(socket.assigns.current_scope, id)
  maybe_track_user(product, socket)

  {:noreply,
   socket
   |> assign(:page_title, page_title(socket.assigns.live_action))
   |> assign(:product, product)}
end
```

In our handle_params/3 function, we look up the product and then add a function, maybe_track_user/2, to conditionally track the user's presence. The word maybe is a convention that marks the function as conditional—we only want to do the user presence tracking if the live view is loading with the :show (as opposed to the :edit) live action and if the live view is connected over WebSockets. Let's look inside that function now.

distributed_dashboard/pento/lib/pento_web/live/product_live/show.ex
```
def maybe_track_user(
      product,
      %{assigns: %{live_action: :show, current_scope: current_scope}} =
        socket
    ) do
  if connected?(socket) do
    Presence.track_user(self(), product, current_scope.user.email)
  end
end

def maybe_track_user(_product, _socket), do: nil
```

We've prepared the live view's plumbing for tracking. We'll implement the presence tracking details within the Presence.track_user/3 function. We pass the process ID of the live view, the product they're viewing, and the email of the user we're tracking.

We want a list of product names and a list of users interacting with each product. Presence allows us to store a top-level key pointing to a map of metadata. We'll use the product name as the top-level key, and the metadata map will contain the list of present users who are viewing that product. Our Presence data structure will ultimately look like this:

```
%{
  "Chess" => %{
    metas: [
      %{phx_ref: "...", users: [%{email: "bob@email.com"}]},
      %{phx_ref: "...", users: [%{email: "terry@email.com"}]}
    ]
  }
}
```

The Presence.track/4 gives us the means to store and broadcast exactly that. Here's what we call .track/4 with:

- The PID of the process we want to track, the Product Show live view.
- A PubSub message topic used to broadcast messages.
- A key representing the presence, in this case the product name.
- The metadata to track for each presence, in this case the list of users.

Let's dive into the usage of the track/4 function now. To track a user for a product name, you can use the track/4 function:

```
topic = "user_activity"
Presence.track(
  some_pid,
  topic,
  "Chess",
  %{users: [%{email: "bob@email.com"}]}
)
```

Presence will store this data:

```
%{
  "Chess" => %{
    metas: [
      %{phx_ref: "...", users: [%{email: "bob@email.com"}]},
    ]
  }
}
```

Notice how the last argument we provided to track/4 becomes part of the Presence data store's list of :metas—the metadata for the given presence.

The PentoWeb.Presence module provides the perfect home for this code. Open up that module now and define a function, track_user/3, that looks like this:

distributed_dashboard/pento/lib/pento_web/presence.ex
```
@user_activity_topic "user_activity"

def track_user(pid, product, user_email) do
  track(
    pid,
    @user_activity_topic,
    product.name,
    %{users: [%{email: user_email}]}
  )
end
```

Beautiful. The code calls our new custom PentoWeb.Presence function with the PID of the current live view, the product, and the user's email. Now, the tracking side of the chain is complete. ProductLive.Show.handle_params/3 calls maybe_track_user/2, and that code invokes our presence tracking in Presence.track_user/3. Phoenix takes care of maintaining a list for us.

Now that we're tracking user presence for a given product, let's move on to the work of displaying those presences and making sure they update in real time.

Display User Tracking

We've come a surprisingly long way with user activity tracking, but there's still work to do. We'll implement a live component, UserActivityLive, that will use its update/2 callback to ask Presence for the list of products and their present users. It will store this list in state via the socket assigns. Then we'll render that list in our component's template. This component doesn't need to implement any event handlers, so we *could* use a function component here. But we want to take advantage of the live component life cycle to make it easy to update our component in real time.

Let's kick things off by defining our component. Create a new file, lib/pento_web/live/admin/user_activity_live.ex, and add in this component definition:

```
defmodule PentoWeb.Admin.UserActivityLive do
  use PentoWeb, :live_component
  alias PentoWeb.Presence

  def update(_assigns, socket) do
    # coming soon!
  end
end
```

We know that the component needs to fetch a list of presences when it first renders. Later, we'll teach the component to update whenever a new presence is added to the `PentoWeb.Presence` data store. As you might guess, we'll have the parent live view, `Admin.DashboardLive`, receive a message when this happens and respond by telling the component to update. So we want to use the component's update/2 function to fetch the presence list and store it in state rather than the mount/3 function. This way we ensure that the presence list is re-fetched when the component updates later on (more on this update flow later). Let's build our update/2 function now.

distributed_dashboard/pento/lib/pento_web/live/admin/user_activity_live.ex
```elixir
def update(_assigns, socket) do
  {:ok,
   socket
   |> assign_user_activity()}
end
```

As usual, we extract the code to build a user activity list to a reducer function called assign_user_activity/1. That function's only job is to fetch a list of products and their present users from `PentoWeb.Presence` and assign it to the :user_activity key. Before we take a closer look at this reducer, let's build out the `PentoWeb.Presence` functionality for listing products and their present users.

Once again, we rely on the `PentoWeb.Presence` module to wrap up the code for interacting with Phoenix Presence. We'll define a function, list_products_and_users/0, that will fetch the list of presences and shape them into the correct format for rendering. Then we'll call on that function in our component's assign_user_activity/1 reducer.

First, open up the `PentoWeb.Presence` module and add in the following code to define the list_products_and_users/0 function:

distributed_dashboard/pento/lib/pento_web/presence.ex
```elixir
def list_products_and_users do
  list(@user_activity_topic)
  |> Enum.map(&extract_product_with_users/1)
end

defp extract_product_with_users({product_name, %{metas: metas}}) do
  {product_name, users_from_metas_list(metas)}
end

defp users_from_metas_list(metas_list) do
  Enum.map(metas_list, &users_from_meta_map/1)
  |> List.flatten()
  |> Enum.uniq()
end

def users_from_meta_map(meta_map) do
  get_in(meta_map, [:users])
end
```

We start with a call to Presence.list/1 to list the present data for the given topic. That returns something that looks like this:

```
%{
  "Chess" => %{
    metas: [
      %{phx_ref: "...", users: [%{email: "bob@email.com"}]},
      %{phx_ref: "...", users: [%{email: "terry@email.com"}]}
    ]
  }
}
```

Then we iterate over the key/value pairs of this map and pattern match out the list of metas. From there, we iterate over the list of meta maps and collect the value of the :users key from each map. We flatten the results, and we make them unique to account for any duplicate entries (for example, if the same user has the same product show page open in multiple tabs). Finally, we return a list of tuples that looks like this:

```
[{"Chess", [%{email: "bob@email.com"}, %{email: "terry@email.com"}]}]
```

Now we're ready to call on PentoWeb.Presence.list_products_and_users/0 in our component's reducer, like this:

distributed_dashboard/pento/lib/pento_web/live/admin/user_activity_live.ex
```
def assign_user_activity(socket) do
  assign(socket, :user_activity, Presence.list_products_and_users())
end
```

We can now implement the component's template, which iterates over the @user_activity list of tuples to display the product names and their present users:

distributed_dashboard/pento/lib/pento_web/live/admin/user_activity_live.html.heex
```
<div class="user-activity-component ml-8">
  <h2>User Activity</h2>
  <p>Active users currently viewing games</p>
  <div :for={{product_name, users} <- @user_activity}>
    <h3>{product_name}</h3>
    <ul>
      <li :for={user <- users}>{user.email}</li>
    </ul>
  </div>
</div>
```

We find no surprises in this template. Two for comprehensions iterate over first the products in @user_activity and then their users. Then we render the name of the product followed by a list of users, and we're done.

The last step is to render this component. We'll need an :id to make it stateful, so we need to add the new id to lib/pento_web/live/admin/dashboard_live.ex:

```
...
{:ok,
 socket
 |> assign(:survey_results_component_id, "survey-results")
 |> assign(:user_activity_component_id, "user-activity")}
...
```

The Admin.DashboardLive live view needs to hold on to awareness of the component's ID so that it can use it to tell the component to update later on (more on that in a bit).

Now, the Admin.DashboardLive template can render the component:

```
distributed_dashboard/pento/lib/pento_web/live/admin/dashboard_live.html.heex
<div class="container mx-auto p-6">
  <h1 class="text-3xl font-bold mb-6">Admin Dashboard</h1>
  <.live_component
        module={PentoWeb.Admin.SurveyResultsLive}
        id={@survey_results_component_id} />

  <.live_component
        module={PentoWeb.Admin.UserActivityLive}
        id={@user_activity_component_id} />
</div>
```

The code is simple and direct. It renders a component, passing only the new id from @user_activity_component_id. Go ahead and try it out. Open a few different browser sessions for different users and navigate each to a product show page. Then point yet another browser to /admin/dashboard, and you'll see the user activity component in all its glory, as shown here:

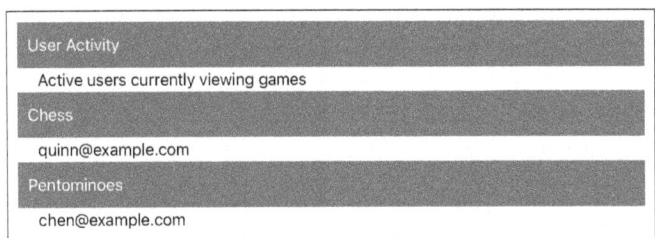

Now our site admins can see users engaging with products. So far, so good. A problem arises, though. When new users interact with the site, you won't be able to see them. Similarly, if a user navigates away from a given product's show page, the user activity list won't update in real time. Admins need to refresh the page to get the latest list of active users. Fortunately, an easy remedy exists, and it has to do with PubSub.

Subscribe to Presence Changes

Recall that when we defined our `PentoWeb.Presence` module, we configured it to use our application's PubSub server. This means that whenever we change the state of the data in the Presence data store—for example, with a call to the `track/4` function—a "presence_diff" event will get broadcast over the specified topic.

So all we need to do is subscribe the `Admin.DashboardLive` view to the "user_activity" topic we provided in our call to `Presence.track/4`. Then we'll implement a `handle_info/2` function in `Admin.DashboardLive` and teach it to respond to messages over this topic by updating the `UserActivityLive` component. When the component updates, it will call `update/2` again, which will re-fetch the latest list of present users.

Let's put the plan into action.

Add a module attribute with the "user_activity" topic to `Admin.DashboardLive` and update the `mount/3` to subscribe to this topic:

```
distributed_dashboard/pento/lib/pento_web/live/admin/dashboard_live.ex
def handle_info(%{event: "presence_diff"}, socket) do
  send_update(
    UserActivityLive,
    id: socket.assigns.user_activity_component_id
  )

  {:noreply, socket}
end
```

With that done, all that remains is responding to the PubSub broadcasts via `handle_info/2`. Let's finish this feature and put a bow on it.

Respond to Presence Events

Now that `Admin.DashboardLive` is subscribed to the "user_activity" topic, we'll implement the `handle_info/2` function for the "presence_diff" event, like this:

```
distributed_dashboard/pento/lib/pento_web/live/admin/dashboard_live.ex
def mount(_params, _session, socket) do
  if connected?(socket) do
    Endpoint.subscribe(@survey_results_topic)
    Endpoint.subscribe(@user_activity_topic)
  end

  {:ok,
   socket
   |> assign(:survey_results_component_id, "survey-results")
   |> assign(:user_activity_component_id, "user-activity")}
end
```

We call the send_update/3 function, providing the component name and ID. This tells the UserActivityLive component to update, invoking its update/2 function.

Remember, the update/2 function already invokes the assign_user_activity/1 reducer. That function fetches a fresh list of user presences per product, so we're done!

With a few dozen lines of code, we've implemented an interactive distributed solution for tracking user activity. It's a solution that will work equally well on a stand-alone server or a worldwide distributed cluster. The following figure shows what's happening.

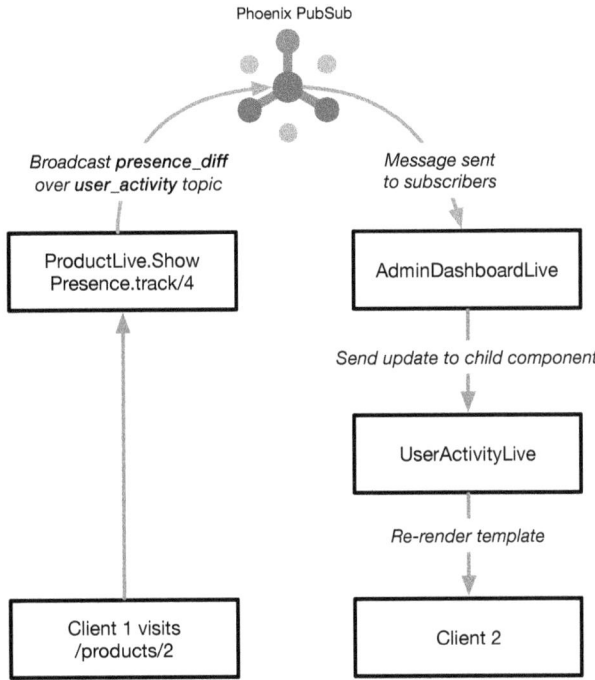

This figure shows exactly what happens when a new user visits a product page. First, the Presence.track/4 function is invoked. This tracks the given user based on the running process, updating the Presence data store accordingly. With this change to Presence state, the Presence service sends out a message via PubSub. When that happens, the Admin.DashboardLive view tells the UserActivityLive component to update.

With just a few lines of code to respond to a PubSub message, the UserActivityLive component updates! That's the beauty of Presence, and of LiveView. Presence and PubSub allow us to supercharge our live view with the ability to reflect the state of our distributed application, while writing very little new code.

It's been a short chapter, but an intense one. It's time to wrap up.

Your Turn

Developers can extend single-page apps to react to distributed events with incremental effort. Phoenix PubSub and Presence bring the powerful capabilities of distributed Elixir to LiveView. They seamlessly integrate into LiveView code to allow you to build live views that represent the state of your entire application. You can even maintain your beautifully layered LiveView components alongside these technologies by using the send_update/3 function to communicate distributed state changes to child components. LiveView components and Phoenix PubSub work together to support complex distributed state management systems with ease.

Now, you can put these skills to work.

Give It a Try

This problem lets you use Presence and PubSub to update a view:

- Use PubSub and Presence to track the number of people taking a survey.
- Add a new component to the admin dashboard view to display this total list of survey-taking users.
- What happens when a user navigates away from a survey page? Did your list of survey-taking users update on its own, without you writing any new code to support this feature? Think through why this is.

Next Time

With a working distributed dashboard, the admin features of the site are now complete. Next, we'll build a set of test cases to make sure the site doesn't regress as new features are released. We'll use the CRC strategy to build test cases that are organized, are easy-to-read, and that scale well to cover a wide range of scenarios. Keep this ball rolling by turning the page!

CHAPTER 10

Test Your Live Views

You've now seen most of what LiveView has to offer. You've used generators to build and customize a full-fledged CRUD feature set. You've built individual forms with and without schemas behind them to express inputs and validation. You've composed complex views with simpler components. You've even extended live views with Phoenix PubSub for real-time updates in your distributed system.

So far, our workflow has consisted of writing tiny bits of code and verifying them by running IEx sessions and looking at browser windows. This flow works well in this book because it offers excellent opportunities for teaching dense concepts. In reality, most developers *build tests as they go*. By writing tests, you'll gain the ability to make significant changes with confidence that your tests will catch breakages as they happen. In this chapter, you'll finally get to write some tests.

Testing for live views is easier than testing for most web frameworks for several reasons. First, the CRC pattern lends itself nicely to robust unit testing because we can write individual tests for the small, single-purpose functions that compose into the CRC workflow. LiveView's test tooling makes a big difference too. Though LiveView is young, the LiveViewTest module offers a set of convenience functions to exercise live views without fancy JavaScript testing frameworks. You'll use this module directly in your ExUnit tests, which means that all of your live view tests can be written in Elixir. As a result, your live view tests will be fast, concurrent, and stable, which differs markedly from the experience of working with headless browser testing tools that introduce new external dependencies and can make consistency difficult to achieve.

Tests instill confidence; unstable tests erode that confidence. Building as much of your testing story as possible on pure Elixir will pay dividends in your confidence and help you move quickly when building your LiveView applications.

In this chapter, we're not going to spend much time beyond the narrow slice of testing where ExUnit meets our LiveView code. If you want to know more about Elixir testing, check out *Testing Elixir [LM21]* by Andrea Leopardi and Jeffrey Matthias. If you're writing full applications using LiveView, you'll eventually need to take a deeper dive into Elixir testing, and that book is a great place to start.

For now, we'll test the survey results feature on the admin dashboard page to expose you to the testing techniques you'll need when building live views.

What Makes CRC Code Testable?

Think of a test as a scientific experiment. The target of the experiment is a bit of code, and the thesis is that the code is working. Logically, each test is an experiment that does three things:

- Sets up preconditions.
- Provides a stimulus.
- Compares an actual response to expectations.

That definition is broad and covers a wide range of testing strategies and frameworks. We're going to write three tests, of two specific types. Both types of tests will follow this broad pattern. One of the tests will be a *unit test*. We'll write it to verify the behavior of the independent functions that set up the socket. We'll also write two *integration tests* that will let us verify the interaction between components: one to test interactions *within* a live view process and another to verify interactions *between* processes.

You might be surprised that we *won't* be testing JavaScript. A big part of the LiveView value proposition is that it pushes much of the JavaScript interactions into the infrastructure, so we don't have to deal with them. Because the Pento application has no custom JavaScript integrations, we don't have to worry about testing JavaScript if we trust the LiveView JavaScript infrastructure.

Instead, the integration tests we write will interact with LiveView machinery to examine the impact of page loads and events that flow through a live view. A good example of such a test is simulating a button click and checking the impact on the re-rendered live view template. Integration tests have the benefit of catching *integration problems*—problems that occur at the integration points between different pieces of your system, in this case the client and the server.

These integration tests are certainly valuable, but they can be brittle. For example, if the user interface changes the button into a link, then your test must be updated as well. That means this type of test is costly in terms of long-term maintenance. Sometimes it pays to isolate specific functions with complex behavior—like our live view reducer functions—and write pure tests for them. Such tests are called *unit tests* because they test one specific unit of functionality. Let's discuss a testing strategy that addresses both integrated and isolated tests.

Isolation vs. Integration

Pure unit tests call one function at a time and then check expectations with one or more assertions. If you've designed your code well, you should find lots of opportunities for unit tests. By filling up your application's functional core with pure, predictable functions and by adhering to the CRC pattern, you'll find yourself with many small, isolated functions that can be tested with small, isolated unit tests, as illustrated here:

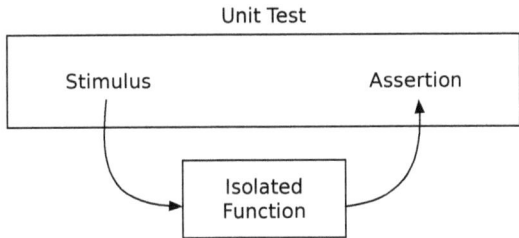

Unit tests encourage *depth*. Such tests don't require much ceremony, so programmers can write more of them and cover more scenarios quickly and easily. Unit tests also allow *loose coupling* because they don't rely on specific interactions. Building code that's friendly to unit tests also lets you take advantage of other techniques, such as property-based testing. This technique uses generated data to verify code and makes it even easier to create unit tests that cover an in-depth range of inputs. Read more about it in *Property-Based Testing with PropEr, Erlang, and Elixir [Heb19]* by Fred Hebert.

In contrast, integration tests check the *interaction between application elements*, as seen here:

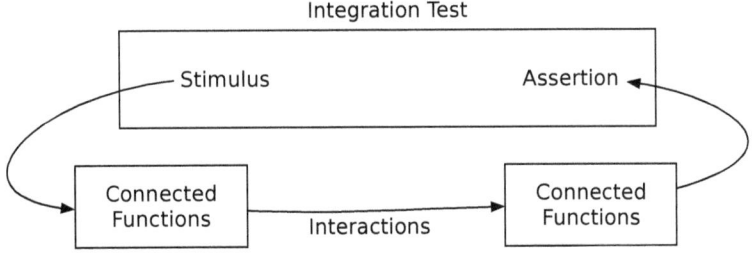

As the figure shows, integration tests check interactions between different parts of the same system. These kind of tests offer testing *breadth* by exercising a wider swath of your application. The cost is tighter coupling, since integration tests rely on specific interactions between parts of your system. Of course, that coupling will exist whether we test it or not.

So which types of tests should you use? In short, good developers need both. In this chapter, you'll start with some unit tests written with pure ExUnit. Then you'll move on to two different types of integration tests. One will use LiveViewTest features to interact with your live view, and another will use LiveViewTest along with plain Elixir message passing to simulate PubSub messages.

Start with Unit Tests

One of the best ways to make writing unit tests easier is to start with single-purpose, decoupled functions. The CRC pipelines we built throughout this book are perfect for unit tests. You could choose to test each constructor, reducer, and converter individually *as functions* by directly calling them within an ExUnit test without any of the LiveView test machinery. That's a unit test.

By exercising individual complex functions in unit tests with many different inputs, you can exhaustively cover corner cases that may be prone to failure. Then you can write a smaller number of integration tests to confirm that the complex interactions of the system work as you expect them to.

For example, a mortgage calculator is likely to have many tests on the function that computes financial values but only a few tests to make sure that those values show up correctly on the page when a user submits a request.

That's the approach we'll take to test the SurveyResultsLive component. We'll focus on a few of this component's functions that are the most complex and likely to fail: the ones that underpin the component's ability to obtain and filter survey results. Along the way, you'll write advanced unit tests composed of reducer pipelines. Then we'll move on to the integration tests.

Unit Test for Survey Results State

We'll begin with some unit tests that cover the SurveyResultsLive component's ability to manage survey results data in state. First up is the assign_products_with_average_ratings/1 reducer function, which needs to handle both an empty survey results dataset and one with existing product ratings. First, we'll make sure the reducer creates the correct socket state when no product ratings exist. Start by defining a test module in test/pento_web/live/survey_results_live_test.exs, like this:

```
testing/pento/test/pento_web/live/survey_results_live_test.exs
defmodule PentoWeb.SurveyResultsLiveTest do
  use PentoWeb.ConnCase
  alias PentoWeb.Admin.SurveyResultsLive
```

Note the use Pento.ConnCase line. This pulls in the Pento.ConnCase behaviour which provides access to the ExUnit testing functions and provides our test with a connection to the application's test database.

You'll also notice that our module aliases the SurveyResultsLive component. That's the component we're testing in this module. We need to perform a few other aliases too. We'll use them to establish some fixtures and helper functions to simplify the creation of test data, like this:

```
testing/pento/test/pento_web/live/survey_results_live_test.exs
alias Pento.{Accounts, Survey, Catalog}

@create_product_attrs %{
  description: "test description",
  name: "Test Game",
  sku: 42,
  unit_price: 120.5
}
@create_user_attrs %{
  email: "test@test.com",
  password: "passwordpassword"
}
@create_user2_attrs %{
  email: "another-person@email.com",
  password: "passwordpassword"
}
@create_demographic_attrs %{
  gender: "female",
  year_of_birth: DateTime.utc_now().year - 15
}
@create_demographic2_attrs %{
  gender: "male",
  year_of_birth: DateTime.utc_now().year - 30
}
defp product_fixture(scope) do
  {:ok, product} = Catalog.create_product(scope, @create_product_attrs)
  product
end

defp user_fixture(attrs \\ @create_user_attrs) do
  {:ok, user} = Accounts.register_user(attrs)
  user
end
```

```elixir
defp demographic_fixture(scope, user, attrs \\ @create_demographic_attrs) do
  attrs =
    attrs
    |> Map.merge(%{user_id: user.id})

  {:ok, demographic} = Survey.create_demographic(scope, attrs)
  demographic
end

defp rating_fixture(scope, stars, user, product) do
  {:ok, rating} =
    Survey.create_rating(scope, %{
      stars: stars,
      user_id: user.id,
      product_id: product.id
    })

  rating
end

defp create_product(%{scope: scope}) do
  product = product_fixture(scope)
  %{product: product}
end

defp create_user(_) do
  user = user_fixture()
  %{user: user}
end

defp create_rating(scope, stars, user, product) do
  rating = rating_fixture(scope, stars, user, product)
  %{rating: rating}
end

defp create_demographic(scope, user) do
  demographic = demographic_fixture(scope, user)
  %{demographic: demographic}
end

defp create_socket(_) do
  %{socket: %Phoenix.LiveView.Socket{}}
end
```

Test fixtures create test data, and ours use module attributes to create User, Demographic, Product, and Rating records, followed by a few helpers that call on our fixtures and return the newly created records. Later, you'll see these helper functions and their return values in action.

Update Existing Fixtures for Phoenix 1.8

Before we can run our tests, we need to update the existing SurveyFixtures module to work with Phoenix 1.8's scope-based authentication system. Our test helpers will try to create products using product_fixture/0, but this function is defined in the CatalogFixtures module. We need to import it into SurveyFixtures.

Open test/support/fixtures/survey_fixtures.ex and add the import at the top of the module:

testing/pento/test/support/fixtures/survey_fixtures.ex
```
import Pento.CatalogFixtures
```

This import gives us access to the product_fixture/1 function that our rating fixtures need. Phoenix 1.8's scope-based system requires that all context functions receive a scope as their first parameter, and our fixture files need to follow this pattern consistently.

You can see how the existing rating_fixture/2 function uses the imported product_fixture/1:

testing/pento/test/support/fixtures/survey_fixtures.ex
```
def rating_fixture(scope, attrs \\ %{}) do
  product = product_fixture(scope)

  attrs =
    Enum.into(attrs, %{
      stars: 4,
      product_id: product.id
    })

  {:ok, rating} = Pento.Survey.create_rating(scope, attrs)
  rating
end
```

Notice how both product_fixture(scope) and Pento.Survey.create_rating(scope, attrs) follow Phoenix 1.8's scope-first parameter pattern.

Now that our test module is defined and we've updated the fixture dependencies, we're ready to write our very first test. We'll start with a test that verifies the socket state when there are no product ratings. Open up a describe block and add a call to the setup/1 function with the list of helpers that will create a user, product, and socket struct, like this:

testing/pento/test/pento_web/live/survey_results_live_test.exs
```
describe "Socket state" do
  setup [
    :create_user,
    :create_socket,
    :register_and_log_in_user,
    :create_product
  ]

  setup %{user: user, scope: scope} do
    create_demographic(scope, user)
```

```
    user2 = user_fixture(@create_user2_attrs)
    scope2 = Accounts.Scope.for_user(user2)
    demographic_fixture(scope2, user2, @create_demographic2_attrs)
    [user2: user2, scope2: scope2]
  end
```

Let's break it down. The describe function groups together a block of tests. Before each one of them, ExUnit will run the setup callbacks. Think of both setup functions as reducers. Both take an accumulator, called the context, which holds a bit of state for our tests to share. The first setup call provides a list of atoms. Each one is the name of a named setup function.[1] A setup function returns a map of data to merge into the context. The second setup function is a reducer that further transforms the context.

The named setup functions each create bits of data to add to the context. If you look at the create_socket named setup function, you'll see that it's nothing more than a pure Elixir function returning an empty LiveView socket to add to the context. By returning %{socket: %Phoenix.LiveView.Socket{}}, the create_socket setup function will add this key/value pair to the shared test context data structure. The other named setup functions are similar.

After running the named setups, ExUnit calls the setup/1 function in which we establish the demographic records for two test users. The function is called with an argument of the context, and the return value of this function likewise gets added to the context map—this time the key/value pairs from the returned keyword list are added to the context map. The result is that our code builds a map, piece by piece, and passes it into each test in the describe block.

We're finally ready to write the unit test. Create a test block within the describe block that matches the context we created in the named setup. For this test, we only need the socket from the context map, so we pull it out using pattern matching, like this:

```
test "no ratings exist", %{socket: socket} do
  # coming soon!
end
```

Let's pause and think through what we're testing here and try to understand what behavior we *expect* to see. This test covers the function assign_products_with_average_ratings/1 when no product ratings exist. If it's working correctly, the socket should contain a key of :products_with_average_ratings that points to a value that looks something like this:

```
[{"Test Game", 0}]
```

---

1. https://hexdocs.pm/ex_unit/ExUnit.Callbacks.html#setup/1

The result tuples should still exist, but with a rating of 0. That's our expectation. We set up our test assertion:

```
test "no ratings exist", %{socket: socket} do
  socket =
    socket
    |> SurveyResultsLive.assign_products_with_average_ratings()
  assert
    socket.assigns.products_with_average_ratings ==
      [{"Test Game", 0}]
end
```

This test expects that when no ratings exist for a given product, then our underlying query for ratings returns a tuple that looks like this: {"Test Game", 0}. Make sure that your Pento.Catalog.Product.Query.average_ratings/1 function looks like this:

```
# pento/lib/pento/catalog/product/query.ex

defp average_ratings(query) do
  query
  |> group_by([p], p.id)
  |> select([p, r], {p.name, fragment("?::float", avg(r.stars))})
end
```

Okay, back to our test. This test won't work as-is. The assign_products_with_average_ratings/1 function expects that both the :age_filter and :gender_filter keys are present in socket assigns. So we need to establish those keys with the help of a reducer pipeline, as shown here:

```
testing/pento/test/pento_web/live/survey_results_live_test.exs
test "no ratings exist", %{socket: socket} do
  socket =
    socket
    |> SurveyResultsLive.assign_age_group_filter()
    |> SurveyResultsLive.assign_gender_filter()
    |> SurveyResultsLive.assign_products_with_average_ratings()

  assert socket.assigns.products_with_average_ratings == [{"Test Game", 0}]
end
```

Perfect. We use the same reducers to set up the socket state in the test as we used in the live view itself. That's a sign that the code is structured correctly. Building a component with small, single-purpose reducers lets us test some complex corner cases with a focused unit test. Testing a socket with no user ratings is a good example of the kinds of scenarios unit tests handle well.

Let's quickly add another, similar, test of the assign_products_with_average_ratings/1 reducer's behavior when ratings *do* exist:

```
testing/pento/test/pento_web/live/survey_results_live_test.exs
test "ratings exist", %{
  socket: socket,
  product: product,
  user: user,
  scope: scope
} do
  create_rating(scope, 2, user, product)

  socket =
    socket
    |> SurveyResultsLive.assign_age_group_filter()
    |> SurveyResultsLive.assign_gender_filter()
    |> SurveyResultsLive.assign_products_with_average_ratings()

  assert socket.assigns.products_with_average_ratings == [
         {"Test Game", 2.0}
       ]
end
```

Thanks to the composability of our reducer functions, writing tests is quick and easy and can be handled entirely in the world of ExUnit. The same functions that set up the socket within the live views also set up the socket in our tests. We haven't even brought in any LiveViewTest functions, but our tests are already delivering value. This block of code is exactly the type of test that might catch regressions that a refactoring exercise might leave behind.

Cover Corner Cases in Unit Tests

The next core behavior to test is the survey results chart's ability to filter results based on age and gender. The assign_age_group_filter/1 function manages the age group key, and we'll focus our attention there now. Testing the ability of this reducer to manage the :age_group_filter piece of socket state could require significant setup code within integration tests, but several quick assertions in a unit test can make quick work of the problem.

The function's behavior is relatively complex. We'll need to cover several different scenarios:

- When the socket has no :age_group_filter key, assign_age_group_filter/1 should add an :age_group_filter key with all.

- When a socket has the 18 and under value for :age_group_filter, assign_age_group_filter/1 should *not* replace it with all.

- Calling assign_products_with_average_ratings/1 when the socket has an :age_group_filter of 18 and under should add the correct, filtered product ratings to the socket.

Thanks to the reusable and composable nature of our reducers, we can construct a test pipeline that allows us to exercise and test each of these scenarios in one beautiful flow.

Create Unit Tests to Clarify Concepts

The line between unit and integration tests isn't always clear. Sometimes a function tests an isolated *concept* that's broken into multiple closely related functions. In these scenarios, sometimes it's helpful to build a multistage test. Let's see how it works.

Open up test/pento_web/live/survey_results_live_test.exs and add a test block within the existing describe:

```
test "ratings are filtered by age group", %{
    socket: socket,
    user: user,
    product: product,
    user2: user2} do
  create_rating(2, user, product)
  create_rating(3, user2, product)

  # coming soon!
end
```

The test uses our helper function to create two ratings. The first is for a user in the 18 and under demographic, and the other isn't.

Now we're ready to construct our reducer pipeline and test it. We'll start by testing the first of the three scenarios we outlined. We'll test that when called with a socket that doesn't contain an :age_group_filter key, the assign_age_group_filter/1 reducer returns a socket that sets that key to a value of "all". Call SurveyResultsLive.assign_age_group_filter/1 with the socket from the test context, and establish your assertions:

```
test "ratings are filtered by age group",
    %{socket: socket, user: user, product: product, user2: user2} do
  create_rating(2, user, product)
  create_rating(3, user2, product)

  socket =
    socket
    |> SurveyResultsLive.assign_age_group_filter()

  assert socket.assigns.age_group_filter == "all"
end
```

Run the test by specifying the test file and line number, and you'll see it pass:

```
[pento] → mix test test/pento_web/live/survey_results_live_test.exs:109
Excluding tags: [:test]
Including tags: [line: "109"]

.

Finished in 0.1 seconds
3 tests, 0 failures, 2 excluded

Randomized with seed 48183
```

Clean and green. One thing to note is that if you run *just* mix test without specifying the test file, you'll run *all* tests defined in the test suite. If you do that, you'll likely see some failures from generated tests exercising workflows that we've changed significantly since first generating them.

Now we're ready to test our second scenario. When the assign_age_group_filter/1 function is called with a socket that already contains an :age_group_filter key, it should retain the value of that key. We test this scenario by updating the *same* socket from our existing test to use the 18 and under filter, like this:

```elixir
test "ratings are filtered by age group",
    %{socket: socket, user: user, product: product, user2: user2} do
  create_rating(2, user, product)
  create_rating(3, user2, product)

  socket =
    socket
    |> SurveyResultsLive.assign_age_group_filter()

  assert socket.assigns.age_group_filter == "all"

  socket =
    update_socket(socket, :age_group_filter, "18 and under")
    |> SurveyResultsLive.assign_age_group_filter()

  assert socket.assigns.age_group_filter == "18 and under"
end

defp update_socket(socket, key, value) do
  %{socket | assigns: Map.merge(socket.assigns, Map.new([{key, value}]))}
end
```

The update_socket helper function sets the :age_group_filter to 18 and under and pipes the result into assign_age_group_filter/1 before running the last assertion.

Tie Stages Together in a Pipeline

This code works, but we can do better. The same pipes you built in the first part of this book will also work well in unit tests. You need only write a tiny

custom helper function to glue the example together. Open up the test file
and add the following below the update_socket/3 helper:

testing/pento/test/pento_web/live/survey_results_live_test.exs
```
defp assert_keys(socket, key, value) do
  assert socket.assigns[key] == value
  socket
end
```

We created an assertion reducer. This function is different than typical
reducers. Rather than transforming the socket, this reducer's job is to call
the assert macro and then return the socket unchanged. The job of the function
is twofold. It calls the assertion and keeps the integrity of the pipeline intact
by returning the element with which it was called.

Now we can assemble our test pipeline, like this:

testing/pento/test/pento_web/live/survey_results_live_test.exs
```
test "ratings are filtered by age group", %{
  socket: socket,
  user: user,
  product: product,
  user2: user2,
  scope: scope,
  scope2: scope2
} do
  create_rating(scope, 2, user, product)
  create_rating(scope2, 3, user2, product)

  socket
  |> SurveyResultsLive.assign_age_group_filter()
  |> assert_keys(:age_group_filter, "all")
  |> update_socket(:age_group_filter, "18 and under")
  |> SurveyResultsLive.assign_age_group_filter()
  |> assert_keys(:age_group_filter, "18 and under")
  |> SurveyResultsLive.assign_gender_filter()
  |> SurveyResultsLive.assign_products_with_average_ratings()
  |> assert_keys(:products_with_average_ratings, [{"Test Game", 2.0}])
end
```

That's much better! The test now unfolds like a story. Each step is a reducer
with a socket accumulator. Then we use our new helper to check each key.

We can chain further reducers and assertions onto our pipeline to test the
final scenario. The assign_products_with_average_ratings/1 function should populate
the socket with the correct product ratings, given the provided filters, like
this:

```
testing/pento/test/pento_web/live/survey_results_live_test.exs
defp assert_keys(socket, key, value) do
  assert socket.assigns[key] == value
  socket
end
```

We find no surprises here. The extra assertion looks like it belongs. Building in this kind of conceptual density without sacrificing readability is what Elixir is all about.

Now if you run the all of the tests in this file, you'll see them pass:

```
[pento] → mix test test/pento_web/live/survey_results_live_test.exs
...

Finished in 0.2 seconds
3 tests, 0 failures

Randomized with seed 543381
```

The composable nature of our reducer functions makes them highly testable. It's easy to test the functionality of a single reducer under a variety of circumstances or to string together any set of reducers to test the combined functionality of the pipelines that support your live view's behavior. With a little help from our assert_keys/3 function, we constructed a beautiful pipeline to test a set of scenarios within one easy-to-read flow.

Now that we've written a few unit tests that validate the behavior of the reducer building blocks of our live view, let's move on to testing LiveView features and behaviours with the help of the LiveViewTest module.

Integration Test LiveView Interactions

Where unit tests check isolated bits of code, integration tests verify the interactions between parts of a system. In this section, we'll write an integration test that validates interactions within *a single live view*. We'll focus on testing the behavior of the survey results chart filter. In the next section, we'll write another integration test that checks interactions *between processes* that manage live updates when new ratings come in.

We'll write both tests *without any JavaScript*. This statement should get some attention from anyone used to the overhead of bringing in an external JavaScript dependency to write integration tests that are often slow and flaky. So we'll say it again, louder this time. You don't need JavaScript to test LiveView!

We'll use the LiveViewTest module's special LiveView testing functions to simulate LiveView connections without a browser. Your tests can mount and render live views, trigger events, and then execute assertions against the rendered view. That's the whole LiveView life cycle.

You might be concerned about leaving JavaScript untested, but remember—the JavaScript that supports LiveView is part of the LiveView framework itself, so you also don't have to leverage JavaScript to *test* your live views. You can trust that the JavaScript in the framework does what it's supposed to do and focus your attention on testing the specific behaviors and features that you built into your own live view, in pure Elixir.

As a result, the integration tests for LiveView are quick and easy to write, and they run fast and concurrently. Once again, LiveView maintains a focused mindset on the server, in pure Elixir. Let's write some tests.

Write an Integration Test

We've unit tested the individual pieces of code responsible for our component's filtering functionality. Now it's time to test that same filtering behavior by exercising the overall live view. We'll write one test together to introduce LiveView's testing capabilities. Then you can use what you've learned to add more tests to cover additional scenarios. Our test will simulate a user's visit to /admin/dashboard, followed by their filter selection of the 18 and under age group. The test will verify an updated survey results chart that displays product ratings from users in that age group.

Because components run in their parent's processes, we'll focus our tests on the `AdminDashboardLive` view, which is the `SurveyResultsLive` component's parent. We'll use `LiveViewTest` helper functions to run our admin dashboard live view and interact with the survey results component. Along the way, you'll get a taste for the wide variety of interactions that the `LiveViewTest` module allows you to test.

Let's begin by setting up a LiveView test for our `AdminDashboardLive` view.

Set Up the LiveView Test Module

It's best to segregate unit tests and integration tests into their own modules, so create a new file, test/pento_web/live/admin_dashboard_live_test.exs, and key this in:

```
testing/pento/test/pento_web/live/admin_dashboard_live_test.exs
defmodule PentoWeb.AdminDashboardLiveTest do
  use PentoWeb.ConnCase

  import Phoenix.LiveViewTest
  alias Pento.{Accounts, Survey, Catalog}

  @create_product_attrs %{
```

```elixir
    description: "test description",
    name: "Test Game",
    sku: 42,
    unit_price: 120.5
  }
  @create_demographic_attrs %{
    gender: "female",
    year_of_birth: DateTime.utc_now().year - 15
  }
  @create_demographic_over_18_attrs %{
    gender: "female",
    year_of_birth: DateTime.utc_now().year - 30
  }
  @create_user_attrs %{email: "test@test.com", password: "passwordpassword"}
  @create_user2_attrs %{email: "test2@test.com", password: "passwordpassword"}
  @create_user3_attrs %{email: "test3@test.com", password: "passwordpassword"}

  defp product_fixture(scope) do
    {:ok, product} = Catalog.create_product(scope, @create_product_attrs)
    product
  end

  defp user_fixture(attrs \\ @create_user_attrs) do
    {:ok, user} = Accounts.register_user(attrs)
    user
  end

  defp demographic_fixture(scope, user, attrs) do
    attrs =
      attrs
      |> Map.merge(%{user_id: user.id})

    {:ok, demographic} = Survey.create_demographic(scope, attrs)
    demographic
  end

  defp rating_fixture(scope, user, product, stars) do
    {:ok, rating} =
      Survey.create_rating(scope, %{
        stars: stars,
        user_id: user.id,
        product_id: product.id
      })

    rating
  end

  defp create_product(%{scope: scope}) do
    product = product_fixture(scope)
    %{product: product}
  end

  defp create_user(_) do
    user = user_fixture()
```

```
    %{user: user}
  end
  defp create_demographic(scope, user, attrs \\ @create_demographic_attrs) do
    demographic = demographic_fixture(scope, user, attrs)
    %{demographic: demographic}
  end
  defp create_rating(scope, user, product, stars) do
    rating = rating_fixture(scope, user, product, stars)
    %{rating: rating}
  end
```

We're doing a few things here. First, we define our test module. Then we use the PentoWeb.ConnCase behaviour that will allow us to route to live views using the test connection. Using this behaviour gives our tests access to a context map with a key of :conn pointing to a value of the test connection. We also import the LiveViewTest module to give us access to LiveView testing functions. Finally, we throw in some fixtures we'll use to create our test data.

Now that our module is set up, go ahead and add a describe block to encapsulate the feature we're testing—the survey results chart functionality:

testing/pento/test/pento_web/live/admin_dashboard_live_test.exs
```
describe "Survey Results" do
  setup [:register_and_log_in_user, :create_product, :create_user]

  setup %{user: user, product: product, scope: scope} do
    create_demographic(scope, user)
    create_rating(scope, user, product, 2)

    user2 = user_fixture(@create_user2_attrs)
    scope2 = Accounts.Scope.for_user(user2)
    create_demographic(scope2, user2, @create_demographic_over_18_attrs)
    create_rating(scope2, user2, product, 3)
    :ok
  end
```

Two calls to setup/1 seed the test database with a product, users, demographics, and ratings. One of the two users is in the 18 and under age group, and the other is in another age group. Then we create a rating for each user.

We're also using a test helper created for us way back when we ran the authentication generator—register_and_log_in_user/1. This function creates a context map with a logged-in user and their authentication scope, a necessary step because visiting the /admin/dashboard route requires an authenticated user.

Now that our setup is completed, we'll write the body of the test.

Test the Survey Chart Filter

As with the other testing module, this one will group tests together into a common describe block. Add a test within describe, like this:

```
test "it filters by age group", %{conn: conn} do
  # coming soon!
end
```

We'll fill in the details of our test after making a plan. Here's what we need to do:

- Mount and render the live view.
- Find the age group filter drop-down menu and select an item from it.
- Assert that the re-rendered survey results chart has the correct data and markup.

This is the pattern you'll apply to testing live view features from here on out—run the live view, target some interaction, test the rendered result. This pattern should sound familiar. Earlier on in this chapter we said that all of the types of tests will adhere to this pattern:

- Set up preconditions.
- Provide a stimulus.
- Compare an actual response to expectations.

LiveView tests are no different.

To mount and render the live view, we'll use the LiveViewTest.live/2 function. This function spawns a simulated LiveView process. We call the function with the test context struct and the path to the live view we want to run and render:

```
test "it filters by age group", %{conn: conn} do
  {:ok, view, _html} = live(conn, "/admin/dashboard")
end
```

The call to live/2 returns a three element tuple with :ok, the LiveView process, and the rendered HTML returned from the live view's call to render/1. We don't need to access that HTML in this test, so we ignore it.

Remember, components run in their parent's process. That means the test *must* start up the AdminDashboardLive view rather than rendering *just* the SurveyResultsLive component. By spawning the AdminDashboardLive view, we're *also* rendering the components that the view is comprised of. This means our SurveyResultsLive component is up and running and is rendered within the AdminDashboardLive view represented by the returned view variable. So we'll be able to interact with elements within that component and test that it re-renders appropriately within the parent live view in response to events. This is the correct way to test LiveView component behavior within a live view page.

> **Testing LiveView Components**
>
>
> To test the rendering of a component in isolation, you can use the LiveViewTest.render_component/2 function. This will render and return the markup of the specified component, allowing you to write assertions against that markup. This is useful in writing unit tests for stateless components. To test the behavior of a component—that is, how it's mounted within a parent live view and how events impact its state—you'll need to run the parent live view with the live/2 function and target events at DOM elements contained within the component.

The test has a running live view, so we're ready to select the 18 and under age filter. Let's interact with our running live view to do exactly that.

Simulate an Event

The test can trigger LiveView interactions using helper functions from LiveViewTest—all you need to do is identify the page element you want to interact with. For a comprehensive look at the rapidly growing list of such functions, check the LiveViewTest documentation.[2]

We'll use the element/3 function to find the age group drop-down on the page. First, we use the unique ID attribute on the form element so that we can find it with the element/3 function, as you can see here:

```
testing/pento/lib/pento_web/live/admin/survey_results_live.html.heex
<div class="form-control w-full">
  <.form
    for={%{}}
    as={:age_group_filter}
    phx-change="age_group_filter"
    phx-target={@myself}
    id="age-group-form"
  >
    <label class="label">
      <span class="label-text text-sm">By age group:</span>
    </label>
    <select name="age_group_filter" id="age_group_filter"
        class="select select-bordered select-sm w-full">
      <%= for age_group <-
```

---

2. https://hexdocs.pm/phoenix_live_view/Phoenix.LiveViewTest.html#functions

```
      ["all", "18 and under", "18 to 25", "25 to 35", "35 and up"] do %>
        <option value={age_group} selected={@age_group_filter == age_group}>
          <%= age_group %>
        </option>
      <% end %>
    </select>
  </.form>
</div>
```

Now we can target this element with the element/3 function, like this:

```
test "it filters by age group", %{conn: conn} do
  {:ok, view, _html} = live(conn, "/admin/dashboard")
  html =
    view
    |> element("#age-group-form")
end
```

The element/3 function accepts three arguments—the live view whose element we want to select, any query selector, and some optional text to narrow down the query selector even further. If no text filter is provided, it must be true that the query selector returns a single element.

Now that we've selected our element, let's take a closer look. Add the following to your test to inspect it:

```
test "it filters by age group", %{conn: conn} do
  {:ok, view, _html} = live(conn, "/admin/dashboard")
  html =
    view
    |> element("#age-group-form")
    |> IO.inspect
end
```

Run the following test, and you'll see the element dumped on the terminal. Note that the exact line number on which your test is defined may differ depending on your formatting or any code comments you may have added.

```
[pento] → mix test test/pento_web/live/admin_dashboard_live_test.exs:90
Compiling 1 file (.ex)
Excluding tags: [:test]
Including tags: [line: "90"]
...
#Phoenix.LiveViewTest.Element<
  selector: "#age-group-form",
  text_filter: nil,
  ...
>
.
Finished in 0.3 seconds
```

Nice! We can see that the element/3 function returned a Phoenix.LiveViewTest.Element struct. Let's use it to fire a form change event that selects the 18 and under option:

```
test "it filters by age group", %{conn: conn} do
  {:ok, view, _html} = live(conn, "/admin/dashboard")
  html =
    view
    |> element("#age-group-form")
    |> render_change(%{"age_group_filter" => "18 and under"})
end
```

The render_change/2 function is one of the functions you'll use to simulate user interactions when testing live views. It takes an argument of the selected element, along with some params, and triggers a phx-change event.

The phx-change attribute of the given element determines the name of the event, and the phx-target attribute determines which component gets the message. Recall that the age group form element we selected looks like this:

testing/pento/lib/pento_web/live/admin/survey_results_live.html.heex
```
<div class="form-control w-full">
  <.form
    for={%{}}
    as={:age_group_filter}
    phx-change="age_group_filter"
    phx-target={@myself}
    id="age-group-form"
  >
    <label class="label">
      <span class="label-text text-sm">By age group:</span>
    </label>
    <select name="age_group_filter" id="age_group_filter"
        class="select select-bordered select-sm w-full">
      <%= for age_group <-
        ["all", "18 and under", "18 to 25", "25 to 35", "35 and up"] do %>
        <option value={age_group} selected={@age_group_filter == age_group}>
          <%= age_group %>
        </option>
      <% end %>
    </select>
  </.form>
</div>
```

So we'll send the message "age_group_filter" to the target @myself, which is the SurveyResultsLive component. The phx-change event will fire with the params we provided to render_change/2. This event will trigger the associated handler, thus invoking the reducers that update our socket, eventually re-rendering the survey results chart with the filtered product rating data. Here's that code to refresh your memory:

```
testing/pento/lib/pento_web/live/admin/survey_results_live.ex
# Event handler for age group filtering
def handle_event("age_group_filter", %{"age_group_filter" => age_group},
                 socket) do
  {:noreply,
   socket
   |> assign_age_group_filter(age_group)
   |> assign_products_with_average_ratings()
   |> assign_dataset()
   |> assign_chart()
   |> assign_chart_svg()}
end
```

Now that we have our test code in place to trigger the form event, and we know how we expect our component to behave when it receives that event, we're ready to write our assertions.

The call to render_change/2 will return the re-rendered template. Let's add an assertion that the re-rendered chart displays the correct data. Recall that the bars in our survey results chart are labeled with the average star rating for the given product, like this:

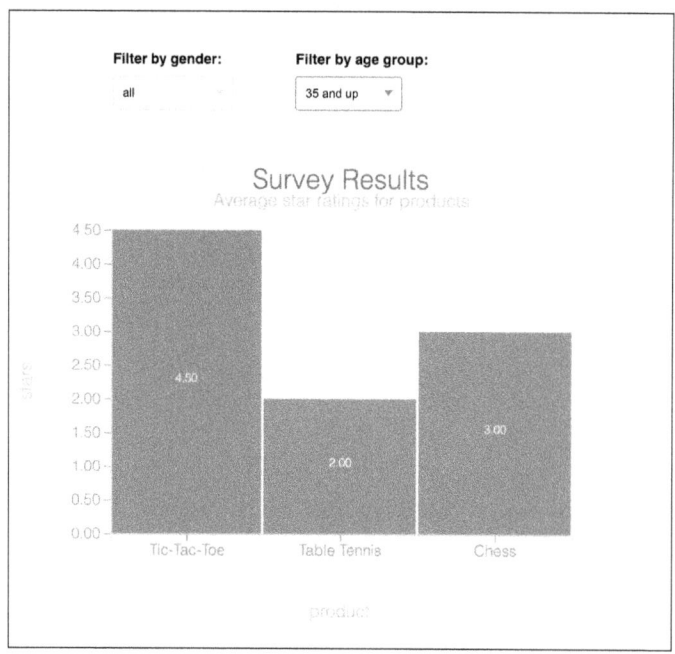

So we'll need to write an assertion that looks for the correct average star rating to be present on the bar for a given game in the selected age group. But how will we select the correct page element to write our assertion?

This is a great time to make use of another LiveViewTest convenience. The open_browser/1 function lets us inspect a browser page at a given point in the run of a test. Let's use it now to inspect the view so we can get a better sense of what test assertion we need to write. Add the following to your test:

```
test "it filters by age group", %{conn: conn} do
  {:ok, view, _html} = live(conn, "/admin/dashboard")
  html =
    view
    |> open_browser()
    |> element("#age-group-form")
    |> render_change(%{"age_group_filter" => "18 and under"})
end
```

Now, run the test via mix test test/pento_web/live/admin_dashboard_live_test.exs:75 and you should see your default browser open and display the following page:

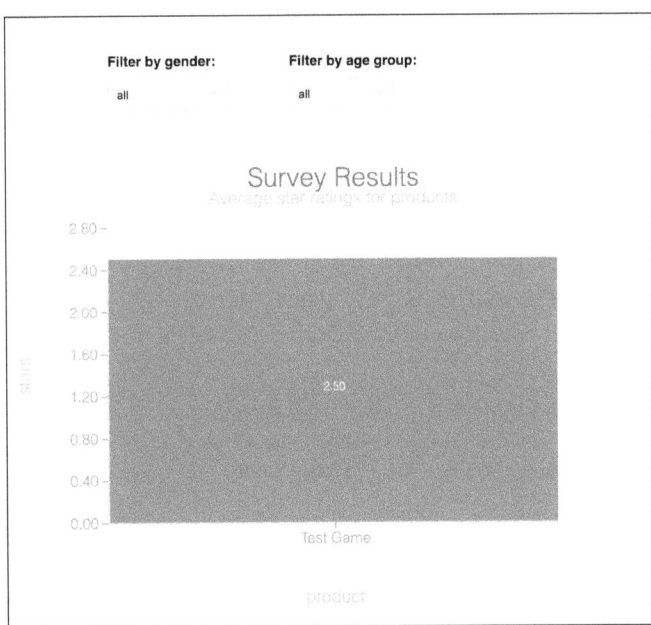

You can open up the element inspector to select the Test Game column's label, like this:

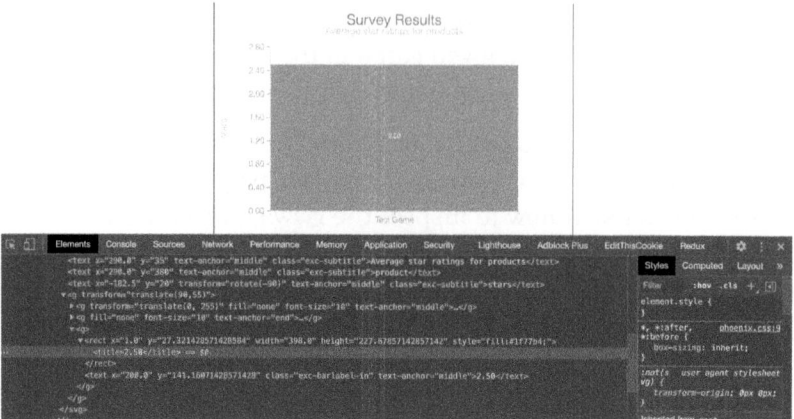

Now you know exactly what element to select—a <title> element that contains the expected average star rating.

So what should that average star rating be? Revisit the test data we established in our setup block here:

```
setup %{user: user, product: product} do
  create_demographic(user)
  create_rating(user, product, 2)

  user2 = user_fixture(@create_user2_attrs)
  create_demographic(user2, @create_demographic_over_18_attrs)
  create_rating(user2, product, 3)
  :ok
end
```

We created two ratings for the test product—a two-star rating for the user in the 18 and under age group and a three-star rating for the other user. So if we filter survey results by the 18 and under age group, we would expect the Test Game bar in our chart to have a title of 2.0. Let's add our assertion here:

testing/pento/test/pento_web/live/admin_dashboard_live_test.exs
```
test "it filters by age group", %{conn: conn} do
  {:ok, view, _html} = live(conn, "/admin/dashboard")
  params = %{"age_group_filter" => "18 and under"}

  assert view
         |> element("#age-group-form")
         |> render_change(params) =~ "<title>2.00</title>"
end
```

Run your test and it'll pass! The LiveViewTest module provided us with everything we needed to mount and render a connected live view, target elements within that live view—even elements nested within child components—and assert the state of the view after firing DOM events against those elements.

The test code, like much of the Elixir and LiveView code we've been writing, is clean and elegantly composed with a simple pipeline. All of the test code is written in Elixir with ExUnit and LiveViewTest functions. This made it quick and easy for us to conceive of and write our test. Our test runs fast, and it's highly reliable. We didn't need to bring in any JavaScript dependencies or undertake any onerous setup to test our LiveView feature. LiveView tests allow us to focus on the live view behavior we want to test—we don't need JavaScript, because we trust that the JavaScript in the LiveView framework will work the way it should.

We only saw a small subset of the LiveViewTest functions that support LiveView testing here. We used element/3 and render_change/2 to target and fire our form change event. Many more LiveViewTest functions allow you to send any number of DOM events—blurs, form submissions, live navigation, and more.

We won't get into all of those functions here. Instead, you can explore more of them on your own. We *will* tackle one more testing task together though. In the last chapter, you provided real-time updates to the admin dashboard with the help of PubSub. LiveViewTest allows us to test this distributed real-time functionality with ease.

Verify Distributed Real-Time Updates

Testing message passing in a distributed application can be painful, but LiveViewTest makes it easy to test the PubSub-backed real-time features we've built into our admin dashboard. That's because LiveView tests interact with views via process communication. Because PubSub uses simple Elixir message passing, testing a live view's ability to handle such messages is a simple matter of using send/2.

In this section, we'll write a test to verify the admin dashboard's real-time updates that fire when it receives a "rating_created" message. We'll use a call to send/2 to deliver the appropriate message to the view and then use the render function to test the result.

Set Up the Test

The real-time survey results chart test will follow the same LiveView test pattern we used earlier on. Remember, these are the steps:

- Mount and render the connected live view.
- Interact with that live view—in this case, by sending the rating_created message to the live view.
- Re-render the view and verify changes in the resulting HTML.

Add the test to test/pento_web/live/admin_dashboard_live_test.exs within the current describe block:

```
test "it updates to display newly created ratings",
    %{conn: conn, product: product} do
  # coming soon!
end
```

That's a basic test that receives the connection and a product. Now, spawn the live view with live/2, like this:

```
test "it updates to display newly created ratings",
    %{conn: conn, product: product} do
  {:ok, view, html} = live(conn, "/admin/dashboard")
end
```

Add a Rating

Before we target our interaction and establish some assertion, let's think about what changes should occur on the page. Thanks to our setup block, we already have one product with two ratings—one with a star rating of 2 and the other with a star rating of 3. So we know our survey results chart will render a bar for the Test Game product with a label of 2.50. We can verify this assumption with the help of the open_browser/0 function, like so:

```
test "it updates to display newly created ratings",
    %{conn: conn, product: product} do
  {:ok, view, html} = live(conn, "/admin/dashboard")
  open_browser(view)
end
```

Perfect. Run the test like this to see the browser state:

```
[pento] → mix test test/pento_web/live/admin_dashboard_live_test.exs:84
```

You'll see the screen shown on the facing page open in the browser.

You can see that the chart does in fact have a bar with a <title> element containing the text 2.50. That's the initial value, but it will change. We'll create a new rating to change this average star rating title and then send the rating_created" message to the live view. Finally, we'll check for the changed <title> element.

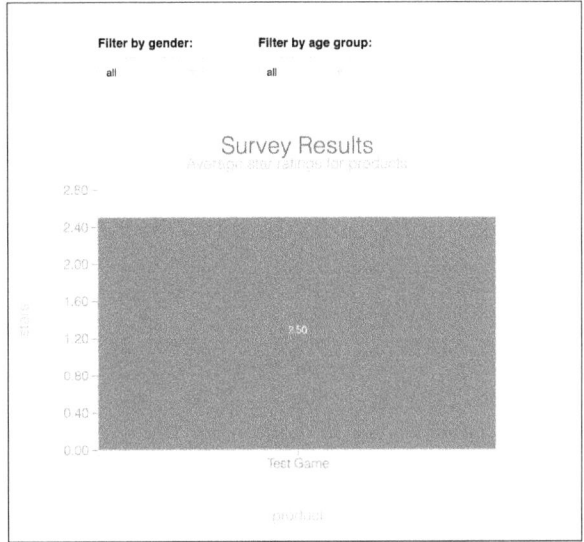

Before making any changes though, the test should verify the initial 2.50 title element, like this:

```
testing/pento/test/pento_web/live/admin_dashboard_live_test.exs
test "it updates to display newly created ratings",
    %{conn: conn, product: product} do
  {:ok, view, html} = live(conn, "/admin/dashboard")
  assert html =~ "<title>2.50</title>"
```

It's a basic assertion to validate the starting state of the page. Now let's create a new user, demographic, and rating with a star value of 3, like this:

```
testing/pento/test/pento_web/live/admin_dashboard_live_test.exs
test "it updates to display newly created ratings",
    %{conn: conn, product: product} do
  {:ok, view, html} = live(conn, "/admin/dashboard")
  assert html =~ "<title>2.50</title>"
  user3 = user_fixture(@create_user3_attrs)
  scope3 = Accounts.Scope.for_user(user3)
  create_demographic(scope3, user3)
  create_rating(scope3, user3, product, 3)
```

Perfect. We're ready to trigger the live view interaction by sending the event to the view.

Trigger an Interaction with send/2

Recall that new ratings trigger PubSub "rating_created" messages to be broadcast over the "survey_results" topic with an empty payload. Since the AdminDashboardLive live view is subscribed to that same topic, it will receive a message that looks like this:

```
%{event: "rating_created", payload: %{}}
```

The AdminDashboardLive view implements the following handle_info/2 event handler for this event:

```
testing/pento/lib/pento_web/live/admin/dashboard_live.ex
def handle_info(%{event: "rating_created"}, socket) do
  send_update(
    SurveyResultsLive,
    id: socket.assigns.survey_results_component_id
  )

  {:noreply, socket}
end
```

To test the admin dashboard's ability to handle this message and update the template appropriately, we can manually deliver the same message with send/2, like this:

```
testing/pento/test/pento_web/live/admin_dashboard_live_test.exs
test "it updates to display newly created ratings",
     %{conn: conn, product: product} do
  {:ok, view, html} = live(conn, "/admin/dashboard")
  assert html =~ "<title>2.50</title>"
  user3 = user_fixture(@create_user3_attrs)
  scope3 = Accounts.Scope.for_user(user3)
  create_demographic(scope3, user3)
  create_rating(scope3, user3, product, 3)

  send(view.pid, %{event: "rating_created"})
  :timer.sleep(2)
```

Notice that we've added a sleep to give the live view time to receive the message, handle it, and re-render before executing any assertions.

We've sent the message, so all that remains is checking the result.

Verify the Result

To view the result, we call render. Then we execute an assertion, like this:

```
testing/pento/test/pento_web/live/admin_dashboard_live_test.exs
test "it updates to display newly created ratings",
     %{conn: conn, product: product} do
```

```
{:ok, view, html} = live(conn, "/admin/dashboard")
assert html =~ "<title>2.50</title>"
user3 = user_fixture(@create_user3_attrs)
scope3 = Accounts.Scope.for_user(user3)
create_demographic(scope3, user3)
create_rating(scope3, user3, product, 3)

send(view.pid, %{event: "rating_created"})
:timer.sleep(2)
assert render(view) =~ "<title>2.67</title>"
```

We render the view, and then execute the assertion that verifies the updated template. It's finally time to run this last test.

Let it fly:

```
[pento] → mix test test/pento_web/live/admin_dashboard_live_test.exs
..

Finished in 0.4 seconds
2 tests, 0 failures

Randomized with seed 678757
```

We've tested a distributed operation and then verified the result. With that, you've seen a lot of what LiveView tests can do. Before we go, we'll give you a chance to get your hands dirty.

Your Turn

LiveView makes it easy to write both unit tests and integration tests. Unit tests call individual functions within a live view in *isolation*. Integration tests exercise interactions *between* functions. Both are important, and LiveView's design makes it easy to do both.

Using the CRC pattern within a live view yields many single-purpose functions that are great testing targets. Unit tests use reducers to set up precise test conditions and then compare those results against expectations in an assertion. Integration tests use the LiveViewTest module to mount and render a view. Then these tests interact with elements on a page through the specialized functions provided by LiveViewTest to verify behavior with assertions.

We only saw a handful of LiveView test features in this chapter, but you're already equipped to write more.

Give It a Try

These tasks will give you a chance to explore unit and integration tests in the context of components.

- Build a unit test that calls render_component/3[3] directly. Test that the stateless RatingLive.Index renders the product rating form when no product rating exists.

- Write another test to verify that the component renders the correct rating details when ratings do exist.

- Test the stateful DemographicLive.Form by writing a test for the parent live view. Ensure that submitting a new demographic form updates the page to display the saved demographic details.

Next Time

This chapter completes our brief tour of testing and closes out Part III, Extend LiveView. In the next part, you'll get to create a new LiveView feature without relying on the help of any generators. We'll build a game to show how a multilayer system interacts across multiple views, starting with a core layer that plots, rotates, and moves points.

---

3. https://hexdocs.pm/phoenix_live_view/Phoenix.LiveViewTest.html#render_component/3

Part IV

Graphics and Custom Code Organization

In Part IV, we'll focus on organizing custom code built from scratch. We'll start with a chapter to provide a detailed look at CRC in Elixir, including a core layer for moving and dropping game pieces. Next, we'll work with a LiveView layer that will render graphics and, finally, work with a boundary layer that handles uncertainty.

CHAPTER 11

Build the Game Core

You now have all of the building blocks you need to build clean, maintainable LiveView applications that handle a wide variety of use cases. In this part of this book, you'll put together what you've learned to build an interactive in-browser game in LiveView, from the ground up.

LiveView might not be the perfect fit for complex in-browser games with lots of interaction or low-latency environments. For such scenarios, it's best to write the full game in a client-side language like JavaScript. But it *is* a good fit for the simple logic game we'll be building if you're not particularly concerned with latency. With LiveView, we can use the CRC pattern to model a game-like domain and present the user with a way to manage changes within that domain. Building a game will give you an opportunity to put into practice just about everything you've learned so far. It's the perfect way to wrap up your adventures with LiveView.

In this chapter, we'll start with our game's functional core, and you'll use the CRC pattern to model the game's basic pieces and interactions.

Remember, the functional core of your application represents certainty. It's the place for all of your predictable code that always behaves the same way, given the same inputs. We'll construct our core out of small, pure functions that will compose into elegant pipelines. These functions will be single-purpose, so they'll be easy to test. And their composable nature makes them flexible—we'll call on the same functions in different orders to construct pipelines that do different things. This will allow us to layer up complex game functionality out of a few simple building blocks.

Before we dive into the details of these building blocks, let's make a plan for our functional core and talk a bit about the game we'll be building.

The Plan

We'll be building the game of Pentominoes—the favorite game of legendary CBS News anchor Walter Cronkite. Pentominoes is something like a cross between Tetris and a puzzle. The player is presented with a set of shapes called pentominoes and a game board of a certain size. The player must figure out how to place all of the pentominoes on the board so that they fit together to evenly cover all of the available space, like a puzzle.

Each pentomino is a shape comprised of five even squares joined together. The game has 12 basic shapes, as shown here:

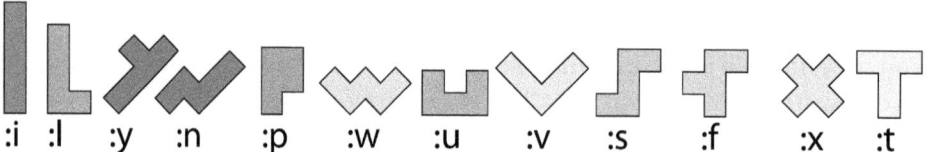

Assuming you're playing a round of Pentominoes with a large rectangular board and *all* of the available pentomino shapes, you might end up with a finished puzzle that looks like this:

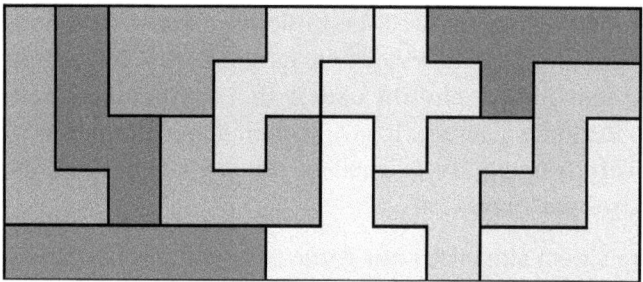

Now, let's say you're playing a round of Pentominoes with a small rectangular board and just three shapes—a :c, a :v, and a :p. You might end up with a finished puzzle that looks like this one:

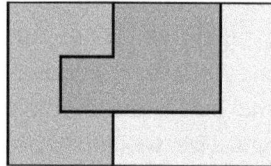

Now that you have a basic idea of how the game works, let's talk about the core concepts of the game that we'll model in code.

The Game Board

Each round of pentominoes solves a different puzzle. This means that each round presents the player with a board of a different size and a new set of pentomino pieces to place.

We'll model the game board with a module that produces Board structs. Each board struct will have the following attributes:

- *points:* All of our puzzles will be rectangles of different shapes. The puzzle shape will be a list of points that make up the grid of our puzzle board.
- *palette:* The set of pentomino shapes that must be placed onto the board to complete the puzzle.
- *completed_pentos:* The pentomino shapes that have already been placed on the board. This will update as the user places more shapes.
- *active_pento:* The pentomino from the palette that the user has selected and is actively in the process of placing on the board.

We'll return to the Board module and its functionality later in this chapter. For now, let's move on to a high-level overview of our next game fundamental, the pentominoes pieces themselves.

The Pentominoes Pieces

We'll define a module, Pentomino, that produces pentominoes structs. Each pentomino struct will have the following attributes:

- *name:* The type of shape—for example, :i or :p.
- *rotation:* The number of degrees that the shape has been rotated.
- *reflected:* A true/false value to indicate whether the user flipped the shape over to place it on the board.
- *location:* The location of the shape on the board grid.

Along with the Pentomino module that represents the placement of a shape on the board, we'll also define another module, Shape, that wraps up the attributes of individual pentominoes shapes. If Pentomino is responsible for representing a shape on the board, Shape is responsible for modeling a given pentomino shape. Each shape struct will have the following attributes:

- *points:* The five points that comprise the given shape.
- *color:* The color associated with the given shape.

We'll take a closer look at the relationship between a Pentomino struct and a Shape struct later on, and we'll see how to use them to model the placement of pentominoes on the game board. Before we move on, however, we have one more game primitive to discuss.

The Pentominoes Points

Each shape is comprised of a set of five points of equal size, and each point will occupy a spot on the board grid. We'll model these points with the Point module. It will produce {x,y} point tuples that represent the x, y coordinates of the point on the game board. It will also implement a set of reducer functions to move these points according to the location, rotation, and reflection of the shape to which a point belongs. To place our pentominoes on the board, we'll apply functions to rotate, reflect, and move that pentomino to all five individual points that make up the pentomino. If that seems a little confusing right now, don't worry. We'll build this out step by step in the following sections.

Now that we have a high-level understanding of the basic building blocks of our game, let's start building the functional core in earnest. Each of the modules we've outlined so far will be implemented in our application's core, and we'll use the CRC pattern to build them. Our core modules will have constructors that create and return the module's data type, reducers to manipulate that data, and converters to transform the data into something that can be consumed by other parts of our application. While not all of our core modules will implement each of these CRC elements, you'll see all of them come into play in the rest of this chapter.

Represent a Shape with Points

The user interface will render each pentomino with a set of points. Before we draw our points on the board, we need to understand *where* we'll be placing those points. To be able to correctly calculate the location of each point in a shape, given that shape's reflection and rotation, we're going to take the following approach:

- Always plot each shape in the center of a 5x5 grid that will occupy the top-left of any given game board.

- Calculate the location of each point in the shape, given its rotation and reflection *within* that 5x5 square.

- Only *then* will we apply the location to move the pentomino's location on the wider board.

We'll dig into this process and the reasoning behind it in greater detail later on. For now, you just need to understand that every shape is comprised of a set of five points, and those five points are located by default in the center of a 5x5 square which is positioned like this:

		1	2	3	4	5	6	7	8	9	10
						X					
	1	1,1	2,1	3,1	4,1	5,1	6,1	7,1	8,1	9,1	10,1
	2	1,2	2,2	3,2	4,2	5,2	6,2	7,2	8,2	9,2	10,2
	3	1,3	2,3	3,3	4,3	5,3	6,3	7,3	8,3	9,3	10,3
	4	1,4	2,4	3,4	4,4	5,4	6,4	7,4	8,4	9,4	10,4
Y	5	1,5	2,5	3,5	4,5	5,5	6,5	7,5	8,5	9,5	10,5
	6	1,6	2,6	3,6	4,6	5,6	6,6	7,6	8,6	9,6	10,6
	7	1,7	2,7	3,7	4,7	5,7	6,7	7,7	8,7	9,7	10,7
	8	1,8	2,8	3,8	4,8	5,8	6,8	7,8	8,8	9,8	10,8
	9	1,9	2,9	3,9	4,9	5,9	6,9	7,9	8,9	9,9	10,9
	10	1,10	2,10	3,10	4,10	5,10	6,10	7,10	8,10	9,10	10,10

Let's do some quick prototyping. Consider the :p shape. If we want to place the :p shape in the center of the 5x5 square, it will look like this:

	1	2	3	4	5	6	7	8	9	10
1	1,1	2,1	3,1	4,1	5,1	6,1	7,1	8,1	9,1	10,1
2	1,2	2,2	**3,2**	**4,2**	5,2	6,2	7,2	8,2	9,2	10,2
3	1,3	2,3	**3,3**	**4,3**	5,3	6,3	7,3	8,3	9,3	10,3
4	1,4	2,4	**3,4**	4,4	5,4	6,4	7,4	8,4	9,4	10,4
5	1,5	2,5	3,5	4,5	5,5	6,5	7,5	8,5	9,5	10,5
6	1,6	2,6	3,6	4,6	5,6	6,6	7,6	8,6	9,6	10,6
7	1,7	2,7	3,7	4,7	5,7	6,7	7,7	8,7	9,7	10,7
8	1,8	2,8	3,8	4,8	5,8	6,8	7,8	8,8	9,8	10,8
9	1,9	2,9	3,9	4,9	5,9	6,9	7,9	8,9	9,9	10,9
10	1,10	2,10	3,10	4,10	5,10	6,10	7,10	8,10	9,10	10,10

So the :p shape can be represented by a list of the following points:

[{3, 2}, {4,2},
{3, 3}, {4, 3},
{3, 4}]

Now that you've seen how a set of points is used to depict a shape on the board, let's build out our very first core module, the Point module.

Define the Point Constructor

Create a file, lib/pento/game/point.ex, and implement the module head, like so:

core/pento/lib/pento/game/point.ex
```
defmodule Pento.Game.Point do
end
```

Now define the constructor function. The core entity that the Point module creates and manages is the point tuple. The first element of the tuple is the x coordinate of the point, and the second value is the y coordinate. So our constructor function will take in two arguments, the x and y values of the point, and return the point tuple, as you can see here:

```
def new(x, y) when is_integer(x) and is_integer(y), do: {x, y}
```

Simple enough. The guards make sure each point has valid data, as long as we create points with the new constructor. If bad data comes in, we let it crash because we can't do anything about that error condition. Now that we have a constructor to create points, let's build some reducers to manipulate those points.

Move Points Up and Down with Reducers

Later, we'll build logic that moves the pentomino shape on the board by applying a change of location to each point in that shape. Right now, we'll start from the ground up by giving our Point module the ability to move an individual point by some amount.

In the Point module, define the move/2 function like this:

```
def move({x, y}, {change_x, change_y}) do
  {x + change_x, y + change_y}
end
```

Here we have a classic reducer. It takes in a first argument of the data type we're manipulating and a second argument of some input with which to manipulate it. Then it returns a new entity that's the result of applying the manipulation to the data. In this case, we take in an amount by which to move each x and y coordinate and return a new tuple that's the result of adding those values to the current x and y coords.

You can already see how easy it will be to create pipelines of movements that change the location of a given point. Since the move/2 reducer takes in a point tuple and returns a point tuple, we can string calls to move/2 together into flexible pipelines.

Tack on an end on your module, and let's see it in action. Open up an IEx session and key this in to create and move a point:

```
iex> alias Pento.Game.Point
Pento.Game.Point
iex> Point.new(2, 2) |> Point.move({1, 0})
{3, 2}
```

Then try moving a point through a pipeline of movements:

```
iex> Point.new(2, 2) |> Point.move({1, 0}) |> Point.move({0, 1})
{3, 3}
```

With this reducer in place, we'll be able to iterate over the points in a shape and move each point by some amount. In this way, we'll move an entire shape according to user input.

Move Points Geometrically with Reducers

Now we have the ability to move points up and down by changing a point's x and y value with the move/2 reducer. That's not enough, though. Users can rotate shapes or flip them over to fit them into the board and solve the puzzle. Here are some of the basic geometric manipulations our users will need to do:

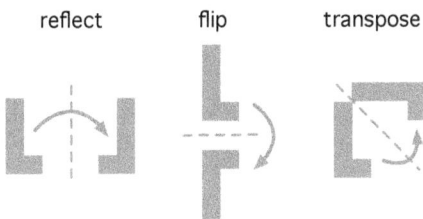

Applying a change in position to a shape means applying that change to each point in the shape. Once again, we'll start from the ground up by giving our Point module the ability to make each type of change. The reflect, flip, and transpose functions will serve as primitives that allow us to do more complex operations like rotations. Later, we'll see this code in action in the context of manipulating the overall shape.

We'll start with the *transpose* movement. Think of transpose as flipping a point over a diagonal line that runs from the upper left to the lower right. To transpose the orientation of a shape on the board, we need to swap the x and y coordinates of each point in the shape. We define a reducer in the Point module that takes in a point tuple and returns a new tuple with the x and y values switched.

Open up the Point module and define a transpose/1 function that looks like this:

```
def transpose({x, y}), do: {y, x}
```

Now let's turn our attention to the *flip* movement. To flip the orientation of a shape on the board, we need to apply the following transformation to each point in the shape:

- Leave the x coordinate alone.
- Subtract the value of the y coordinate from 6.

Here's where our approach of plotting each shape within an initial 5x5 grid comes into play. We take this approach so that we always know how to apply the flip (and later the reflect) transformation on a given shape. If we know that each shape is centered in a 5x5 grid, then we know that flipping it means applying this transformation to each point:

```
{x, 6 - y}
```

This makes it easy to build a reducer to flip a point. By first applying any and all transpose, flip, or reflect transformations to all of the points in a shape centered in a 5x5 grid, we're able to calculate the correct location of each point in accordance with its orientation. Only then can we place the shape (and each of its points) in a provided location on the wider board. We'll take a closer look at this process of manipulating the overall shape and locating it on the board later on. For now, understand that starting with a 5x5 grid let's us define flip/1 and reflect/1 reducers that will always correctly place points according to the orientation of the given shape.

With this in mind, you can define a flip/1 function that takes in a first argument of a point tuple and returns a new tuple, like this:

core/pento/lib/pento/game/point.ex
```
def flip({x, y}), do: {x, 6 - y}
```

Now for our last geometric manipulation—the *reflect* movement. Reflecting a shape means applying this transformation to each point:

```
{6-x, y}
```

Go ahead and define a reflect/1 reducer that takes in an argument of a point tuple and returns a new tuple, like so:

core/pento/lib/pento/game/point.ex
```
def reflect({x, y}), do: {6 - x, y}
```

Let's look at one example of applying one of these reducers to each point in a shape to better understand how we'll use our reducers to manipulate shapes on the board. Let's say you have our :p shape from the earlier example placed in the center of the 5x5 grid, as shown here:

	1	2	3	4	5	6	7	8	9	10
1	1,1	2,1	3,1	4,1	5,1	6,1	7,1	8,1	9,1	10,1
2	1,2	2,2	**3,2**	**4,2**	5,2	6,2	7,2	8,2	9,2	10,2
3	1,3	2,3	**3,3**	**4,3**	5,3	6,3	7,3	8,3	9,3	10,3
4	1,4	2,4	**3,4**	4,4	5,4	6,4	7,4	8,4	9,4	10,4
5	1,5	2,5	3,5	4,5	5,5	6,5	7,5	8,5	9,5	10,5
6	1,6	2,6	3,6	4,6	5,6	6,6	7,6	8,6	9,6	10,6
7	1,7	2,7	3,7	4,7	5,7	6,7	7,7	8,7	9,7	10,7
8	1,8	2,8	3,8	4,8	5,8	6,8	7,8	8,8	9,8	10,8
9	1,9	2,9	3,9	4,9	5,9	6,9	7,9	8,9	9,9	10,9
10	1,10	2,10	3,10	4,10	5,10	6,10	7,10	8,10	9,10	10,10

This shape is made up of the following points:

points = [{3, 2}, {4,2}, {3, 3}, {4, 3}, {3, 4}]

So if we iterate over this list of points and apply the Point.reflect/1 reducer to each one, we end up with the resulting list:

points = [{3, 2}, {2,2}, {3, 3}, {2, 3}, {3, 4}]

Mapped onto the board, we see this:

	1	2	3	4	5	6	7	8	9	10
1	1,1	2,1	3,1	4,1	5,1	6,1	7,1	8,1	9,1	10,1
2	1,2	**2,2**	**3,2**	4,2	5,2	6,2	7,2	8,2	9,2	10,2
3	1,3	**2,3**	**3,3**	4,3	5,3	6,3	7,3	8,3	9,3	10,3
4	1,4	2,4	**3,4**	4,4	5,4	6,4	7,4	8,4	9,4	10,4
5	1,5	2,5	3,5	4,5	5,5	6,5	7,5	8,5	9,5	10,5
6	1,6	2,6	3,6	4,6	5,6	6,6	7,6	8,6	9,6	10,6
7	1,7	2,7	3,7	4,7	5,7	6,7	7,7	8,7	9,7	10,7
8	1,8	2,8	3,8	4,8	5,8	6,8	7,8	8,8	9,8	10,8
9	1,9	2,9	3,9	4,9	5,9	6,9	7,9	8,9	9,9	10,9
10	1,10	2,10	3,10	4,10	5,10	6,10	7,10	8,10	9,10	10,10

By applying our point reducer transformations to each point in a shape, we'll move and orient the shape according to input from the user.

Before we move on, let's do a little more exploration of the code we've built so far. The beautiful thing about our reducers is that we can string them into any combination of pipelines to transform points. Open up IEx, alias Pento.Game.Point, and try out some of the pipelines shown on the next page.

```
iex> Point.new(2, 2) |> Point.move({1, 0})
{3, 2}
iex> Point.new(1, 1) |> Point.reflect
{5, 1}
iex> Point.new(1, 1) |> Point.flip
{1, 5}
iex> Point.new(1, 1) |> Point.flip |> Point.transpose
{5, 1}
```

Next up, we'll use these point movement reducers to create the *rotate point* flow.

Combine Reducers to Rotate Points

We've built out a set of point movement primitives that we'll use to manipulate shapes on the Pentominoes board. But users won't directly provide flip or transpose input. Instead, they'll rotate a shape in increments of 90 degrees. So we'll define a set of rotate/2 reducers that apply the correct pipeline of flip/1 and transpose/1 transformations in accordance with the given degrees of rotation.

Rotating shapes in increments of 90 degrees means that we'll need to apply the following transformations:

- *Rotate 0 degrees:* Do nothing.
- *Rotate 90 degrees:* Reflect and then transpose.
- *Rotate 180 degrees:* Reflect and then flip.
- *Rotate 270 degrees:* Flip and then transpose.

Thanks to the composable nature of our reducer functions, building a set of rotate/2 functions that pattern matches to each of these rotation values and pipes the given point into the correct set of reducers should be easy. Open up the Point module and define these functions:

core/pento/lib/pento/game/point.ex
```
def rotate(point, 0), do: point
def rotate(point, 90), do: point |> reflect |> transpose
def rotate(point, 180), do: point |> reflect |> flip
def rotate(point, 270), do: point |> flip |> transpose
```

Applying these rotate/2 functions to an :l shape, for example, should give you something like the transformations shown at the top of the next page.

Let's walk through what happens if we pipe each of the points in our original :p shape through the rotate/2 function with a degrees argument of 90. Open up IEx and type this in:

```
iex> alias Pento.Game.Point
iex> points = [{3, 2}, {4,2}, {3, 3}, {4, 3}, {3, 4}]
```

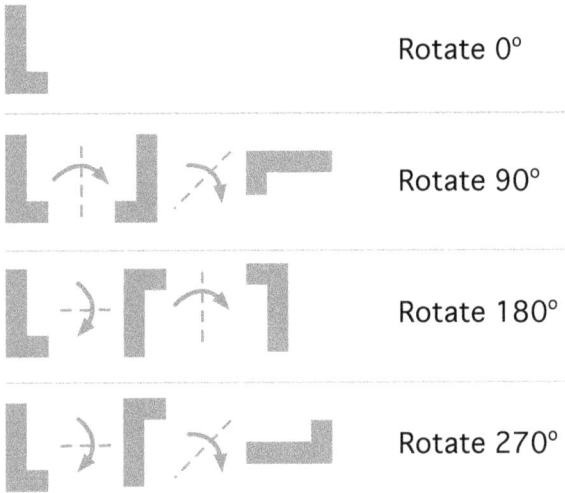

Rotate 0°

Rotate 90°

Rotate 180°

Rotate 270°

```
iex> Enum.map(points, &Point.rotate(&1, 90))
[{2, 3}, {2, 2}, {3, 3}, {3, 2}, {4, 3}]
```

Let's break this down one step at a time. Calling rotate/2 with a second argument of 90 invokes the following pipeline under the hood:

```
point |> reflect |> transpose
```

Taking this one step at a time, calling reflect/1 on each point in the :p points applies the {6-x, y} transformation to each point in the list, returning this:

```
iex> Enum.map(points, &Point.reflect(&1))
[{3, 2}, {2, 2}, {3, 3}, {2, 3}, {3, 4}]
```

Then, calling the transpose/1 reducer with each point in this resulting list swaps each point's x and y values, giving us this:

```
iex> reflected_points = [{3, 2}, {2, 2}, {3, 3}, {2, 3}, {3, 4}]
iex> Enum.map(reflected_points, &Point.transpose(&1))
[{2, 3}, {2, 2}, {3, 3}, {3, 2}, {4, 3}]
```

Putting it all together, calling the rotate/2 reducer with our :p points and an argument of 90 degrees moves the shape to this new location on the board, as shown at the top of the next page.

By applying our rotate/2 reducer to each point in the :p shape, we're moving the shape around within the 5x5 grid. This ensures that we're correctly orienting the shape in the known area of the 5x5 grid. From there, we can place the shape in a given location on the wider board. Let's move on to that task now.

	1	2	3	4	5	6	7	8	9	10
1	1,1	2,1	3,1	4,1	5,1	6,1	7,1	8,1	9,1	10,1
2	1,2	2,2	3,2	4,2	5,2	6,2	7,2	8,2	9,2	10,2
3	1,3	2,3	3,3	4,3	5,3	6,3	7,3	8,3	9,3	10,3
4	1,4	2,4	3,4	4,4	5,4	6,4	7,4	8,4	9,4	10,4
5	1,5	2,5	3,5	4,5	5,5	6,5	7,5	8,5	9,5	10,5
6	1,6	2,6	3,6	4,6	5,6	6,6	7,6	8,6	9,6	10,6
7	1,7	2,7	3,7	4,7	5,7	6,7	7,7	8,7	9,7	10,7
8	1,8	2,8	3,8	4,8	5,8	6,8	7,8	8,8	9,8	10,8
9	1,9	2,9	3,9	4,9	5,9	6,9	7,9	8,9	9,9	10,9
10	1,10	2,10	3,10	4,10	5,10	6,10	7,10	8,10	9,10	10,10

Prepare a Point for Rendering

Let's continue using our :p shape as an example. Imagine we have a :p shape that starts out centered in the middle of the 5x5 square with these default points values:

```
iex> [{3, 2}, {4,2}, {3, 3}, {4, 3}, {3, 4}]
```

Let's apply the following pipeline of transformations to each point in the list:

```
iex> [{3, 2}, {4,2}, {3, 3}, {4, 3}, {3, 4}] \
     |> Enum.map(&Point.rotate(&1, 90)) \
     |> Enum.map(&Point.reflect(&1))
[{4, 3}, {4, 2}, {3, 3}, {3, 2}, {2, 3}]
```

Breaking this down one step at a time, applying the rotate/2 reducer to each point in the shape, just like we did earlier, gives us the following:

	1	2	3	4	5	6	7	8	9	10
1	1,1	2,1	3,1	4,1	5,1	6,1	7,1	8,1	9,1	10,1
2	1,2	2,2	3,2	4,2	5,2	6,2	7,2	8,2	9,2	10,2
3	1,3	2,3	3,3	4,3	5,3	6,3	7,3	8,3	9,3	10,3
4	1,4	2,4	3,4	4,4	5,4	6,4	7,4	8,4	9,4	10,4
5	1,5	2,5	3,5	4,5	5,5	6,5	7,5	8,5	9,5	10,5
6	1,6	2,6	3,6	4,6	5,6	6,6	7,6	8,6	9,6	10,6
7	1,7	2,7	3,7	4,7	5,7	6,7	7,7	8,7	9,7	10,7
8	1,8	2,8	3,8	4,8	5,8	6,8	7,8	8,8	9,8	10,8
9	1,9	2,9	3,9	4,9	5,9	6,9	7,9	8,9	9,9	10,9
10	1,10	2,10	3,10	4,10	5,10	6,10	7,10	8,10	9,10	10,10

Then we call reflect/1 with each of these new points, performing the {6-x,y} transformation and returning this:

	1	2	3	4	5	6	7	8	9	10
1	1,1	2,1	3,1	4,1	5,1	6,1	7,1	8,1	9,1	10,1
2	1,2	2,2	3,2	4,2	5,2	6,2	7,2	8,2	9,2	10,2
3	1,3	2,3	3,3	4,3	5,3	6,3	7,3	8,3	9,3	10,3
4	1,4	2,4	3,4	4,4	5,4	6,4	7,4	8,4	9,4	10,4
5	1,5	2,5	3,5	4,5	5,5	6,5	7,5	8,5	9,5	10,5
6	1,6	2,6	3,6	4,6	5,6	6,6	7,6	8,6	9,6	10,6
7	1,7	2,7	3,7	4,7	5,7	6,7	7,7	8,7	9,7	10,7
8	1,8	2,8	3,8	4,8	5,8	6,8	7,8	8,8	9,8	10,8
9	1,9	2,9	3,9	4,9	5,9	6,9	7,9	8,9	9,9	10,9
10	1,10	2,10	3,10	4,10	5,10	6,10	7,10	8,10	9,10	10,10

Nothing new here so far—we've simply applied a pipeline of reducers to each point in a shape. Now, let's say the provided location of the overall shape on the wider board is {5, 5}. All we need to do is take the updated list of points and apply the Point.move/2 reducer to each one. Let's add to our pipeline now, like so:

```
iex> [{3, 2}, {4,2}, {3, 3}, {4, 3}, {3, 4}] \
     |> Enum.map(&Point.rotate(&1, 90)) \
     |> Enum.map(&Point.reflect(&1)) \
     |> Enum.map(&Point.move(&1, {5, 5}))
[{9, 8}, {9, 7}, {8, 8}, {8, 7}, {7, 8}]
```

Recall that the move/2 reducer takes in a first argument of a point and a second argument of {x_change, y_change}. It returns a new point tuple that's the result of adding the x_change value to the x coordinate and the y_change value to the y coordinate, leaving us with this board:

	1	2	3	4	5	6	7	8	9	10
1	1,1	2,1	3,1	4,1	5,1	6,1	7,1	8,1	9,1	10,1
2	1,2	2,2	3,2	4,2	5,2	6,2	7,2	8,2	9,2	10,2
3	1,3	2,3	3,3	4,3	5,3	6,3	7,3	8,3	9,3	10,3
4	1,4	2,4	3,4	4,4	5,4	6,4	7,4	8,4	9,4	10,4
5	1,5	2,5	3,5	4,5	5,5	6,5	7,5	8,5	9,5	10,5
6	1,6	2,6	3,6	4,6	5,6	6,6	7,6	8,6	9,6	10,6
7	1,7	2,7	3,7	4,7	5,7	6,7	7,7	8,7	9,7	10,7
8	1,8	2,8	3,8	4,8	5,8	6,8	7,8	8,8	9,8	10,8
9	1,9	2,9	3,9	4,9	5,9	6,9	7,9	8,9	9,9	10,9
10	1,10	2,10	3,10	4,10	5,10	6,10	7,10	8,10	9,10	10,10

This calculation is a little off though. Remember that we placed our original :p shape in the center of the 5x5 grid at the top left of our board, meaning the center of the :p shape occupied the {3,3} location on the board. We always take {3,3} as the starting point of the center of any shape we put on the board. This way, we can reliably apply the correct math to calculate the orientation of the shape given the provided rotation, reflection, and so on. So when we move our correctly orientated shape to its final location, we're off by 3. To ensure that the shape is moved to the given location, we need to take the results of applying move(point, {5, 5}) and subtract 3 from every point's coordinates. We'll call this action "centering the point" to account for the {3,3} offset we began with.

Let's implement a center/1 reducer to do that for us now:

core/pento/lib/pento/game/point.ex
```
def center(point), do: move(point, {-3, -3})
```

Now we add a call to center/1 to the end of our pipeline:

```
iex> [{3, 2}, {4,2}, {3, 3}, {4, 3}, {3, 4}] \
     |> Enum.map(&Point.rotate(&1, 90)) \
     |> Enum.map(&Point.reflect(&1)) \
     |> Enum.map(&Point.move(&1, {5, 5})) \
     |> Enum.map(&Point.center(&1))
[{6, 5}, {6, 4}, {5, 5}, {5, 4}, {4, 5}]
```

This leaves us with the following board:

	1	2	3	4	5	6	7	8	9	10
1	1,1	2,1	3,1	4,1	5,1	6,1	7,1	8,1	9,1	10,1
2	1,2	2,2	3,2	4,2	5,2	6,2	7,2	8,2	9,2	10,2
3	1,3	2,3	3,3	4,3	5,3	6,3	7,3	8,3	9,3	10,3
4	1,4	2,4	3,4	4,4	5,4	6,4	7,4	8,4	9,4	10,4
5	1,5	2,5	3,5	4,5	5,5	6,5	7,5	8,5	9,5	10,5
6	1,6	2,6	3,6	4,6	5,6	6,6	7,6	8,6	9,6	10,6
7	1,7	2,7	3,7	4,7	5,7	6,7	7,7	8,7	9,7	10,7
8	1,8	2,8	3,8	4,8	5,8	6,8	7,8	8,8	9,8	10,8
9	1,9	2,9	3,9	4,9	5,9	6,9	7,9	8,9	9,9	10,9
10	1,10	2,10	3,10	4,10	5,10	6,10	7,10	8,10	9,10	10,10

Now our :p shape is correctly orientated according to the given rotation and reflection, and it's correctly placed with its center in the provided location of {5, 5}.

So far, we've strung together our own bespoke pipeline of reducers by iterating over a list of points and calling various combinations of rotate/2, reflect/1 and move/2. Let's take a step back and think about how such a pipeline will be used in the context of placing a shape on the board.

We know that we'll define a module, Shape, that produces structs with these attributes:

- *points:* The list of points that make up the shape.
- *rotation:* The number of degrees the shape user has rotated the shape, between 0 and 270 in increments of 90.
- *reflected:* A true or false value indicating if the user has reflected the shape.
- *location:* The desired location of the shape on the board.

We want a way to apply each of these attributes to a given point, so we'll create a pipeline of reducers in a function, Point.prepare/4, to do exactly that. In lib/pento/game/point.ex, define this function:

core/pento/lib/pento/game/point.ex
```
def prepare(point, rotation, reflected, location) do
  point
  |> rotate(rotation)
  |> maybe_reflect(reflected)
  |> move(location)
  |> center
end
```

Note that we're using a new reducer function, maybe_reflect/2. Here's what that function looks like:

core/pento/lib/pento/game/point.ex
```
def maybe_reflect(point, true), do: reflect(point)
def maybe_reflect(point, false), do: point
```

The maybe_reflect/2 reducer takes in a first argument of a point and a second argument of true or false. It calls the reflect/1 reducer if the second argument is true and simply returns the unchanged point if it's false.

This prepare/4 function is where the CRC pattern shines. We can manipulate *one point* in the pentomino, according to the set of rules that we'll later encapsulate in the Shape struct. Then we can use the same prepare/4 function to move *all of the points* according to the same rules.

Later we'll use Point.prepare/4 to move all the points in a pentomino shape at once. Now, let's move on to building out that Shape module.

Group Points Together in Shapes

The Shape module is responsible for modeling pentomino shapes. It will wrap up the attributes that describe a shape and implement some functions that manage the behavior of shapes. In this section, we'll define the Shape module and implement its constructor function. We'll use the Point.prepare/4 function we just built to prepare a shape for rendering in the correct location, given some input.

Represent Shape Attributes

Let's begin with the attributes that describe a shape. Each shape will have a distinct color and a list of points. The Shape module will wrap up these attributes in a struct. We'll build this out first. Create a file, lib/pento/game/shape.ex, and define the module like this:

```elixir
defmodule Pento.Game.Shape do
  defstruct color: :blue, name: :x, points: []
end
```

Our module implements a call to defstruct to define what keys the struct will have, along with their default values. Now, if we open up IEx, we can create new Shape structs like this:

```
iex> alias Pento.Game.Shape
Pento.Game.Shape
iex> Shape.__struct__
%Pento.Game.Shape{color: :blue, points: [], name: :x}
```

Great. Now we have a module that produces structs that represent shapes. Let's make our module a little smarter. We'll implement a set of functions that represent each shape's points and colors.

Add these functions to your module to represent the colors associated with each shape:

```elixir
# core/pento/lib/pento/game/shape.ex
defp color(:i), do: :dark_green
defp color(:l), do: :green
defp color(:y), do: :light_green
defp color(:n), do: :dark_orange
defp color(:p), do: :orange
defp color(:w), do: :light_orange
defp color(:u), do: :dark_gray
defp color(:v), do: :gray
defp color(:s), do: :light_gray
defp color(:f), do: :dark_blue
defp color(:x), do: :blue
defp color(:t), do: :light_blue
```

Then add these functions to represent the list of points that make up each shape:

```
core/pento/lib/pento/game/shape.ex
defp points(:i), do: [{3, 1}, {3, 2}, {3, 3}, {3, 4}, {3, 5}]
defp points(:l), do: [{3, 1}, {3, 2}, {3, 3}, {3, 4}, {4, 4}]
defp points(:y), do: [{3, 1}, {2, 2}, {3, 2}, {3, 3}, {3, 4}]
defp points(:n), do: [{3, 1}, {3, 2}, {3, 3}, {4, 3}, {4, 4}]
defp points(:p), do: [{3, 2}, {4, 3}, {3, 3}, {4, 2}, {3, 4}]
defp points(:w), do: [{2, 2}, {2, 3}, {3, 3}, {3, 4}, {4, 4}]
defp points(:u), do: [{2, 2}, {4, 2}, {2, 3}, {3, 3}, {4, 3}]
defp points(:v), do: [{2, 2}, {2, 3}, {2, 4}, {3, 4}, {4, 4}]
defp points(:s), do: [{3, 2}, {4, 2}, {3, 3}, {2, 4}, {3, 4}]
defp points(:f), do: [{3, 2}, {4, 2}, {2, 3}, {3, 3}, {3, 4}]
defp points(:x), do: [{3, 2}, {2, 3}, {3, 3}, {4, 3}, {3, 4}]
defp points(:t), do: [{2, 2}, {3, 2}, {4, 2}, {3, 3}, {3, 4}]
```

Define the Shape Constructor

A shape will be constructed with a provided name, rotation, reflection, and location. The Shape constructor will use the name to select the correct set of points and the correct color for the shape. It will apply the rotation, reflection, and location values to each point and return an updated points list that's correctly oriented and placed on the board.

This last part might sound challenging, but we already built out all of the code we need in the previous section. The Point.prepare/4 function takes in a point, rotation, reflection, and location and does all the work of orienting, moving, and centering a point on the board. All our constructor needs to do is iterate over the points that make up the shape and call Point.prepare/4 with each one. This will return a new list of correctly updated points. Let's build it.

First, remember to alias the Pento.Game.Point module, like this:

```
core/pento/lib/pento/game/shape.ex
defmodule Pento.Game.Shape do
  alias Pento.Game.Point
end
```

Then implement the constructor as shown here:

```
core/pento/lib/pento/game/shape.ex
def new(name, rotation, reflected, location) do
  points =
    name
    |> points()
    |> Enum.map(&Point.prepare(&1, rotation, reflected, location))

  %__MODULE__{points: points, color: color(name), name: name}
end
```

Go ahead and test out your new constructor function. Open up IEx and key this in:

```
iex> Pento.Game.Shape.new(:p, 90, true, {5, 5})
%Pento.Game.Shape{
  color: :orange,
  points: [{6, 5}, {5, 4}, {5, 5}, {6, 4}, {4, 5}],
  name: :p
}
```

You can see how the layers of our functional core are starting to come together. Given some information about a pentomino—its name, rotation, reflection, and location—we generate a struct that represents the shape's color, with all of the points in the right place thanks to the reducer pipeline in the Point.prepare/4 function. This struct wraps up everything we'll need to render the shape on the board later on.

Track and Place a Pentomino

The Shape constructor takes in a rotation, reflection, and location value and returns the struct that represents the orientation and location of that shape on the board. This rotation, reflection, and location will be the result of a user selecting a shape and moving it around the board before finally dropping it into place. A user may do any combination of rotating the shape, reflecting the shape, or moving it up and down on the board before deciding to place it. So we need a way to track all of these user inputs in one place before feeding the final rotation, reflection, and location values into our Shape constructor. We'll implement the Pentomino module to do exactly that.

Like the Shape module, the Pentomino module will produce structs that know the shape name, rotation, reflection, and location. Most importantly, however, the Pentomino module will implement a series of reducers that we can string together given a set of user inputs to change the rotation, reflection, and location of the pentomino. Then the pentomino will be converted into a shape in order to be placed on the board at the correct set of points.

If you're thinking that this process—creating a Pentomino struct, transforming it with a series of reducers, and then converting it into a shape that can be displayed to the user—sounds a lot like CRC, you're right!

Let's implement our new module.

Represent Pentomino Attributes

Create a new file, lib/pento/game/pentomino.ex, and define a module that looks like this:

```
defmodule Pento.Game.Pentomino do
  @names [:i, :l, :y, :n, :p, :w, :u, :v, :s, :f, :x, :t]
  @default_location {8, 8}

  defstruct [
    name: :i,
    rotation: 0,
    reflected: false,
    location: @default_location
  ]
end
```

Great. Now if you load up IEx, you should be able to create a new pentomino with the default values, like this:

```
iex> alias Pento.Game.Pentomino
Pento.Game.Pentomino
iex> Pentomino.__struct__
%Pento.Game.Pentomino{
  location: {8, 8},
  name: :i,
  reflected: false,
  rotation: 0
}
```

Now we're ready to define the constructor.

Define the Pentomino Constructor

Our constructor is simple. All it needs to do is implement a function, new/1, that takes in an argument of a keyword list and uses it to return a new Pentomino struct. Go ahead and add this function in now:

core/pento/lib/pento/game/pentomino.ex
```
def new(fields \\ []), do: __struct__(fields)
```

Now, recompile your IEx session and practice creating a new pentomino, like so:

```
iex> recompile()
iex> Pentomino.new(location: {11,5}, name: :p, reflected: true, rotation: 270)
%Pento.Game.Pentomino{
  location: {11, 5},
  name: :p,
  reflected: true,
  rotation: 270
}
```

With the constructor in place, we can move on to the reducers.

Manipulate Pentominoes with Reducers

A pentomino struct will hold the state of the pentomino as we transform that state with input from the user. A user will be able to do the following:

- Rotate the pentomino in increments of 90 degrees.
- Flip the pentomino.
- Move the pentomino up, down, left, or right one square at a time.

Each of these interactions will update the pentomino's rotation, reflected, or location attributes, respectively. When a user is done moving the pentomino and is ready to place it on the board, we'll take the final values of each of these attributes and use them to create a Shape struct that knows its correct points locations.

Let's start with the rotate/1 reducer. This reducer takes in an argument of a pentomino and updates its rotation attribute in increments of 90 by performing the following calculation: rem(degrees + 90, 360). This ensures that we rotate the pentomino 90 degrees at a time, returning the value to 0 rather than exceeding 270. Open up the Pentomino module and add this in:

```
core/pento/lib/pento/game/pentomino.ex
def rotate(%{rotation: degrees} = p) do
  %{p | rotation: rem(degrees + 90, 360)}
end
```

Here, we return a new pentomino struct with all of the original struct's values, along with the updated :rotation value.

Next up, implement the flip/1 reducer. This reducer takes in an argument of a pentomino and returns a new struct with an updated :reflected value that's the opposite of the present value. So if the pentomino is *not* flipped, flipping it will set :reflected to true. If it *is* flipped, flipping it *again* will set :reflected to false. Open up the Pentomino module and add this in:

```
def flip(%{reflected: reflection} = p) do
  %{p | reflected: not reflection}
end
```

Lastly, we implement a set of reducers to move the pentomino up, down, left, and right by one square at a time. In other words, moving a pentomino up should change its location by {x, y-1}, and so on.

A pentomino's location represents the x and y coordinates of the center point of the pentomino's shape. We already have a function that knows how to move a point—Point.move/1. We'll reuse it here. First, open up the Pentomino module and alias Pento.Game.Point at the top of the module. Then add in these reducers:

```
core/pento/lib/pento/game/pentomino.ex
def up(p) do
  %{p | location: Point.move(p.location, {0, -1})}
end

def down(p) do
  %{p | location: Point.move(p.location, {0, 1})}
end

def left(p) do
  %{p | location: Point.move(p.location, {-1, 0})}
end

def right(p) do
  %{p | location: Point.move(p.location, {1, 0})}
end
```

That's it for our reducers. Now for the final step—creating the converter function.

Convert a Pentomino to a Shape

A pentomino knows its rotation, reflection, and location based on a set of user input. To place that pentomino on the board, we convert it to a shape. Recall that creating a new shape struct with a call to the Shape.new/4 constructor does a few things:

- Gets the list of default points that make up the given shape.
- Iterates over that list of points and calls Point.prepare/4 to apply the provided rotation, reflection, and location to each point in the shape. Collects the newly updated list of properly oriented and located points.
- Returns a shape struct that knows its name, color, and this updated list of points.

In this way, we convert a pentomino into a shape that can be placed on the board, with the correct orientation, in the correct location, with the correct color.

Let's build that constructor now. Open up the Pentomino module and add this in:

```
core/pento/lib/pento/game/pentomino.ex
def to_shape(pento) do
  Shape.new(pento.name, pento.rotation, pento.reflected, pento.location)
end
```

Now it's time to test drive it.

Test Drive the Pentomino CRC Pipeline

Let's run through a few examples of the Pentomino CRC pipeline. We'll create a new pentomino struct with the constructor, apply some transformations with various combinations of reducers, and convert the pentomino into a shape that knows its points and can be placed on a board.

Open up IEx and try this out:

```
iex> Pentomino.new(name: :i) |> Pentomino.rotate |> Pentomino.rotate
%Pento.Game.Pentomino{
  location: {8, 8},
  name: :i,
  reflected: false,
  rotation: 180
}
```

We've constructed a new pentomino and rotated it twice. Just like with our previous reducer pipelines, we can string together any combination of reducers to change the state of our entity. By calling Pentomino.rotate/1 twice, we first update the default rotation from 0 to 90 and then from 90 to 180.

Let's keep adding to our reducer pipeline, as shown here:

```
iex> Pentomino.new(name: :i) \
      |> Pentomino.rotate \
      |> Pentomino.rotate \
      |> Pentomino.down
%Pento.Game.Pentomino{
  location: {8, 9},
  name: :i,
  reflected: false,
  rotation: 180
}
```

This time, we add an additional step to our reducer pipeline, the call to Pentomino.down/1. This changes the location by applying the transformation: {x, y+1}.

Finally, let's convert our pentomino to a shape, like this:

```
iex> Pentomino.new(name: :i) \
      |> Pentomino.rotate \
      |> Pentomino.rotate \
      |> Pentomino.down \
      |> Pentomino.to_shape
%Pento.Game.Shape{
  color: :dark_green,
  points: [{8, 11}, {8, 10}, {8, 9}, {8, 8}, {8, 7}],
  name: :i
}
```

We end up with a shape that has a correctly populated :points value, given the rotation, reflection, and location of the transformed pentomino.

Now that we can create pentominoes, move them, and convert them to shapes that can be placed on a board, it's time to build out the last piece of our functional core—the game board.

Track a Game in a Board

The Board module will be responsible for tracking a game. It will produce structs that describe the attributes of a board and implement a constructor function for creating new boards when a user starts a game of Pentominoes. Later, it will implement reducers to manage the behavior of a board, including commands to select a pento to move, rotate or reflect a pento, drop a piece into place, and more.

Represent Board Attributes

A board struct will have the following attributes:

- *points:* The points that make up the shape of the empty board that the user will fill up with pentominoes. All of our shapes will be rectangles of different sizes.

- *completed_pentos:* The list of pentominoes that the user has placed on the board.

- *palette:* The provided pentominoes that the user has available to solve the puzzle.

- *active_pento:* The currently selected pentomino that the user is moving around the board.

Let's start by defining our module, along with a defstruct to define the Board structs to have these attributes. Create a new file, lib/pento/game/board.ex, add this in, and then close your module with an end:

```
core/pento/lib/pento/game/board.ex
defmodule Pento.Game.Board do
  alias Pento.Game.{Pentomino, Shape}

  defstruct active_pento: nil,
            completed_pentos: [],
            palette: [],
            points: []
end
```

Next up, we'll diverge from the CRC pattern and define a function that returns the list of puzzle shapes we'll support:

def puzzles(), **do**: ~w[default wide widest medium tiny]a

This function will be called later on in LiveView when we generate a new game for a user to play.

Now we're ready to implement the constructor.

Define the Board Constructor

Define a constructor function, new/2, that takes in two arguments, an atom that indicates the palette size (how many pentominoes to give the user) and a list of points that will form the board grid. Here's a look at the new/2 function:

core/pento/lib/pento/game/board.ex
```elixir
def new(palette, points) do
  %__MODULE__{palette: palette(palette), points: points}
end

def new(:tiny),    do: new(:small, rect(5, 3))
def new(:widest),  do: new(:all, rect(20, 3))
def new(:wide),    do: new(:all, rect(15, 4))
def new(:medium),  do: new(:all, rect(12, 5))
def new(:default), do: new(:all, rect(10, 6))
```

Here, we define two functions called new. The new/1 function will be called with a board size atom. Each new/1 function calls the new/2 constructor with a different palette size and list of board points, depending on the provided board size.

Let's take a look at the palette/1 and rect/2 helper functions used by our constructors now.

Define Constructor Helper Functions

The rect/2 function takes in a board width and height and uses a for loop to return the list of points that make up a rectangle of that size. Open up the Board module and add this in:

core/pento/lib/pento/game/board.ex
```elixir
defp rect(x, y) do
  for x <- 1..x, y <- 1..y, do: {x, y}
end
```

Now, define two versions of a palette/1 function that pattern match on the available :all or :small atoms to return a list of pentomino shapes, like this:

core/pento/lib/pento/game/board.ex
```
defp palette(:all), do: [:i, :l, :y, :n, :p, :w, :u, :v, :s, :f, :x, :t]
defp palette(:small), do: [:u, :v, :p]
```

These functions work together to produce the correct set of board points and list of pentomino shapes for a given board size. Let's test drive our new constructor function.

Open up IEx and create a tiny board, like this:

```
iex> alias Pento.Game.Board
Pento.Game.Board
iex> Board.new(:tiny)
%Pento.Game.Board{
  active_pento: nil,
  completed_pentos: [],
  palette: [:u, :v, :p],
  points: [{1, 1},{1, 2},{1, 3},{2, 1},{2, 2},{2, 3},...{5, 3}]
}
```

You can see that we've created a board struct with the correct list of points describing the board rectangle, the correct (small) list of pentominoes for the user to place, and the correct default values to active_pentos and completed_pentos. With our basic board in place, let's move on to discuss how we'll manipulate the board given user input during game play.

Manipulate the Board with Reducers

We won't be building the Board reducers in this chapter. We'll take that on in the next chapter as we build out our game live view. But let's think through this problem now.

Users will be able to do a few things with pentominoes on the board:

- *choose:* Pick an active pentomino from the palette to move around the board. This should update a board struct's active_pento attribute.

- *drop:* Place a pentomino in a location on the board. That should update the list of placed pentominoes in the completed_pentos attribute of a given board struct.

We'll also need to make Board smart enough to know if a pentomino *can* be dropped in a given location. We'll support these interactions with our boards:

- *legal?:* Returns true if the location a user wants to drop a pentomino in is in fact on the board.

- *droppable?:* Returns true if the location a user wants to drop a pentomino in is in fact unoccupied by another piece.

Lastly, we'll want to give the Board module the ability to tell us if the game is over. We'll implement this behavior:

- *status:* Indicates if all of the pentominoes in the palette have been placed on the board. In other words, are all of the pentominoes in the palette listed in the completed_pentos list of placed pieces?

We need two more abstractions before we're ready to move on and build the graphical representation of our game in the UI. One will gather up all of the shapes on a given game board so that they can be rendered, and the other will provide a utility to tell us whether or not a given shape is the actively selected one being placed by the user. Let's start with that first abstraction now.

Translate a Board into Shapes for Presentation

We already have a Pentomino.to_shape/1 function that translates a pentomino into a shape to be placed on the board. Now we need to build a list of *all* of the shapes that make up a game (the board shape, along with the set of pentominoes used to solve that particular puzzle). In the next two chapters, we'll take this list of shapes and render them on the board in the UI.

We'll start by implementing a new helper function, Board.to_shape/1, to convert the board struct into a shape that can be rendered.

First off, define the new converter function, Board.to_shape/1, that takes in an argument of a board struct and returns a Shape struct representing that board, like this:

core/pento/lib/pento/game/board.ex
```
def to_shape(board) do
  Shape.__struct__(color: :purple, name: :board, points: board.points)
end
```

Here, we create a new Shape struct with a default color of :purple, a name of :board, and the list of points that comprise the puzzle board. Now that we know how to create the shape representing the board, we're ready to implement another converter function that returns the list of *all* of the shapes that represent a full game—the board shape, the list of placed pentomino shapes, and the active pentomino shape.

Define another function Board.to_shapes/1, like this:

```
def to_shapes(board) do
  board_shape = to_shape(board)
  pento_shapes = [board.active_pento|board.completed_pentos]
end
```

Here, we convert the board into a shape with the Board.to_shape/1 converter that we just built to get the shape of the puzzle board. Then we start constructing our list. We create a variable, pento_shapes, that points to a list of the active pento, followed by the completed pentos that have already been placed on the puzzle board.

Before we add our board shape to this list of pento shapes, let's think about our goal. We want to *layer* the shapes so that the board shape is always in the background. Any completed pentos that have been placed *cover up* board squares, and the active pento that is highlighted covers up any *placed* pentos that a user might place the active pentos on top of. That way, the user will be able to move the active pento around the board, hiding the pieces beneath, until they're ready to drop the pento into position.

To render shapes in this specific order, our list needs to be ordered correctly with the board shape at the head, followed by the placed pentos, and ending with the active pento. We achieve this by reversing our list of pento_shapes before adding them to the tail of a new list that begins with the board_shape. We also want to filter the list to handle the scenario in which there's no actively selected pento and board.active_pento evaluates to nil. Then we need to convert this list of pentos into shapes. Putting it all together gives us something like this:

```elixir
# core/pento/lib/pento/game/board.ex
def to_shapes(board) do
  board_shape = to_shape(board)
  pento_shapes =
    [board.active_pento | board.completed_pentos]
    |> Enum.reverse()
    |> Enum.filter(& &1)
    |> Enum.map(&Pentomino.to_shape/1)

  [board_shape | pento_shapes]
end
```

Here it is, summed up:

- Convert the board into the single shape representing the puzzle.
- Construct a list of the board's active pento and completed pentos.
- Reverse the order of those items.
- Strip out the nils in case the active pento is not set.
- Convert them into shapes.
- Assemble the final list of shapes in the correct order for rendering.

We have one more abstraction we need to build into our core Board module before moving on to the next chapter—a board should be able to tell us which one of its pentos is the active pento currently being placed by the user. We'll use this later on the presentation layer to highlight and manipulate the active pento.

Highlight the Active Pento

We've already given our core board structs awareness of which pento is active by providing a board attribute, :active_pento. Now we'll build a function that takes in an argument of a board and a given pento on that board and tells us if that pento is the active one.

Define two versions of a Board.active?/2 function with two different function heads—one to handle a shape name that's a string and one to handle a shape name that's an atom. Both functions will return true if the given shape name matches board.active_pento and false if not. Your code should look like this:

core/pento/lib/pento/game/board.ex
```elixir
def active?(board, shape_name) when is_binary(shape_name) do
  active?(board, String.to_existing_atom(shape_name))
end

def active?(%{active_pento: %{name: shape_name}}, shape_name), do: true
def active?(_board, _shape_name), do: false
```

Great. Now our game core has everything we need to represent the board in the UI. Let's wrap up.

Your Turn

In this chapter, you built out a solid functional core for our new Pentominoes game feature. You layered together four pieces of our core functionality to represent pentomino pieces, manipulate their orientation and location, and convert them into something that can be placed on a pentomino game board.

The Point module represents points. It constructs {x, y} tuples and manipulates them with reducers. We strung these reducers together into a pipeline in the Point.prepare/4 function.

The Shape module builds structs that have a color, name, and the list of points in that shape. It uses Point.prepare/4 to apply these attributes to every point in the shape.

The Pentomino module tracks the transformations to a shape that a user will apply during game play. Its constructor produces structs with the shape name, rotation, reflection, and location attributes. Its reducers take in some user input and update these attributes. Its converter returns shapes with the correctly located set of points, given these attributes.

The Board module represents the shape of the puzzle board, along with the state of the game as a whole. It knows the list of points that comprise the board and can convert those points into a shape to be rendered. It also knows the list of placed pentominoes and which pento is currently active and in the process of being placed. It can assemble this full list of shapes for rendering.

We've covered a lot of complex logic in this chapter, and the CRC pattern made it all possible. By creating a set of modules that modeled the different elements of our game, we were able to break out the logical concerns of game play. By applying the CRC pattern to each of these game elements, we were able to neatly model the attributes and behaviors of the game. By layering these game elements, we assembled the near-complete behavior of a round of pentominoes.

Now it's time for you to work with these concepts on your own.

Give It a Try

These exercises let you better understand the core by writing tests. You'll also have a chance to extend the core by adding some new kinds of boards and creating a reducer to add an optional direction to turn a pentomino.

- Write tests for the core. Focus on writing unit tests for the individual reducer functions of our core modules. Maybe reach for the reducer testing pipelines we used in Chapter 10, Test Your Live Views, on page 303, to keep your tests clean, flexible, and highly readable.
- Add a skewed rectangle[1] puzzle and a function called Board.skewed_rect/2, like Board.rect/2, to support it.
- Add an optional direction argument to Pentomino.rotate/1 that allows both clockwise and counterclockwise rotation.

Up Next

We're going to depart from the approach we've taken in building out features so far and turn our attention to the UI *before* we build the application boundary. With our functional core firmly in place, we've perfectly set the stage for building out the UI in LiveView. In the next chapter, we'll focus on rendering a board and shapes by composing a series of LiveView components. We'll build *almost* the full game-play functionality, adding in new Board reducers along the way. Only then will we build the application boundary that will enforce some necessary game rules and validations on the UI.

---

1. http://puzzler.sourceforge.net/docs/pentominoes.html

CHAPTER 12

Render Graphics with SVG

You've built the conceptual processing engine of our game into the application's functional core. Now it's time to turn your attention to the presentation layer.

Good software is built in layers. Not only are we layering our interface on top of a solid functional core, we're also going to compose the interface itself out of layers of components. We'll represent each part of our game UI with a component that renders some SVG markup. Components and SVG are the perfect tools for building our game. Components will make it easy for us to build and layer Pentominoes game elements. SVG, a library for presenting graphics with text, will let us draw game shape images that can be diffed and re-rendered by LiveView. After all, SVG presents images as text, and LiveView knows exactly how to make efficient updates to a UI made from text-based markup.

Before we jump in to writing code, let's make a plan.

Plan the Presentation Layer

When we built the admin dashboard, we used the Contex library to produce SVG. That approach hid graphics presentation details from us. Now it's time to attack those graphical details. We'll divide the game into layers and represent each part of the game with its own component. Most of our components will be function components. Just one, our board, will process events to move, rotate, and drop pentominoes.

Each of these components will construct and render some hand-crafted SVG markup.

The overall game display will consist of the game's puzzle board along with the palette of available shapes. The entry point for this display will be a live view, GameLive. This live view will render a stateful top-level component, Board. The Board component will, in turn, render some stateless children—a Canvas component to display the puzzle board and a Palette component to display the pentomino shapes that the user can use to solve the puzzle.

Here's a look at the overall architecture of our layered components:

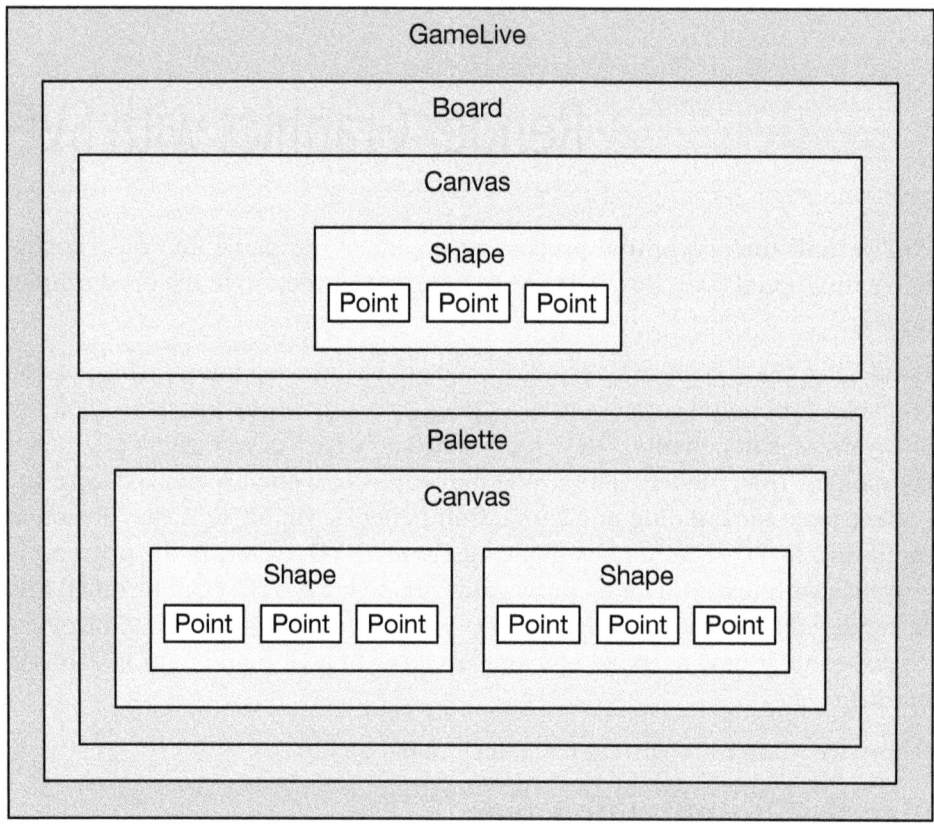

This layered design will let us focus on one bit of complexity at a time, while the ergonomic syntax for component rendering will make it easy to layer our components in code. We'll define and layer slim, single-purpose function components that represent the different parts of our game. This might seem abstract, so let's take a moment to make the concepts more concrete.

Working from the inside out, the smallest level of abstraction in our presentation layer is the point, which we'll represent with a Point component. In our game display, points are colored squares, and each point square will be positioned somewhere in a grid that represents the user's viewport. So a point will have x and y coordinates in addition to a width and a color attribute. Eventually, we'll also need to apply a phx-click to the collection of points that make up a shape so users can interact with puzzle pieces. A component is the perfect interface for wrapping up a point's attributes and functionality so that we can display a point to the user and let a user interact with a group of points.

Say we have a plain Phoenix Component.point/1 function component that renders the SVG for a single point. In the live views and live components that make use of them, we'll make sure to import the components in the Component module. That way, we can call them like this:

```
<.point
    x={ @x }
    y={ @y }
    fill={ @fill }
    name={ @name } />
```

Beautiful. With this approach, we can wrap the SVG to draw a point inside a small, single-purpose component, and we can render that component with a lightweight syntax that's easy to read and write. We'll see this and our other components in action later on in this chapter when we build and layer the series of components outlined above. Let's take a more detailed look at that design now.

The point/1 function component is the lowest level of abstraction in our game design. We'll wrap up calls to render sets of point/1 function components within a stateless shape/1 function component. We'll also build a live Board component to display a single rectangular Shape representing the puzzle board alongside another function component, .palette/1, that renders the list of pentomino shapes that can be placed to solve the puzzle. The Board needs to be live, although we won't take advantage of a live component's ability to handle user input in this chapter. In the next chapter, we'll teach it to handle the user interactions that make up our game.

Now that we have a high-level understanding of the components we'll build and how they fit together, it's time to start coding.

Define a Skinny GameLive View

Most of the game will happen in the components and application core files, but you *will* need a live view to serve as the entry point of the Pentominoes game. This live view will be slim—it won't do much more than render the top-level Board live component that renders our game display and handles game events. Start by creating a new route in your routes.exs file, like this:

graphics/pento/lib/pento_web/router.ex
```
live "/game/:puzzle", GameLive
```

Note that we've given our route a dynamic segment of :puzzle. We'll use this URL parameter to let users pick a puzzle shape.

Next, we need a subdirectory, lib/pento_web/live/game_live, to house the Pentominoes UI. Add a new file, lib/pento_web/live/game_live/game_live.ex, and define this live view:

```
defmodule PentoWeb.GameLive do
  use PentoWeb, :live_view

  def mount(_params, _session, socket), do: {:ok, socket}
  def render(assigns) do
    ~H"""
    <section class="mx-auto max-w-4xl px-4 py-8">
      <h1 class="font-heavy text-3xl mb-6">Welcome to Pento!</h1>
    </section>
    """
  end
end
```

Now, if you run the server and point your browser at /game/medium, you should see this:

Welcome to Pento!

With that out of the way, let's build our first component, the .point/1 function component.

Render Points with SVG

The .point/1 function component will be the foundation of our game's presentation layer. We'll use points both to construct pentomino shapes for our palette and to draw the single rectangular puzzle board shape. We'll render an individual point with SVG, but before we write that code, let's take a moment to dig into what SVG is and how it works.

SVG[1] stands for Scalable Vector Graphics. It's a text-based markup language for describing vector graphics that can be rendered cleanly at any size. Vector graphics are different from those rendered by formats like JPEG, PNG, and GIF. Raster graphics light up individual points, called pixels, in a specified color. With vector graphics, on the other hand, you'll use text to specify and assemble shapes. Since SVG uses text to build shapes and images, it's the

---
1. https://developer.mozilla.org/en-US/docs/Web/SVG

perfect fit for rendering images with LiveView. Changes to the live view's state will cause the template to re-render, allowing LiveView to update just the part of the text-based SVG image that needs changing.

It's time to write your own SVG, starting with a 10x10 square SVG point. We'll start by rendering a simple SVG square. Then we'll wrap that SVG markup in a small function component.

Build the SVG Point

First up, let's render an SVG square directly in the GameLive view. Open up the GameLive module and add the square below the title, like this:

```
# lib/pento_web/live/game_live/game_live.ex
~H"""
<section class="mx-auto max-w-4xl px-4 py-8">
  <h1 class="font-heavy text-3xl mb-6">Welcome to Pento!</h1>
</section>
<svg viewBox="0 0 100 100">
  <rect x="0" y="0" width="10" height="10" />
</svg>
"""
```

Here, we define an SVG image with opening and closing <svg> tags. We use the SVG viewBox attribute to specify the position and dimension of the SVG viewport in user space. The viewBox attribute points to a list of four numbers: min-x, min-y, width, and height. Together, these data points specify a rectangle that's mapped to the bounds of the SVG element's viewport. So by giving the viewBox the values 0 0 100 100, we're going to render a 100x100 pixel space within which to place our SVG shape.

The self-closing <rect /> tag implements a rectangle shape with width and height properties of 10 pixels each. The x and y attributes define the horizontal and vertical positions of the rectangle, respectively. So, all together, this SVG markup defines a viewport and draws a 10x10 rectangle within that viewport. Point your browser at /game/medium to see this rectangle on the page:

Great. With our single point in place, we're ready to draw collections of points.

Dynamically Draw Points with SVG <defs>

Now you know how to draw one SVG square, but we'll need lots of them to build our shapes. We'll use the SVG <defs> element to define reusable square-shaped templates. Then we'll use LiveView to dynamically render collections of squares in our game display.

The <defs> SVG element stores graphical objects for rendering later. Objects created inside a <defs> element are not rendered directly. Instead, they're rendered when they are referenced by a <use> element later on. Think of it like defining a function that you call on later. Let's take a look at an example.

Open up GameLive and replace the <rect> we built earlier with this code to render four similar squares:

```
# lib/pento_web/live/game_live/game_live.ex
<svg viewBox="0 0 100 100">
  <defs>
    <rect id="point" width="10" height="10" />
  </defs>
  <use xlink:href="#point" x="0" y="0" fill="blue" />
  <use xlink:href="#point" x="10" y="0" fill="green" />
  <use xlink:href="#point" x="0" y="10" fill="red" />
  <use xlink:href="#point" x="10" y="10" fill="black" />
</svg>
```

First, we use <defs> to define a reusable <rect> shape with an ID of "point". Then we render that same shape four times by calling <use> and setting the xlink:href attribute to the #point ID. Each time we render the <rect> implemented in our <defs> element, we assign a different set of x and y coordinates and a different color. Open your browser at /game/medium to see the result.

In the next section, we'll move this logic into two components—a canvas/1 function component that defines the reusable rectangle shape with <defs> and the point/1 function component that renders this shape with <use>. Later, we'll use LiveView to dynamically render the correct set of point/1 function components for a given shape.

Prepare a Module for Components

We'll keep the function components for the Pentominoes game all in one place. The game will need to support concepts for a single point, a grouping of points called a shape, a grouping of shapes on a canvas, and so on.

This Component module will house function components that manage our SVG details. These components will wrap increasingly complex concepts, starting with a point, then a shape composed of points, and then a palette composed of shapes. We'll also build a function to wrap an SVG canvas. Create the file lib/pento_web/live/game_live/component.ex, and key this much in:

```
graphics/pento/lib/pento_web/live/game_live/component.ex
defmodule PentoWeb.GameLive.Component do
  use Phoenix.Component
  alias Pento.Game.Pentomino
  import PentoWeb.GameLive.Colors

  @width 10
end
```

Our component module uses Phoenix.Component to declare our intention to build function components. By virtue of that use directive, we get the ~H sigil for HEEx templates, the attr macro for defining attributes, and the slot macro for defining slots. We also import the core components we need and set the @point module attribute with our point width.

The next step is to start churning out the components to render the SVG our code will use.

Build the Point Component

The point/1 functional component will only be responsible for rendering one single <use> element with the appropriate x, y, and fill based on the assigns we pass in. The <defs> element that implements the reusable rectangle will be implemented in another component entirely. We'll deal with those details later. For now, declare the point/1 function using the ~H sigil to render an SVG <use> element:

```
graphics/pento/lib/pento_web/live/game_live/component.ex
attr :x, :integer, required: true
attr :y, :integer, required: true
attr :fill, :string
attr :name, :string
attr :"phx-click", :string
attr :"phx-value", :string
attr :"phx-target", :any

def point(assigns) do
  ~H"""
  <use
    xlink:href="#pento-point"
    x={convert(@x)}
    y={convert(@y)}
    fill={@fill}
    phx-click="pick"
```

```
        phx-value-name={@name}
        phx-target="#board-component"
    />
    """
end
```

By looking at the attr definitions, you can immediately see the attributes our components can use. This ceremony has a price. It nearly doubles the length of our function on the page, and that's more code we need to maintain and understand. It also has tremendous value. Those attributes will let our compiler catch errors our eyes cannot. For now, set aside the phx-click, phx-value-name, and phx-target attributes. We'll need those later so the user can interact with shapes on the page by name.

Shift your focus to the other keys the SVG graphic requires. The point/1 function creates a single <use> string with the SVG fill attribute set to the value of the @fill assignment and the x and y attributes set to the appropriate numbers, given the @x and @y assignments and adjusted by the convert/1 function. Let's dive a little deeper into the convert/1 function that will help position the point correctly. Here's a closer look at that helper function:

graphics/pento/lib/pento_web/live/game_live/component.ex
```
defp convert(i) do
  (i - 1) * @width + 2 * @width
end
```

The convert/1 function takes in the value of the x or y coordinate and does some math to build the x and y offsets of the square. The math serves to center each pentomino within its 5x5 box. The i - 1 part is important because the x and y values in our pentominoes start at 1, but the values on our canvas will start at zero. We multiply the position by the width and then adjust the component to keep it centered on the canvas. Don't worry about any other details for now. Keep your focus on the component structure.

Our .point/1 function component is complete. Now we need a wrapper around an SVG canvas to implement the <defs> element for the reusable <rect> SVG shape. We'll implement the .canvas/1 function component to take care of this.

Render a Canvas with a Slot

The .canvas/1 function component will manage a few responsibilities:

- Define an SVG viewport with a top-level <svg> element.
- Define the reuseable <rect> shape with a <defs> element.
- Provide a component slot we can use to render custom content with the correct set of points based on the state of our game.

We'll brush up on component slots in a bit. For now, just think of a slot as a predefined container in a template that can hold our custom content. The function is surprisingly small:

graphics/pento/lib/pento_web/live/game_live/component.ex
```
attr :view_box, :string
slot :inner_block, required: true
def canvas(assigns) do
  ~H"""
  <svg viewBox={@view_box}>
    <defs>
      <rect id="pento-point" width="10" height="10" />
    </defs>
    {render_slot(@inner_block)}
  </svg>
  """
end
```

A first glance over the attributes doesn't tell us much. We're going to pass our view_box attribute straight through to the viewBox attribute required by SVG. Our code also supports an @inner_block, meaning we're expecting code between the <.canvas ...> and </canvas> tags. The code between tags is a *slot*, and the code between the component's tags is called the *inner block*. Now, shift your attention to the function body.

Here, we render an <svg> element with the viewBox attribute set to @view_box component assignment. The <svg> element contains a reusable <rect> shape with a static width and height of 10px and an id of "point". Calls to point/1 will render a rect because the xlink:href attribute in the point/1 function matches the id in the rect tag within the canvas definition.

Next, we'll test the Canvas by rendering a set of points via some calls to render the .point/1 function component. Our Canvas is flexible because users can customize its inner_block slot. To support custom content, LiveView components provide a feature called slots.

Now we can render the .canvas/1 function component with some custom content. Open up GameLive and import the new function components:

```
# lib/pento_web/live/game_live.ex
import PentoWeb.GameLive.Component
```

Next, update render/1, like this:

```
# lib/pento_web/live/game_live.ex
def render(assigns) do
  ~H"""
```

```
    <section class="mx-auto max-w-4xl px-4 py-8">
      <h1 class="font-heavy text-3xl mb-6">Welcome to Pento!</h1>
      <.canvas view_box="0 0 200 30">
        <.point x={0} y={0} fill="blue" name="a" />
        <.point x={1} y={0} fill="green" name="b" />
        <.point x={0} y={1} fill="red" name="c" />
        <.point x={1} y={1} fill="black" name="d" />
      </.canvas >
    </section>
    """
end
```

Visit /game/medium to see .canvas/1 render the .point/1 function components in the render_slot placeholder:

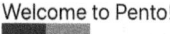

This eloquent syntax makes it easy to assemble complex layers of components. Child components go between opening and closing parent component tags, maintaining a beautiful and clear separation between the parent and child. You can click a point if you want, but the corresponding handle_event/3 function isn't implemented yet, so you'll get the predictable crash.

Now we have a .canvas/1 function component that knows how to render a collection of points and a .point/1 function component that draws a single point. With the code we've written so far, we could draw both the game's board and the palette by calling the .canvas/1 function with the right set of points. But we can do better. In the next section, we'll build some intermediate layers with groupings of points.

Compose with Components

In the remaining sections of this chapter, we'll use the .point/1 and .canvas/1 function components to render more complex graphics. We'll roll up a collection of points with common colors and names into shapes represented by a .shape/1 function component. Then we'll assemble shapes to display the palette of pentominoes for a game. We'll also use a single rectangular shape of a given size to represent the game's puzzle board. When we're done, the design of our components will look something like this:

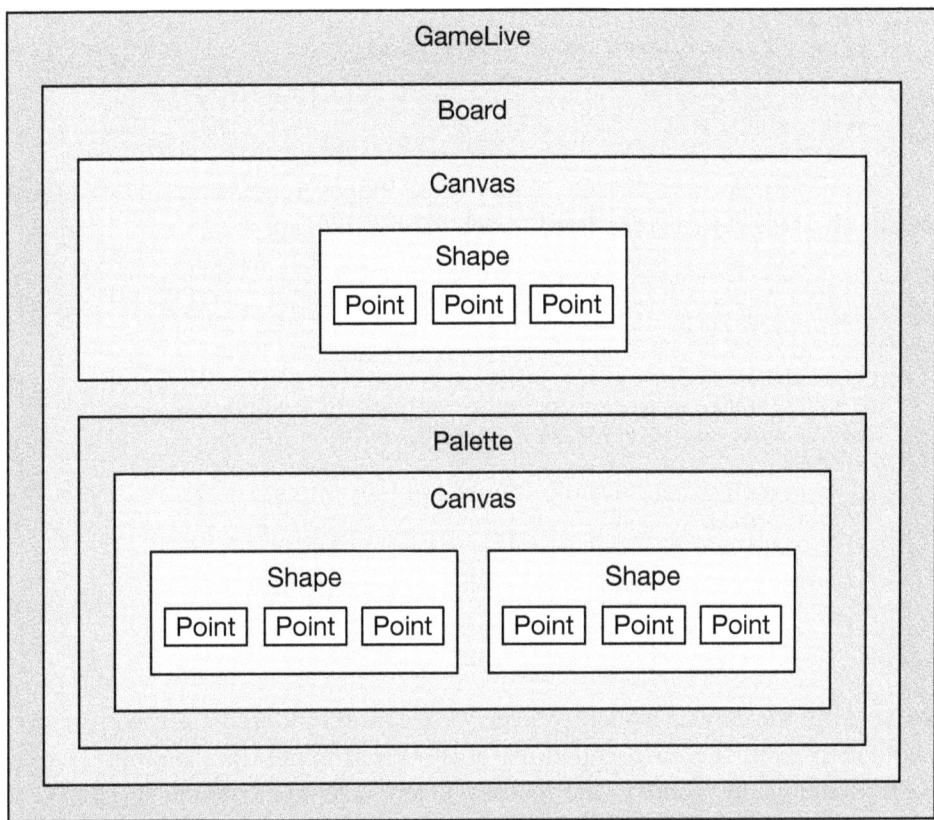

The Board live component contains a call to .canvas/1 that renders a single .shape/1 component depicting our puzzle board and one more .shape/1 component for each pentomino on the board. It also renders the Palette containing a .canvas/1 function call to display the set of .shape/1 components representing the pentominoes a user can place for a particular puzzle. Let's start building out this structure now.

Render Shapes with Multiple Points

First up, we'll build a .shape/1 function component that knows how to render the list of points that make up a given shape. Create a new file, lib/pento_web/live/game_live/component.ex. In it, define your shape function to display the list of points with the shape's fill and name attributes, like this:

```
graphics/pento/lib/pento_web/live/game_live/component.ex
attr :points, :list, required: true
attr :name, :string, required: true
attr :fill, :string, required: true

def shape(assigns) do
  ~H"""
```

```
    <%= for {x, y} <- @points do %>
      <.point x={x} y={y} fill={@fill} name={@name} />
    <% end %>
  """
end
```

The .shape/1 function can already render basic shapes in GameLive. Update render/1 to call on .shape/1 with some hard-coded values, like so:

```
# lib/pento_web/live/game_live.ex
def render(assigns) do
  ~H"""
  <section class="mx-auto max-w-4xl px-4 py-8">
    <h1 class="font-heavy text-3xl mb-6">Welcome to Pento!</h1>
    <.canvas view_box="0 0 220 70">
      <.shape
        points={ [{3, 2}, {4, 3}, {3, 3}, {4, 2}, {3, 4}] }
        fill="orange"
        name="p" />
    </.canvas>
  </section>
  """
end
```

We've given the canvas a slightly larger viewBox and rendered a .shape/1 function component with the hard-coded list of points that make up a :p shape. Later, we'll dynamically render the points given a shape name. If you visit /game/medium, you'll see a P shape rendered in bright orange. That shape would make a good logo—let's build a simple logo with SVG rect primitives. While we're at it, we'll use native SVG to render a P-shape in place of the Phoenix logo, like this:

```
graphics/pento/lib/pento_web/components/layouts/root.html.heex
<a href="/">
  <svg viewBox="0 0 55 55" class="h-6">
    <rect x="0" y="0" width="55" height="55" fill="#DDD" />
    <rect x="10" y="5" width="30" height="30" fill="#689042"></rect>
    <rect x="10" y="35" width="15" height="15" fill="#689042"></rect>
  </svg>
</a>
<p class="px-2 text-[0.8125rem] font-heavy leading-6">
  Pentominos
</p>
```

This P shape made of nothing but three SVG boxes serves as a nice little logo, and we tack on a description in a p tag. Visit /game/medium to see the shape displayed on the page, as shown here:

Pentominos   bruce@grox.io   Dashboard   Products   Survey   Settings   Log out

Welcome to Pento!

Success! The canvas renders the shape using a slot full of points, ultimately rendering several different <rect> elements that together make up a :p shape. We can also see the shiny new logo.

Now let's make those hard-coded lists of shapes dynamic. The next step is to use our core code to calculate the shapes to build. The end user needs an easy way to select a pentomino to place on the board. We can use the .canvas and .shape components to render a list of all pentomino shapes a user can use to solve the puzzle. We'll wrap that idea in a function component called .palette/1. The palette will wrap a list of shapes in .canvas tags. We'll do that next.

Build a Palette from Shapes

It's time to build a palette. Recall from the previous chapter that each new core Game.Board struct has an attribute called palette with a value like :medium. That palette defines the list of shapes allowed in a puzzle. Here's a fresh look at the Game.Board constructor function:

```
graphics/pento/lib/pento/game/board.ex
def new(palette, points) do
  %__MODULE__{palette: palette(palette), points: points}
end

def new(:tiny),    do: new(:small, rect(5, 3))
def new(:widest),  do: new(:all, rect(20, 3))
def new(:wide),    do: new(:all, rect(15, 4))
def new(:medium),  do: new(:all, rect(12, 5))
def new(:default), do: new(:all, rect(10, 6))
```

And here's the palette/1 helper function returning the corresponding list of shape names:

```
defp palette(:all), do: [:i, :l, :y, :n, :p, :w, :u, :v, :s, :f, :x, :t]
defp palette(:small), do: [:u, :v, :p]
```

Later, we'll initialize a new core Board struct in LiveView and invoke the palette/1 function to build a canvas with all of the available shapes. The palette will have two primary attributes. The shape_names list will hold all available pentominoes for a puzzle. The user will pick up pentominoes from the palette and place them on the board. The second attribute is a list of completed shapes. Once the user places pentominoes on the board, we'll use this second list to render the pentomino in a different color. To show the pentominoes on the board, we'll rely on the core module we already built to convert shape *names* into shape *structs*.

The core Pentomino module implements the new/2 constructor, taking a shape name and location. The new/2 function returns a Pentomino struct. The Pentomino module also implements a converter function that converts a pentomino struct into a core Shape struct. Each Shape struct knows its list of points and their correct location. So our .palette/1 function component will take a shape name and use it to construct a Pentomino struct. Then it will convert *that* into a core Shape struct. Finally, we'll render the points in the shape by calling .shape/1. We'll do that next.

Our palette/1 function will use the initial shape_names and completed_shape_names assignments to build a list of pentomino shapes at the right location and in the right color. Start by defining your palette/2 function to extract the :shape_names from assigns, like this:

```
# lib/pento_web/live/game_live/component.ex
attr :shape_names, :list, required: true
attr :completed_shape_names, :list, default: []
def palette(%{shape_names: shape_names}=assigns) do
  # coming soon!
end
```

We start with a list of shape names on the palette and a list of completed shapes. These attributes determine the API for our function component. Here's how we'll render the palette:

```
graphics/pento/lib/pento_web/live/game_live/component.ex
attr :shape_names, :list, required: true
attr :completed_shape_names, :list, default: []

def palette(assigns) do
  ~H"""
  <div id="pento-palette">
    <svg viewBox="0 0 500 125">
      <defs>
```

```
        <rect id="palette-point" width="10" height="10" />
      </defs>
      <%= for shape <- palette_shapes(@shape_names) do %>
        <.palette_shape
          points={shape.points}
          fill={color(shape.color, false, shape.name in @completed_shape_names)}
          name={shape.name}
        />
      <% end %>
    </svg>
  </div>
  """
end

attr :points, :list, required: true
attr :name, :string, required: true
attr :fill, :string, required: true

def palette_shape(assigns) do
  ~H"""
  <%= for {x, y} <- @points do %>
    <.palette_point x={x} y={y} fill={@fill} name={@name} />
  <% end %>
  """
end

attr :x, :integer, required: true
attr :y, :integer, required: true
attr :fill, :string, required: true
attr :name, :string, required: true

def palette_point(assigns) do
  ~H"""
  <use
    xlink:href="#palette-point"
    x={convert(@x)}
    y={convert(@y)}
    fill={@fill}
    phx-click="pick"
    phx-value-name={@name}
    phx-target="#board-component"
  />
  """
end
```

We start with a canvas wrapped in a div and then iterate over each of the shapes from the palette_shapes/1 helper function. The only tricky bit is using the color/3 function to determine the color. If the piece has been placed, we want to notify the user by turning the piece black. Now let's do the hard part. We need to translate the list of shape names to actual shapes in the right location.

We need to somehow take all of the shape names and convert that list to points on the page. Sometimes, with a complex problem, it pays to break down one larger step into several smaller ones. It's too much work to find the precise location of every point from every pentomino, but we *can* find the position of each pentomino in the list. For now, build a list of shapes with indexes (and save the hard part for another function):

graphics/pento/lib/pento_web/live/game_live/component.ex
```
defp palette_shapes(names) do
  names
  |> Enum.with_index()
  |> Enum.map(&place_pento/1)
end
```

We take one small step toward the goal. We start with a list of shape names. The Enum.with_index/1 function translates the list of names to a list of tuples like {:p, 0} with a name and an index. Then we map over *that* list to place each of the shapes on the canvas. Next, we write the place_pento/1 function to take one more small step toward the goal:

graphics/pento/lib/pento_web/live/game_live/component.ex
```
defp place_pento({name, i}) do
  Pentomino.new(name: name, location: location(i))
  |> Pentomino.to_shape()
end
```

Now that we have an individual shape, it's a trivial matter to convert that to a pentomino, and we can convert that one to a list of shapes. We still don't have to solve the whole problem. We save the math for determining the precise {x, y} location of each pentomino on the palette until a later function, called location/1.

Before we move on, let's think about this location calculation. If a palette has all of its pentominoes, we'll display the pentominoes that make up our palette in two rows and six columns. Given an index, we can get the *row* (the y value) by dividing the index by 6 and leaving off the remainder: div(i, 6). Similarly, we can get the *column* (the x value) by calculating the remainder of the index divided by 6: rem(i, 6). So, for example, if we're operating on the first shape at index 0 of the palette, we'll get the following {x, y} location:

```
iex> i = 0
0
iex> {rem(i, 6), div(i,6)}
{0, 0}
```

The next shape at index 1 will get this {x, y} location:

```
iex> i = 1
0
iex> {rem(i, 6), div(i,6)}
{1, 0}
```

As div(i, 6) where i is less than six is *always* zero, every shape at indices 0–5 will get a y value of 0 and be placed in the first row. Meanwhile, the remainder used to calculate the y value counts upward from 0. It gets bigger for each index, until it reaches six when it starts over at zero. Play around with a few more examples in IEx by setting i to various numbers until you get the hang of it.

We still need to adjust our {x, y} values. The widest pentomino is 3 points, and we need to have space between each one. We'll need to multiply each x value by four. Similarly, we'll allow enough vertical space if we assume a height of 5. Then we shift each unit by 3 points down and right so our first pentomino won't hang off of the canvas. Here's the code we use to determine the precise location:

graphics/pento/lib/pento_web/live/game_live/component.ex
```
defp location(i) do
  x = rem(i, 6) * 4 + 3
  y = div(i, 6) * 5 + 3
  {x, y}
end
```

This code builds in the calculations we discussed. Don't get bogged down in the details. If the math is a little confusing to you, try making the 4 and 5 factors slightly smaller or greater and see what changing the values does to the display. Then try adjusting the + 3 adjustment. You'll see how each number impacts the overall calculation. The real takeaway, though, is that the .palette/1 function component knows how to take a list of shape *names* and convert them into shape *structs* that know their name and location. With the shapes behind us, let's write the helpers that translate the generic core colors into precise colors supported by the browser.

Add Helpers for Showing Colors

In the core, we used colors like :dark_green and :light_orange to describe our pentominoes. That's fine for the core, but we're going to need more detail in the user interface. We'll need a precise color code for our fill attributes for points and shapes, and also some overrides for those colors in case a pentomino is selected or one from the palette is already in use. Review the fill assigns for the .palette/1 component:

```
fill={ color(shape.color, false, shape.name in @completed_shape_names) }
```

Notice the fill attribute is populated with a call to a color/3 function, but we haven't implemented such a function yet. We need to build functions to translate the color field from the core struct into HTML-friendly hex codes. We'll do so in the PentoWeb.GameLive.Colors helper module. Create lib/pento_web/live/game_live/colors.ex now:

```
graphics/pento/lib/pento_web/live/game_live/colors.ex
defmodule PentoWeb.GameLive.Colors do
  def color(c), do: color(c, false, false)

  def color(_color, true, _completed), do: "#B86EF0"
  def color(_color, _active, true), do: "#000000"
  def color(:green, _active, _completed), do: "#8BBF57"
  def color(:dark_green, _active, _completed), do: "#689042"
  def color(:light_green, _active, _completed), do: "#C1D6AC"
  def color(:orange, _active, _completed), do: "#B97328"
  def color(:dark_orange, _active, _completed), do: "#8D571E"
  def color(:light_orange, _active, _completed), do: "#F4CCA1"
  def color(:gray, _active, _completed), do: "#848386"
  def color(:dark_gray, _active, _completed), do: "#5A595A"
  def color(:light_gray, _active, _completed), do: "#B1B1B1"
  def color(:blue, _active, _completed), do: "#83C7CE"
  def color(:dark_blue, _active, _completed), do: "#63969B"
  def color(:light_blue, _active, _completed), do: "#B9D7DA"
  def color(:purple, _active, _completed), do: "#240054"
end
```

The pentominoes all have their own color mappings. In addition, a user will place one pentomino on the board at a time, and later we'll apply a highlighted color to this active shape. Finally, we want to show pentominoes as black once they've been placed on the palette.

The Colors module calculates color codes with nothing but pattern matching. When the second argument of the color/3 function is true, it will return a bright pink color, "#B86EF0", to denote the piece currently in play. Similarly, a true value for the third argument will return the #000000 black color. Otherwise, each pentomino returns a unique color code based on the provided fill atom. The color/1 function is just a convenience function for inactive pentominoes. While it may not seem that there's anything specific to LiveView in this module, it belongs in the lib/pento_web/live/ directory because it has user-interface issues, and only live views and components will call it.

Okay, let's put it all together and render the .palette/1 component from within GameLive now. Replace the content under our <h1> component in the render/1 function with this:

```
def render(assigns) do
  ~H"""
  <section class="mx-auto max-w-4xl px-4 py-8">
    <h1 class="font-heavy text-3xl mb-6">Welcome to Pento!</h1>
    <.palette shape_names={ [:i, :l, :y, :n, :p, :w,
                             :u, :v, :s, :f, :x, :t] } />
  </section>
  """
end
```

Here, we're calling the .palette/1 function component with a hard-coded list of shape names. If you point your browser at /game/medium, you should see this neat display of your palette:

Welcome to Pento!

With the palette in hand, we're ready to present a board. The Board live component will wrap up all of the game elements we've built so far. Let's build it now.

Put It All Together

The Board live component will render the .canvas/1 function representing the puzzle board shape, along with the .palette/1 function we just built. The Board will also manage the state of the game based on user interactions. It will be a stateful component that knows how to receive events and update the game's state in response to a user selecting, moving, and placing pentominoes. We'll build that behavior in the next chapter. For now, we'll focus on the component props and the render function that will present the game display to the user.

Render the Board Component

Before we dive into the code for our component, let's take a look at how GameLive will render it. Open up GameLive and start by updating the aliases and mount/3 function, as shown on the following page.

```
graphics/pento/lib/pento_web/live/game_live.ex
defmodule PentoWeb.GameLive do
  use PentoWeb, :live_view

  alias PentoWeb.GameLive.Board

  def mount(%{"puzzle" => puzzle}, _session, socket) do
    {:ok, assign(socket, puzzle: puzzle)}
  end
```

We match the puzzle name in params and store it in the socket. We'll need it to render the Board component with the correct puzzle board shape and palette of pentomino shapes. Now update the render/1 function to call live_component/1 to render our Board live component. It should call on the component with a puzzle assigns set equal to the @puzzle assignment and an id assigns set equal to "game":

```
graphics/pento/lib/pento_web/live/game_live.ex
def render(assigns) do
  ~H"""
  <section class="mx-auto max-w-4xl px-4 py-8">
    <h1 class="font-heavy text-3xl mb-6">Welcome to Pento!</h1>
    <.live_component module={Board} puzzle={@puzzle} id="board-component" />
  </section>
  """
end
```

Our new code is simple and elegant. The GameLive view takes some info from the params and renders one component. Next, we'll use the Board to display elements of our game.

Define the Board Component

Create a file, lib/pento_web/live/game_live/board.ex, and define a stateful component with the usual imports and aliases:

```
graphics/pento/lib/pento_web/live/game_live/board.ex
defmodule PentoWeb.GameLive.Board do
  use PentoWeb, :live_component

  alias Pento.Game.{Board, Pentomino}
  import PentoWeb.GameLive.{Colors, Component}
end
```

Unlike the function components in GameLive/Component, the Board has state that users update by interacting with the elements on the board. It's a live_component, so our initial module setup has the use PentoWeb, :live_component directive. We then import the function components and colors that we need to present the user interface. We also need access to the Game.Board and Game.Pentomino models because they represent the state that this board will hold in its socket.

Next, we need to establish a constructor. Our update/2 will establish the initial state of the initial params, the board that holds the logical representation of our game, and the list of shapes that we'll render. The function will add those values to the component's socket with some handy reducers, like this:

graphics/pento/lib/pento_web/live/game_live/board.ex
```elixir
def update(%{puzzle: puzzle, id: id}, socket) do
  {:ok,
   socket
   |> assign_params(id, puzzle)
   |> assign_board()
   |> assign_shapes()}
end
```

The id and the puzzle come from the assigns that we'll pass in when we render the Board component from its parent live view, GameLive. So we'll group them together in a single reducer:

graphics/pento/lib/pento_web/live/game_live/board.ex
```elixir
def assign_params(socket, id, puzzle) do
  assign(socket, id: id, puzzle: puzzle)
end
```

We'll use the :id assignment when we render (more on that later), and we'll use the :puzzle assignment to create a new board struct.

Let's move on to our next two reducers. The board assignment will track the *conceptual* state of the game and the shapes assignment will represent the data we'll render. Define a reducer, assign_board/1, that takes in the socket and pattern matches the puzzle type out of socket assigns. Then add in the following hard-coded data to describe an active pentomino as well as a list of completed, or placed, pentominoes, like this:

```elixir
def assign_board(%{assigns: %{puzzle: puzzle}} = socket) do
  active = Pentomino.new(name: :p, location: {3, 2})
  completed = [
      Pentomino.new(name: :u, rotation: 270, location: {1, 2}),
      Pentomino.new(name: :v, rotation: 90, location: {4, 2})
    ]

  # coming soon!
end
```

For now, we'll hard-code a rich set of data to mimic an in-progress game. This technique is common in LiveView development. By hard-coding in some more complex data, we can prototype our rendering capabilities while we work on the underlying features.

Now, let's use this dummy data to construct a new core Board struct and add it to the component's state, like this:

```
graphics/pento/lib/pento_web/live/game_live/board.ex
def assign_board(%{assigns: %{puzzle: puzzle}} = socket) do
  active = Pentomino.new(name: :p, location: {7, 2})

  completed = [
    Pentomino.new(name: :u, rotation: 270, location: {1, 2}),
    Pentomino.new(name: :v, rotation: 90, location: {4, 2})
  ]

  # atom must exist!
  _puzzles = Board.puzzles()

  board =
    puzzle
    |> String.to_existing_atom()
    |> Board.new()
    |> Map.put(:completed_pentos, completed)
    |> Map.put(:active_pento, active)

  assign(socket, board: board)
end
```

Let's break down this last bit of our assign_board/1 reducer, as it's more complex. Recall that our core Board module's constructor expects to be called with a puzzle type that's an atom. So we need to convert the *string* puzzle type from our component's assigns into an atom and use *that* to initialize a new board struct. We use to_existing_atom to make sure we don't create new atoms, which could eventually result in an exhausted atom table, a hard crash, and an overnight support issue. We pipe this argument into a call to Board.new/1, then we pipe our new board struct into two successive calls to Map.put/3. The first call adds the list of completed pentominoes, and the second adds the active pentomino. This leaves us with a board struct that has all of the elements we need to build out the game-rendering functionality: a background describing the shape of the board, an active pento, and a list of completed pentos.

We have one more reducer to go—the assign_shapes/1 reducer. This function is responsible for converting the board struct into a set of shapes for rendering. Define your function to look like this:

```
# lib/pento_web/live/game_live/board.ex
def assign_shapes(%{assigns: %{board: board}} = socket) do
  shapes = Board.to_shapes(board)
  assign(socket, shapes: shapes)
end
```

Now we need to render these shapes.

Render the Board

The Board component's render function will loop over the list of shapes we placed in socket assigns and render each one of them. This will in turn render the points that make up each shape, thereby drawing the SVG squares that make up our game display.

Fill out the Board component's render/1 function with these details:

```
graphics/pento/lib/pento_web/live/game_live/board.ex
def render(assigns) do
  ~H"""
  <div id={@id} phx-window-keydown="key" phx-target={@myself}>
    <.canvas view_box="0 0 200 70">
      <%= for shape <- @shapes do %>
        <.shape
          points={shape.points}
          fill={color(shape.color, Board.active?(@board, shape.name), false)}
          name={shape.name}
        />
      <% end %>
    </.canvas>
    <hr />
    <.palette
      shape_names={@board.palette}
      completed_shape_names={Enum.map(@board.completed_pentos, & &1.name)}
    />
  </div>
  """
end
```

This rendering accomplishes three things: it provides a single <div> that holds the component so we can collect keystrokes and attach a unique ID, it renders a .canvas/1 function with the board's shapes, and it renders a .palette/1 function so the user can pick up pieces to place in the puzzle. We don't have to work too hard to establish the color of the pentominoes on the board or in the canvas. We're making use of the color/3 function to calculate the color of the pentomino within the fill attribute. To acommodate the color/3 function in the palette, we pass the list of completed shapes to the .palette/1 function component.

It's time to see our code in action. Open up your browser, visit /game/tiny, and you should see something like the image on the next page.

This code is picking up steam! Now we have everything we need to bring some life to this game. We've covered a lot of ground in this chapter. It's time to wrap up and give you a chance to put what you've learned into practice.

Pentominos   **bruce@grox.io**   Dashboard   Products   Survey   Settings   Log out

Welcome to Pento!

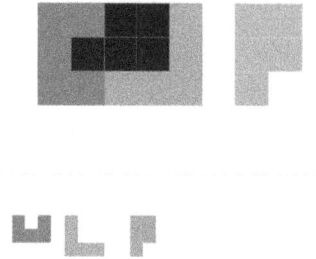

Your Turn

So far, we've implemented a stateful Board component that renders the single shape of the puzzle board along with the board's palette of pentominoes. By layering the .point/1, .shape/1, .canvas/1, and .palette/1 function components in various ways, we built out a complex UI in a simple manner that will be easy to read and maintain, even as the complexity of our game grows.

This layered approach was helped along by a few things. Our robust application core made it easy to map core concerns to the UI components that render them. We defined simple converter functions in the application core and called on them in single-purpose reducer functions in LiveView to produce data for rendering. When it came time to render this data, the combination of LiveView components and SVG provided us with the perfect toolkit. We used SVG to define reusable shapes, components to wrap these shapes in single-purpose components, and LiveView to dynamically render the correct set of SVG shapes for each piece of the game display. SVG and LiveView components are a winning combo for building complex, layered, and interactive UIs.

Now it's time for you to build some new features on your own.

Give It a Try

You'll put your new skills to work with three different challenges. The first challenge will give you a chance to define and use your own function component.

Build a Game Instructions Component

Define a new function component, GameInstructions.show/1, that renders a paragraph with some game instructions. Then render this component within the GameLive view, between the title and the board.

Add a New Puzzle

This challenge will give you an opportunity to work in both the application's functional core and the UI layer. You'll add a new puzzle type to the Pento.Board core module and trace the code flow that draws the puzzle shape in the UI.

First, add a new function head for the Board.new/1 constructor that pattern matches a first argument of :small. This constructor should return a new board struct with the small palette and a set of points representing a rectangle of some size between the existing Tiny and Medium puzzles. The exact size is up to you. To play around with the puzzle size, render your new board in the UI by visiting /game/small. Once you're satisfied with the puzzle size, trace the code flow from the game's entry point in GameLive and answer the following questions:

- How does the PentoWeb.GameLive.Board component know the shape of the puzzle board?
- How does the PentoWeb.GameLive.Board component render the list of points that make up the puzzle board?
- How does the PentoWeb.GameLive.Board component know what shapes make up the palette?
- How does the PentoWeb.GameLive.Board component render the palette?
- How does the .palette/1 function component render the correct list of shapes?

Build a Pentomino Control Panel

This challenge will give you a chance to work with more complex SVG shapes. You'll build a Control Panel with four arrows that will allow the user to move a selected shape up, down, left, or right. But don't worry about building that behavior just yet. For now, focus on building the control panel display. You'll end up with something like this:

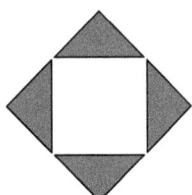

Build a stateless component, .control_panel/1, that uses SVG <defs> to define a reusable SVG polygon element. It should implement a viewBox prop and define the default slot. It should render the <defs> for a triangle shape, like this:

```
def control_panel(assigns) do
  ~H"""
  <svg viewBox={ @viewBox }>
    <defs>
      <polygon id="triangle" points="6.25 1.875, 12.5 12.5, 0 12.5" />
    </defs>
    <slot/>
  </svg>
  """
end
```

Next, build another function component, .triangle/1. You can expect to call it with the following assigns:

- An x and y prop that will hold the positioning values.
- A fill prop that will be set equal to some color.
- A rotate prop that will be set equal to the degrees by which the shape will be rotated to form your control panel display.

Implement .triangle/1 to render the <use> element that draws the triangle shape, like this:

```
def triangle(assigns) do
  ~H"""
    <use
      x={ @x }
      y={ @y } transform="rotate( @rotate, 100, 100)"
      href="#triangle"
      fill={ @fill } />
  """
end
```

Here, we're using the SVG transform[2] attribute to specify a rotation[3] of a given number of degrees around an x, y point of 100, 100. You may want to play around with the x, y values given to the rotate function once you start displaying your triangles. Check out the linked documentation to learn more.

Now render the .control_panel/1 function component from GameLive with a viewBox value of 0 0 200 40. Then place four calls to .triangle/4 within the opening and closing <ControlPanel> tags. The first triangle should set the rotate prop to "0", the second should set it to "90", the third should set it to "180", and the fourth

---

2. https://developer.mozilla.org/en-US/docs/Web/SVG/Attribute/transform
3. https://developer.mozilla.org/en-US/docs/Web/SVG/Attribute/transform#rotate

should set it to "270". Finally, play around with the x/y prop values until your triangles are positioned correctly.

Next Time

In the next chapter, we'll give users the ability to select, move, and place pentominoes on the board. We've already built a lot of this logic into our application core—we have functions that can move, rotate, and flip pentomino shapes. We'll use these functions when we model this behavior in the UI.

As we build this behavior into our game UI, we'll find that we want to enforce some rules. For example, a user shouldn't be able to drop a piece outside the bounds of the puzzle board or on top of a piece that is already placed. These kinds of validity checks belong in the application boundary. We'll build that boundary layer and use it to write the code that enforces game rules on user input. When we put it all together, we'll have a fully functioning Pentominoes game in which users can select their puzzle size, place pentominoes within that puzzle, and win the game.

We're almost done with our game. Keep reading, and we'll build out the final functionality.

CHAPTER 13

Establish Boundaries and APIs

You've built the game logic in the application core and the presentation layer in LiveView, but our game live view doesn't respond to the user yet. Now it's time to put the pieces together to assemble our fully functioning game of Pentominoes. We'll bring our live view to life by teaching it to respond to user input. You'll build on everything we've covered so far to achieve the following:

- Integrate event processing into our live view to capture keystrokes and mouse clicks.
- Create new core functions to pick up, move, and drop a pentomino piece on the board.
- Model uncertainty in our application's boundary layer, using a Phoenix context.
- Present a clean API to the user.

This chapter will be more fast-paced than the previous ones. At this point, you're familiar with all of the LiveView techniques and tools we'll use here, and you're getting comfortable with designing pure, functional application cores while keeping code that deals with external input and uncertainty in the boundary. So we'll trust you to deep-dive into code samples on your own and take you through building the final pieces of our game play at a higher-level. As always, we'll begin with a plan.

It's Alive: Plan User Interactions

In the previous two chapters, we built code to do the following:

- Represent our game's functionality in the application core.
- Establish a game UI with layered LiveView components.
- Set the initial game state and render it in LiveView.

Now we need to let users interact with the live view to bring our game to life. Allowing user input, however, means dealing with uncertainty. Users will try to move pieces in ways that should fail—for example, by placing a piece out of bounds of the board or on top of another piece that's already placed. You'll put the code for handling these interactions in a brand-new boundary layer we'll build for our game. The boundary is the home for code that deals with external input and uncertainty. We'll model our game's boundary layer in a single Phoenix context, allowing us to provide a unified API for game play.

Before we write any of the code though, let's outline each of the user interactions that make up our game. The basic rules of our game work like this:

- The user can pick up pieces, manipulate them, and drop them on the board.
- The user can place pieces until the whole puzzle board is covered.

Let's dig into the logic that governs these specific interactions. We'll describe our game logic in the following format:

When the event occurs, *if* the conditions are met, *then* the event is applied to the state of the game. If the conditions aren't met, we'll fail the interaction.

Here's our game logic:

When: The user clicks a point.
- *If:* The point is part of a shape on the palette *and* there's no active shape,
- *Then:* Make the clicked shape the active shape and center it on the board.

When: The user clicks a point.
- *If:* The point is part of an existing shape placed on the board *and* there's no active shape,
- *Then:* Make the clicked shape the active shape and center it on the board.

When: The user types an arrow key to move or the user types the shift key to rotate or the user types the enter key to flip.
- *If:* The middle point of the pentomino is on the board,
- *Then:* Move the pentomino,
- *Else:* Don't move the pentomino and report an error.

When: The user hits the space bar to drop a pentomino.
- *If:* All points cover the board *and* no points overlap existing pentominoes,
- *Then:* Drop the pentomino,
- *Else:* Don't drop the pentomino and report an error.

When: The user clicks anything else on the SVG.
- *Then:* Do nothing.

In the remainder of this chapter, we'll build a game boundary layer that handles these rules. The boundary layer will receive user input through the live view, execute some new core functions to apply user input to game state, and return tagged tuples for the live view to act on. Let's begin by building some new core functions for processing user input.

Process User Interactions in the Core

We'll begin with the first user interaction on our list: a user picks a pentomino to move. Recall that our core Board module produces board structs with an attribute, :active_pento, that holds the actively selected pentomino shape. So, to model the interaction of a user selecting a pentomino, all we need to do is update the board's :active_pento. We need to support three scenarios here:

- If the user clicks the board background instead of a pentomino piece from the palette or from among the pieces already placed on the board, we should ignore it.
- If the shape clicked is already the active pento, we deselect it by setting :active_pento back to nil.
- If there's no active pento, and the piece selected is a valid piece, then we should set :active_pento to that piece.

Let's start with the first scenario: ignoring the action if the selected shape name is :board. A simple pattern match should take care of this case. Define a function, Board.pick/2, that takes in a first argument of the board struct and a second argument of the shape name. In the first head, we'll ignore clicks on points that are not part of an actual pentomino. These clicks are easy to identify because the shape name is :board, to represent the conceptual board beneath the pentominoes. Match the shape_name argument in the first head, like this:

boundary/pento/lib/pento/game/board.ex
```
def pick(board, :board), do: board
```

In this first clause, we ignore the user's action by simply returning the unchanged board struct.

Next up, we'll handle the second scenario. The user clicks a pentomino, but an active pentomino is already selected. In that case, if the user clicks the active one, we want to release it. Otherwise, we do nothing, like this:

```elixir
boundary/pento/lib/pento/game/board.ex
def pick(%{active_pento: pento} = board, sname) when not is_nil(pento) do
  if pento.name == sname do
    %{board | active_pento: nil}
  else
    board
  end
end
```

The function clause does much of the work. This clause matches clicks when the active pentomino is not nil. Then it's a small matter of checking to see if the user has clicked the active one again. If so, we release it back to the palette by setting the active pentomino to nil. Otherwise, we return the board unchanged because a user shouldn't be able to pick up a second pentomino.

Okay, on to our last scenario: there's no active pento, and the shape is not the underlying :board. That means the user is picking up a pentomino. It might be one that has already been solved. If so, we remove it from the completed list and let them place it again. If not, we simply make it the active pentomino. We can cover both conditions at once by implementing yet another pick/2 function head, like this:

```elixir
def pick(board, shape_name) do
  active =
    board.completed_pentos
    |> Enum.find(&(&1.name == shape_name))
    |> Kernel.||(new_pento(board, shape_name))

  completed = Enum.filter(board.completed_pentos, &(&1.name != shape_name))

  %{board | active_pento: active, completed_pentos: completed}
end
```

Let's break this down. Generally, we calculate the active pentomino, calculate the solved pentominoes, and then add both to our socket. To build the active pentomino, we look to see if the one the user clicked is already on the board. If it is, we find it in the list of pentominoes that've already been placed. Otherwise, we build a new one by piping the result of Enum.find/2 to the Kernel.|| function. This means that if Enum.find/2 returns a pento, then the whole pipeline will return that pento. If Enum.find/2 returns nil, then we use the new_pento/2 function to return a newly created pentomino with the correct location at the center of the board. Finally, we filter out the pentomino the user has picked up from the ones that have already been placed, and then we return the socket.

Let's build out this new_pento/2 helper function now.

Implement the new_pento/2 function to take in a first argument of the board and a second argument of the selected shape name. The function will use the Pentomino.new/2 constructor function we already built to return a new Pentomino struct with the correct shape name and centered location—any newly selected pentomino will be placed in the center of the board so that the user can move it around from there. Your new_pento/2 function should look like this:

boundary/pento/lib/pento/game/board.ex
```elixir
defp new_pento(board, shape_name) do
  Pentomino.new(name: shape_name, location: midpoints(board))
end

defp midpoints(board) do
  {xs, ys} = Enum.unzip(board.points)
  {midpoint(xs), midpoint(ys)}
end

defp midpoint(i), do: round(Enum.max(i) / 2.0)
```

We find no surprises in Pentomino.new/2. The hardest part is calculating the new location that's centered in both dimensions. The midpoints/1 helper accomplishes this task by dividing each set of dimensions by two and rounding. That completes the code we need to handle the "select an active pento" interaction.

Now let's build out the code to handle the "drop the active pento" interaction. Define two versions of the drop/2 function—one that handles the scenario in which there's no active pento to drop and one that handles the valid drop scenario, like this:

boundary/pento/lib/pento/game/board.ex
```elixir
def drop(%{active_pento: nil} = board), do: board

def drop(%{active_pento: pento} = board) do
  board
  |> Map.put(:active_pento, nil)
  |> Map.put(:completed_pentos, [pento | board.completed_pentos])
end
```

The first function head is easy. If there's nothing to drop, we return the board unchanged. For the valid drop scenario, we first reset the board's :active_pento attribute to nil. Then we add the dropped pento to the board's list of :completed_pentos. Finally, we return the updated board struct.

It'll be up to the boundary layer to determine whether a drop is legal and proceed accordingly, but we'll build the "legal drop checking" logic into our application core. Then we'll call on it later in our game's boundary layer. Since we implement pentominoes with individual points, our job will be relatively easy. If any of the points from the existing pentominoes are in the selected one, the move should be illegal. Also, users can't drop pentominoes off of the board, meaning all active points need to be board points. Implement a converter function, Board.legal_drop?/1, that takes in an argument of a board and returns a Boolean. You'll have two versions of the function, as shown here:

boundary/pento/lib/pento/game/board.ex
```
def legal_drop?(%{active_pento: pento}) when is_nil(pento), do: false

def legal_drop?(%{active_pento: pento, points: board_points} = board) do
  points_on_board =
    Pentomino.to_shape(pento).points
    |> Enum.all?(fn point -> point in board_points end)

  no_overlapping_pentos =
    !Enum.any?(board.completed_pentos, &Pentomino.overlapping?(pento, &1))

  points_on_board and no_overlapping_pentos
end
```

The first version simply returns false if the board has a nil active pento. The second version is a little more complex. Let's break it down.

First, we use the Pentomino.to_shape converter to create a list of all of the points that make up the active pento. Then we check to see if all of the pentomino's points are contained in the board's list of points. We capture this check in a variable, points_on_board. Then we make sure that there are no placed pentominoes in the space in which the user is dropping the active pento. To accomplish this, we use the help of a new function on the Pentomino module, overlapping?/2, that looks like this:

boundary/pento/lib/pento/game/pentomino.ex
```
def overlapping?(pento1, pento2) do
  {p1, p2} = {to_shape(pento1).points, to_shape(pento2).points}
  Enum.count(p1 -- p2) != 5
end
```

This performs a straightforward check by first converting each pentomino to a shape with the existing Pentomino.to_shape/1 converter function and then using list subtraction to remove any points from the two lists that are the same. If any points are removed, then the resulting count will be less than five, which means that the pieces *do* overlap.

Once we calculate whether or not the pieces overlap, we tell the Board.legal_drop/1 function to return true if all the points in the active pento are on the board *and* none of the points in the active pento overlap a piece that's already placed. Otherwise, it returns false.

Now that we have a core function to compute whether or not a *drop* is illegal, we need to implement a core function to determine whether or not a *move* is illegal. The boundary layer will use this function later on to determine if a move can be processed. Implement a function, Board.legal_move/1, that returns true if the center of the active pento is present on the board, like this:

boundary/pento/lib/pento/game/board.ex
```
def legal_move?(%{active_pento: pento, points: points} = _board) do
  pento.location in points
end
```

The function is surprisingly simple—it checks to see if the location of the active pento is in the board's list of points.

Now that we've added the necessary functions to our core, let's build out a game boundary layer that knows how to use it.

Build a Game Boundary Layer

Let's face it. Games are fun because of the constraints built into the rules. One role of a boundary layer is to handle uncertainty. Our code will need to return error conditions when users make illegal moves. The user interface will then take on the job of informing the user. The game boundary layer will receive user input through the live view, validate it, and return an error-tagged tuple if anything is illegal. This is the pattern you've seen encapsulated in changesets within the boundary layer. Boundaries are the place to handle input from the external world and deal with uncertainty, all while providing a clean, unified API for use in our presentation layer—the live view.

Let's start with the boundary layer ceremony. Create a new file, lib/pento/game.ex, and implement the boundary module, like this:

boundary/pento/lib/pento/game.ex
```
defmodule Pento.Game do
  alias Pento.Game.{Board, Pentomino}

  @messages %{
    out_of_bounds: "Out of bounds!",
    illegal_drop: "Oops! You can't drop out of bounds or on another piece."
  }
end
```

Here, we alias the Board and Pentomino core modules that we'll need to rely on throughout our boundary. We also add some messages for users and store them in a map for now. We can extract them later if we need to.

With that out of the way, we're ready to implement our first boundary function, the maybe_move/2 function. The "maybe" in the function name indicates that it *could* fail. The function will work like this:

- Take in a board struct and some attempted move.
- If the move is legal, apply it to the board state and return an ok-tagged tuple with the new board struct.
- If the move is *not* legal, return an error-tagged tuple with the unchanged board struct.

We'll create a few different versions of this function to handle various scenarios. First up, implement a maybe_move/2 function in case our board struct has no active pento, like this:

boundary/pento/lib/pento/game.ex
```
def maybe_move(%{active_pento: p} = board, _m) when is_nil(p) do
  {:ok, board}
end
```

Next up, define another version of maybe_move/2, as follows:

boundary/pento/lib/pento/game.ex
```
def maybe_move(board, move) do
  new_pento = move_fn(move).(board.active_pento)
  new_board = %{board | active_pento: new_pento}

  if Board.legal_move?(new_board),
    do: {:ok, new_board},
    else: {:error, @messages.out_of_bounds}
end
```

Here, we look up the move function with a helper function, move_fn/1, and invoke it with an argument of the active pento. This returns a new pento with the updated location—more on the move_fn/1 function in a bit. Then we update the board's :active_pento attribute, setting it equal to the newly located pento. Next up, we call our new Board.legal_move?/1 core function to determine if the new location of the active pento is valid. If it is, we return an ok-tagged tuple. If not, we return an error-tagged tuple. This pattern of validating input and returning an ok-tagged or error-tagged tuple is a common one for the boundary layer. Our boundary is doing the job of taking in some input, validating it, and either returning a tuple with updated state or an error. The presentation layer can use these tuples to update the UI appropriately.

Let's take a closer look at the move_fn/1 function now. This function is responsible for using the move input to look up and return the appropriate Pentomino move function. We use a simple case statement to accomplish this, as you can see here:

boundary/pento/lib/pento/game.ex
```
defp move_fn(move) do
  case move do
    :up -> &Pentomino.up/1
    :down -> &Pentomino.down/1
    :left -> &Pentomino.left/1
    :right -> &Pentomino.right/1
    :flip -> &Pentomino.flip/1
    :rotate -> &Pentomino.rotate/1
  end
end
```

That's it for the maybe_move/2 function. Now we're ready to build out the maybe_drop/2 function. This function is responsible for determining if the active pento can be dropped in the desired location. To do so, it need only delegate out to the Board.legal_drop/1 function and return the appropriate tuple, like this:

boundary/pento/lib/pento/game.ex
```
def maybe_drop(board) do
  if Board.legal_drop?(board) do
    {:ok, Board.drop(board)}
  else
    {:error, @messages.illegal_drop}
  end
end
```

The complex rules around determining the legality of a drop are handled in the core. This is the essence of the boundary layer—it does as little work as possible while still implementing all of the machinery to process user input and handle uncertainty.

With our boundary up and running, its time to hook up our live view to handle user events.

Extend the Game Live View

We've already built all of the presentation logic we need to render the full game state. This is thanks to a common flow we followed for building our live view—we hard-coded some complex game state into our live view and rendered it in the previous chapter. This allowed us to scaffold out the framework we needed to send events and render the various possible states of our live view. Now, we need only bring it to life by teaching the live view to handle these events.

In the last chapter, we promised that the stateful Board component would handle all of the user events and game state changes. It's time to build out that functionality now. Open up your PentoWeb.Pento.Board live component and make sure you have the following aliases and props, including the Pento.Game alias:

boundary/pento/lib/pento_web/live/game_live/board.ex
```elixir
defmodule PentoWeb.GameLive.Board do
  use PentoWeb, :live_component

  alias Pento.Game.Board
  alias Pento.Game
  import PentoWeb.GameLive.{Colors, Component}
```

It's a good idea to review the various imports and aliases when we start working with our API. We'll still have a direct call to the Game.Board.new core function, but we'll remove the direct calls to our Game.Pentomino. Eventually, we'll abstract away the need to directly alias and call on the Game.Board module by adding additional functionality to the Pento.Game boundary layer. No modules that are nested *underneath* the boundary layer, or context module, should be directly exposed in LiveView. We want our boundary layer to provide the single API through which the presentation layer will interact with the game.

For now, we'll leave Game.Board where it is and remove Game.Pentomino. We can also remove the hard-coded active and completed pentominoes from assign_board/1, like this:

boundary/pento/lib/pento_web/live/game_live/board.ex
```elixir
def assign_board(%{assigns: %{puzzle: puzzle}} = socket) do
  board =
    puzzle
    |> String.to_existing_atom()
    |> Board.new()

  assign(socket, board: board)
end
```

We'll be making changes to the active pentomino and the completed ones through the Game layer, as it should be. With the setup out of the way, let's begin by adding handlers to process keystrokes and mouse clicks. Recall that we already added these phx-click and phx-key events to the appropriate bits of SVG markup when we built our components in the previous chapter. Now, we need an event handler for the "pick" mouse click event and the "key" keyboard press event. Add them in to the Board live component as follows:

boundary/pento/lib/pento_web/live/game_live/board.ex
```elixir
def handle_event("pick", %{"name" => name}, socket) do
  {:noreply, socket |> pick(name) |> assign_shapes}
end

def handle_event("key", %{"key" => key}, socket) do
  {:noreply, socket |> do_key(key) |> assign_shapes}
end
```

These event handlers are relatively simple. They call reducers to process the event and update the board's socket state accordingly. Let's take a closer look at the reducer for handling the key-press event:

boundary/pento/lib/pento_web/live/game_live/board.ex
```elixir
def do_key(socket, key) do
  case key do
    " " -> drop(socket)
    "ArrowLeft" -> move(socket, :left)
    "ArrowRight" -> move(socket, :right)
    "ArrowUp" -> move(socket, :up)
    "ArrowDown" -> move(socket, :down)
    "Shift" -> move(socket, :rotate)
    "Enter" -> move(socket, :flip)
    "Space" -> drop(socket)
    _ -> socket
  end
end
```

Each key press does some work—arrows apply a directional move, the "enter" key flips the piece, the "shift" key rotates the piece, and the "space" key drops it. Implement the move/2 reducer now to call on the Game.maybe_move/2 boundary function and update socket state based on the returned tuple, like this:

```elixir
def move(socket, move) do
  case Game.maybe_move(socket.assigns.board, move) do
    {:error, message} ->
      put_flash(socket, :info, message)

    {:ok, board} ->
      socket |> assign(board: board) |> assign_shapes
  end
end
```

The game's boundary layer does all the work, and our live view only needs to update state based on the results.

Now implement the drop/1 reducer to behave in a similar manner. As shown here, it calls out to the Game.maybe_drop/1 boundary function and updates state based on the tuple that's returned:

```elixir
defp drop(socket) do
  case Game.maybe_drop(socket.assigns.board) do
    {:error, message} ->
      put_flash(socket, :info, message)

    {:ok, board} ->
      socket |> assign(board: board) |> assign_shapes
  end
end
```

We're seeing the benefit of small, single-purpose reducers in action here. By implementing reducers that take in a board, apply some state change, and return an updated board, our code remains clean and highly readable, not to mention easy to test.

Next up, we'll implement the pick/2 reducer that our "pick" event handler calls on. Define the function to take in an argument of the socket and a shape name, and return an updated socket that contains a new core Pento.Board struct with the newly active pento. You can see the completed function here:

boundary/pento/lib/pento_web/live/game_live/board.ex
```elixir
defp pick(socket, name) do
  shape_name = String.to_existing_atom(name)
  update(socket, :board, &Board.pick(&1, shape_name))
end
```

The call to Pento.Board.pick/2 is an excellent candidate for some code that should be moved into our boundary layer to keep our API consistent—we want to direct *all* game interactions through the single Pento.Game API. You can tackle that refactor as an exercise.

Our Board live component can now handle the pick, move, and drop events, thereby completing the full functionality of our Pentominoes game! Try it out by firing up the server, directing your browser at /game/medium, and playing a few rounds. Next, we can give the user a little guidance when playing the game. Let's offer some directions in the parent game_live.ex live view.

Add Help with JavaScript

Sometimes, simple tasks like showing or hiding JavaScript information pop-ups is a job better managed on the client without the help of LiveView. We can take advantage of JavaScript hooks for this purpose. We'll offer a clickable Help icon for that purpose. As usual, we'll do most of our work in components. Let's start with the GameLive.render/1 function:

boundary/pento/lib/pento_web/live/game_live.ex
```elixir
def render(assigns) do
  ~H"""
  <section class="mx-auto max-w-4xl px-4 py-8">
    <div class="grid grid-cols-2">
      <div>
        <h1 class="font-heavy text-3xl text-center mb-6">
          Welcome to Pento!
        </h1>
      </div>
      <.help />
    </div>
```

```
    <.live_component module={Board} puzzle={@puzzle} id="board-component" />
  </section>
  """
end
```

Most of this page is the same, with a couple of exceptions. First, we wrap our playing area in a two-column grid. The Tailwind class grid denotes a grid layout, and the grid-columns-2 sets the names of the columns. The left column will hold our game and the right one our help button and help.

We also call the .help function component to render our help system, like this:

boundary/pento/lib/pento_web/live/game_live.ex
```
def help(assigns) do
  ~H"""
  <div class="relative">
    <.help_button />
    <.help_page />
  </div>
  """
end
```

That component simply calls two others, one to build the button and one to build the hidden help page. Look at the .help_button/1 next:

boundary/pento/lib/pento_web/live/game_live.ex
```
attr :class, :string, default: "h-8 w-8 text-slate hover:text-slate-400"

def help_button(assigns) do
  ~H"""
  <button
    phx-click={JS.toggle(to: "#info", in: "fade-in", out: "fade-out")}
    class="text-slate hover:text-slate-400">
    <.icon name="hero-question-mark-circle-solid" class="h-8 w-8" />
  </button>
  """
end
```

A lot's going on in this simple button component, which takes a class with a default value. Setting up the attributes with a default helps keep the markup clear but also brings attention to important attributes at a glance. Going from the inside out, the .icon function component is defined in CoreComponents. It returns a <span> element that uses an SVG-driven library provided by Phoenix in assets/vendor/heroicons. That library is bundled within your compiled app.css by the plugin in your generated assets/tailwind.config.js file. Check out the definition of this .icon function component in the code on the next page.

```
boundary/pento/lib/pento_web/components/core_components.ex
attr :name, :string, required: true
attr :class, :string, default: "size-4"

def icon(%{name: "hero-" <> _} = assigns) do
  ~H"""
  <span class={[@name, @class]} />
  """
end
```

You can use the official Heroicons website[1] as a reference for what CSS classes you can apply to render various icons. By setting the name attribute to "hero-question-mark-circle-solid", we're rendering the symbol with a question mark in a circle. Note that we append -solid to get a solid line around the icon. Additionally, the default class we provided gives us a decent default size for our purposes and also a hover attribute that sets a default color when the mouse is over it. The icon code is rich, but the real magic happens in the wrapping button.

Notice the phx-click attribute on the button. It handles the chore of showing and hiding the help div. The code fragment JS.toggle(to: "#info") will show the div with an info ID if it's hidden and hide it if it's visible. This JavaScript interop is implemented in Elixir but calls convenient utility functions[2] already supported on the client. In this way, you can show or hide individual components and apply transitions using JavaScript, but without writing custom code.

Now all that remains is to build the .help_page/1 component:

```
boundary/pento/lib/pento_web/live/game_live.ex
def help_page(assigns) do
  ~H"""
  <div id="info"
       class="absolute right-0 top-10 bg-white border-2 border-gray-300
              p-4 z-10 w-80 shadow-lg rounded hidden">
    <ul class="list-disc list-inside">
      <li>Click on a pento to pick it up</li>
      <li>Drop a pento with a space</li>
      <li>Pentos can't overlap</li>
      <li>Pentos must be fully on the board</li>
      <li>Rotate a pento with shift</li>
      <li>Flip a pento with enter</li>
      <li>Place all the pentos to win</li>
    </ul>
  </div>
  """
end
```

---

1. https://heroicons.com
2. https://hexdocs.pm/phoenix_live_view/Phoenix.LiveView.JS.html#content

The code is dead simple. It renders a list wrapped in a div. The outer div has most of the magic. It has a solid white background and Tailwind styles to establish a fixed position. Based on the JS.toggle(to: "#info") function that shows the help pop-up, we add id="info" to the div. The rest of the code is a static list.

Now the user can click the ? to see the Help screen:

- Click on a pento to pick it up
- Drop a pento with a space
- Pentos can't overlap
- Pentos must be fully on the board
- Rotate a pento with shift
- Flip a pento with enter
- Place all the pentos to win

The contents may not be perfect yet, but the button works with minimal effort. Better yet, our users can see instructions for playing the game without requiring us to write custom JavaScript and without our code making unnecessary calls to the server.

We still have some user-interface work to do, though. Right now, the user can play the game, but they must type the URL. Let's build a picker that lets them preview games and choose one to play.

Build a Picker to Control Navigation

The picker will be a live view, but it won't need to process any events. We'll start with each of the available puzzles. For each one, we'll show the puzzle's outer shape and a palette so the player can select an appealing game from a graphical list. With LiveView and a few function components, it's going to go quickly. Let's write the code from the top down, starting with the pento_web/live/game_live/picker.ex module:

```
boundary/pento/lib/pento_web/live/game_live/picker.ex
defmodule PentoWeb.GameLive.Picker do
  use PentoWeb, :live_view

  alias Pento.Game.Board
  import PentoWeb.GameLive.{Colors, Component}
```

We don't need much in this module. We need the board for the list of puzzles and also to generate the shape of the puzzle. We import the components to give us access to the .canvas/1 and .palette/1 function. We use both of those components to provide a graphical representation of each puzzle.

Now we set up the data we need. Each row needs the name of the puzzle we'll use in the URL and also the board itself so we can render the outer shape and component. Load that data in one list, like this:

boundary/pento/lib/pento_web/live/game_live/picker.ex
```
def mount(_params, _session, socket) do
  {:ok, assign_boards(socket)}
end

def assign_boards(socket) do
  assign(
    socket,
    :boards,
    Board.puzzles()
    |> Enum.map(&{&1, Board.new(&1)})
  )
end
```

We map over the puzzle names and build a tuple for each one of those in the form &{&1, Board.new(&1)}. This capture syntax works like this: the initial & means we're building a function. We represent the first argument with &1. If we had a second argument, we'd represent it with &2, and so on. In this way, we build a tuple with the puzzle name and a starting board for the puzzle. Next, we map over those in the render/1 function:

boundary/pento/lib/pento_web/live/game_live/picker.ex
```
def render(assigns) do
  ~H"""
  <h1 class="font-heavy text-4xl text-center mb-6">
    Choose a Puzzle
  </h1>
  <%= for {puzzle, board} <- @boards do %>
    <.row board={board} puzzle={puzzle} />
  <% end %>
  """
end
```

Keeping our functions short, we render nested divs for a grid with two columns and a heading in each one. Within the grid, we map over the @board.rows with a for comprehension, calling the .row/1 function component for each one. We pass both the puzzle and the board to the function component. We leave the details of the picker to row/1:

boundary/pento/lib/pento_web/live/game_live/picker.ex
```
attr :board, :any, required: true
attr :puzzle, :atom, required: true

def row(assigns) do
  ~H"""
  <.link navigate={~p"/game/#{@puzzle}"}>
```

```
    <div class="grid grid-cols-2 hover:bg-slate-200">
      <div>
        <h3 class="text-2xl">Pieces</h3>
      </div>
      <div>
        <h3 class="text-2xl">
          {@puzzle |> to_string |> String.capitalize()} Puzzle
        </h3>
      </div>
      <.palette shape_names={@board.palette} />
      <.board board={@board} />
    </div>
  </.link>
  """
end
```

The function has two important jobs and handles each one with a function component. The .link component wraps the entire row in the <.link> tags and sets up LiveView navigation to the verified route ~p"/game/#{@puzzle}". That code will navigate our user to the right place when they click on the div. The hover:hover:bg-slate-300 class adds a nice visual effect when the user highlights the div.

The second job is to show a row. Each row has two columns, the palette and the shape of the puzzle. We render the first with the existing .palette and the other with another custom function component called board/1:

boundary/pento/lib/pento_web/live/game_live/picker.ex
```
attr :board, :any, required: true

def board(assigns) do
  ~H"""
    <div>
      <.canvas view_box={"0 0 400 #{height(@board) * 10 + 25}"}>
        <.shape
          points={Board.to_shape(@board).points}
          fill={color(:purple)}
          name="board"
        />
      </.canvas>
    </div>
  """
end
```

We tweak the height in the view_box of each cell with a helper function, allowing 10 pixels for each point and an added buffer of 25 for white space. We've already done the lion's share of the work to show the puzzle shape elsewhere. We have a function called Board.to_shape/1 to build a shape from a board. All we need to do to show the board is render it with the .shape/1 function component.

This last bit of code does the basic work of rendering a shape in a canvas. Let's look at the helper to calculate the height, in points, of a board:

```
boundary/pento/lib/pento_web/live/game_live/picker.ex
defp height(board) do
  board.points
  |> Enum.map(fn {_, y} -> y end)
  |> Enum.max()
end
```

The helper pulls the maximum y value from the list of points making up each board. Add the /play route to router.ex beneath the "/game/:puzzle" route, like this:

```
boundary/pento/lib/pento_web/router.ex
live "/game/:puzzle", GameLive
live "/play", GameLive.Picker
```

Run it and you'll see a list of palettes and puzzles. You can choose a puzzle to play. We can do better, though. All of the puzzles are rectangles. We can build a list of more interesting puzzles with a few small tweaks to our game/board.ex module.

Add Some Puzzles to the Board

We're looking for some low-lying fruit. We want some interesting puzzles, but we don't want to work too hard to get them. With just a little effort, we can subtract a few points from a rectangle to get some pretty marvelous effects. To accommodate the additional size of our new puzzles, we need a taller display canvas in game_web/live/game_live/board.ex, achieved like this:

```
<.canvas view_box="0 0 200 140">
```

We also need to make some tweaks to lib/game/board.ex. Start by adding the names of the new puzzles.

```
boundary/pento/lib/pento/game/board.ex
def puzzles(), do: ~w[tiny small ball donut default wide widest medium]a
```

We changed the order and added small, ball, and donut. Now, tweak the constructor to allow an optional hole. In the constructor, we subtract the hole from the base rectangles to make an overall puzzle, like this:

```
boundary/pento/lib/pento/game/board.ex
def new(palette, points, hole \\ []) do
  %__MODULE__{palette: palette(palette), points: points -- hole}
end
```

We use simple set subtraction to process the additional parameter. For example, [1, 2, 3, 4] -- [2, 3] would remove the elements in the second list from the first, leaving [1, 4]. Now we can build our extra puzzles:

boundary/pento/lib/pento/game/board.ex
```
def new(:small), do: new(:medium, rect(7, 5))

def new(:donut) do
  new(:all, rect(8, 8), for(x <- 4..5, y <- 4..5, do: {x, y}))
end

def new(:ball) do
  new(:all, rect(8, 8), for(x <- [1, 8], y <- [1, 8], do: {x, y}))
end
```

These smaller rectangles will be subtracted from the bigger ones. Don't worry about the details now—you'll see the results shortly. Next, add the extra :medium palette for the intermediate-sized puzzles, like this:

boundary/pento/lib/pento/game/board.ex
```
defp palette(:medium), do: [:t, :y, :l, :p, :n, :v, :u]
```

We add the extra function head with seven shapes. This :medium palette is used to solve our :small puzzle. And we're finally ready to test.

Point your browser to localhost:4000/play. Though no one element of the user interface is complex, the result is beautiful and striking:

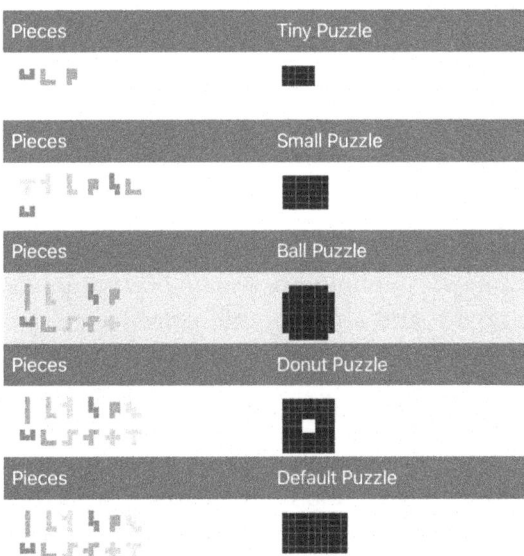

This is the crowning jewel of our work. We took advantage of the background core modules to build a board. Then we rendered the resulting list of boards with a few basic components and a couple of dozens of lines of code. Now, you can use what you've learned to put LiveView through its paces.

Your Turn

Teaching our live view to handle and respond to user input brought our game to life, but it also introduced uncertainty into our application. Building a boundary layer to handle user input and deal with uncertainty allowed us to find a home for all of our game behavior and quickly deliver the full functionality we needed. We added the complex, but certain, logic for processing different types of user input to the application core. And we implemented the Pento.Game context module to act as our boundary—taking in user input from the live view, choosing whether and how to apply that input to update the game's state, and returning the appropriate tuple that LiveView can use to update the UI. Finally, we put it all together in our live view by teaching the Board live component to handle user interactions by calling on the boundary layer, updating the socket, and re-rendering as needed, based on the info returned by the boundary.

Here are a few more exercises you can try out to round out our Pentominoes application and deepen your knowledge.

Give It a Try

- First, refactor our Pentominoes game by removing all references to Pento.Game.Board from the Board live component. Instead, the component should only call on Pento.Game, which can in turn call on Pento.Game.Board. This allows our live view to confine all of its interactions with our gaming logic to the single Pento.Game API, reaching only *one level deep* into the game's abstractions.

- Now, implement a score-keeping feature that tracks a user's score as they play a single game of Pentominoes. Assign 500 points for each piece that's placed on the board, and subtract one point for every move. A user gets a higher score for solving the puzzle in fewer moves.

- Next, build a button that allows a user to Give Up. When the button is clicked, the game ends.

- Build a You've Won page to motivate the user. If all the pieces are placed on a page, let the user know they've won. What can you show them to celebrate their success?

What's Next?

With the conclusion of our game, you have everything you need to build complex, sophisticated UIs with LiveView in the wild. You built a brand-new LiveView application from the ground up, including authentication, with the help of generators. You layered components to build fast, responsive, fully interactive single-page apps, and you designed clean, maintainable code across the core, boundary, and presentation layers of your Phoenix application.

With the help of LiveView, you quickly and easily built a wide variety of complicated interactive features, including an entire browser-based game. LiveView's many benefits have become apparent over the course of this book—it provides fast interactivity and high performance while also empowering us as developers to be highly productive. LiveView gave us fast development cycles by allowing us to focus our minds entirely on the server-side, even when writing tests. And it provided everything we needed to support complicated user interactions in the browser—from interactive forms to distributed real-time UIs to a full in-browser game.

With all of these benefits, it's not surprising that LiveView is being adopted fast. Teams are reaching for LiveView to handle fast prototyping of complex features and apps and to deliver the interactive and real-time features that the modern web demands. With LiveView, teams can deliver SPAs that are comprehensively tested, resilient to failure, easy to debug, and lightning fast—and they can do it quicker than ever before.

The LiveView framework will have a big impact on web development and Elixir adoption as more and more teams and businesses reach to take advantage of its many benefits. With this book under your belt, you're ready to be a part of that growth.

Bibliography

[Alm18]   Ulisses Almeida. *Learn Functional Programming with Elixir*. The Pragmatic Bookshelf, Dallas, TX, 2018.

[Heb19]   Fred Hebert. *Property-Based Testing with PropEr, Erlang, and Elixir*. The Pragmatic Bookshelf, Dallas, TX, 2019.

[IT19]   James Edward Gray, II and Bruce A. Tate. *Designing Elixir Systems with OTP*. The Pragmatic Bookshelf, Dallas, TX, 2019.

[LM21]   Andrea Leopardi and Jeffrey Matthias. *Testing Elixir*. The Pragmatic Bookshelf, Dallas, TX, 2021.

[McC15]   Chris McCord. *Metaprogramming Elixir*. The Pragmatic Bookshelf, Dallas, TX, 2015.

[MTV19]   Chris McCord, Bruce Tate, and José Valim. *Programming Phoenix 1.4*. The Pragmatic Bookshelf, Dallas, TX, 2019.

[Tho18]   Dave Thomas. *Programming Elixir 1.6*. The Pragmatic Bookshelf, Dallas, TX, 2018.

[WM19]   Darin Wilson and Eric Meadows-Jönsson. *Programming Ecto*. The Pragmatic Bookshelf, Dallas, TX, 2019.

Thank you!

We hope you enjoyed this book and that you're already thinking about what you want to learn next. To help make that decision easier, we're offering you this gift.

Head on over to https://pragprog.com right now, and use the coupon code BUYANOTHER2026 to save 30% on your next ebook. Offer is void where prohibited or restricted. This offer does not apply to any edition of *The Pragmatic Programmer* ebook.

And if you'd like to share your own expertise with the world, why not propose a writing idea to us? After all, many of our best authors started off as our readers, just like you. With up to a 50% royalty, world-class editorial services, and a name you trust, there's nothing to lose. Visit https://pragprog.com/become-an-author/ today to learn more and to get started.

Thank you for your continued support. We hope to hear from you again soon!

The Pragmatic Bookshelf

Advanced Functional Programming with Elixir

Combine advanced functional programming concepts with production-ready Elixir and proven domain-driven design techniques to write cleaner, more thoughtful software. You'll explore foundational ideas like equality, ordering, predicates, monoids, and monads—then go beyond syntax as you develop intuition for composing logic, modeling behavior, and growing systems. With a focus on maintainable, declarative code over theory, you'll gain practical, composable patterns you can apply right away.

Joseph Koski
(250 pages) ISBN: 9798888651797. $53.95
https://pragprog.com/book/jkelixir

Ash Framework

Ash Framework is the game-changing toolkit for Elixir developers. With modular, plug-and-play building blocks, Ash slashes development time, effort, and complexity, letting you do more with less code. Design declarative, customizable domain models that are easy to maintain and optimized for performance. Shift your focus to what to build, instead of how, using Ash's intuitive design principles. Tackle bigger challenges and build scalable, future-proof web applications with confidence. Elevate your Elixir skills and revolutionize your workflow with Ash.

Rebecca Le and Zach Daniel
(294 pages) ISBN: 9798888651520. $53.95
https://pragprog.com/book/ldash

Programming Elixir 1.6

This book is *the* introduction to Elixir for experienced programmers, completely updated for Elixir 1.6 and beyond. Explore functional programming without the academic overtones (tell me about monads just one more time). Create concurrent applications, but get them right without all the locking and consistency headaches. Meet Elixir, a modern, functional, concurrent language built on the rock-solid Erlang VM. Elixir's pragmatic syntax and built-in support for metaprogramming will make you productive and keep you interested for the long haul. Maybe the time is right for the Next Big Thing. Maybe it's Elixir.

Dave Thomas
(410 pages) ISBN: 9781680502992. $47.95
https://pragprog.com/book/elixir16

Engineering Elixir Applications

The days of separate dev and ops teams are over—knowledge silos and the "throw it over the fence" culture they create are the enemy of progress. As an engineer or developer, you need to confidently own each stage of the software delivery process. This book introduces a new paradigm, *BEAMOps*, that helps you build, test, deploy, and debug BEAM applications. Create effective development and deployment strategies; leverage continuous improvement pipelines; and ensure environment integrity. Combine operational orchestrators such as Docker Swarm with the distribution, fault tolerance, and scalability of the BEAM, to create robust and reliable applications.

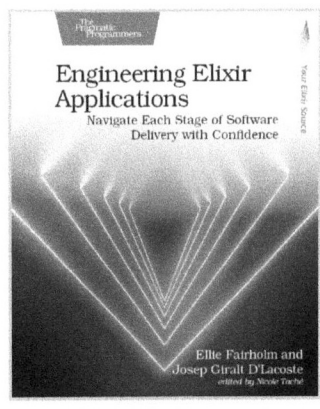

Ellie Fairholm and Josep Giralt D'Lacoste
(458 pages) ISBN: 9798888650677. $61.95
https://pragprog.com/book/beamops

Testing Elixir

Elixir offers new paradigms, and challenges you to test in unconventional ways. Start with ExUnit: almost everything you need to write tests covering all levels of detail, from unit to integration, but only if you know how to use it to the fullest—we'll show you how. Explore testing Elixir-specific challenges such as OTP-based modules, asynchronous code, Ecto-based applications, and Phoenix applications. Explore new tools like Mox for mocks and StreamData for property-based testing. Armed with this knowledge, you can create test suites that add value to your production cycle and guard you from regressions.

Andrea Leopardi and Jeffrey Matthias
(262 pages) ISBN: 9781680507829. $45.95
https://pragprog.com/book/lmelixir

Build a Weather Station with Elixir and Nerves

The Elixir programming language has become a go-to tool for creating reliable, fault-tolerant, and robust server-side applications. Thanks to Nerves, those same exact benefits can be realized in embedded applications. This book will teach you how to structure, build, and deploy production grade Nerves applications to network-enabled devices. The weather station sensor hub project that you will be embarking upon will show you how to create a full stack IoT solution in record time. You will build everything from the embedded Nerves device to the Phoenix backend and even the Grafana time-series data visualizations.

Alexander Koutmos, Bruce A. Tate, Frank Hunleth
(90 pages) ISBN: 9781680509021. $26.95
https://pragprog.com/book/passweather

Metaprogramming Elixir

Write code that writes code with Elixir macros. Macros make metaprogramming possible and define the language itself. In this book, you'll learn how to use macros to extend the language with fast, maintainable code and share functionality in ways you never thought possible. You'll discover how to extend Elixir with your own first-class features, optimize performance, and create domain-specific languages.

Chris McCord
(128 pages) ISBN: 9781680500417. $17
https://pragprog.com/book/cmelixir

Genetic Algorithms in Elixir

From finance to artificial intelligence, genetic algorithms are a powerful tool with a wide array of applications. But you don't need an exotic new language or framework to get started; you can learn about genetic algorithms in a language you're already familiar with. Join us for an in-depth look at the algorithms, techniques, and methods that go into writing a genetic algorithm. From introductory problems to real-world applications, you'll learn the underlying principles of problem solving using genetic algorithms.

Sean Moriarity
(242 pages) ISBN: 9781680507942. $39.95
https://pragprog.com/book/smgaelixir

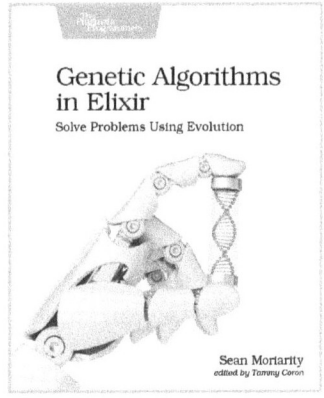

The Pragmatic Bookshelf

The Pragmatic Bookshelf features books written by professional developers for professional developers. The titles continue the well-known Pragmatic Programmer style and continue to garner awards and rave reviews. As development gets more and more difficult, the Pragmatic Programmers will be there with more titles and products to help you stay on top of your game.

Visit Us Online

This Book's Home Page
https://pragprog.com/book/liveview
Source code from this book, errata, and other resources. Come give us feedback, too!

Keep Up-to-Date
https://pragprog.com
Join our announcement mailing list (low volume) or follow us on Twitter @pragprog for new titles, sales, coupons, hot tips, and more.

New and Noteworthy
https://pragprog.com/news
Check out the latest Pragmatic developments, new titles, and other offerings.

Save on the ebook

Save on the ebook versions of this title. Owning the paper version of this book entitles you to purchase the electronic versions at a terrific discount.

PDFs are great for carrying around on your laptop—they are hyperlinked, have color, and are fully searchable. Most titles are also available for the iPhone and iPod touch, Amazon Kindle, and other popular e-book readers.

Send a copy of your receipt to support@pragprog.com and we'll provide you with a discount coupon.

Contact Us

Online Orders:	*https://pragprog.com/catalog*
Customer Service:	*support@pragprog.com*
International Rights:	*translations@pragprog.com*
Academic Use:	*academic@pragprog.com*
Write for Us:	*http://write-for-us.pragprog.com*

www.ingramcontent.com/pod-product-compliance
Ingram Content Group UK Ltd.
Pitfield, Milton Keynes, MK11 3LW, UK
UKHW051848210426
5322IPUK00024B/599